AF577080

TALL BUILDINGS

of Europe, the Middle East and Africa

TALL BUILDINGS

of Europe, the Middle East and Africa

Edited by **Georges Binder**

Foreword by **Norman Foster**

images
Publishing

Published in Australia in 2006 by
The Images Publishing Group Pty Ltd
ABN 89 059 734 431
6 Bastow Place, Mulgrave, Victoria 3170, Australia
Tel: +61 3 9561 5544 Fax: +61 3 9561 4860
books@images.com.au
www.imagespublishing.com

The Images Publishing Group Reference Number: 551

National Library of Australia Cataloguing-in-Publication entry:

Tall buildings of Europe, the Middle East and Africa.

Includes index.
ISBN 1 876907 81 9.

1. Tall buildings. 2. Skyscrapers. I. Binder, Georges.

720.483

Edited by Robyn Beaver

Designed by The Graphic Image Studio Pty Ltd, Mulgrave, Australia
www.tgis.com.au

Digital production by Splitting Image Colour Studio Pty Ltd, Australia
Printed by Everbest Printing Co. Ltd. in Hong Kong/China

IMAGES has included on its website a page for special notices in relation to this and our other publications.
Please visit www.imagespublishing.com

CONTENTS

Appendix

FOREWORD

The urge to build tall is not new. Indeed, I would argue that it is a historical imperative. If you look back five thousand years to the pyramids, five hundred years to the medieval cathedrals, or fifty years to the iconic skyscrapers, such as the Seagram Building in New York, you find that they are all – plus or minus a few metres – the same height. They all stretched the technology of their time to the absolute vertical limit. When I see my children stacking building blocks, or people striving to ascend mountains for the pleasure of looking down, I think that the urge to build and climb high is inherent within us.

In one sense there is a delight in making technology and materials work as hard as possible simply because we can. However, at the beginning of the twenty-first century there are far more urgent reasons for building tall: cultural, demographic, economic and environmental. Two vital factors are global population growth and the increasing rate of urbanisation. The world's population has doubled to six billion since 1960 and is currently growing at the rate of seventy-eight million a year – a pattern that is expected to continue for at least the next decade.

Hand-in-hand with this trend is a worldwide shift towards living in cities. It is estimated that by 2030 two thirds of the world's population will be urbanised. While the established giants such as London continue to expand, a new generation of mega-cities in excess of twenty-five million people is predicted in the next fifteen years. The major challenge in such cities is to accommodate more and more people, at greater densities than before, while seeking to create a higher quality of urban life. The tall building may not be the only key, but with finite resources, and with less and less land on which to build, it is a vital component of the future city.

Energy consumption and pollution are also key factors. In the developed world, buildings account for half the energy we consume, with transport and industry together accounting for the rest. If you analyse that breakdown further, you find that energy consumption and urban density are inextricably linked. As cities spread horizontally and their populations spend more time in their cars travelling to and from work, levels of energy consumption and pollution rise. By building to greater densities and to higher levels of energy efficiency in urban centres with established public transport systems we can reduce the reliance on the car. We can also improve the quality of urban life, bringing down travel times and allowing people to live, work and spend their leisure time in close proximity.

There are many myths propagated about density. For example, people imagine that density is somehow equated with poverty. But that does not follow. Monaco and Macau are two of the world's densest communities, yet they are at the opposite ends of the spectrum socially and economically.

It is interesting to note the shifting geographical spread of tall buildings in the last two decades and the changing attitudes to skyscrapers around the world. The established centres in the West have fast been overtaken by the rush to build tall in Asia and the Pacific Rim. China alone has twenty-two of the world's hundred tallest buildings, second only to the United States, and cities such as Shanghai have been transformed beyond recognition. In ten years, Pudong, Shanghai's business district, has gained the kind of skyline that took fifty years to achieve in New York and thirty years in Hong Kong.

While few people would welcome the arrival of the skyscraper in sensitive historic city centres such as Florence or Istanbul, the last few years have witnessed a radical change in attitudes to tall buildings in some of Europe's oldest cities. Madrid and Barcelona, for example, have plans for a series of towers to meet their shortage of flexible modern office space.

London, long resistant to upward growth, now anticipates the construction of a wave of tall buildings. The headquarters for Swiss Re, in the City, can be seen as a herald of this trend. Other progressive new developments on the horizon include Renzo Piano's London Bridge Tower, which offers living and working accommodation for 8000 people, sited above one of the busiest transport hubs in the capital. The low-rise, low-density alternative to schemes such as this would be to accommodate all those people in conventional developments in the suburbs or the green belt, thus creating additional congestion and pollution and consuming up to twenty times the amount of land.

This book comes at a crucial moment in the development of our cities. It presents an argument in favour of taller structures, not because they are the ultimate expression of Modernism, or of a particular aesthetic, but because they can help to achieve higher densities and to solve the problem of growth in our cities.

Norman Foster

INTRODUCTION

The early years in Europe

Selected early tall buildings

While the 11-storey Witte Huis office building in Rotterdam, The Netherlands, (Willem Molenbroek, **1898**) is usually regarded as the first tall building in Europe, it was in Antwerp, Belgium in **1932** that the 26-storey Torengebouw (now KBC) became Europe's first skyscraper, remaining its tallest until the 1950s. Designed by Vanhoenacker, Smolderen and Van Averbeke, its style was reminiscent of the great early American skyscrapers.

In Amiens, France, architects-contractors Perret were asked by the authorities in 1942 to design the new plaza fronting the railway station. The Tour Perret was to be a landmark entry comprising shops and offices. Construction began in **1949** and was interrupted about three years later. People were not ready to live in such a structure. Construction resumed in 1959 and the 26-storey 101-metre building, which was eventually designed as a residential project, was completed in 1960. In Madrid, Spain Torre de Madrid (Otamendi, 1957), became the tallest building in Western Europe at 142 metres. In Milan, Italy in **1958** the 28-storey Torre Velasca (B.B.P.R.) recalled a historical Milan typified by the tower of the Sforzesco Castle. It is one of the few contextual towers built at a time when Europe was invaded by a series of pure Modernist tall buildings such as the Pirelli Building, also in Milan (Gio Ponti, Pier Luigi Nervi, **1960**). The same year in Paris, France, the 23-storey residential Edouard Albert building (Edouard Albert, Henri Boileau, Roger Labourdette), became the first high-rise building in Paris. The 22-storey Royal SAS Hotel (now Radisson SAS Royal Hotel) in Copenhagen, Denmark designed by Arne Jacobsen, was also completed in 1960.

Torengebouw, Antwerp, Belgium, Jan Vanhoenacker, Jos Smolderen and Emiel Van Averbeke, 1932, 26 storeys

Photography: *Courtesy KBC Archives*

Tour Perret, Amiens, France, Auguste and Gustave Perret, 1949–1960, 26 storeys; glass-lantern addition by architect Thierry Van de Wyngaert in 2005

Photomontage: *Thierry Van de Wyngaert*

Selected early regional high-rise zones

Most of the very early tall buildings in Europe were either residential, hospitality or mixed-use projects. It was not until the mid-1960s, and the accompanying office real estate boom, that the European skyscraper became predominantly an office building. Isolated office or hotel towers were usually in city centres, with low- to middle-income housing tower blocks on the periphery of the same cities. These housing tower blocks contributed to the poor image of the tall building in Europe that lingered for decades, a result of poor construction standards and ineffective urban planning.

In **London, United Kingdom,** several projects completed in the 1960s and 1970s, which at the time provoked outcry from some and disdain from others, are now listed projects, thus proving that only time can allow for reasonable judgment when it comes to architecture and urbanism. A good example is the 35-storey Centre Point located on Tottenham Court Road (R. Seifert & Partners, 1966). It has been a grade II listed building since 1995 and is now an integral part of the London skyline. The use of special precast capstone units, as both structure and finish, permitted rapid construction; however, the slender elegant reinforced concrete tower was infamous for being empty for a long time in the 1970s.

Modernist tall buildings for public housing spread around the whole country. The 31-storey residential Trellick Tower (Ernö Goldfinger, 1972), epitomises the low-income 'tower blocks' built at the time although most were less stylish than this example. It has been a grade II listed building since 1998. Other grade II listed tall buildings in London include

Centre Point, London, United Kingdom, R. Seifert & Partners, 1966, 35 storeys

Photography: *G. Binder, courtesy Buildings & Data SA*

Trellick Tower, London, United Kingdom, Ernö Goldfinger, 1968, 31 storeys

Photography: *G. Binder, courtesy Buildings & Data SA*

the Barbican towers, part of the 2000-unit Barbican housing ensemble designed in 1956 by Chamberlin, Powell and Bon, and built between 1963 and 1982. The Barbican is part of a series of European large-scale centrally located projects designed in the 1950s that comprise tall buildings erected above vast pedestrian concrete slabs, such as the Tour Maine-Montparnasse in Paris and the Cité Administrative de l'Etat in Brussels. Over the years, the Barbican has been connected via elevated pedestrian walkways to many other adjacent buildings, thus making the area one of the major European urban automobile-free ensembles.

The Commercial Union building (now Aviva Tower), in the heart of the financial centre of London, is one of the purest pieces of high-rise

Hotels as skyscraper catalysts in Europe and the Middle East

Until the early 1970s, many of the high-rise buildings in major **European** cities were hotels. Many were American, such as the 29-storey London Hilton (1963); and Brussels' Knott's Westbury (23 storeys, 1963) and Brussels Hilton (29 storeys, 1967). In 1974, the 33-storey Concorde Lafayette and the 31-storey Paris Sheraton Hotel (now Méricien Montparnasse) were the second- and third-tallest buildings in Paris, behind the Tour Maine-Montparnasse. Hotels in Berlin, Frankfurt and Hamburg were the tallest buildings in those cities at the time of completion in the 1960s and 1970s. Moscow's 34-storey 198-metre-high Ukraina Hotel, constructed in 1957, remains Europe's tallest hotel almost 50 years after its completion. One of the most famous of these early European hotels is the 22-storey Royal SAS Hotel (now Radisson SAS Royal Hotel) in Copenhagen, designed by Arne Jacobsen and the city's tallest building at time of completion in 1960.

Hilton introduced tall buildings in locations such as Israel with the 17-storey Hilton Tel Aviv in 1965 and in 1974, the 21-storey Jerusalem Hilton (now Crowne Plaza Hotel), which remains the tallest building in the Israeli capital. Both hotels were designed by Yacov Rechter Architect.

The 14-storey Istanbul Hilton, (Gordon Bunshaft, Skidmore, Owings & Merrill, 1955) was the first European Hilton and was probably the first building to bring the International Style on a grand scale to the commercial scenery of Europe. It was also the tallest building in town when completed. The Hilton hotel chain, followed by CP Hotels, InterContinental, Holiday Inn and Sheraton – albeit often with less architectural panache – played a major role in the foundation of the high-rise building in Europe as an established building type. Many of these hotels remain as stand-alone towers, often in central locations facing parks or gardens where tall buildings would not be permitted to be built today. Examples include the Hilton hotel in Brussels, facing the Parc d'Egmont and the London Hilton, facing Hyde Park.

In **Africa**, hospitality towers have also historically been among the tallest buildings. Examples include the Hilton in Nairobi (1969), the Hôtel du 2 Février in Lomé (1980), the 36-storey Ramses Hilton in Cairo (1980), the Sheraton Harare (1986), the Ambassador Hotel in Harare (1995), and the Hôtel Ivoire InterContinental in Abidjan.

In Dubai, in the **Middle East**, the 321-metre Burj Al Arab became the world's tallest hotel when it opened at the end of 1999. In 2000, the Emirates Towers (now Jumeirah Emirates Towers), a twin-tower project composed of a 355-metre office tower and a 309-metre atrium hotel, also brought international media attention to Dubai. These projects, initiated by the then Crown Prince Sheikh Mohammed bin Rashid Al Maktoum, now Ruler of Dubai, focused attention on Dubai as a new destination for tourism and business, in much the same way as the Petronas Towers did for Kuala Lumpur. The 67-storey, 333-metre Rose Rotana Suites continues this trend. The current wave of tall hotels in the Middle East is also a reflection of newly created Middle East-based hotel chains such as Jumeirah (Burj Al Arab, Jumeirah Emirates Towers), whose brand extends well beyond the boundaries of the Middle East, with the Jumeirah Carlton Tower in London and the Jumeirah Essex House in New York City.

Royal SAS Hotel (now Radisson SAS Royal Hotel), Copenhagen, Denmark, Arne Jacobsen, 1960, 22 storeys
Photography: Courtesy Radisson SAS Royal Hotel

Jerusalem Hilton (now Crowne Plaza), Jerusalem, Israel, Yacov Rechter, 1974, 21 storeys
Photography: Coll. G. Binder/Buildings & Data SA

Istanbul Hilton, Istanbul, Turkey, Gordon Bunshaft of Skidmore, Owings & Merrill with Sedad H. Eldem, 1955, 14 storeys
Photography: Coll. G. Binder/Buildings & Data SA

Burj Al Arab, Dubai, United Arab Emirates, WS Atkins, 1999, 52 storeys
Photography: Courtesy Atkins

Espace Nord (originally Quartier Nord), Brussels, Belgium, recent view
***Photography:** Airprint Business Communication*

Front de Seine, Paris, France, recent view
***Photography:** Courtesy Valode & Pistre Architectes*

architecture of the International Style in Europe. The timeless 28-storey cantilevered tower was designed in 1969 by Gollins Melvin Ward and Partners and was the first of a cluster of towers still under progress today.

Belgium has played a major role in the history of tall buildings on the Old Continent: Antwerp's Torengebouw was the first major skyscraper in Europe, but in 1961 **Brussels** put its mark on the high-rise scene with the 30-storey Centre International Rogier. Designed by Jacques Cuisinier, it was one of the first early extensive mixed-use projects. The project was successful in its early years but faded away in the 1970s. Demolished in 2001, it was recently replaced by a new 145-metre office building. No doubt, the next generation will understand the mistake of demolishing this building.

In 1966, the 37-storey Tour du Midi was, at 149.2 metres, the tallest building in Belgium and in Western Europe. The cantilevered tower structure, using 38-metre long Preflex beams, was designed by civil engineer Abraham Lipski. It is interesting to note that this tallest building in Belgium was a government initiative housing a public administration.

In 1967 a master plan was designed for the Quartier Nord (now Espace Nord) area of Brussels. Created by Groupe Structures at the request of the Brussels authorities, the plan covered a 53-hectare area next to the Gare du Nord (one of Brussels' main railway stations, rebuilt in the mid 1950s) and called for a series of buildings on an orthogonal plan. The towers were to be linked by bridges and the traffic was to remain underneath the pedestrian platforms. There was no political vision at the time to adopt this plan in a coherent way and the city authorities allowed tall buildings to be built at the same time in many locations around town, so few occupants were willing to settle in the Quartier Nord dedicated high-rise area, a factor compounded by the 1973 economic crisis. By the mid 1980s, only a few towers, including the World Trade Center, had been completed. By the end of the 1980s, the second generation in charge of the privately run development company CDP Group, historically the area's primary developer, had gradually transformed the Quartier Nord (renamed Espace Nord in the early 1990s) as the place to build large-scale projects in Brussels. With a government ministry office building and JP Morgan's Euroclear building completed in the early 1990s, the Espace Nord was on track for continuing success. The overall project has been amended and the concrete pedestrian platforms and highways scheduled in the 1967 plan now accommodate a landscaped promenade designed by Wirtz International.

Paris, France with the well-known exception of the 58-storey Tour Maine-Montparnasse (1973), does not have a lot of tall buildings within the Paris city limits. Most have been built in specifically designed areas, such as the Front de Seine and the Quartier d'Italie for residential tall buildings. Office towers are within the 3,420,000-square-metre La Défense area which, although designed for office towers, has a few residential towers at its periphery, such as the 46-storey Défense 2000 completed in 1974, France's tallest residential building. La Défense epitomises its architects' and urban planners' early visions of living in tall buildings located high above a vast landscaped concrete slab, with motor vehicle circulation below.

The Tour Maine-Montparnasse, designed by Eugène Beaudouin, Urbain Cassan, Louis de Hoym de Marien and Jean Saubot with A. Epstein and Sons as consulting architect, is part of a larger urban project comprising the reconstruction of the Montparnasse railway station. After the reconstruction, the station was hidden behind three large tower blocks so that the identifying feature of the station is now the Tour Maine-Montparnasse office tower. The 58-storey skyscraper is a major European project not only because it was the tallest in Western Europe from 1973 till 1990 but because it combines generic ideas such as creating a tall urban signal or totem, often found opposite a major railway station as it is the case here, in addition to the large esplanade which comes with so many tall buildings conceived in those times.

The Front de Seine, following a master plan by Raymond Lopez together with Henry Pottier, is a tall buildings area erected along the Seine River on a former industrial site, not far from the Eiffel Tower. It was also built in accordance with urban planning ideals of the 1960s: tall buildings erected above a landscaped platform with traffic underneath. Comprising some 20 residential towers and a few commercial buildings, the one-kilometre long, 25-hectare project, which also features retail space, was mostly built between 1968 and 1978. Most of the cantilevered towers are about 100 metres high and the first four levels are recessed to allow more free space around the buildings along the esplanade, while giving the Front de Seine its own architectural identity.

The 19-storey Unité d'Habitation in **Marseilles** (Le Corbusier, 1952) was a new vision for social housing, providing communal amenities for the building occupants. This project was probably the catalyst for the building of many tower blocks in many locations in the following 25 years.

The 24-storey Mannesmann-Hochhaus in **Düsseldorf, Germany** (Paul Schneider von Esleben, 1956) is one of the early Modernist tall buildings in Europe. Also in Düsseldorf and still one of the country's greatest is the Thyssenhaus, originally known as Phoenix Reinrhor, designed in 1960 by Hentrich and Petschnigg, the architects who formed HPP. Its

Paris La Défense: a unique tall buildings vision

In 1960, EPAD, the *Etablissement Public pour l'Aménagement de la Défense,* the public body responsible for developing the La Défense area, proposed a master plan along a major Parisian historical development axis towards the west. This major axis includes the Champ Elysées and the Arc de Triomphe. The master plan was designed by architects Robert Camelot, Jean de Mailly, and Bernard Zerhfuss. The plan was drawn according to the principles of the Charter of Athens as proposed by Le Corbusier. Approved in December 1964, 850,000 square metres of offices were scheduled in the new plan by Auzelle, Herbé, Camelot, de Mailly and Zehrfuss. The same year, oil company Esso completed the first office building in La Défense; it became the first modern office building in Paris.

The main idea behind the plan was to separate car traffic and pedestrian circulation routes. Offices were to be housed in tall buildings while people were to live in low-rise structures with square courtyards and inner gardens. The office towers were initially planned as 25-storey, 100-metre-tall buildings, aligned two by two, with a gross typical floor plate of 24 metres x 42 metres (1008 square metres) for a total of 27,000 square metres while the residential buildings were not be taller than 12 levels. Buildings were to be located on both sides of a vast landscaped 1.5-kilometer-long, 12-hectare esplanade known as *la dalle*. Later, both the office and residential buildings were conceived with a wider variety of shapes and scope. About 25,000 people and hundreds of businesses had to be relocated to make room for the new urban ensemble.

In 1966, the Tour Nobel (now Tour Initiale) was the first high-rise office building to open in La Défense and the Paris area. In 1970, there was a need for more office space; a new master plan was approved in 1972 allowing the construction of taller and larger buildings, such as Tour GAN (44 storeys, 1973), by Harrison, Abramovitz and Bisseuil and Tour Fiat (now Tour Areva, 46 storeys, 1974) by Skidmore, Owings & Merrill associated with Saubot-Jullien. These towers responded to the increased demand for office space and the requirement of large open-plan work areas. While the early towers had 1000-square-metre floor plates, too small for the real estate demand, the new buildings had up to and over 2000-square-metre floor plates. In 1972, when the concrete core of the Tour GAN under construction appeared through the Arc de Triomphe when seen from the Champs Elysées perspective, there was a chorus of criticism about the height of these new towers; while Valéry Giscard d'Estaing, then Minister of Finance, wanted to shorten the new towers, President Georges Pompidou eventually decided to retain the height of the new tall buildings as planned. The oil and economic crisis of 1973 halted the development of new projects but a series of buildings were still under construction.

In 1981, Les Quatre Temps, then the largest shopping mall in Europe, opened and President Mitterrand placed Tête Défense on the *Grands projets* list. A competition was organized and the Grande Arche project, designed by Johan von Spreckelsen, was completed by Paul Andreu in 1989. In the mid-1990s, the construction of the Tour EDF, designed by Henry Cobb of Pei Cobb Freed & Partners and developed by Hines, brought optimism to the La Défense district and was soon followed by a new series of successful projects completed or still under progress.

With the exception of three sites (CNIT, Esso/Coeur Défense and Septentrion/Europlaza) built prior to the La Défense master plan where owners have title to the land, ownership of the early generation of the so-called '24 x 42 towers' is limited to the exact size of the building footprint at the esplanade level, without any additional area around the building. The ownership of the next generation of towers, beginning in the early 1970s, evolved with what makes the La Défense project so unique – the building owners do not own the land under the towers or endless volumes towards the sky but rather 'volumetric divisions' above and below the esplanade with a pre-set limit below and above. EPAD is thus selling 'construction rights' to developers; this in turn has allowed it to finance infrastructural works. La Défense is a living development area where development sites may be optimized or newly created, such as in the case of the recently completed Tour CBX or slightly expanded, such as the former Tour du Crédit Lyonnais, which was renovated and renamed Opus 12 with larger typical floor plates as EPAD sold additional 'volumetric divisions' to the developer allowing the floor expansion required by the market demand.

According to EPAD, 150,000 people work at La Défense and 20,000 people reside there; more are scheduled in the coming years with 110,000 square metres of new housing proposed. The 160-hectare area of La Défense currently includes 3,420,000 square metres of current office space, 210,000 square metres of retail space, 2800 hotel rooms, 31 hectares of platforms and promenades, 11 hectares of landscaped gardens, 90,000 square metres of roads (of which 60,000 square metres are covered), 46,000 underground parking spaces and more than 60 monumental art pieces by noted artists, including Agam, Calder and Miro. All this has made La Défense a truly unique urban environment on a scale that epitomises the dream of many architects and urban planners of the previous century.

EPAD has recently proposed to the French Government in its programme for the next 15 years that in addition to 110,000 square metres of new housing, an additional 500,000 square metres of offices be built, 350,000 square metres be renovated and a 400-metre tower be erected as a strong architectural gesture for the district. The additional built space would bring the La Défense FAR to 3.7 (*La Défense 2015 – Le sens de l'avenir*, EPAD, 2006), the same as the well-known Triangle d'Or – or Golden Triangle area – near the Champs Elysées.

Finally, of note are two major historical projects never built, but which attracted much attention to the La Défense area: a 324-metre stainless steel sculpture named Tour Lumière Cybernétique by Hungarian-born artist Nicolas Schöffer, was first unveiled in 1963 and was intended to become a new lighthouse beacon for Paris; the 100-storey Tour sans fins, designed by Jean Nouvel & Associés in 1989 was another dazzling proposal for the area.

Paris La Défense, France, recent view
Photography: *Michael Hierner*

Moscow State University, Moscow, Russia, Lev Rudnev, Sergei Tchernitchev, Pavel Abrosimov, Alexander Khriakov, 1953, 36 storeys
Photography: *Airprint Business Communication, Brussels*

One Canada Square (centre) at Canary Wharf, Cesar Pelli & Associates, 1991, 48 storeys
Photography: *Courtesy Canary Wharf PLC*

rational articulated floor plan can be seen in many other projects. In 1960 Alvar Aalto designed his only tall building, Bremen's Neue Vahr, a 22-storey residential building whose plan opens out like a fan in order to allow all studios, each with its own loggia, to face towards light while the service core is relegated along the other façade.

A fact not widely known is that the tallest building in Europe from 1953 until 1990, was in **Moscow, Russia**. The 240-metre, 36-storey Moscow State University was part of series of seven high-rise projects begun in Moscow in the late 1940s according to a plan supported by Stalin. A similar project, the Palace of Culture and Science, was built in **Warsaw, Poland** in 1955. This was a gift of Stalin, from the 'mother country' to Poland. These Moscow and Warsaw projects were designed by a team led by Lev Rudnev. All the early Russian skyscrapers – which were not to be lookalikes of their American counterparts – may be interpreted as smaller versions of a plan of the late 1930s to build the Palace of the Soviets not far from the Kremlin. The 416-metre project – taller than the Empire State Building – designed by Iofan, Chtchouko, Guelfreikh and Merkoulov, was expected to be topped by a huge 100-metre statue to the glory of Lenin that was never built.

Europe today

Northern Europe is not known as a tall buildings zone. However, Santiago Calatrava and the City of **Malmö, Sweden** attracted much attention with the award-winning 190-metre, 54-storey residential HSB Turning Torso with its nine rotating building units towering high above the city. It is interesting to note that the city that choose to support the construction of a super-tall tower – as it is seen locally – is also generally regarded as the densest city in Sweden.

Rotterdam, The Netherlands, a city destroyed during World War II was, along with Frankfurt, one of the few European cities where political leaders and urban planners have demonstrated their shared belief in the benefits offered by tall buildings. The tallest towers spread from the Central Station in the Weena area where in 1992 the Delftse Poort (ING) became the country's tallest building at 151 metres. Across the street, the project was followed in 2000 by the Millennium, which houses offices atop a Westin hotel. It was one of the first major mixed-use towers built in the city. Others include De Rotterdam (Rem Koolhaas, OMA), to be built at Kop van Zuid on former docks between towers by Foster and Piano. De Rotterdam will be one of the most diverse mixed-use high-rise ensembles ever built in the country. Steps away, the mixed-use Montevideo recently became the tallest tower in The Netherlands at 152.3 metres. These buildings should in the future be topped by the 51-storey mixed-use Coolsingel Tower designed by PPKS Architects. This project may well epitomise a new way of life in continental Europe, integrating hotel, housing and office in a single 215-metre glass tower. High-rise living is becoming part of Rotterdam's urban environment.

Most tall buildings in **Amsterdam** have been built on the outskirts of the city, especially in the Zuidas – or South Axis – area, which features tall

In Germany, the pencil tower is queen; in Europe and the Middle East, the gherkin is king

RWE, Essen, Germany, Ingenhoven Overdiek und Partner, 1996, 31 storeys

Photography: Courtesy Ingenhoven und Partner Architekten

Victoria-Haus, Düsseldorf, Hentrich Petschnigg & Partner (HPP), 1998, 29 storeys

Photography: Manfred Hanisch

Westhafen Tower, Frankfurt, Germany, schneider+schumacher, 2003, 29 storeys

Photography: Waltrand Krase

Peachtree Plaza, Atlanta, Georgia, USA, John Portman & Associates, 1976, 73 storeys

Photography: Coll. G Binder/Buildings & Data SA

Following the completion of the cylindrical RWE tower in Essen in 1996, a number of pencil towers have appeared around Germany, as though every single city in the country wanted its own landmark cylindrical tower. Examples include Victoria-Haus, Düsseldorf, Hentrich Petschnigg & Partner (HPP), 1998; DLZ Trendpark (TDS-turm), Neckarsulum, Ziltz + Partner, 1999; Business Tower, Nuremberg, Dürschinger and Biefang with Spengler, 2000; Main Tower, Frankfurt which is actually made up of a circle and a square, Architekten Schweger + Partner, 1999; Intershop-Tower, Jena, Plannungsgruppe Geburtig, Büro Weimar und Architekturbüro Ruhland, 2001; Sparkassen Pforzheim Calw, Pforzheim, archis, 2001; Munich City Tower, Munich, Heinz A. Musil, 2003; and Westhafen Tower, Frankfurt, schneider+schumacher, 2003.

All the abovementioned towers are office buildings. In the past, most of the few cylindrical towers have been hospitality projects, such as the 40-storey Washington Plaza (now The Westin Seattle) in Seattle, Washington (John Graham Associates, 1969) or the 73-storey Peachtree Plaza (now The Westin Peachtree Plaza) in Atlanta, Georgia in 1976 – then the world's tallest hotel – designed by John Portman & Associates.

Could it be that the cylindrical pencil tower epitomises the German landmark tall building while the gherkin shape epitomises the pan European–Middle East tall building on the international scene? There is indeed a special attitude from the public towards such projects, which began following the publicity, well before construction, of Foster and Partners' 30 St Mary Axe in London and Barcelona's Torre Agbar, completed in 2005 and designed by Jean Nouvel with b720 Arquitectos. Nouvel has also designed a new tower of similar iconic shape, which is under construction in Doha, Qatar and scheduled for completion in 2007. Both Torre Agbar and 30 St Mary Axe are among the most widely published buildings over the last 20 years. Returning to the German circular towers, it should also be noted that the RWE tower by Ingenhoven Overdiek und Partner is one of the most widely published European tall buildings of the 1990s – can this partly explain the incredibly large series of German cylindrical towers that followed and why then only in Germany when the building became famous well beyond the German boundaries?

Perhaps French architect André Bruyère, who designed an egg-shaped skyscraper in the early 1970s – such a project was also proposed to house the Centre Georges Pompidou cultural and art centre in Paris – found the secret to building successful tall buildings as he said once with a sense of humour: *'There is a campaign against skyscrapers which quite often prevents their construction. The principle of them pleases me more than the way in which they are sometimes handled. I noted that there is no campaign against eggs.'* (André Bruyère, *L'Oeuf/The Egg*, Albin Michel, Paris, 1978).

Eggs and gherkins share an almost perfect form, easily readable by all, however complex the geometric form of those objects can be. Those organic-shaped towers lead perhaps to their wide acceptance among the general public and public authorities.

30 St Mary Axe, London, United Kingdom, Foster and Partners, 2003, 41 storeys

Photography: Nigel Young/Foster and Partners

Torre Agbar, Barcelona, Spain, Ateliers Jean Nouvel with b720 Arquitectos, 2005, 35 storeys

Photography: Rafael Vargas

Doha High-rise Building, Doha, Qatar, Ateliers Jean Nouvel with Arab Engineering Bureau, 2007, 44 storeys

Rendering: Courtesy Ateliers Jean Nouvel

The Egg, André Bruyère, 1978, 36 storeys

Rendering: *Reproduced from André Bruyère,* The Egg/L'Oeuf, *Albin Michel, Paris, 1978, coll. G Binder/Buildings & Data SA*

buildings designed by many noted architects. Zuidas is located on either side of the south circular road, within easy reach of the Schipol Airport and is linked to the centre of Amsterdam by a metro line. The Dutch Government, the City of Amsterdam and the property sector reached an agreement to bring roads and rail tracks underground. The amount of free space created above the infrastructure along 1.2 kilometres will be used to create a very dense mixed-use area with 100-metre towers.

The Hague boasts a series of projects by American firms, including the Zurichtoren (Cesar Pelli & Associates), the Castalia, a 1967 office building rebuilt around its original shell by Michael Graves and the award-winning Hoftoren (Kohn Pedersen Fox Associates). The Hoftoren, located next to the main railway station, has become a city beacon.

Frankfurt, Germany, which leads German cities in terms of skyscrapers, has a main axis along which the tallest buildings have been built since the early 1970s. This axis, along Mainzer Landstrasse, forms a major urban ensemble, linking the railway station to the heart of the financial district. In some ways, Frankfurt owes the initial attention brought to tall building architecture to American or American-based architectural firms such as Murphy/Jahn with the MesseTurm (1990), and to Kohn Pedersen Fox Associates with the 1993 DG Bank (now DZ Bank) and later to other international firms such as Foster and Partners with the Commerzbank. The city is proud of its skyline and uses it as a tool to attract tourists and business travellers. Main Tower, completed in 1999, brought back a top-floor skydeck open to tourists as a city attraction, an amenity which up to then was considered more as an old-fashioned feature, proving that a building and a skyscraper in particular can bring life and enjoyment to an area. The adjacent 32-storey Eurotheum adds life to the central business district with its 74 residential units located in the building's upper levels and its six glass-enclosed elevators.

Several German tall buildings are accessible to the general public, including the atriums of the DZ Bank and the Commerzbank, and the penthouse restaurant atop Main Tower, all located in Frankfurt. Several feature amenities on the roof (instead of the usual blind mechanical roof levels) such as the landscaped terrace of the RWE Hochhaus in Essen or the rooftop atrium in Uptown München in Munich. Perhaps these contribute to the generally wide acceptance of the tall building in Germany.

Vienna, Austria which didn't have many tall buildings until a decade ago, now features several high-rise buildings, mainly in the Donau City area located on the left bank of the Danube. The first project, completed in 1979, was UNO-City (United Nations Offices) at the 24-storey Y-shaped Vienna International Centre. Donau City has since evolved into an urban ensemble comprising both office and residential towers.

Among the first real major tall buildings in **London, United Kingdom** was the Centre Point tower, designed by Richard Seifert in 1966. Seifert also put his name to what was the tallest tower in London until Canary Wharf came along: the National Westminster Tower, later known as NatWest Tower and now renamed Tower 42. The National Westminster Tower, which in 1980 became the tallest tower in the United Kingdom at 183 metres, was also probably the world's tallest cantilevered building. Its construction actually began in 1971 and took about 10 years to be completed. Until the completion in 1991 of Canary Wharf's One Canada Square, almost a generation passed without any newly conceived major tall building in London.

Canary Wharf is the revitalization of a vacated Port of London Docklands site, providing office, recreational and retail facilities. Skidmore, Owings & Merrill developed the master plan, which included design guidelines, infrastructure design and the establishment of development parcels. The plan includes high-rise office towers in the central core of the site with low- to mid-rise buildings oriented to the waterfront around the core.

The Leadenhall Building, London, United Kingdom, The Richard Rogers Partnership, planning consent granted, 47 storeys
***Rendering:** Cityscape, courtesy The British Land Company PLC*

From 1981 to 1998, the London Docklands Development Corporation was an urban development corporation originally established by Michael Heseltine, then Secretary of State for the Environment, and an instrumental figure in the creation of the Canary Wharf development.

In the year 2000, London's first-ever elected mayor, Ken Livingstone, wanted to boost the economy as much as he wanted to create new urban environments. He believed that creating high-rise landmark statements such as the future 288-metre Bishopsgate Tower, designed

Madou Plaza, Brussels, Belgium, ASSAR, lead and design architect Archi 2000, 2006, 34 storeys
Photography: *ASSAR*

by Kohn Pedersen Fox Associates, would reinforce the fact that the heart of the economic city centre should remain as such and evolve in accordance with the times. With a rooftop restaurant scheduled, the tower can also be a part of London's entertainment scene. The new towers will add density to the city: as an example, the 55-storey 55,000-square-metre Leadenhall Building designed by the Richard Rogers Partnership and scheduled to replace the existing 1969 122 Leadenhall Street building will have a floor capacity increased by more than three times when comparing both buildings. In addition to recent corporate towers, there are a growing number of new residential tall buildings such as the 46-storey Pan Peninsula Tower designed by Skidmore, Owings & Merrill in the Canary Wharf area, scheduled to become the tallest residential building in the country when completed in 2007.

These dramatic changes in London's urban development have occurred in parallel with other changes in the city, such as the long-delayed redevelopment around Paternoster Square, completed in 2003. London authorities, while encouraging the construction of carefully designed tall buildings in specific areas, have also been encouraging the demolition of older 1960s tall building eyesores such as those at Paternoster Square, one of the areas much debated by Prince Charles in the late 1980s. Today, London demonstrates one of the most coherent political visions in terms of building tall in Europe. Tall buildings are symbolic of the regeneration and new urban development in London, led by mayor Ken Livingstone.

Other cities in the United Kingdom have created their own flagship buildings, such as the 48-storey Beetham Tower in **Manchester**, which encompasses a Hilton hotel with residential units in the upper levels, and the 39-storey Holloway Circus Tower in **Birmingham,** accommodating housing and a Radisson SAS hotel. Both projects are by Ian Simpson Architects.

Brussels, Belgium, as it was in 1965–1975, is again involved in a high-rise construction boom, but in this case it is a matter of managing the legacy of the past. Projects comprise either the construction of tall buildings that were part of master plans drawn up in the 1960s, as in the case of the Espace Nord, or involve renovation or reconstruction of existing buildings. A failure in its early years, the 53-hectare Espace Nord area is now close to completion, with its majestic landscaped promenade featuring sculptures by internationally acclaimed artists. Among the projects recently completed or under progress within or immediately alongside the Espace Nord limits, are North Galaxy, Ellipse Building, Brussels Tower, Zenith Building, Dexia Tower and Covent Garden, and not too far away, the Tour de la Cité Administrative is under renovation, thus making the area one of the most active tall building construction sites in Europe. Also in Brussels is the 34-storey 2006 MIPIM Award winner Madou Plaza, which has been rebuilt around its original 1965 shell. Madou Plaza, designed by ASSAR in association with Archi 2000 is probably the city's most ambitious renovated tower. The double-skinned building occupied by the European Commission has been totally transformed in terms of volume and texture and its relation to the urban environment with a newly built plaza. It is worth noting that Madou Plaza would not have received planning permission today if the plan had involved the construction of a new tall building rather than the transformation of an existing one.

In **France,** one location is predominant in terms of tall buildings. Over the last 30 years, most French tall buildings have been erected in the Paris La Défense area. Recent and current projects include towers designed by French architects including Atelier Christian de Portzamparc, Valode & Pistre Architectes and Jean-Paul Viguier and American firms such as Arquitectonica, Kohn Pedersen Fox Associates and Pei Cobb Freed & Partners. Kohn Pedersen Fox Associates will renovate, transform and expand the 1974 Tour Axa, the former Tour Assur, forming an impressive sight at the entrance to the La Défense district and expected to become France's tallest building.

In the early to mid 1990s in **Lille**, Euralille, a large urban ensemble around the new railway station and a new shopping mall, was constructed as part of a master plan by Rem Koolhaas. The taller buildings are the Tour Lilleurope (Claude Vasconi architecte) and the Tour du Crédit Lyonnais (Atelier Christian de Portzamparc). Both projects, completed in 1995, form a bridge structure spanning across the railway tracks while a series of lower buildings designed by Jean Nouvel are also part of the overall project that signals the city's urban

An architect's view of London

London is a global city. It attracts tens of thousands of new residents every year and there is little evidence that this will subside anytime soon. London is not a typical British city, as New York is not particularly American; it is multicultural, polycentric and economically focused. This is an important part of London's character. Like other global cities, London is under tremendous urban pressure. As a modern city it is subject to change and in need of constant renewal. Global cities cannot resist change if they are to maintain their status and clearly, London's strategy to embrace growth by promoting a more dense and compact city is correct. The challenge for London is how to do this while maintaining a high quality of life that is enjoyable and affordable. The solutions to these issues are never simple; however, I would offer that part of a solution lies in London promoting a more diversified built form and I would suggest that tall buildings form an important part of that diversity, not because they are tall and attract attention, but because if developed properly, they provide a more sustainable long-term use of land and resources.

London is an ancient city, built on layers of history. The scale of its streets, the proportion of its building plots and its medieval figure ground all form part of its unique identity. Its parks, great monuments and its river help contribute to this uniqueness. Both its physical context and its political context play a role in deciding the architecture of London's tall buildings. London is not a vertical city and in my opinion it is unlikely that it will become a city dominated by verticality. But this does not mean that tall structures cannot be integrated into its landscape. Because it is not a vertical city, its policies on promoting verticality are in stark contrast to those of other cities. New York is a vertical city. It has a grid iron figure ground and promotes the development of tall buildings with a clear zoning policy. Hong Kong is similar in that respect. Designing tall buildings under such policies and in this context will naturally influence the way one approaches the solution and clearly the results.

In London, at times one can sense the tension between old and new, almost a distrust of the modern. Given its history and the independence of each of its boroughs, London does not have a unified policy on the built environment or tall buildings. This tends to frustrate mostly everyone involved and at times it seems as though its politicians are trying to achieve the impossible – compose the skyline of a modern city.

The Bishopsgate Tower (centre), London, United Kingdom, Kohn Pedersen Fox Associates, planning consent granted, 60 storeys
Rendering: *Courtesy KPF and Cityscape*

Along with others, our work in designing tall buildings in London has been primarily focused within the 'City of London', the Square Mile.

- The City of London's context is challenging. Its medieval pattern and early Roman origins juxtapose the ancient and the modern.
- 'The City' has a goal of creating a cluster of tall buildings and has clearly defined an area in which tall buildings could be built.
- It has stated a desire to improve its skyline.
- It is a strong proponent of good design.

We must recognise that we are undoubtedly dealing with a period of strong visual change on London's skyline. This in itself is a provocative issue. As a generation of buildings, London's current crop of tall buildings present a unique opportunity in both scale and content for a 21st-century European model that responds to scale and context and an aspirational agenda for excellence in architecture.

Lee Polisano
President
Kohn Pedersen Fox Associates

Torre Repsol YPF, Madrid, Spain, Foster and Partners, 2008, 53 storeys
Rendering: *Courtesy Foster and Partners*

renewal. Construction of the Tour CMA CGM, designed by Zaha Hadid, is expected to begin soon in **Marseilles**, in the south of France. The headquarters project of the world's third-largest maritime shipping company should again highlight the architecture of Marseilles, more than fifty years after the completion of the Unité d'Habitation by Le Corbusier.

Early tall buildings in **Spain** included the Edificio Espana and later the concrete curvilinear-shaped residential Torres Blancas and Banco de Bilbao by Francisco Javier Saenz de Oiza, both in **Madrid**. There were few other major projects until 1988 when the 157-metre Torre Picasso (Minoru Yamasaki and Associates), became the tallest tower in Spain. In 1992–1994, the high-tech 45-storey Hotel Arts Barcelona in **Barcelona** designed by Bruce Graham of Skidmore, Owings & Merrill was completed. Another building of note in Barcelona is the recently completed Torre Agbar (Jean Nouvel with b720 Arquitectos). This long-awaited project was one of the most featured European tall buildings in architecture publications and one of the most talked about ever. With Torre Agbar accommodating the local water company, Barcelona authorities demonstrated that an iconic skyscraper can play a major role as a catalyst for a new commercial and business zone without disturbing the city historic core.

Following the lead of the twin leaning Puerta de Europa towers (John Burgee Architect with Philip Johnson as consultant,1996), is another series of prestigious high-rise buildings designed by noted architects. These include Torre de Cristal with its shining glass-enclosed roof garden (Pelli Clarke Pelli Architects), Torre Espacio (Pei Cobb Freed & Partners) and Torre Repsol YPF (Foster and Partners). The 53-storey 250-metre Torre Repsol YPF will top Torre Picasso by almost 100 metres. These projects will put Madrid on the European tall buildings map on a scale not seen before. In the housing area, Madrid is also thinking tall: the 21-story Mirador project (MVRDV), completed in 2005 in the Sanchinarro area can perhaps be seen as a revisited colourful contemporary vision of the ideal of Le Corbusier's Unité d'Habitation with its open air promenade deck on the 13th level as a high communal space.

While **Italy** had a few major tall buildings icons in the 20th century, such as the mixed-use Torre Velasca by B.B.P.R. and the sleek Pirelli Building by Gio Ponti completed in the late 1950s in **Milan**, the area – and Italy in general – didn't become a tall buildings zone in the way that might have been expected when these projects were completed. However the new 45-storey curvilinear glass Regione Lombardia headquarters (Pei Cobb Freed & Partners), destined to become Italy's tallest tower when completed in 2008, and new projects designed for Milan's Fair, will perhaps act as high-rise catalysts. The situation may also change when the unique trio of towers designed by Zaha Hadid Architects, Studio Daniel Libeskind, Arata Isozaki & Associates and Pier Paolo Maggiora is built in a few years. Elsewhere in Italy, noteworthy among the few tall buildings completed in the early 1990s in Naples are the ENEL twin towers (Pica Ciamarra Associati), characterised by their futuristic glass-enclosed elevators that travel along the main façade.

Eastern Europe today

In **Warsaw, Poland,** apart from the 231-metre high Palace of Culture and Science completed in 1955, there were few tall buildings until the late 1990s when American architects arrived with projects such as the 35-storey Warsaw Financial Center (Kohn Pedersen Fox Associates, 1999), the 43-storey Warsaw Trade Tower (RTKL, 2000) and the 22-storey Westin Warsaw hotel (John Portman & Associates, 2003). Among the most recent tall buildings in Warsaw are the 46-storey InterContinental Warszawa, Poland's tallest hotel (Tadeusz Spychala with Wojciech

Zlota 44, Warsaw, Poland, Studio Daniel Libeskind (centre), design 2005, 45 storeys in between the Palace of Culture and Science (left), Lev Rudnev, 1955, 43 storeys and the InterContinental Warszawa (right), Tadeusz Spychala with Wojciech Poplawski and Willibald Fürst, 2004, 46 storeys

Rendering: *Courtesy Studio Daniel Libeskind*

Triumph-Palace, Moscow, Russia, TROMOS, 2005, 57 storeys

Photography: *Courtesy DON-Stroy*

Poplawski and Willibald Fürst), which stands out with its corner pillar exposed along the lower half of the building. In the future, next to the InterContinental hotel, the 45-storey Zlota 44 project designed by Studio Daniel Libeskind and developed by Orco Property Group will be, at 192 metres, Europe's second-tallest residential high-rise building. The Libeskind design for the residential project may lead other developers

Burj Dubai, Dubai, United Arab Emirates, Adrian Smith of Skidmore, Owings & Merrill, 2008, more than 150 storeys

Rendering: *Courtesy Skidmore, Owings & Merrill LLP*

National Commerce Bank, Jeddah, Saudi Arabia, Gordon Bunshaft of Skidmore, Owings & Merrill, 1983, 27 storeys

***Photography:** Courtesy Skidmore, Owings & Merrill LLP*

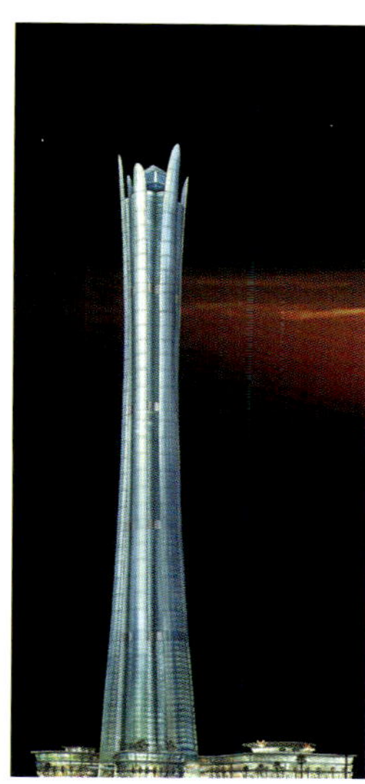

Burj Al Alam (The World Tower), Dubai, United Arab Emirates, Nihon Sekkei and Teo A. Khing Design Consultants, scheduled completion 2009, 108 storeys

***Rendering:** Courtesy Fortune Group*

in Poland and elsewhere to propose advanced-design residential towers since when it comes to tall buildings, the most innovative proposals have often been reserved for office and hotel projects.

Moscow, Russia leads the way in eastern Europe when it comes to tall buildings. Moscow State University remained the city's tallest for 50 years until recently with the completion of the 264.1-metre Triumph-Palace, a residential project designed by Andrey Trofimov of TROMOS in the same spirit as the early Moscow skyscrapers. DON-Stroy, the developer of Triumph-Palace, has recently completed other residential tall buildings such as Alye Parusa and Vorobyovy Hills, also designed by TROMOS, and more are in the pipeline. The following super-tall projects, designed in Moscow by a series of foreign-based architectural firms, are currently under construction: the 448-metre Federation Tower (Federation Tower Planning Association); the 286-metre twin-towered Capital City (NBBJ) and the 300-metre Moscow International Business Center (Swanke Hayden Connell Architects). Unveiled in March 2006, the Moscow City Towers is a 118-storey 600-metre mixed-use building designed by Foster and Partners and is scheduled to join the abovementioned towers in the most active super-tall buildings construction site area in Europe. The Moscow-City development, where most of the current super-tall buildings are located, is an initiative of the city authorities. Since some of the Moscow projects are financed by state-owned banks, some of these tall gestures can be seen to be in line with what is happening in several Asian and Middle East locations but at the same time, are also reminiscent of the Moscow towers approved by Stalin in an attempt to establish the former USSR by means of impressive buildings.

The Middle East

Istanbul, Turkey introduced the first International Style hospitality building to Europe with the 1955 Istanbul Hilton, and may well play a major role on the tall buildings scene over the next years. While the current tallest building in Istanbul is the 52-storey Is Bank headquarters, designed in 2000 by Swanke Hayden Connell Architects in the Levent tall buildings area, several super-tall high-rise projects currently at design phase or under progress may well radically transform the Istanbul skyline in the future.

With the limited availability of land and the anticipated expansion of the population, **Israel** can be expected to see an increase in the number its tall buildings. In Ramat Gan, in the **Tel-Aviv** area, the 68-storey mixed-use Moshe Aviv Tower (AMAV Planning/A. Niv–A.Schwartz Architects, 2003) is perhaps an indication of the future of such Israeli super-tall buildings.

Middle Eastern countries did not produce many tall buildings until the late 1990s. In 1983 in **Jeddah**, **Saudi Arabia** the 27-storey National Commerce Bank (Gordon Bunshaft, Skidmore, Owings & Merrill) was one of the Middle East's first great early high-rise projects. The stone-clad tower, comprising three stacked V-shaped elements which could be described as open-air atria, created a subtle working environment, protecting the building's occupants from the sun. A decade later, also in Jeddah, Nikken Sekkei showed an equally contextual approach with the 21-storey Islamic Development Bank Headquarters with its octagonal open-air inner light-court and the narrow vertical windows of the perimeter façades providing protection from the sun.

The 39-storey Dubai International Trade Centre (now World Trade Centre) designed by John R Harris Partnership in 1979 was the precursor to the impressive tall buildings era of the **United Arab Emirates**, particularly **Dubai,** that began with the Burj Al Arab in 1999, and the 305 and 355-metre hotel and office Emirates Towers, now known as the Jumeirah Emirates Towers, in 2000.

At the same time, the 302.3-metre-high mixed-use Kingdom Centre (Ellerbe Becket and Omrania & Associates) and the 267-metre Al Faisaliah complex (Foster and Partners) were completed in **Riyadh, Saudi Arabia**. Many of these super-tall buildings were initiated by the ruling families, as was the case in 1979 with the Dubai International Trade Centre. In **Dubai,** several super-tall residential towers such as the 90-storey 23 Marina or the 102-storey Princess Tower and of course the multi-use Burj Dubai, scheduled to be the world's tallest building at more than 150 storeys high, will create a brand new standard of living. The Burj Dubai crowns a series of super-tall projects initiated by or with the help of the man who became in January 2006 the new Ruler of Dubai. In a recent *Time* magazine devoted to 'the world's most influential people', the role of Mohammed bin Rashid Al Maktoum was recognised in the publication's 'builders and titans' category: 'Sheik Mo's bold vision of transforming Dubai (pop. 240,000, not including a million or so foreign workers) into another Singapore and raising GDP from $8 billion to $37 billion in 15 years is urban planning on a cosmic scale'. (*Time*, 8 May, 2006)

The 270,000-square-metre Burj Dubai literally takes the imagination to new heights. With more than 150 storeys at a height of well over 700 metres, can anyone really imagine what life will be like in such a building? And while most of the super-tall buildings of the past were predominantly office buildings, the Burj Dubai is predominantly a residential project, but also includes the first Armani-branded hotel and offices. We can certainly speak here of a new lifestyle. In Dubai – a city that is coming to rely more and more on tourism – some of the very tall buildings are hotels that have become destinations in their own right such as the Burj Al Arab or the Jumeirah Emirates Towers.

Not only does Dubai stand out through the pace of new super-tall skyscrapers being built or planned, but also through the very scale of the projects. The Jumeirah Beach Residences towers, developed by Dubai Properties and designed by Wimberly Allison Tong & Goo are 'only' 55 storeys high, but there are 36 towers, mostly residential ones, to be built in one single phase. On a similar scale is the 108-storey, 484-metre mixed-use Burj Al Alam (The World Tower) designed by Nihon Sekkei and Teo A. Khing Design Consultants and scheduled to be completed by the end of 2009. Of the many super-tall projects under progress in Dubai, it is one of the few that is predominantly an office tower. The project, which includes a hotel in the upper levels, is part of Business Bay, destined to become a major corporate address in Dubai.

While favouring building towards the sky, the Roads and Transport Authority of Dubai is also preparing state-of-the-art transportation infrastructures. The fully automated driverless Dubai Metro will be running via elevated viaducts going underground in areas such as the city centre. By the end of 2009, the first phase of the 70-kilometre Dubai Metro should be operational.

Kuwait City, Kuwait shows strong signs that Dubai's race to the sky is meant to be followed by others in the same direction. There are currently three tall buildings of more than 300 metres under construction in Kuwait City. In **Manama, Bahrain**, the Atkins-designed Bahrain World Trade Center tapers to a height of 240 metres and will feature three suspended electricity-generating wind turbines between the twin sail-shaped towers. The 260-metre Dual Towers at Bahrain Financial Harbour, (Ahmed Janahi Architects), will add a waterfront-type ensemble to the new skyline. In Makkah, Saudi Arabia, the 485-metre 76-storey Abraj Al Bait Towers and Shopping Center project designed by Dar Al-Handasah (Shair and Partners), scheduled for completion in 2008, promises to be an impressive, lively multi-use ensemble comprising six residential towers and a five-star hotel comprising 1.7 million square metres, just steps away from the Holy Mosque.

The Dubai and Middle East super-tall projects are intended not only to provide hospitality, residential or (less often) office space, but to also transform the whole image of a region to attract tourism and business on a scale not seen before. If the image of a city like Dubai has already been radically transformed in recent years and the 'super-tall effect' proves to be efficient, can the same strategy be duplicated all over the Middle East with the same success?

Standard Bank Centre, Johannesburg, South Africa, Hentrich-Petschnigg & Partner (HPP), 1970, 35 storeys

***Photography:** Manfred Hanisch*

Africa

In the 1950s, in **Cairo, Egypt**, architect Naoum Shebib designed several tall buildings, among which was the imposing radio and television complex comprising a central 30-level tower along the Nile. But it is perhaps the 36-storey Ramses Hilton, the 27-storey El Gezira Sheraton and the 32-storey Semiramis InterContinental hospitality towers, completed in 1980, 1984 and 1988 respectively that began the city's race to the sky. Dozens of residential tall buildings were erected in the following years, most of them lacking any architectural interest. In recent years, several new hospitality and mixed-use tall buildings have been completed or are in progress – one ambitious project is Nile City, a project designed with a regionalist approach by Atelier d'Art Urbain Architects, encompassing two 143-metre office towers, a shopping mall, movie theatres and a five-star 100-metre Fairmont hotel. Apart from Cairo and the elegant 30-storey Casablanca Twin Center in **Casablanca, Morocco** (Ricardo Bofill, Taller de Arquitectura, 1999), not many major tall buildings have been constructed in Africa in recent years.

In **Johannesburg, South Africa** the listed 20-storey Anstey's, (Emley & Williamson, 1937) was the tallest building in Africa at the time of completion. The ziggurat-shaped Art Deco apartment building was named after the well-known department store located in the four-level podium.

Nile City, Cairo, Egypt, Atelier d'Art Urbain Architects, 2003/2007, 25 & 39 storeys

***Rendering:** Patrick Van Der Stricht*

The ubiquitous 'tower above a podium' is also found in Africa: the African Guarantee Building designed in 1960 by Monty Sack, and the Santam Building designed in 1967 by Stauch, Vorster and Partners, are fine examples of this. The 35-storey Standard Bank Centre (Hentrich-Petschnigg & Partner (HPP), 1970) is one of the most impressive cantilevered tall buildings ever built and its fully glass-enclosed lobby makes the building appear to be rising from the ground and floating above the plaza, especially at night. Since 1973, the 50-storey mixed-use Carlton Centre designed by Skidmore, Owings & Merrill and W. Rhodes-Harrison, Hoffe and Partners is Africa's tallest building while the dark-tinted glazed, 22-storey IBM Building (Arup Associates and Abramovitz, Sacks, Moss, Sack, Feldman, Associates, 1976) is another refined project built by IBM, which was known at the time for erecting many quality buildings around the world. The IBM Building remains distinctive with its circular nine-elevator service tower located on the northeast corner of the building. The timeless blue-glazed 11 Diagonal completed in 1986, together with **Durban's** 88 on Field, both designed by Helmut Jahn, are among the remaining famous tall buildings of South Africa. However, an optimistic sign is that two tall buildings are currently under construction in Durban.

Other African tall buildings areas include **Abidjan, Ivory Coast** where a booming economy contributed to a number of tall buildings completed between 1975 and 1984 in the Plateau area. Since then, few buildings of that scale have been built and the current political situation is not conducive to new projects. It is worth noting that tall buildings as governmental imagery have been seen in recent years in Africa; the tallest buildings in **Kenya** and in **Zimbabwe** are the 140-metre Central Bank completed in 1997 in **Nairobi** and the 120-metre Reserve Bank of Zimbabwe completed in 1997 in **Harare**. Harare is one of the few African cities to have tall buildings constructed in the last decade. In **Cairo**, the 143-metre Ministry of Foreign Affairs tower became the tallest building in the city when completed in 1994. Cairo took over the role as the capital of today's African skyscrapers with the 143-metre Nile City project

MesseTurm, Frankfurt, Germany, Murphy/Jahn, 1990, 63 storeys

Photography: *Roland Halbe*

DG Bank (now DZ Bank), Frankfurt, Germany, Kohn Pedersen Fox Associates, 1993, 52 storeys

Photography: *Dennis Gilbert*

Conclusion: a towering Middle East, a European high-rise revival and a rather quiet Africa

Although a few pre-war or immediately post-war skyscrapers existed, high-rise buildings mainly arrived on the European scene during the 1965–1975 decade. At the time, tall buildings in **Europe** were mainly isolated commercial towers in city centres and low- to middle-income housing tower blocks at the periphery. These residential tall buildings, being often poorly designed and badly built, are probably responsible to a large extent for the poor image of the European tall building. After this time, until the early 1990s, there were few such projects in Europe. In many places, such as Brussels, London or Paris, this is partly explained by a combination of the economic climate that followed the 1973 oil crisis and possibly the social situation that followed the so-called '68 events' which occurred in Paris and other places. The emergence of 'green' political parties in Europe and the general public's concern for the environment are other likely contributors. There followed almost 20 years when the tall building was seen as an antisocial and anti-urban object. The situation obviously changed in the early 1990s.

While many of the early 1960s and 1970s European tall buildings were hotels, particularly hotels managed (and sometimes owned) by well-known North American hotel chains, a new series of taller buildings, also with a North American flavour emerged in the 1990s, but this time because of

Tour Maine-Montparnasse, Paris, France, Beaudouin, Cassan, Le Hoym de Marien and Saubot; A Epstein and Sons, consulting architect, 1973, 58 storeys

Photography: *Courtesy Montparnasse 56*

the origin of their architects and, in some cases, their developers. While few of the first wave of architects were originally respected for their tall buildings works – although a series of recently listed 1960s tall buildings in London shows that time may prove that some early judgments may have been misguided – the architects of this new series of major tall buildings were American-based stars such as Murphy/Jahn (MesseTurm), Kohn Pedersen Fox Associates (DG Bank, now DZ Bank) and Cesar Pelli & Associates (One Canada Square at Canary Wharf). The MesseTurm was an initiative of New York-based Tishman Speyer Properties and Canary Wharf was initiated by Toronto-based developer Olympia & York. These projects have been widely published and may have changed the European perception of tall buildings; coincidence or not, since that time there has been an increased interest and acceptance of tall buildings in Europe, which are in fact growing taller and taller.

This was first evident in Frankfurt and in Rotterdam, two cities largely destroyed during World War II, where there was not much to save and therefore little argument against tall buildings. In Europe, the demolition of the old urban fabric has often been confused with the construction of tall buildings, which are totally different phenomena except that in some cases, they may occur at the same place. Other cities such as London, or more recently, Madrid and Barcelona have shown a particular interest in building high-profile iconic tall buildings with a global urban vision.

In Germany almost every major city has begun to erect tall buildings, in many cases starting with a cylindrical tower as a landmark building, while France's main and only active tall buildings area – Paris La Défense – should remain as such for many years. More conservative cities like Brussels will mainly renovate existing tall buildings or build the few already planned in the 1960s with the exception of a few newly conceived residential buildings.

Heading east, Moscow seems to be the European city that is most strongly demonstrating its belief in high-rise residential tall buildings and mixed-use super-tall buildings, whether from a developer's or public authority's point of view. A 118-storey mixed-use tower designed by Foster and Partners, scheduled to become the tallest building in Europe, will surpass the United States for the first time since the Chrysler Building surpassed the Eiffel Tower in 1930.

In **Africa**, the first wave of tall buildings in the 1960s appeared in locations such as Johannesburg and Durban and later in locations such as Abidjan and Harare. Changing political and economic situations almost put an end to any such construction 20 years ago. A large country like Egypt is an exception, however, because of its demography and economy, and could well see many other tall buildings appearing in the future, as several have been built successfully in Cairo in recent years.

Just ten years ago, there were very few moderately tall buildings and tourism was not part of daily life in locations such as Dubai in the **Middle East**. But, before the end of the current decade most of the tallest buildings of the Europe/Middle East/Africa zone will be located in the Middle East. The Middle East, and Dubai in particular, have decided to create a new regional image by creating iconic super-tall towers, in several cases starting first with hotel and mixed-use projects that become a destination on their own, often supported by the ruling family members or public authorities.

The concept of constructing super-tall buildings at the initiative of public leaders appeared a decade ago in Kuala Lumpur and in Shanghai, with projects such as the Petronas Twin Towers and the Jin Mao Tower. However, many tall buildings have been developed or supported by governments; these include the Moscow State University in 1953, the Paris La Défense high-rise district master plan initiated by the French Government, or the 104-metre Tour Perret in Amiens in 1952 which was an initiative of the French Ministry of Reconstruction and Town Planning. The 149-metre Tour du Midi in Brussels in 1966 and the 209-metre Tour Maine-Montparnasse in Paris in 1973 were both the tallest in Western Europe at time of their completion. The Brussels building was, and still is, a government-owned ministry building while the Paris Tour Maine-Montparnasse, though jointly developed by a duo of French and American developers, was encouraged by President Georges Pompidou. Did Pompidou, who was a Modern Art lover, by expressing his belief in the Tour Maine-Montparnasse and other tall buildings approved by him in Paris La Défense, champion the notion of the tall building as the expression of modernity?

Moscow City Towers, Moscow, Russia, Foster and Partners, 2006 (design unveiled), 118 storeys
Rendering: *Courtesy Foster and Partners*

With the example of the Tour-Maine Montparnasse (often known today as Tour Montparnasse), we can also confirm that density and height are not always on par. In a March-April 1975 issue devoted to the Gratte-Ciel (Skyscraper), the French architecture review *L'Architecture d'Aujourd'hui* published an article by architect Robert Auzelle. Auzelle illustrates his article with plans of the Tour Maine-Montparnasse, with a

Burj Mubarak Al Kabir at Madinat Al Hareer (City of Silk), Kuwait City, Kuwait, Eric R. Kuhne & Associates, design phase, 250 storeys
Rendering: *Eric R. Kuhne & Associates*

hypothetical scheme of a series of 6-storey buildings erected on the 270-metre by 91-metre site where the current 58-storey tower and its adjoining low-rise slab stand. The architect concludes that tall buildings are being erected for reasons of prestige, availability of finance and precariousness (the fact that buildings can be demolished and rebuilt is not widely recognized on the European scene), while demonstrating that his low-rise scheme features more square metres than the tall building scheme actually built.

The introductory pages of *Highrise Building and Urban Design* by Hans Aregger and Otto Glaus (Frederick A. Praeger, 1967) state: 'After a controversial beginning and a period of reluctant toleration, Europe seems to have accepted high-rise building. Objections on aesthetic grounds, warning of its disruptive effect on established townscapes, made no impression'. The authors could obviously not predict the future and foresee the next generation that didn't accept the tall building in Europe.

Therefore, the current boom of European tall buildings is an interesting sign but it is perhaps still too early to make any deductions regarding the future of tall buildings on the Old Continent. Moscow is the exception, with its seemingly unstoppable adoption of tall buildings. The race to the sky is alive in Europe since Paris La Défense will probably have a 400-metre tower erected during the next decade if the proposal is approved by the French Government.

The unprecedented scope of super-tall buildings under progress in the Middle East will not only allow locations such as Dubai to create a skyline in a single decade, but for the first time, people will be living in buildings of heights not seen before, in some cases higher than the highest mountain of some countries. Other works of pharaonic scale are underway in the region, such as man-made resort islands along the coasts of Doha and Dubai. In Dubai, the Palm Islands concept and the resort islands are expected to confirm Dubai as a major tourist and resort destination; another such project is The World, 300 man-made islands strategically positioned to form the shape of the world map.

The Middle East region and Dubai as a forerunner – Dubai should accommodate about 15 towers of more than 300 metres before the end of the decade – have demonstrated a political and urban vision. In many cases those skyscrapers are not stand-alone towers as most of the North American super-tall skyscrapers, but are part of larger mixed-use ensembles. Super-tall residential and mixed-use buildings seem to be becoming the norm in the Middle East and as such could actually prefigure an entirely new way of living: sharing more common amenities, implementing new energy systems such as co-generation systems, and preserving land use.

Europe and the Middle East have a long history of building tall: fine examples are the 72 houses-towers in San Gimignano, Italy (13th and 14th century) of which 15 still exist today; the construction of the minaret of the Great Mosque in Kairouan, Tunisia (8th–9th century); or the belfries and bell-towers of Bruges, Belgium (14th century) or Venice, Italy (10th/16th century, rebuilt in 1912 after it collapsed), which are both tall as a 25-storey building. Tall buildings will always be ambassadors of technological success, powerful political vision or private entrepreneurial optimism. Until the late 1970s, the tall building in Europe was not meant to impress, with the exception of the Russian high-rises of the 1950s. In the early 1990s, One Canada Square gave Canary Wharf a majestic air in order to face the attractive power of the City of London, while the MesseTurm in Frankfurt confirmed the reputation of the city as a leading financial centre in Europe, thus proving to be a sign of its 'international' nature.

While super-tall buildings in Europe remind us of or confirm the historic grandeur of the location where they sit, the super-tall buildings of the Middle East promote a sort of grandeur in the making, with high-rise towers which are in many cases the jewel in the crown of growing mixed-use urban ensembles. The Burj Mubarak Al Kabir at Madinat Al Hareer – City of Silk – in Kuwait City is a mixed-use tower designed by Eric R. Kuhne & Associates. Still at design phase, the project is scheduled to reach 1001 metres, a figure obviously related to the *Thousand and One Nights* tale. The tower is designed to house a series of vertical villages combining offices, hotels, leisure and residences into a vertical city centre of 250 storeys.

It appears that European and Middle Eastern super-tall buildings of scales not seen before are becoming the norm, providing a shared experience and a view to a brighter future, whether consolidating the past as in Europe, or confronting the future as in the Middle East. As such, the tall building is now playing a much bigger role than just accommodating people: to impress people from a city point of view, as was the case at the time of belfries and campaniles, from a country point of view as was the case in Europe in the early 1990s, or from a continental or regional perspective as is the case today, people have always resorted to tall buildings. The future will always retain an element of our past.

Georges Binder
Managing Director
Buildings & Data SA
Brussels, Belgium, 2006

LOVA

NI D A AB

THE N HERLA S

GYPT

U N D K IN

SWEDE S A

ISRAEL N M

BEL M

PROJECTS

COLORIUM DÜSSELDORF GERMANY

The Colorium is a dramatic 18-storey multicoloured tower on the waterfront in Düsseldorf's revivified harbour. Although designed as a commercial building for a private client, Ibing Immobilien Handel GmbH & Co.Hochhaus KG, this new £11-million landmark will play an integral part in the regeneration programme that is progressively transforming Düsseldorf's disused port and dock area into a Media Harbour, incorporating a galaxy of international architectural talent.

Located on an extremely constricted site on the Speditionsstrasse peninsula, formerly home to a waterfront silo, the 12,400-gross-square-metre building takes the form of a dramatic 62-metre-high tower with two basement levels. The treatment of the external façade of the building, an intricate patchwork of coloured glass, transforms what could be a conventional office into a towering mosaic artwork. The regularity of the floor pattern is broken down and blurred by the sophisticated and sensuous façade treatment using advanced glass technology and only 17 distinct types of panels. To ensure an intense external colour appearance, the artwork is screen printed onto the glass with a reduced percentage of printed area in the vision panels.

Overlaying the concrete frame, the mosaic façade distorts the internal structure, scale and perspective of the building, creating a highly elusive and pictorial presence on the waterfront. The plant installation at roof level is transformed into a red light box cantilevering out over the water.

1

2

Colorium | **Location** Düsseldorf, Germany | **Completion date** 2001 | **Architect** Alsop Architects | **Client** Ibing Immobilien Handel GmbH; Hochhaus KG | **Structural engineer** Arup GmbH | **Mechanical engineer** Intecplan GmbH | **Landscape architect** Alsop Architects | **Contractor** Arbeitsgemeinschaft Hamelmann Heine | **Height** 62 m/203 ft | **Above-ground storeys** 18 | **Use** Office | **Area of above-ground building** 12,400 sq m/133,424 sq ft | **Cost** DM34 M

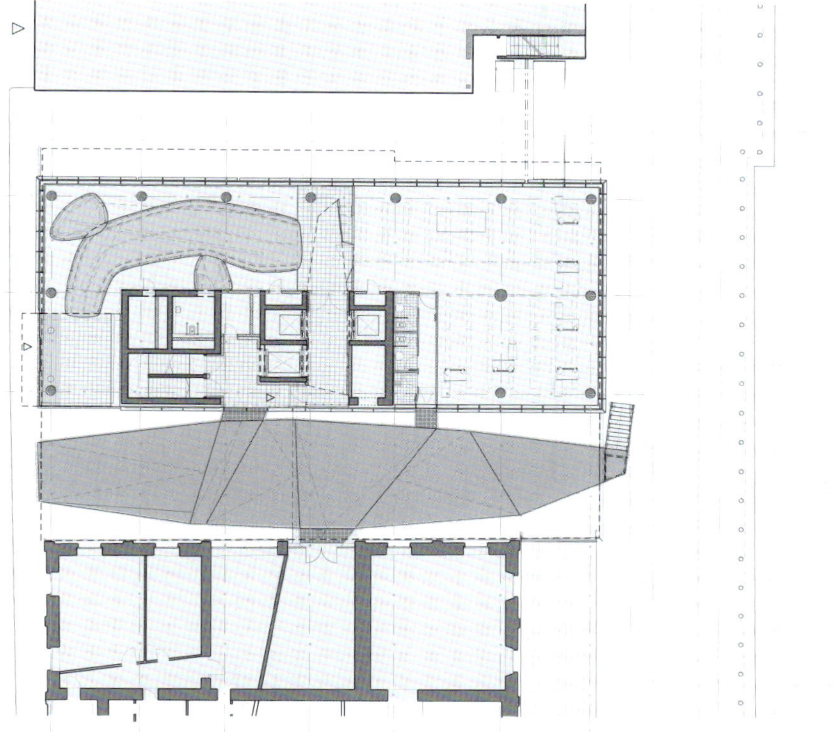

3

1 *Quayside view*
2 *Northwest elevation from Speditionsstrasse*
3 *Site plan*
4 *View of entrance from west*
5 *View from across the dock*

Photography: *Christian Richters*

4

5

ITÄMERENTORI HELSINKI FINLAND

The Itämerentori office building lies near the centre of Helsinki City, on the borough's main square. It consists of a 16-storey tower, which forms a dominant centre point to the area and to the gateway from the west. In the urban silhouette of Helsinki it has become one of a pair with an older landmark tower in the east of the city.

The Itämerentori building is a joint office building for SITRA, the Finnish National Fund for Research and Development and the Finnish offices of multinational firm PricewaterhouseCoopers. The building accommodates approximately 600 office workers.

The lower part of the building is reserved for SVH PricewaterhouseCoopers. It consists of three five-storey office wings that enclose an inner courtyard. The offices open onto a gallery space that is covered by a large glass roof of nearly 1000 square metres. The tower contains the SITRA premises, with conference facilities and saunas at the top. The office layout is open and flexible; the partitioning system is portable and HEPAC technology is easy to alter.

The ground floor consists of lobby areas with associated conference facilities and a pedestrian gallery providing a café-restaurant and shops. The main entry is from the Itämerentori Square. Two basement floors accommodate storage space as well as technical and staff facilities and 370 car parking spaces.

The frame of the building consists of steel columns and beams and precast concrete slabs. The basement is cast in situ. The elevations consist mainly of a double skin structure. The materials include glass and Corten weatherproof steel and acid-proof steel.

1

2

3

4

Itämerentori | **Location** Helsinki, Finland | **Completion date** 2001 | **Architect** Helin & Co Architects | **Clients** SITRA The Finnish National Fund for Research and Development, LEL-työeläkekassa (now Etera Mutual Pension Insurance Company) and TaEL, the Pension Fund for Performing Artists and Certain Groups of Employees (now under Etera) | **Structural engineer** Finnmap Consulting Oy Ltd | **Mechanical engineer** JP-Talotekniikka – JP Building Engineering | **Contractor** YIT-Yhtymä Oyj – YIT Group | **Height** 67 m/220 ft | **Above-ground storeys** 16 + ventilation engine rooms | **Basements** 3 | **Mechanical levels** 1 | **Use** Offices and commercial | **Site area** 7108 sq m/76,510 sq ft | **Area of above-ground building** 18,900 sq m/203,400 sq ft | **Structural materials** Steel, reinforced concrete, double skin elevation, mainly constructed of Corten steel, acid-proof steel | **Other materials** (exterior) Corten steel panels and glass; (interior) wood, glass, steel, natural stone | **Cost** approx €71 M

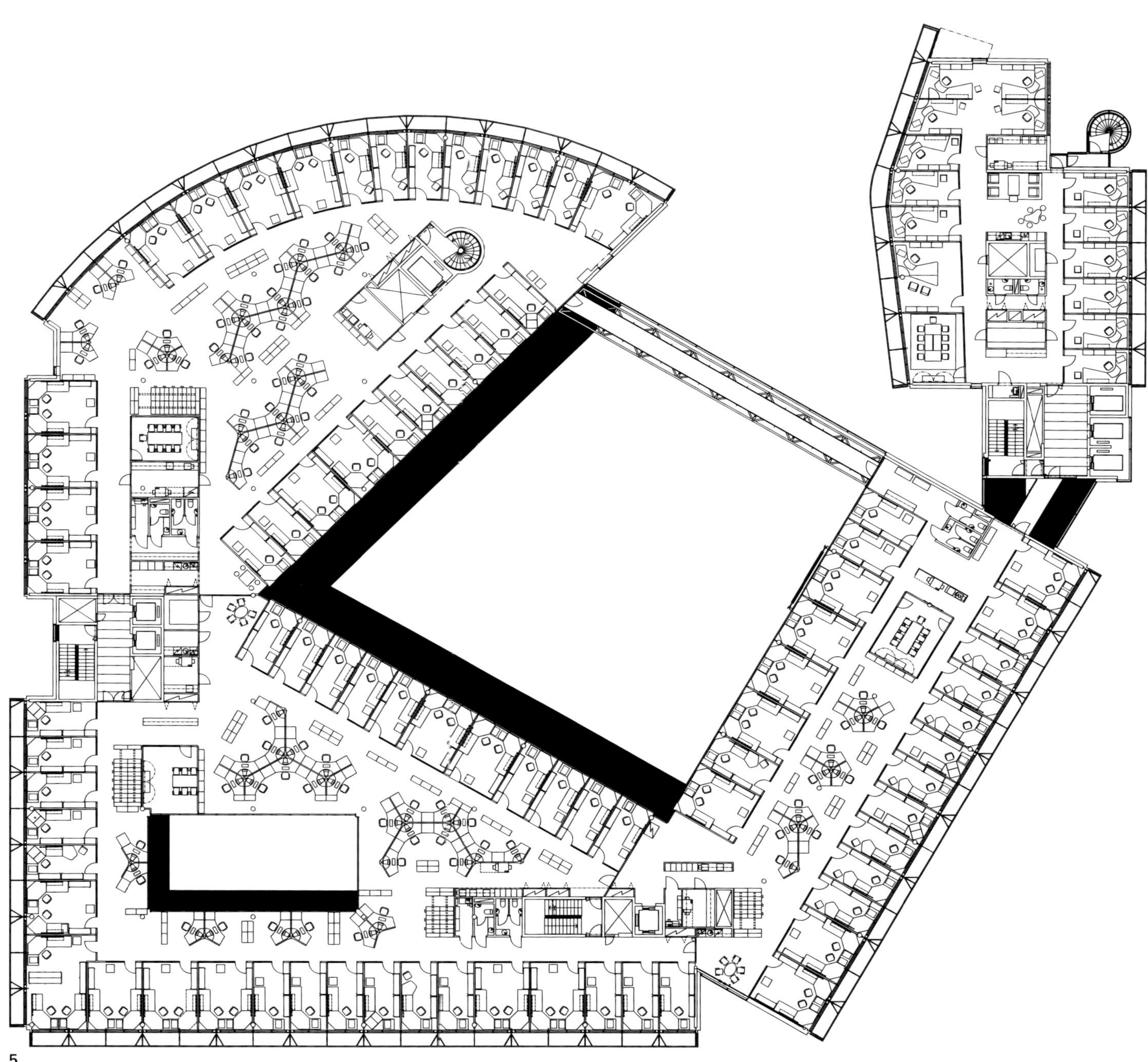

5

1 *The landmark of Ruoholahti*

2 *A light-filled, glazed gallery is left in the middle of the surrounding building masses*

3 *A stucco-surfaced blue shaft connects the tower to the lower building masses*

4 *Detail of double façade*

5 *Typical office floor plan*

Photography: *Titta Lumio (2,4); Voitto Niemelä (1,3)*

MALIETOREN

THE HAGUE
THE NETHERLANDS

The office tower stands at a prominent point above a motorway, where it marks the transition from urban area to green zone and serves as a city gateway for the motorway traffic. The gateway role is strengthened by the direction the transparent glass façades give the building. These fold inward, leaving the steel structure freely visible. The resultant shadow effects and dynamics can be seen by motorists passing underneath.

The side walls, with glass that continues right up to the overhanging roof, feature clear strips of fenestration. Above each of these, a band of figured and reflecting glass acts as a sunbreak; round glass blocks in the concrete inner leaf spot the façade with points of light. Wing-shaped aluminium slats screen off the parking space that occupies the first five floors. These slats alternate above the entrance, allowing the garage function to be seen. The ambience of the main entrance hall owes much to the exposed load-bearing girders.

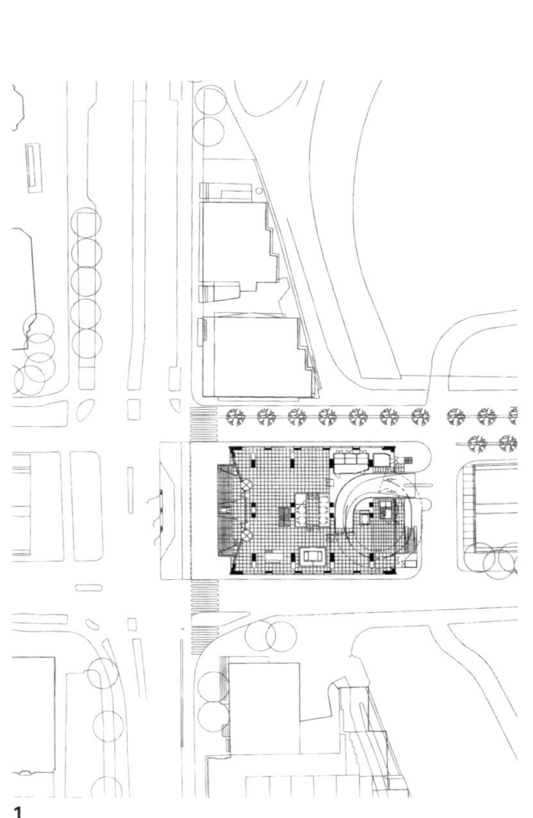

1

2

Malietoren | **Location** The Hague, The Netherlands | **Completion date** 1996 | **Architect** Benthem Crouwel Architekten BV bna | **Client** AM Development (formerly Multi Vastgoed bv) | **Structural engineer** Ove Arup & Partners International Ltd., London and Corsmit Raadgevend Ingenieursbureau BV, Rijswijk | **Mechanical engineer** Technical Management, Rijswijk | **Contractor** Wilma Bouw bv, The Hague | **Height** 70 m/230 ft | **Above-ground storeys** 19 | **Above-ground useable levels** 19 | **Mechanical levels** 1 | **Use** Office | **Area of above-ground building** 25,000 sq m/269,100 sq ft (offices 14,000 sq m/150,700 sq ft; parking 5500 sq m/59,200 sq ft; other 5500 sq m/59,200 sq ft) | **Structural materials** Glass, steel, aluminium slats | **Cost** €22.7 M

3

4

1 *Site plan*
2 *General view of Malietoren*
3 *Façade detail*
4 *Plinth detail*
5 *Interior*
6 *Entrance*

Photography: *Jannes Linders*

5

6

KONE BUILDING ESPOO FINLAND

The Kone Building is located on the shoreline in Espoo near Helsinki. A basic block-like shape was sought for the 18-storey tower building. All protruding structures, such as the ventilation and maintenance systems of the façades were placed under the eaves. 'Breathing spaces' have been created within the basic volume in the form of the two-storey entrance vestibule, as well as the 16th-floor outdoor terrace bordered by glass walls. The main building materials are glass and steel, with Finnish wood used in the interior in different forms. All these materials are technically durable, timeless and classic, and immune to fashion trends.

The main vertical connections in the building, the south-facing panoramic lifts, run along a lift shaft extending the entire height of the building. This lift shaft acts as a heat valve for the offices, controlling the heat gains from the glazed south façade. The base and the top of the lift shaft have automatic ventilation hatches through which excess heat is removed. In designing the façade, visible diagonal bracing has been avoided, so that there are no competing motifs in the horizontal landscape or in the vertical lift theme.

On the east and west sides of the building natural light is supplied to the offices through a 2.3-metre-tall strip window. These façades also have an outer secondary glazed façade, which with its silk-screened laminated glass, prevents excessive heat from penetrating the office spaces. Further, the double façade 'raincoat' guarantees maximum durability against the increased wind and water pressure higher up in the tower-like building.

1

2

3

4

Kone Building | **Location** Espoo, Finland | **Completion date** 2001 | **Architect** SARC Architects | **Client** Management Co. KONE Building | **Structural engineer** Magnus Malmberg Ltd. | **Mechanical engineer** Olof Granlund Ltd. | **Interior architect** K & Y Wiherheimo | **Contractor** Skanska | **Height** 72.6 m/238 ft | **Above-ground storeys** 18 | **Above-ground useable levels** 16 | **Mechanical levels** 2 | **Use** Office | **Site area** 2916 sq m/31,376 sq ft | **Area of above-ground building** 9787 sq m/105,308 sq ft | **Structural materials** Steel, reinforced concrete, aluminium curtain wall | **Other materials** Silk screen printed glass, corrugated aluminium, birch wood | **Cost** €20 M

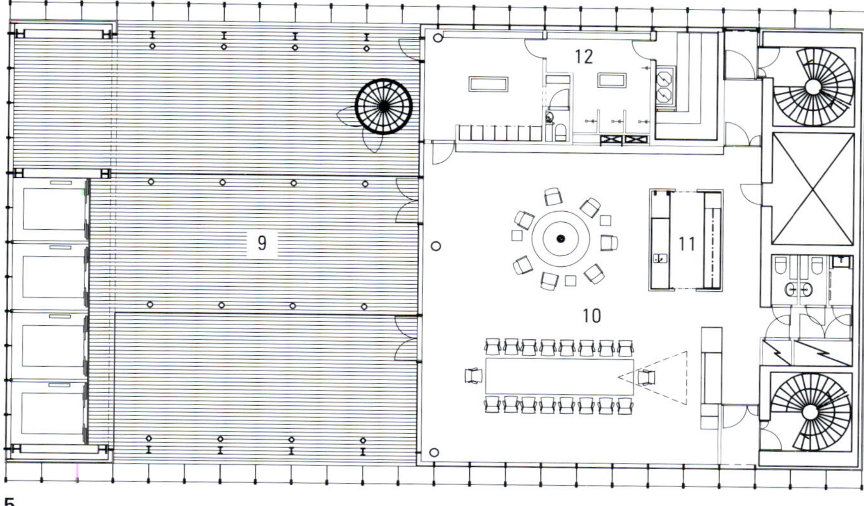

5

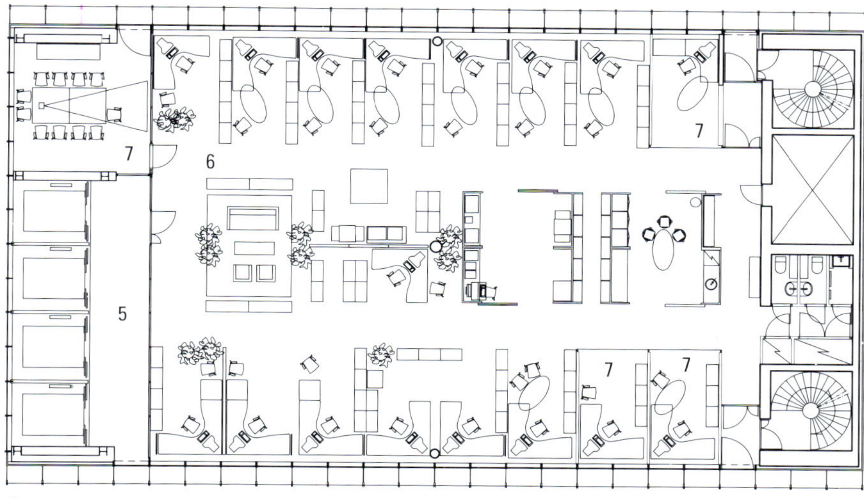

6

1 *Kone Building seen from seaside boulevard to the east*

2 *View from northeast with corrugated aluminium-clad façade*

3 *Terrace on 15th floor with glazed lift shaft*

4 *Lobby*

5 *15th floor plan*

6 *Typical office floor plan*

7 *1st floor plan*

Photography: *Jussi Tiainen*

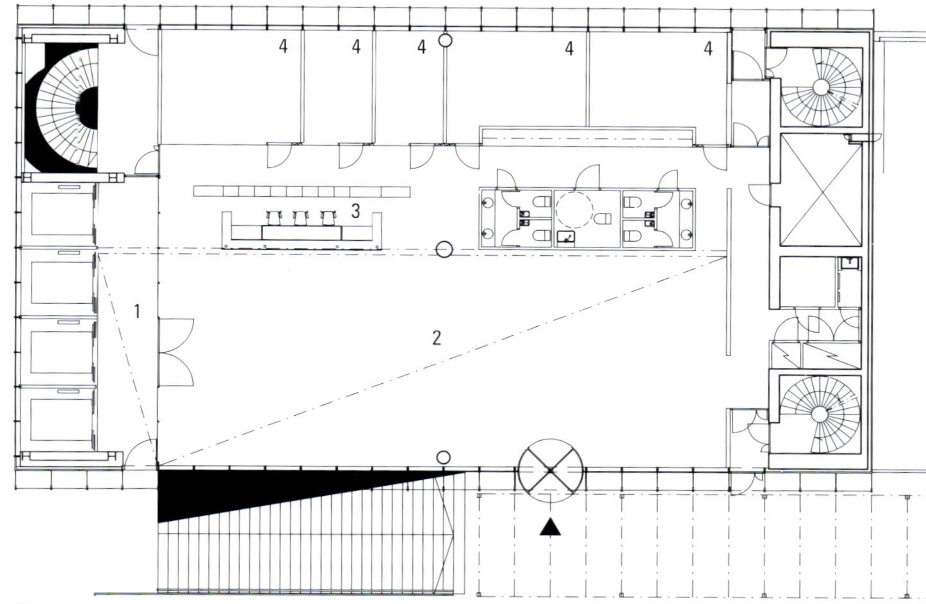

7

1 Lift lobby
2 Lobby
3 Reception
4 Meeting room
5 Lift lobby
6 Office landscape
7 Office room
8 Meeting room
9 Terrace
10 Conference room
11 Kitchen
12 Sauna

11 DIAGONAL STREET

JOHANNESBURG SOUTH AFRICA

The program called for 360,000 square feet of speculative office space with an average of 20,000 square feet on a typical floor, and below-grade parking for 175 vehicles.

The mechanical gridiron geometric pattern of streets in Johannesburg provided a perfect context for a geometric building. The site for this building is a full block development in Newton, an area adjacent to the central business district of Johannesburg.

Within the greater context of South African history, with its Calvinist traditions and the diamond industry association of the developer's parent company, the building establishes its own strong identity. The building is crafted like a diamond to conform to the sloping height restrictions of the city's building ordinance. The completed composition recalls the imagery of early 20th-century skyscrapers.

The building enclosure consists of a double skin. The inner wall consists of 50 percent glass with the glass in a continuous strip, butt jointed and silicone sealed. The mullionless glass allows complete flexibility in locating interior partitions along the exterior wall. The space between the inner wall and the exterior wall provides an environmental buffer that is naturally ventilated. The exterior wall is actually a sun shade to reduce the extremely high solar radiation factor due to the thin, clear air at 6000 feet above sea level. The exterior wall is a panelised curtainwall system, utilising a combination of three colours of reflective glass. Prior to installation, the glass was sealed to the aluminium frames with structural silicone and then the completed panel assembly was erected and attached to the structure. The structural system is concrete, designed to facilitate a slip-form core and flying forms for floor construction.

The HVAC system consists of six packaged air conditioning units on each floor supplying conditioned air to the ceiling plenum. A separate duct provides a zone of heated and/or chilled air along the perimeter.

1

2

11 Diagonal Street | **Location** Johannesburg, South Africa | **Completion date** 1986 | **Architect** Murphy/Jahn, Inc. in association with Louis Karol Architects | **Structural engineer** Ove Arup & Partners | **Mechanical engineer** Biederman, Finn, Beekhuizen & Associates | **Height** 80 m/262 ft | **Above-ground storeys** 20 | **Use** Office | **Area of above-ground building** 33,450 sq m/360,000 sq ft | **Structural materials** Concrete, glass, aluminium

3

4

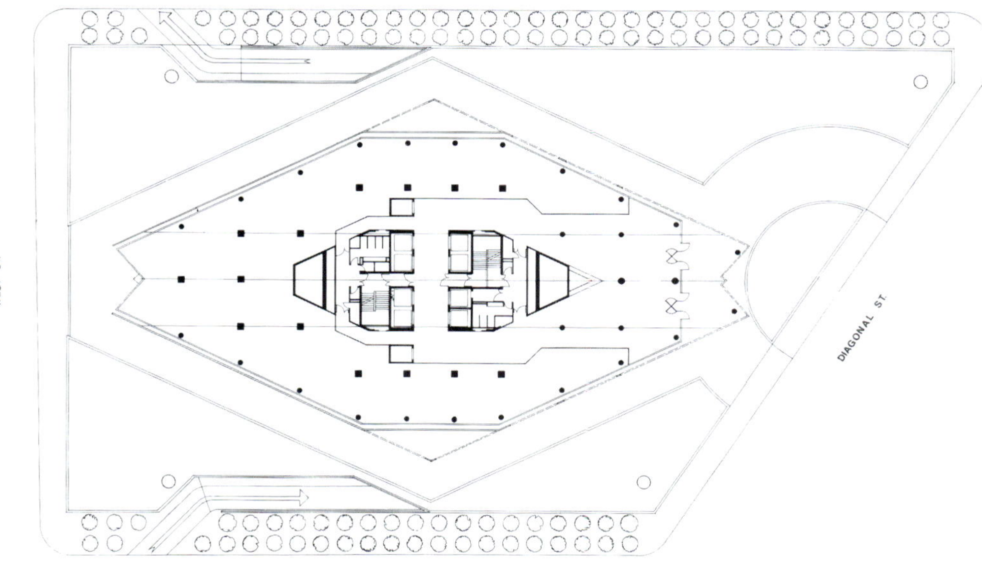

5

1 *Side elevation*
2 *Overall front view*
3 *Façade detail*
4 *Lobby*
5 *Ground floor plan*

Photography: *Michael Meyersfeld*

STADTSPARKASSE HEADQUARTERS

DÜSSELDORF
GERMANY

The architects converted the Düsseldorf headquarters of the Stadtsparkasse into a financial 'department store', complete with ATM stations and customer consultation areas, offices for insurance brokers, kiosk, travel agency, internet café, auditorium, refreshment facilities and bistros, thoroughly overhauling the staid image of the savings bank. Open client service areas promote a friendly interactive atmosphere. This concept seeks to dissolve the barrier between the bank and its clientele, lowering the inhibition threshold. Consultation and communication are the priorities.

Built in 1964, the building was subsequently expanded in 1990, but remained isolated, was not energy efficient, and had lost its aesthetic appeal. Following its 1997 win in an international competition, Ingenhoven und Partner set about transforming the building, enveloping it in a breathing glass climate skin, which contributes to reducing energy costs. The glazed atrium, planted with large olive trees, and the glass cube on Steinstrasse, designed by structural engineer Werner Sobek, create high-quality internal space.

The building was stripped down to the load-bearing structure and the brown parapet slabs were replaced with floor-to-ceiling clear glass windows with slender aluminium frames. The windows are now openable behind the floor-height double façade, although the low ceiling heights remain.

A free-standing glass screen, which extends the full length of Berliner Allee between Stein and Grünstrasse, offers an unfettered view onto a transparent 'bankscape'. The screen serves as a noise buffer, transforms the solitary building into a glazed block edge development and integrates all building sections.

The architects have urbanised the building and brought the city into it, a concept they refer to as 'public reclamation'. All the better if the 'reclamation' also contributes to urban renewal and energy conservation.

1

2

3

4

5

Stadtsparkasse Headquarters | **Location** Düsseldorf, Germany | **Completion date** (renovation and transformation) 2001 | **Architect** Ingenhoven Overdiek und Partner Architekten | **Client** Stadtsparkasse Düsseldorf | **Structural engineer** KKK Ingenieurgesellschaft mbH | **Landscape architect** Ingenhoven Overdiek und Partner Architekten | **Height** 80 m/262 ft | **Above-ground storeys** 21 | **Basements** 2 | **Above-ground useable levels** 21 | **Use** Office | **Area of above-ground building** 35,021 sq m/114,904 sq ft | **Structural materials** Mixed | **Other materials** Glass, aluminium

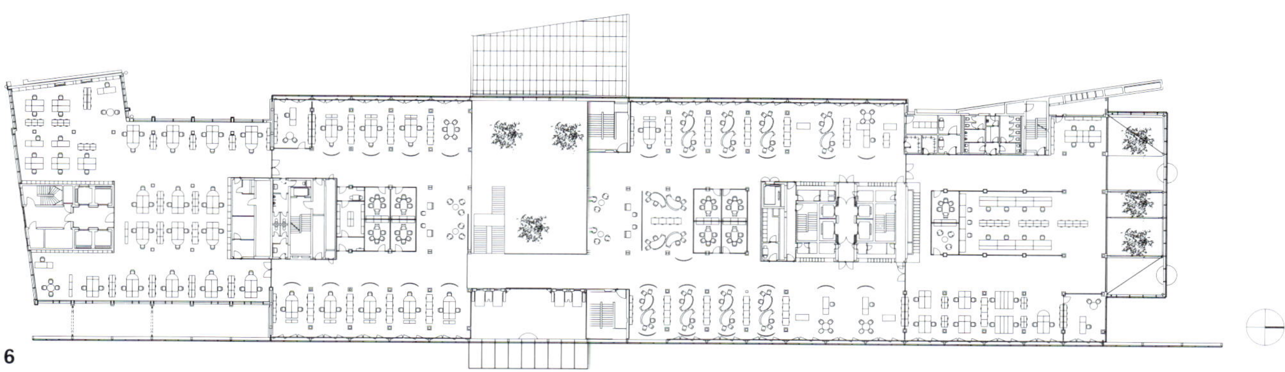

6

7

8

9

1–3 *General views*

4 *Façade screen*

5 *Glass cube*

6 *Ground floor plan*

7,8 *Façade screen on Berliner Allee*

9 *The 1964 tower designed by FW Kraemer and H Rosskotten before its 2001 renovation and transformation*

Photography*: HG Esch, Holger Knauf, courtesy Ingenhoven und Partner Architekten*

FERRING INTERNATIONAL CENTER

COPENHAGEN
DENMARK

The Ferring Pharmaceutical company's new headquarters in Ørestaden houses both research laboratories and traditional headquarters facilities. Because it is crucial that the laboratories are not subject to vibration of any kind, the company requested that the height of the research department not exceed three storeys. This, together with the permitted building-to-site ratio in the area, resulted in the balance of the headquarters facilities being housed in an 80-metre tower. The basic concept was that the tall building, when seen from a distance, should be experienced as a simple form without any pronounced detail, while the buildings appear more varied when viewed close up. A great deal of attention was given to the light and shadow effects on the façades to achieve a variation in relationship to the solar elevation and viewpoint.

The building consists of a three-winged 'comb' scheme that houses laboratories, and a 20-storey tower rising from one end of the comb's three 'teeth'. The tower is supported by 16 steel columns, pulled back 0.5 and 2.7 metres respectively from the side and end façades. This construction principle gives the building the character of being airborne while providing openness in the floor plans. The floor plans, with few partitions, are primarily subdivided by black, hip-high metal filing cabinets, providing a sense of calm that is a necessity at these heights where the floor-to-ceiling windows provide one of Copenhagen's most intoxicating views.

Along the climate screen runs a half-metre-wide installation pit covered by a black steel grid. The openness and transparency of the tower building is repeated in the laboratory wing, where the offices are separated from the corridors by matte glass partitions. This makes the corridors surprisingly pleasant leisure areas that allow a more varied usage than in traditional buildings.

1

2

3

4

Ferring International Center | **Location** Copenhagen, Denmark | **Completion date** 2001 | **Architect** Henning Larsens Tegnestue A/S | **Client** Ferring A/S | **Structural engineer** Moe & Brødsgaard A/S | **Landscape architect** Schønherr Landscape | **Contractor** M.T. Højgaard A/S | **Height** 80 m/263 ft | **Above-ground storeys** 21 | **Basements** 2 | **Above-ground useable levels** 20 | **Mechanical levels** 1 | **Use** Offices, laboratories | **Area of above-ground building** 16,700 sq m/179,800 sq ft | **Structural materials** Steel | **Other materials** Steel, glass, wood, stone | **Cost** DKK 320 M

1. *Ferring International Center*
2. *Administration tower and research laboratory wing*
3. *Administration area subdivided by hip-high metal filing cabinets*
4. *Administration area overlooking Copenhagen*
5. *Level 10 floor plan*
6. *Level 1 floor plan*
7. *Level 0 floor plan*
8. *Aerial view*
9. *Element mouldings and fixed louvres are of black anodised aluminium*

Photography: *Jens Lindhe*

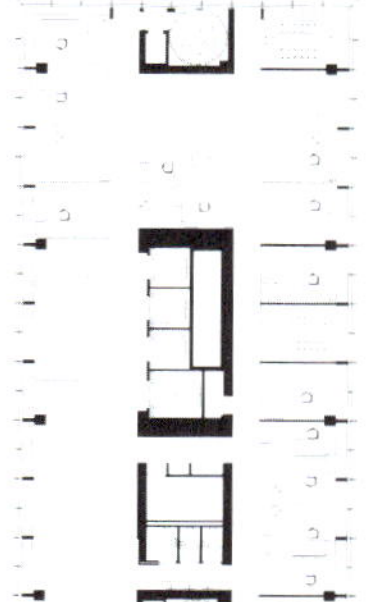
5

8

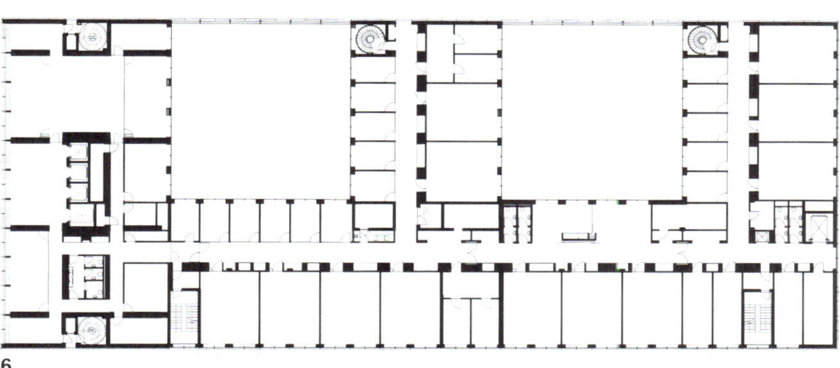
6

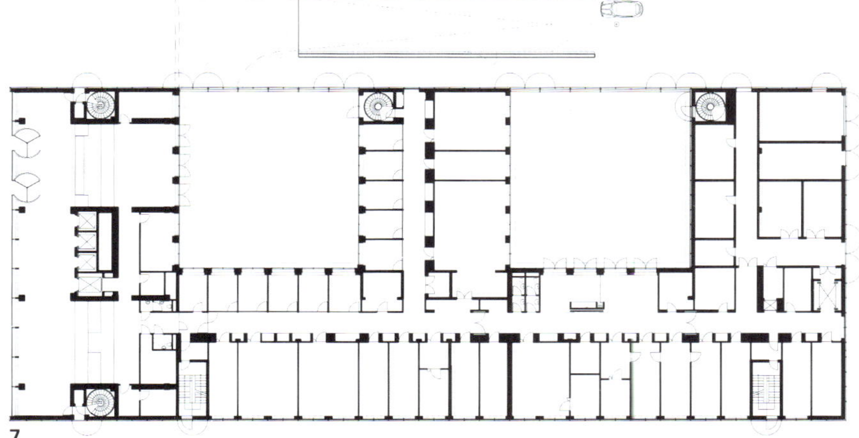
7

9

GSW HEADQUARTERS BERLIN GERMANY

This design forms the extension to an office tower that was one of the first projects to be built during the reconstruction of Berlin in the 1950s. The design endeavours to combine the remaining fragments of the city into a three-dimensional composition through which the existing building is reintegrated into its context. The idea of conglomerate growth is not only accepted but put forward as a model for urban development.

The new ensemble responds as much to the baroque logic of the street plan as it does to the rules of 19th-century urbanism. It also absorbs the object-like quality of the 1950's tower and registers the confrontational space that had developed between the high-rises either side of the Berlin Wall. In this combination of the disparate spatial configurations of consecutive generations, the new high-rise slab is the element associated with the present and the future.

The design of the high-rise slab is generated by a concern for the workplace in the city, and by a commitment to an architecture that is economical with the (built and natural) resources of the environment. This building not only offers an exemplary working environment in its passive control of energy consumption, but at the same time it redefines an architecture in which the value of sensuous space is reassessed.

1

2

3

GSW Headquarters | **Location** Berlin, Germany | **Completion date** 1999 | **Architect** sauerbruch hutton architects | **Client** GSW Gemeinnützige Siedlungs- und Wohnungsbaugesellschaft Berlin mbH | **Structural engineer** Dewhurst MacFarlane and Partners, London (competition); Arup GmbH, Berlin (design development); ARGE Arup GmbH, Berlin with IGH mbH, Berlin (site supervision) | **Environmental engineer** Ove Arup + Partners, London (low energy concept, competition); Arup GmbH, Berlin (design development); ARGE Arup GmbH, Berlin with IGH mbH, Berlin (site supervision) | **Mechanical engineer** competition (low energy concept): Ove Arup + Partners, London | **Landscape architect** ST raum a, Berlin | **Contractor** ARGE Rohbau, Züblin AG, Berlin with Bilfinger + Berger, Berlin | **Height** 80.38 m/263.7 ft | **Above-ground storeys** 23 | **Basements** 1 + mechanical parking system | **Above-ground useable levels** 21 (including ground floor) | **Mechanical roof levels** 2 | **Use** offices, shops, public areas, conference rooms and restaurants | **Site area** 8382 sq m/90,220 sq ft | **Area of above-ground building** 7997 sq m/86,080 sq ft | **Floor area** 47,873 sq m (gross area)/515,300 sq ft | **Structural materials** (high-rise) Post-stressed RC edge beam, prefabricated floor elements with an in-situ concrete topping with composite steel and concrete beams | **Other materials** (exterior) Glass and aluminium façade (high-rise), terracotta tiles with graphite coloured glazing (low-rise), corrugated metal panels (pillbox), fibre-cement panels (matching the existing tower) | **Other materials** (interior) Exposed concrete, glass, wood (American cherry, beech), stone (granite, basaltina, colombina) | **Cost** DM160 M

1–3 *General and detailed views of GSW building*
4 *Third floor plan*
5 *Ground floor plan*

***Photography**: Annette Kisling*

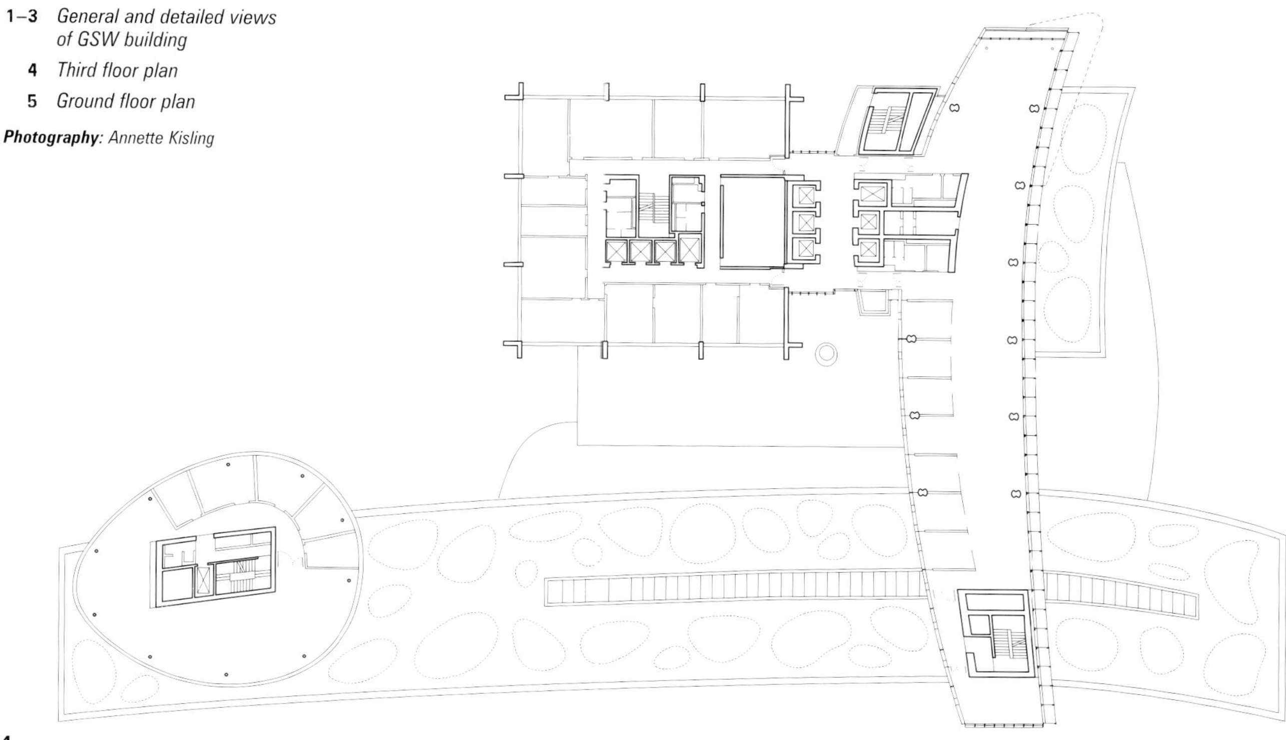

4

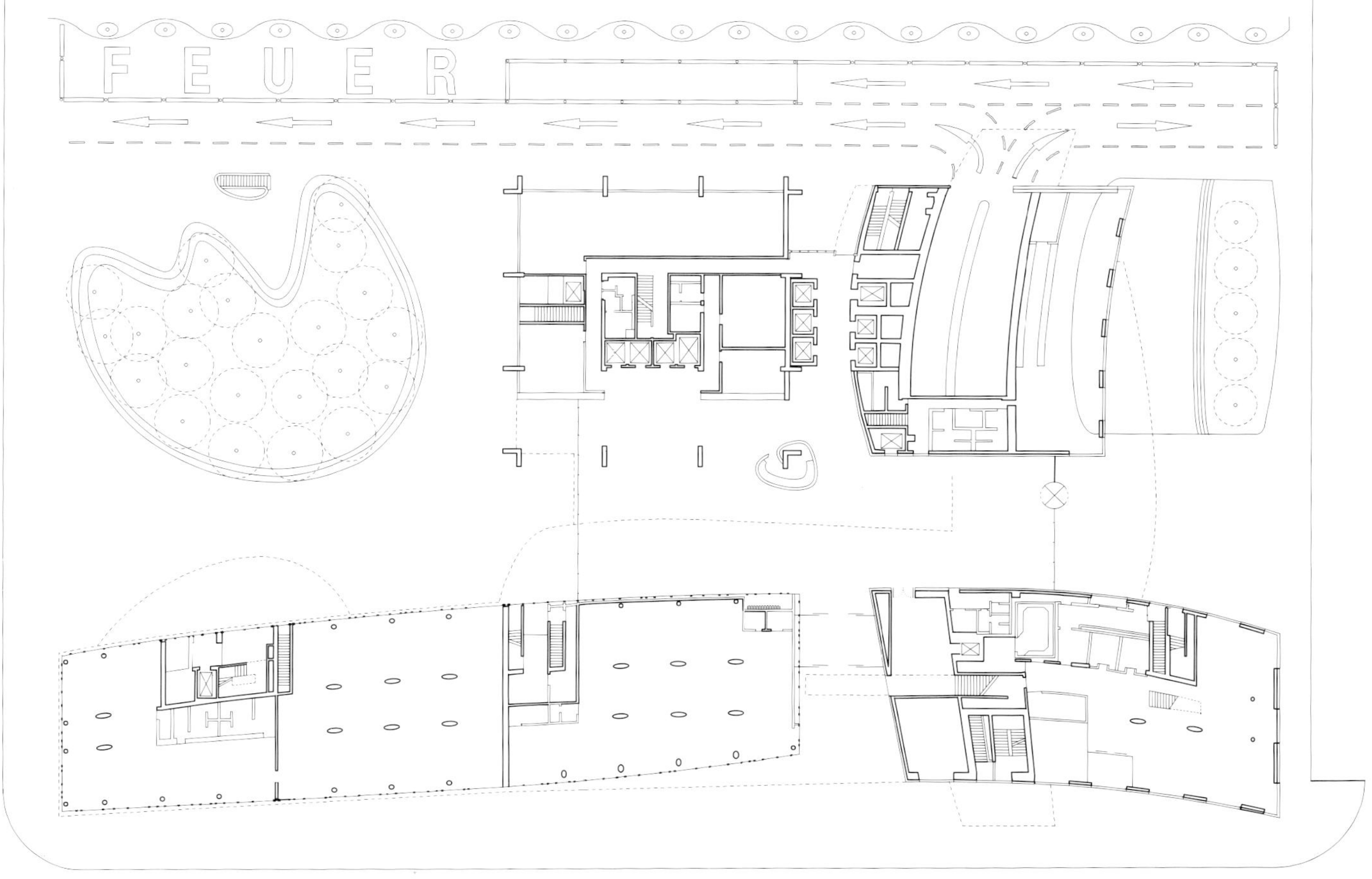

5

TORRES BLANCAS MADRID SPAIN

Located on the outskirts of Madrid along a major thoroughfare, the undulating Torres Blancas appears as a series of concrete shafts. External balconies provide effective solar protection to most apartments in the residential building. Solar shading is also provided by louvred shutters on most windows.

The 21 levels designed for housing are distributed as follows: six levels contain eight apartments per level; nine levels contain four apartments per level; six levels contain two apartments per level. Originally, a restaurant and a service centre were built on the top 24th and 25th levels.

A sunken plaza around the building creates a garden for the residents, and differentiates this building from the typical urban apartment blocks in Madrid. Today, the tower remains an isolated object in its urban context but its unusual organic shape helps it blend into the city.

1&2 *General views*
3 *Façade detail*
4 *Section*

Photography: *G Binder, courtesy Buildings & Data SA*

1

2

Torres Blancas | **Location** Madrid, Spain | **Completion date** 1968 | **Architect** Francisco Javier Saenz de Oiza | **Client** Hisa | **Structural engineer** Carlos Fernandez Casado and Javier Manterola Armisén | **Contractor** Huarte y Cia | **Height** 81 m/266 ft | **Above-ground storeys** 25 | **Easements** 2 | **Use** Residential, restaurant | **Structural materials** Concrete | **Other materials** Concrete

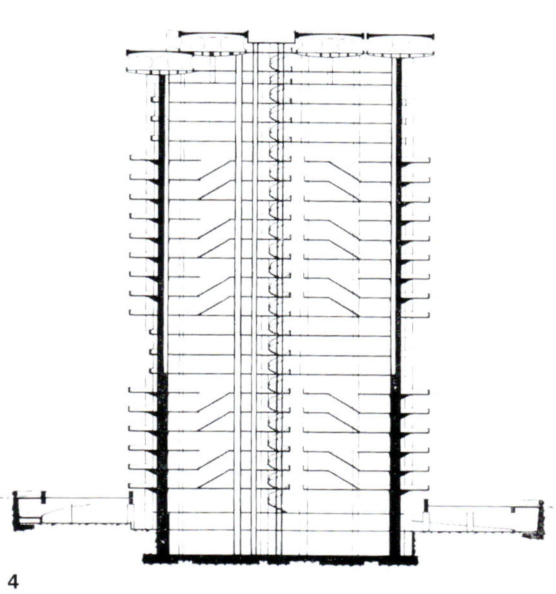

4

3

IBM HOUSE (NOW EUROPE–ISRAEL TOWER)

TEL AVIV
ISRAEL

This tower was built between 1973 and 1978 to serve as the Israeli headquarters of IBM. The building is located in the northern civic centre of Tel Aviv, across the street from the regional courthouse and Tel Aviv Museum of Art. The mosaic-clad tower blends harmoniously with its surroundings and has served as a major urban focal point on Tel Aviv's skyline for almost 30 years. A few years ago it became the focus of a public call for preservation after its new owners intended to change its façades and clad it with glass and marble curtain wall. The protest was successful and in 2002 the building was renovated and preserved in its original form.

The unique plan of the building – a triangle with curved sides – provides both an efficient utilisation of the floor area, and a more comfortable working environment. The curved sides fit with the curves of the adjoining streets and the freeflowing lines of the adjacent Asia House, providing most of the offices with an optimal north–south orientation.

The structure is 'cup' shaped, with a central core that contains lifts, staircases, toilets and service shafts. This central core rises from a foundation core 30 metres in diameter that penetrates through four large basement floors. The 23 office floors above the ground surround the core and hang from it.

Placing the building on a single foundation proved to be an efficient and safe solution against earthquakes and wind forces, and resulted in large unobstructed underground areas for halls, storage and parking. The core was cast continually using slip forms, whereas most other building components, including walls, columns, ceilings, and balustrades, were prefabricated and brought to the site for assembly, resulting in time and cost savings.

The building sits on a large raised plaza, paved with cast in-situ granolite and covered with large beds of colourful flowers. The entrance lobby is surrounded with floor-to-ceiling glass walls that provide continuity from the plaza into the lobby and make the entrance welcoming and friendly.

1

2

3

1 *View across plaza from east*
2 *General view from north*
3 *Glass lobby as seen from street*
4 *West façade*
5 *Typical floor plan*
6 *Section from foundation mat to first typical floor*

***Photography:** Yaki Assayag*
***Plans:** A Lipski; courtesy G Binder/Buildings & Data SA*

IBM House (now Europe–Israel Tower) | **Location** Tel Aviv, Israel | **Completion date** 1978 | **Architect** Yasky and Partners Architects – A Yasky, J Sivan | **Client** IBM | **Structural engineer** S Ben Avraham Engineers Ltd; structural consultant: A Lipski, Engineer, Belgium | **Mechanical engineer** Ofir-Ronen Engineers Ltd. (air conditioning); A Gilad and Partners (electrical engineers) | **Landscape architect** A Brant Landscape Architecture Ltd. | **Contractor** Solel Bone Ltd. | **Height** 84 m/276 ft | **Above-ground storeys** 25 | **Basements** 4 | **Above-ground useable levels** 24 | **Mechanical levels** 2 | **Use** Office | **Site area** 4000 sq m/43,040 sq ft | **Area of above-ground building** 30,000 sq m/322,800 sq ft | **Structural materials** Reinforced concrete | **Other materials** External façades: prefabricated concrete elements with ceramic mosaic cladding; interior walls: plasterboard, fibreglass decorative ceilings

4

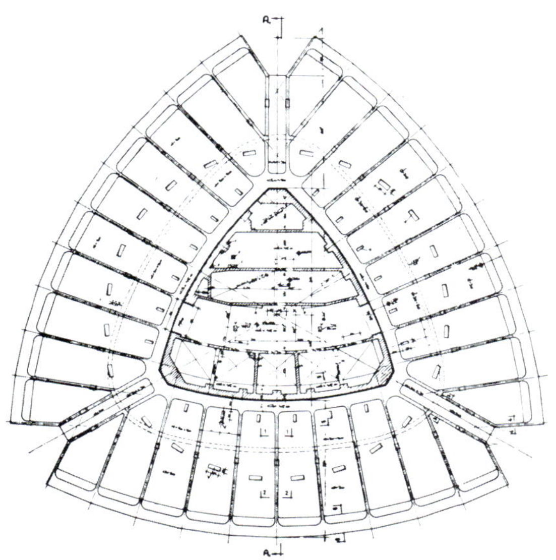

5

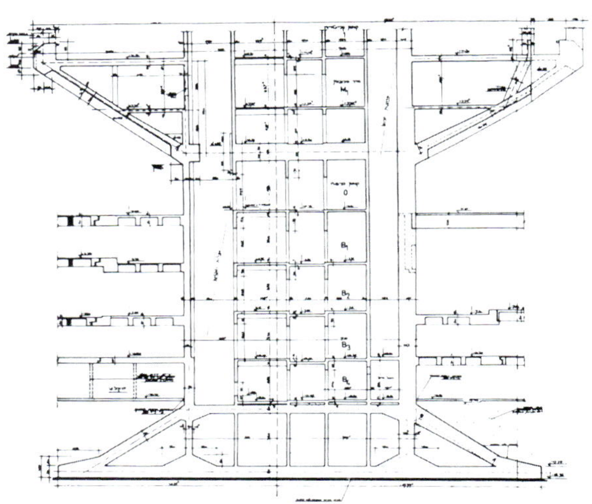

6

ELLIPSE BUILDING BRUSSELS BELGIUM

The Ellipse Building is one of the last major high-rise buildings to be developed within the Espace Nord area of Brussels. The original 1967 masterplan for this area included a series of tall buildings. The Ellipse Building has been designed to form a link between buildings of different scales and uses that are already completed or are soon to be built.

Set above a landscaped garden, the central glass-enclosed promenade at ground level gives access to all the low- and high-rise units that make the Ellipse Building a unique part of the downtown skyline of Brussels. The 23-storey tower – curved on one side and flat on the other, to complement another tower across the road – has been designed so that it will not impede the views enjoyed by the occupants of a nearby residential tall building.

The horizontal streamlined texture of the building accentuates the curve of the design and creates an interesting focal point at the end of the Espace Nord main axis.

1,3,4 *General views*
2 *Typical floor plan*
5 *Lobby*

Photography: *Marc Detiffe (3,4)*
Digital renderings: *Détrois SA (1); Montois Partners (5)*

1

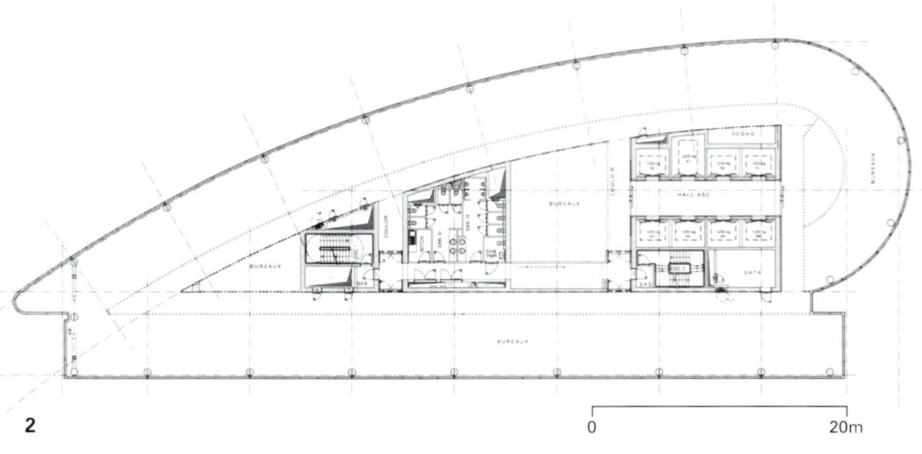

2

Ellipse Building | **Location** Brussels, Belgium | **Completion date** 2006 | **Architect** Montois Partners Architects; Art & Build Architects | **Client** Fortis Real Estate; Immomills Development | **Construction manager** Fortis Real Estate Construction Management; Progex | **Structural engineers** Ingénieurs Associés; B.CEC | **Mechanical engineers** Technum; Tractebel Development Engineerinng; Geocal | **Acoustical consultant** Venac | **Contractor** Cordeel | **Height** 85 m/279 ft | **Above-ground storeys** 23 | **Basements** 3 | **Above-ground useable levels** 22 | **Mechanical levels** 1 | **Use** Offices, retail | **Area of above-ground building** 46,198 sq m/497,090 sq ft (typical floor 1434 sq m/15,430 sq ft) | **Structural materials** Reinforced concrete | **Other materials** Glass curtain wall, granite

3

4

5

THE WESTIN WARSAW

WARSAW
POLAND

The Westin Warsaw Hotel, located at a major intersection in the Wola central business district, is one of Poland's most dynamic hotel environments. The five-star, 22-storey hotel is equipped to accommodate international business travellers by offering all the amenities needed to conduct 21st-century commerce.

Designed to be one of Poland's most dynamic hotel environments, the hotel includes 366 elegantly appointed rooms, a 530-square-metre ballroom, 445 square metres of meeting space and boardrooms, and a signature restaurant. The glazed vertical atrium, which houses the glass observation elevator cabs, provides an exhilarating experience for guests, presents a kinetic sculpture for the citizens of Warsaw, and acts as a beacon for this hub of business activity.

Other amenities include a bar, fitness centre, and a 150-square-metre presidential suite on the 20th floor with panoramic views of the city. Joining Portman in the execution of the design of the hotel were the architects Design Office Kazimierski and Ryba of Warsaw, Poland and Skanska Teknik Ab of Sweden. The interiors were designed by Wilson & Associates Inc. of Dallas, Texas.

The hotel tower's L-shape utilises an efficient double-loaded corridor design. At the corner between the two legs, a glass atrium serves as the focal point of the building. It is also the point where the tower's vertical circulation is located.

Situated in the heart of the business and financial center of Warsaw on one of the city's prime thoroughfares, the hotel serves as the centre point of the existing Atrium North and South complex, developed by Skanska International and Portman Holdings. The importance of the hotel's location at the corner of Grzybowska Street and Jana Pawla II Boulevard motivated the creation of the dramatic glazed tube.

1

2

1 *General view, night*
2 *General view at sunrise*
3 *The 'tube'*
4 *Suspended glass staircase*
5 *Floor plan*

Photography: *Jaime Ardiles-Arce, courtesy Westin Warsaw (1–3); Michael Portman (4)*

The Westin Warsaw | **Location** Warsaw, Poland | **Completion date** 2003 | **Architect** John Portman & Associates | **Local architect** Design Office Kazimierski and Ryba | **Client** Hotel Atrium Sp. ZO.O. | **Structural engineer** Skanska Teknik AB | **Mechanical engineer** Skanska Teknik AB | **Contractor** Skanska Polska Sp. ZO.O. | **Height** 89.9 m/294.8 ft | **Above-ground storeys** 22 | **Basements** 1 | **Above-ground useable levels** 21 | **Mechanical levels** 1 | **Use** Hotel | **Site area** 1997 sq m/21,500 sq ft | **Area of above-ground building** 25,950 sq m/279,322 sq ft | **Structural materials** Poured-in-place concrete, structural steel | **Other materials** Walnut, French limestone Italian marble, Egyptian alabaster

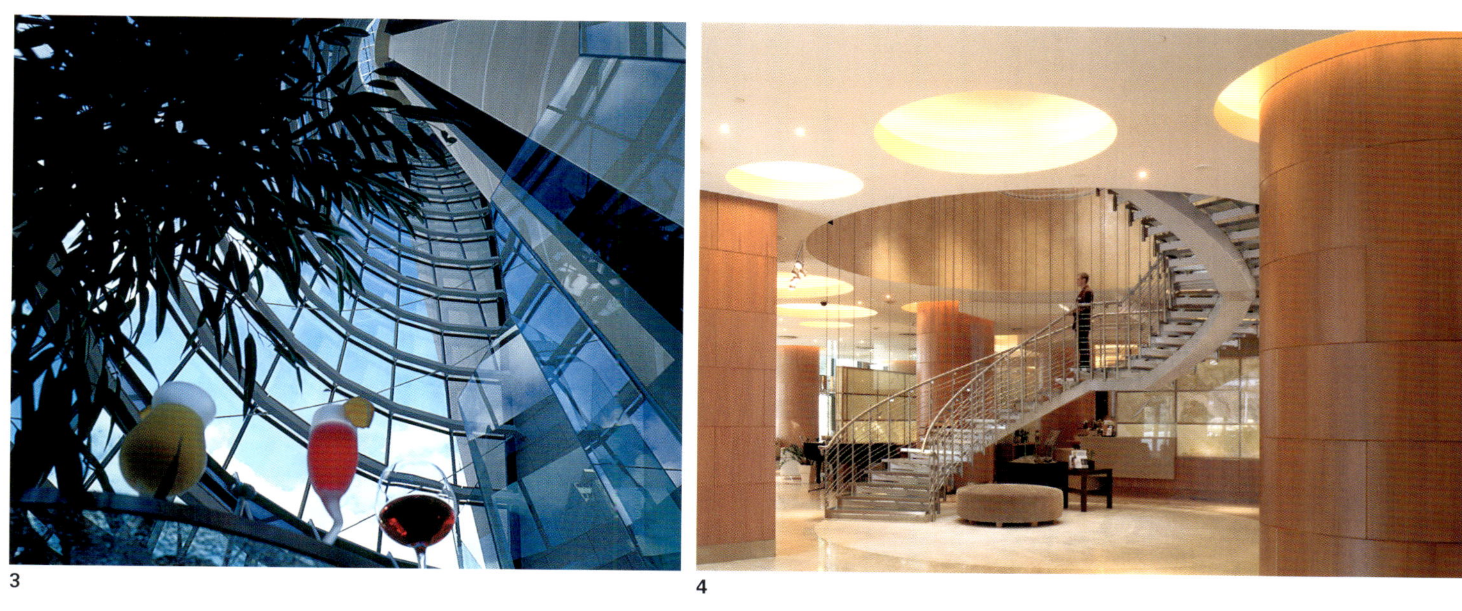

3

4

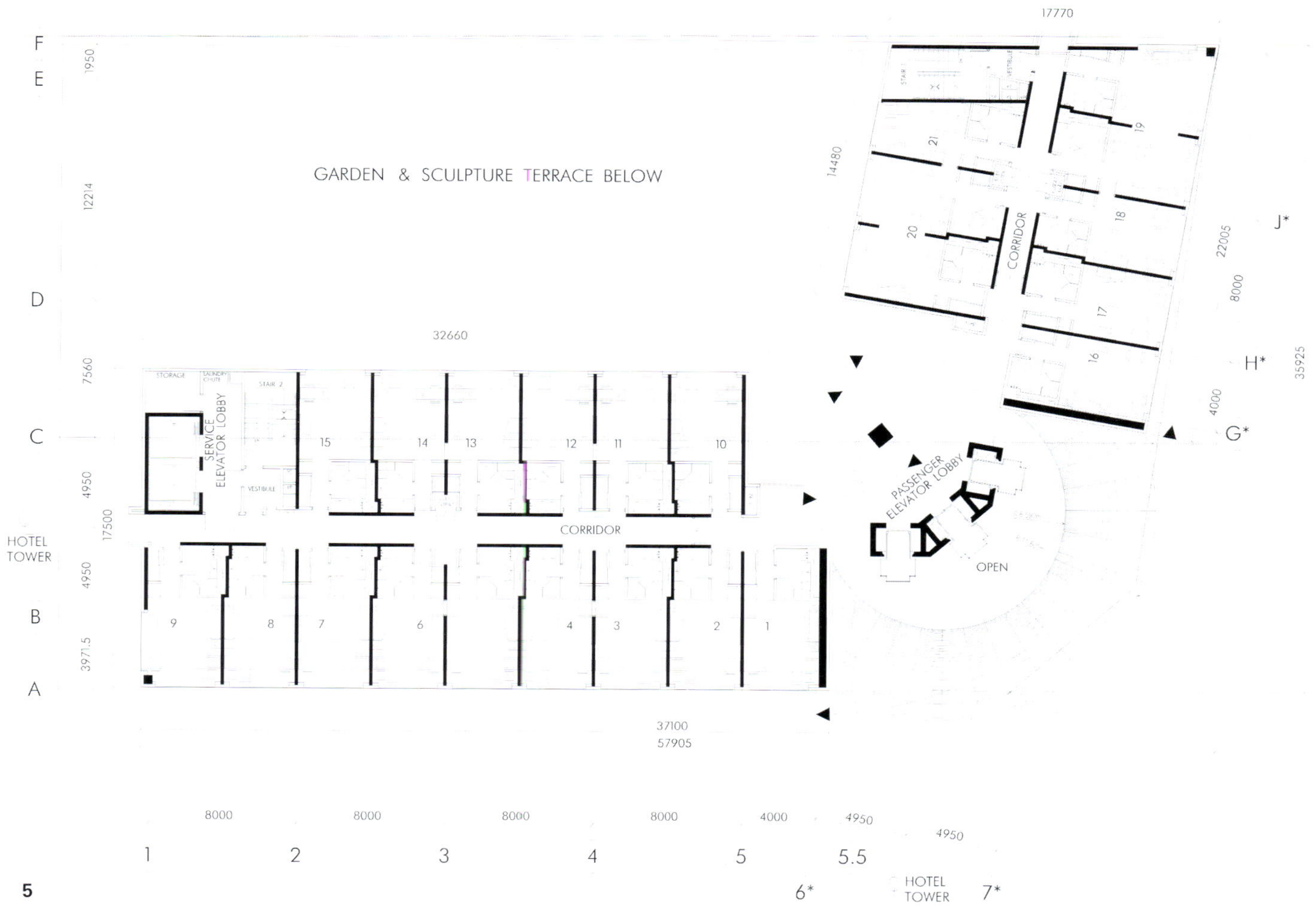
GARDEN & SCULPTURE TERRACE BELOW
CORRIDOR
SERVICE ELEVATOR LOBBY
PASSENGER ELEVATOR LOBBY
OPEN
HOTEL TOWER
HOTEL TOWER
17770
32660
37100
57905
8000
8000
8000
8000
4000
4950
4950
22005
35925
F
E
D
C
B
A
J*
H*
G*
1
2
3
4
5
5.5
6*
7*
5

BERLINER TOR CENTER HAMBURG GERMANY

The Berliner Tor Center occupies a very prominent position within Hamburg's urban fabric. As an important landmark on the traffic artery leading to the main station and the Rathausmarkt, the triad of skyscrapers is visible from a great distance and is a distinct feature of the city skyline. The dramatic urban ensemble is composed of two buildings of similar size alongside the existing skyscraper. Both new high-rise slabs rise up from a seven-storey horizontal block construction that defines the local topography of streets and buildings. The colour variations chosen for the design of the double façade lend the new buildings a specific identity, making them distinctive orientation points within the city. The pillar-supported office ring and the unique design of the ground-floor buildings beneath them provide fluid urban space for public use. The buildings accommodate offices, apartments and commercial tenants.

The building envelope was conceived as an internal climate moderator to achieve optimum energy efficiency, as well as providing the option for workers to control their individual office climates. All offices are equipped with floor-to-ceiling sliding windows, allowing for individual ventilation. Movable louvres are positioned as shading devices between the outer and inner façades and are centrally controlled according to the weather. The double-skin façade concept avoids overheating the building in summer due to the lower night temperatures, allowing the building to cool down.

Two basement storeys with 950 parking spaces as well as service, installation and storage spaces are located underneath the building complex. The installation of double and triple parking systems as well as sliding parking units allowed for an increased number of parking spaces and optimised floor efficiency.

1

1 *View of offices from southeast*
2 *Third floor plan*
3 *IBM Tower*
4 *View of apartments from garden*

Photography: *Klaus Frahm, Hamburg (1,3,4)*

Berliner Tor Center | **Location** Hamburg, Germany | **Completion date** 2004 | **Architect** Jan Störmer Partner | **Client** Becken Investitionen Vermögensverwaltung | **Structural engineer** Phillip Holzmann Planungsgesellschaft | **Mechanical engineer** Ridder & Meyn Ingenieurges mbH | **Landscape architect** GHP Landschaftsarchitekten | **Façade consultant** PBI Planungs Büro für Ingenieurleistungen GmbH | **Contractor** Imbau; Bilfinger + Berger | **Height** 90 m/295 ft | **Above-ground storeys** 23 | **Basements** 2 | **Use** Offices, apartments, commercial | **Site area** 21,000 sq m/226,000 sq ft | **Area of above-ground building** 75,000 sq m/807,300 sq ft | **Structural materials** Reinforced concrete, steel | **Other materials** Glass, aluminium | **Cost** €95 M

2

3

4

OPUS 12 PARIS LA DÉFENSE FRANCE

Located on the southern side of the La Défense esplanade, Paris's primary business development, the Opus 12 tower advances slightly relative to neighbouring towers. It has been the subject of a complete and total reconstruction of an early 1970's office tower. Gone is the heavy and visually restrictive concrete exterior wall structure, replaced by a lighter load-bearing steel structure and curtain wall. The typical floor plate width has been increased by 5 metres. The subsequent gain in area and volume provides increased workspace and the incorporation of modern building systems adapted to contemporary needs.

The new tower has been rebuilt on the old, including an extensive six-level building platform shared by nearly all construction at La Défense. At its base, a sunken patio exposes the building's substructure while generous glazing provides views and light to newly created shared building facilities such as restaurants, cafés and a conference centre. Previously unproductive space has been cleverly transformed, thanks to the dynamic vertical entry hall shared by the tower's occupants and visitors. Lower levels communicate with the exterior by way of the vast and high entry hall, opening from below onto the La Défense esplanade and its teeming pedestrian environment.

Enveloped in a double skin of clear and opalescent glass, the building takes on a new significance. Entirely glazed upper floors offer occupants a broad view of Paris and the Grande Arche. Morning and evening, the tower's rounded corners capture and diffract the sun's rays, reflecting the colours of changing light – a jewel-like object in a vertical universe.

1

1 *Main façade as seen from the La Défense Esplanade*

2&3 *Axonometric views and typical floor plans showing the renovation conceptual design. The former Crédit Lyonnais tower designed in 1973 by Dubuisson and Jausserand can be seen before renovation on both drawings.*

***Photography**: K Khalfi*

Opus 12 | **Location** Paris La Défense, France | **Completion date** Initial construction 1973/renovation 2004 | **Architect** (2004) Valode et Pistre Architectes | **Client** AXA | **Structural engineer** SETEC | **Mechanical engineer** OTH | **Landscape architect** Michel Desvignes | **Contractor** Bouygues | **Height** 90 m/295 ft | **Above-ground storeys** 27 | **Basements** 6 | **Above-ground useable levels** 27 | **Mechanical levels** 1 | **Use** Office, restaurants, conference facilities | **Site area** 1850 sq m/19,906 sq ft | **Area of above-ground building** 30,200 sq m/324,952 sq ft | **Structural materials** Steel, concrete | **Other materials** Aluminium and glass curtain wall featuring a fully glazed spandrel fire break | **Cost** €84 M

2

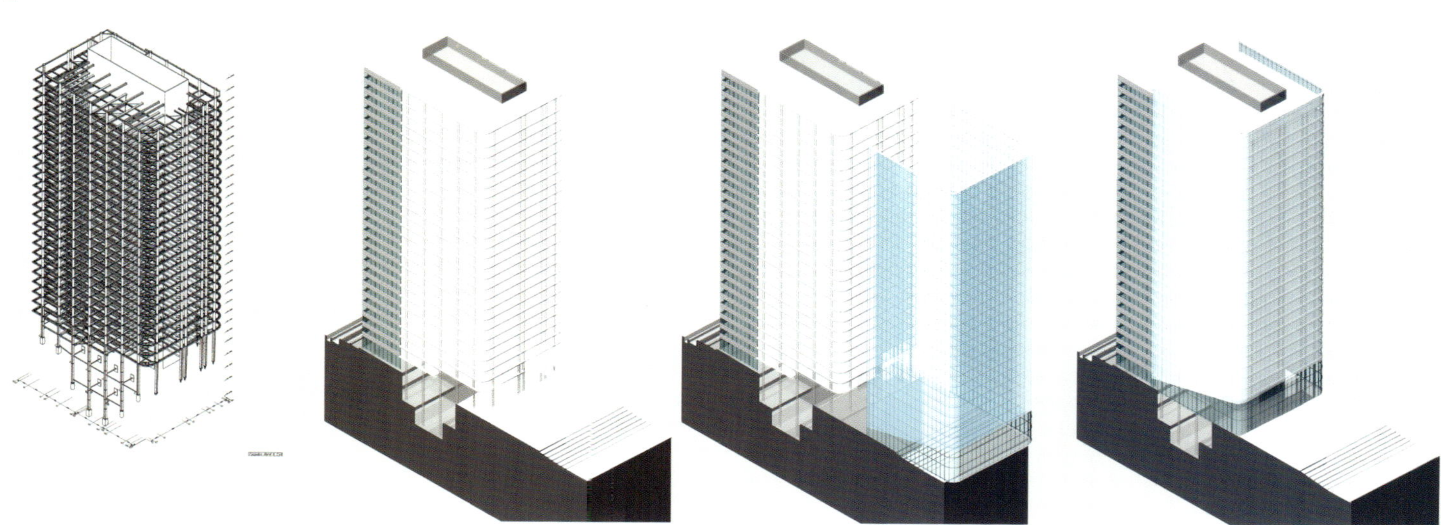

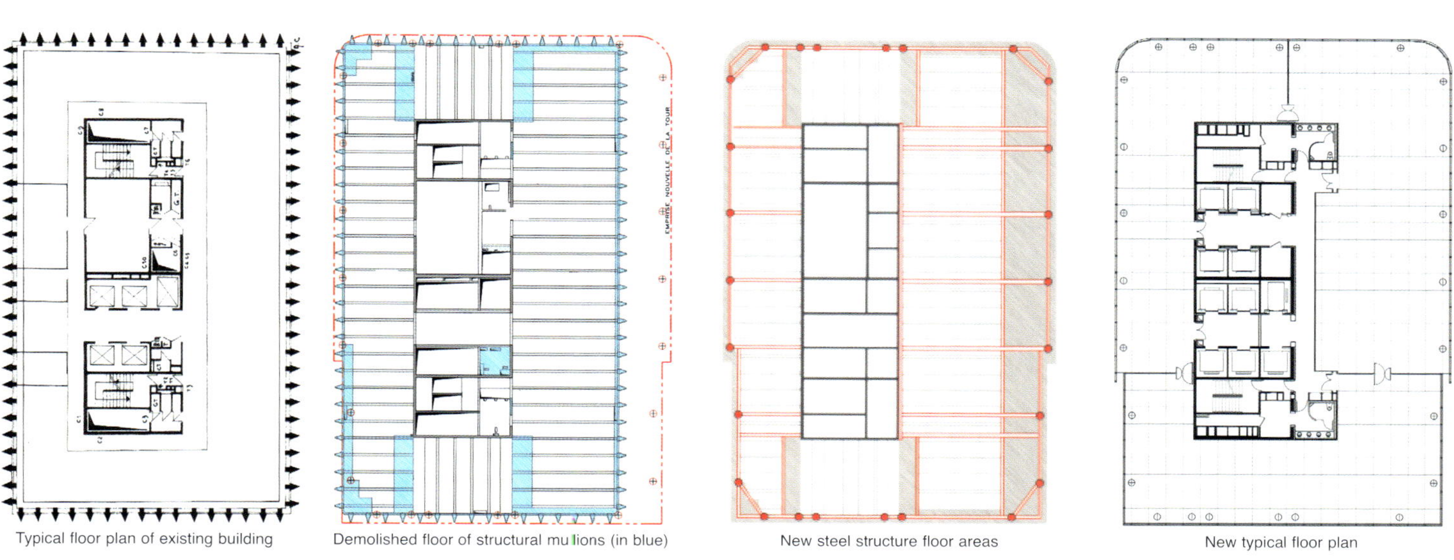

Typical floor plan of existing building

Demolished floor of structural mullions (in blue)

New steel structure floor areas

New typical floor plan

3

MAHLER 4, BUILDING 3BH

AMSTERDAM THE NETHERLANDS

The Mahler 4 office tower is part of a high-rise urban development south of Amsterdam. Located close to the city centre and with direct access to the urban network of public transport and motorways, the project has the potential to benefit from its unique location. The ambitious programming incorporates a lively, high-density mixture of offices, housing, retail and public space, designed by nine international architects, all contributing to an exceptional project of metropolitan scale.

The urban concept for this location, as developed by De Architecten Cie, is based on a vertical layered structure with the anatomical analogy of legs, torso and head. The Mahler 4 office tower challenges this masterplan further and proposes to create an explicit tactile and emotional experience out of the stacked block structure. Both an innovative composition of shifted volumes and a transformation from a light to heavy materialisation, it creates an impressive landmark that appears different from every angle.

Each of the three sections of the building reveals its own character and material expression and offers space suited to potentially different tenant requirements. Spacious office floors are combined with internal voids to enhance internal connections and spatial quality. Carefully defined lines of vision offer views to the surrounding environment. The overall image contributes to the creation of innovative and outstanding office facilities at this location.

1

2

3

1 *Close-up of rocky top*
2 *View of glass section*
3 *View from east side*
4 *Level 7 floor plan*
5 *Level 1 floor plan*
6 *Section through void*

Renderings: *Steven Simons, Peter Heavens, A2 Studio*

Mahler 4 | **Location** Amsterdam, The Netherlands | **Completion date** 2007 | **Architect** (EEA) Erick van Egeraat associated architects | **Client** Mahler 4 consortium | **Structural engineer** Arup; Engineersgroup Van Rossum; Van der Vorm | **Mechanical engineer** Techniplan | **Contractor** G & S Vastgoed bv | **Height** 90.7 m/298 ft | **Above-ground storeys** 24 | **Basements** 3 | **Above-ground useable levels** 24 | **Mechanical levels** 2 | **Use** Office | **Site area** 1750 sq m/18,840 sq ft | **Area of above-ground building** 31,089 sq m/ 334,600 sq ft | **Principal structural materials** Reinforced concrete | **Other materials** Glass façade partially printed, natural stone, aluminium

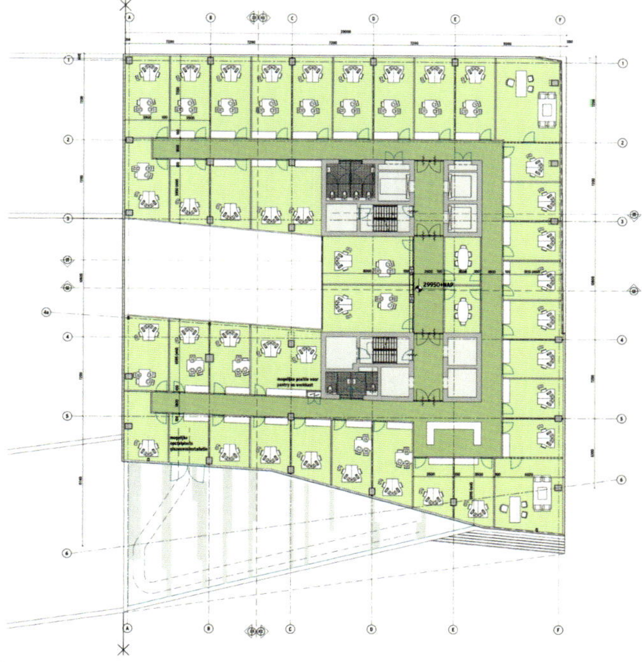

4

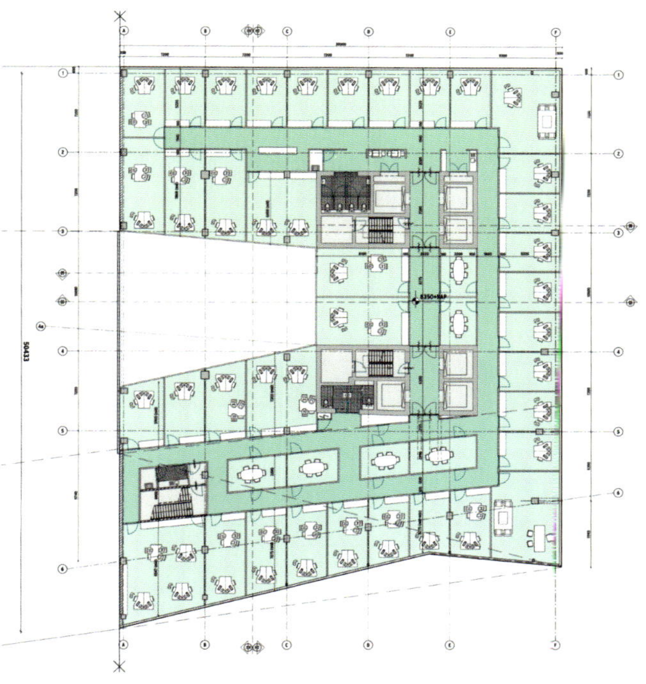

5

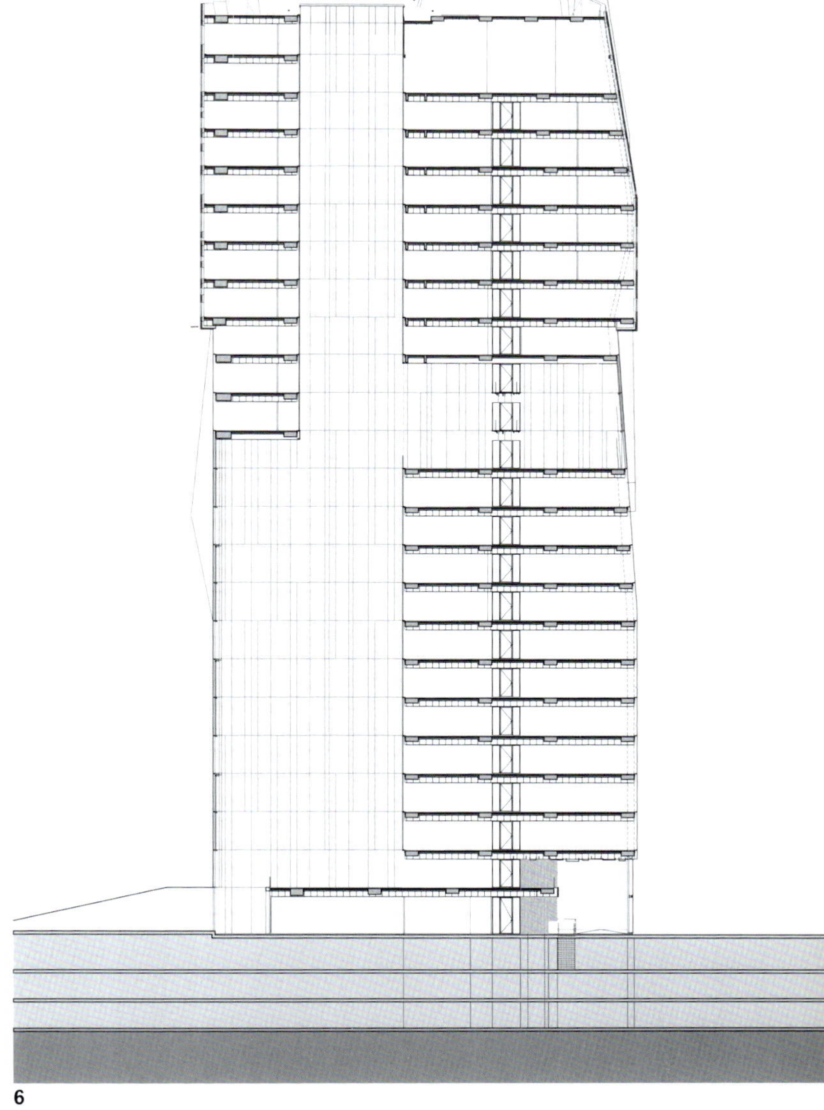

6

MAHLER 4 AMSTERDAM THE NETHERLANDS

Rafael Viñoly Architects, and eight other architects, were invited to participate in the design of this mixed-use development in the South Axis of Amsterdam. The master plan defined the sites, program, and areas, and set the design criteria, of each building to ensure coherence of the overall development and to create a new urban focal point for Amsterdam. The master plan broke with traditional urban design composition, based on uniformity and aesthetic cohesiveness, to achieve a rich urban environment that is as vibrant as it is unpredictable.

The subdued reflective qualities of the glass and the blank anodised aluminium give this building a unified sense of mass that reflects even the subtlest of changes in the weather conditions. The vertical mullions change grid dimensions on each face of the building. This creates a varying density, depending on the point of view, and a dynamic, constantly changing image. The total combined effect encourages the perception of the building not as a planar composition but as a sculptural element in perpetual motion.

The building reinterprets the horizontal data of the project into a more dynamic geometry that results from the trace of an exterior fire escape that wraps around the building. The open stair subtracts a spiral volume from the building. Offering a fair-weather alternative to the two elevator cores, the stairs create exterior spaces that office workers can use as informal gathering spaces in addition to a few gardens and outdoor plazas that punctuate the façade.

'The Diagonal,' the main pedestrian axis of the master plan, provides access to the ground floor of the south façade, which contains retail units. Two large lobbies contain reception areas and are connected to the underground parking level. The external stairs allow visitors access to a large public garden on the roof of the wider six-storey lower portion of the building. A second, smaller terrace at the 16th floor of the narrower portion of the tower is for private use only.

1

2

3

4

1 *Night view showing neon illumination of external stair cut*
2 *Night view from the main highway (A10)*
3 *Southern entrance and base of external staircase*
4 *External stair cut detail*
5 *Detail showing corner conditions of external staircase*
6 *Level 19 floor plan*
7 *Level 8 floor plan*
8 *Level 2 floor plan*
9 *Ground level floor plan*

Photography: *Raoul Suermondt*
Drawings: *Courtesy Rafael Viñoly Architects*

Mahler 4 | **Location** Amsterdam, The Netherlands | **Completion date** 2005 | **Architect** Rafael Viñoly Architects PC | **Associate architect** Van den Oever Zaaijer & Partners | **Client** Mahler 4 Consortium, G&S Vastgoed | **Structural engineer** Van Rossum Raadgevende Ingenieurs | **Mechanical engineer** Deerns Raadgevende Ingenieurs | **Landscape architect** Ruwan Aluvihare – DRO Amsterdam | **Contractor** G&S Bouw | **Height** 91 m/300 ft | **Above-ground storeys** 26 (including mezzanine) | **Basements** 3 | **Above-ground useable levels** 25 | **Mechanical levels** 1 | **Use** Office | **Site area** (entire development) 160,000 sq m/1,721,600 sq ft | **Area of above-ground building** 32,259 sq m/347,240 sq ft | **Structural materials** Concrete, steel | **Other materials** Glass, aluminium | **Cost** US$46.5 M

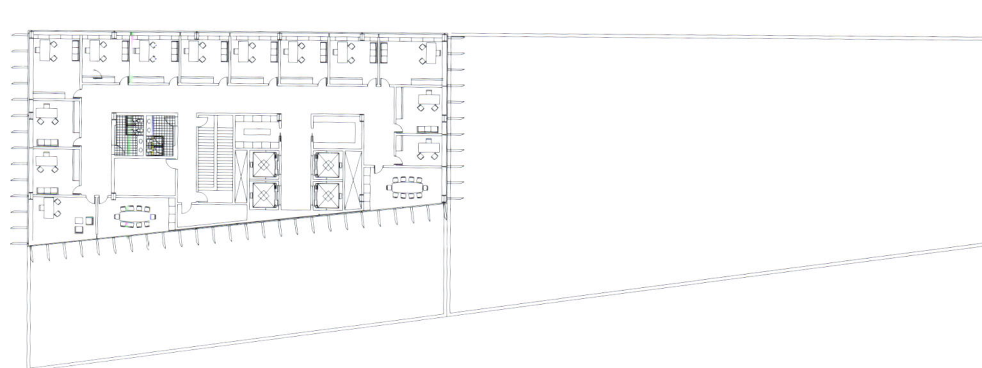

6

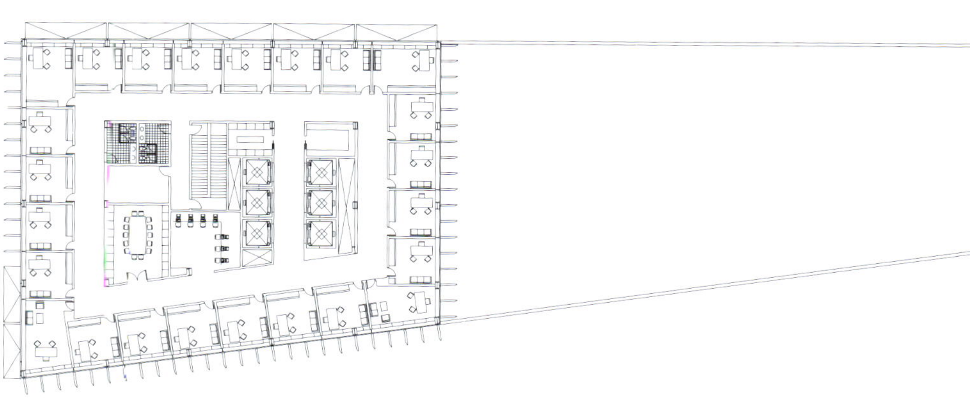

7

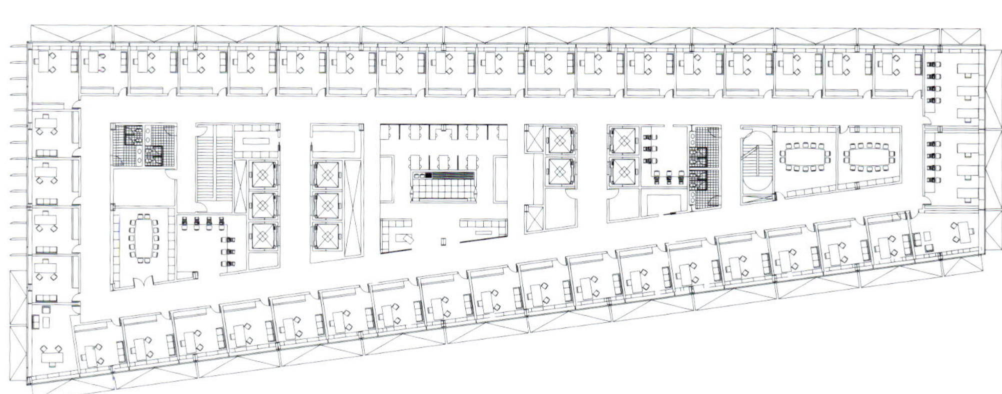

8

5

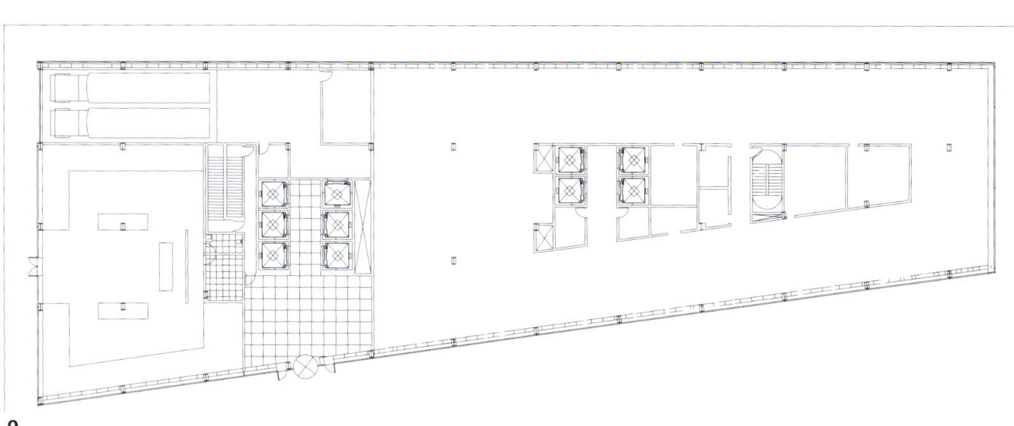

9

SONY CENTER BERLIN GERMANY

In the reconstruction of Berlin, the Sony Center represents a new technical vision and order. Surrounded by traditional urban streets and spaces, it is a new type of covered, urban forum for a changing culture.

The construction components emphasise transparency, lightness and layering and state-of-the-art technology. The skins employ sophisticated glass and lightweight steel technologies. The façades of the office buildings at each corner of the site are constructed with load-bearing glass mullions. The visible metal on the façade is reduced to a minimal band at the slab edge.

The Forum buildings (Filmhaus, IMAX/Forum Apartments and Bürogebäude Bellevuestrasse) take on a more constructed appearance through components of formed metal and metal mullions. This system is overlaid with wintergardens, open walkways in the Forum apartments, full-height pivot windows in the Bellevue offices and a woven metal screen for projection in the Filmhaus. Through these devices the Forum façades assume a rich texture and layering.

The Esplanade Residence has a glass façade with full-height doors leading to continuous exterior balconies, interrupted by cantilevered glass bays that allow panoramic views.

The roof is an elliptical umbrella providing shading and protection from the elements and displays state-of-the-art cable, membrane and glass technology. One third of the roof is glazed, assuring views to the outside, ecological and economical construction and desired contrast and interesting lighting. The remaining two-thirds of the roof is a cable-reinforced fibreglass membrane, ensuring transparency, long life and economy.

A shared aim for all the buildings is to maximise daylight and views, and to provide various options for natural ventilation with or without mechanical assistance. The office buildings have different systems, based on tenants' requirements, with various degrees of control for windows, shades and temperature. The apartments use floor heating and fan coils for cooling. The large glazed spaces like the Filmhaus Atrium and Sony Wintergarden and Skygarden act like transitional buffer zones and are naturally ventilated.

1

1 *Bahn Tower general view*
2 *Site plan*
3 *Sony Center Forum*
4&5 *Bahn Tower façade detail*

Photography: *Engelhardt/Sellin, Aschau i.CH (1&3); H.G. Esch (4); John Linden (5)*

Sony Center | **Location** Berlin, Germany | **Completion date** 2000 | **Architect** Murphy/Jahn, Inc. | **Client** Sony with partners TishmanSpeyer Properties and Kajima | **Structural engineers** Ove Arup, New York (Roof Forum); BGS Ingenieursozietät, Berlin (Buildings) | **Mechanical engineers** Jaros Baum & Bolles, New York; Ingenieurgesellschaft Höpfner mbH, Berlin | **Landscape architect** Peter Walker & Partners, Berkeley, California; Rheims + Partner, Krefeld, Germany | **Height** Tower 94 m/308 ft | **Above-ground storeys** Tower 26 | **Use** Mixed: office, residential, cinema, entertainment, retail | **Site area** 26,444 sq m/284,600 sq ft | **Area of above-ground building** 132,500 sq m/1,426,000 sq ft | **Structural materials** Steel, glass | **Cost** approx DM1.5 billion

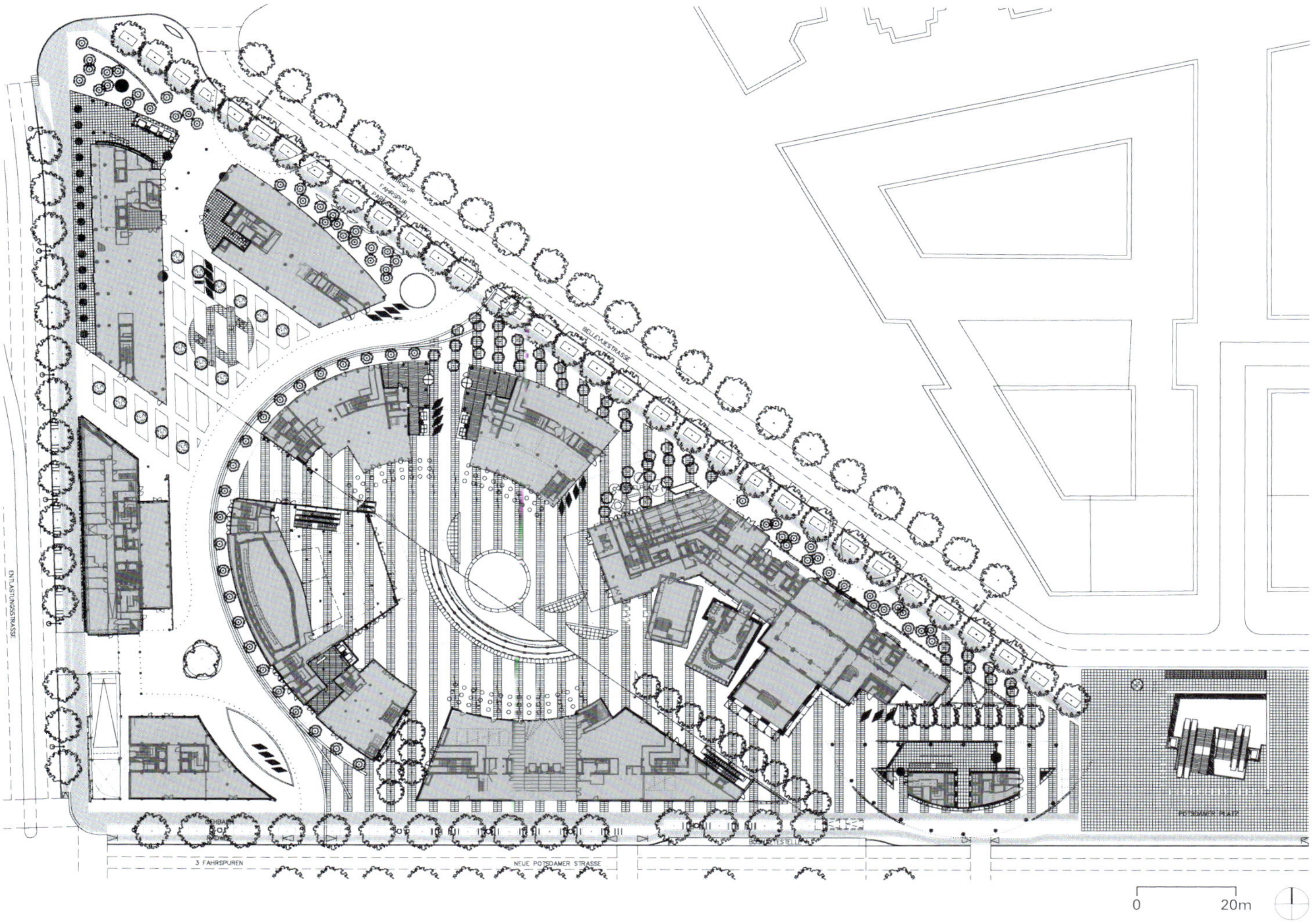

0 20m

2

3

4

5

HILTON BRUSSELS

BRUSSELS
BELGIUM

The Hilton Brussels (originally Brussels Hilton) was one of the first international hotels to be built in Brussels and a truly multipurpose project. The building consisted of a Hilton International Hotel, 10,000 square metres of offices and an upscale art and retail gallery. Due to the success of the hotel, which rapidly became a popular meeting point in Brussels, the tower is now fully used by the hotel, (with the exception of one office level) which has expanded from 308 rooms to 431 today. From the beginning the project was designed to suit several purposes, including hotel accommodation, office space and retail. The design philosophy proved to be highly efficient as the multipurpose aspect evolved gradually over the years.

The 29-storey Hilton project includes a two-level platform and a 27-storey high-rise section. The platform contains the lobby at ground level, the coffee shop, bar and retail gallery; the upper level houses the ballroom, the gourmet restaurant and an art gallery. Immediately above the platform the recessed level is used for mechanical equipment; the sleek shaft of the tower rises from the third level. The topmost level was originally designed to accommodate the *En plein Ciel* rooftop restaurant, the highest public viewpoint in Brussels.

As in many of the projects designed by Henri Montois, the Hilton hotel features artworks by an array of internationally recognised artists including Vic Gentils, Jean-Pierre Ghijsels, Emile Souply and Victor Vasarely, among many others. The combination of art with architecture is characteristic of Henri Montois' vision and personal approach to buildings.

1

2

Hilton Brussels | **Location** Brussels, Belgium | **Completion date** 1967 | **Architect** Henri Montois | **Client** Hilton International – Compagnie Hôtelière de Belgique | **Developer** Herpain | **Structural engineer** Gilbert Lesage | **Mechanical engineer** Marcq & Roba | **Contractor** Entreprises Herpain et Fils | **Height** 94.12 m/308.8 ft | **Above-ground storeys** 29 | **Basements** 4 | **Mechanical levels** 2 | **Use** Hotel, office, retail | **Site area** 2770 sq m/29,805 sq ft | **Area of above-ground building** 30,000 sq m/322,800 sq ft | **Structural materials** Reinforced concrete, slipformwork | **Other materials** Prefabricated concrete, aluminium window frames

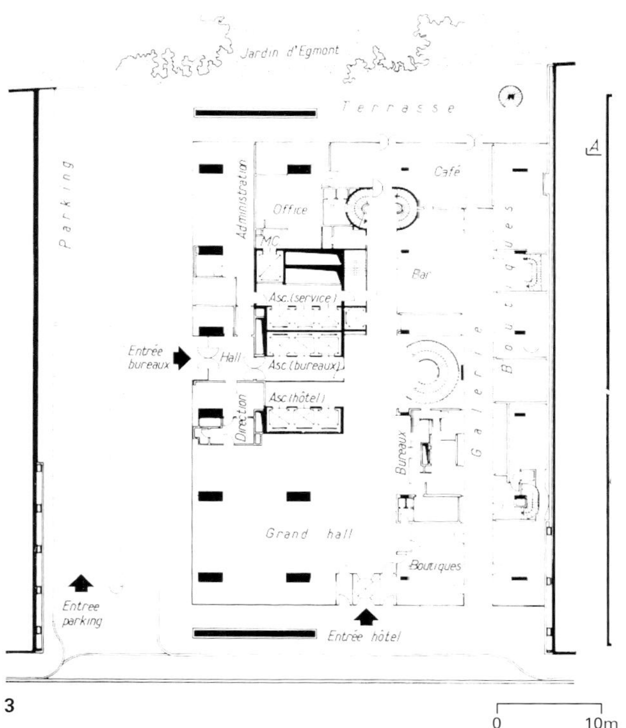

3

4

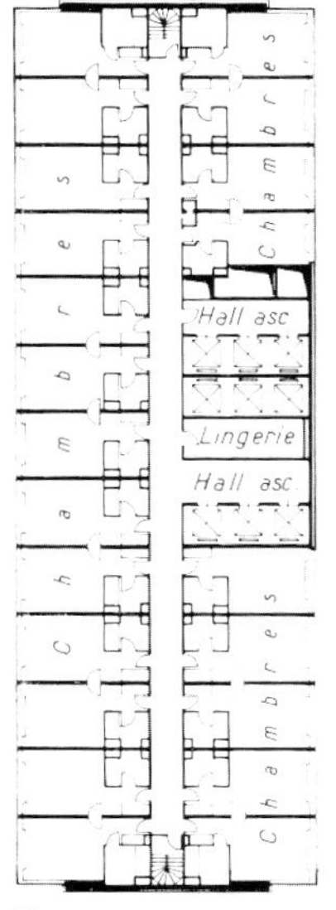

5

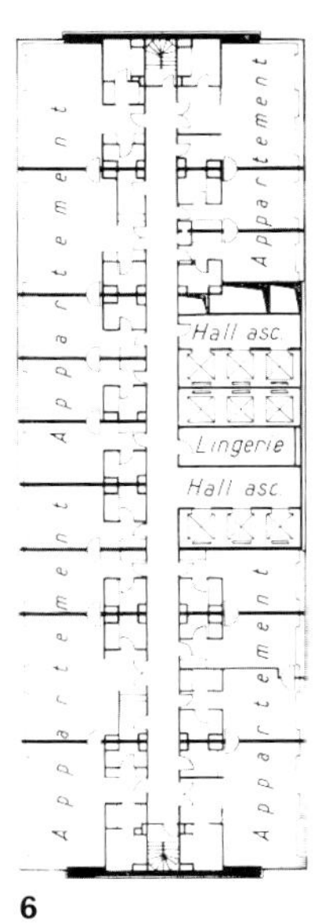

6

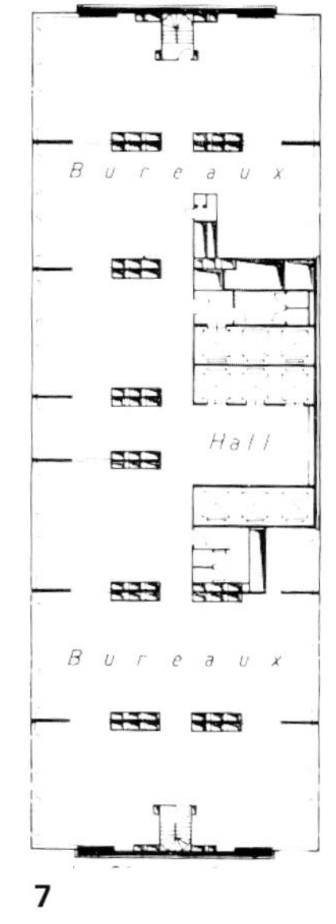

7

1 General view seen from Place Louise
2 General view with Law Courts on the left
3 Ground floor plan
4 Main entrance canopy, now demolished
5 Typical hotel rooms, low-rise floor plan
6 Suites level floor plan
7 Typical office level, high-rise floor plan

***Photography:** Bauters sprl, courtesy G Binder/Buildings & Data SA*
***Plans:** Reproduced from* La Technique des Travaux, *May–June 1971; courtesy G Binder/Buildings & Data SA*

THYSSENHAUS DÜSSELDORF (ORIGINALLY PHOENIX-RHEINROHR)

DÜSSELDORF
GERMANY

The so called 'Dreischeibenhaus', a name that conveys the design idea of discs, is based on a prize-winning competition design. The building volume is divided into three staggered discs, with the central one rising three storeys above the outer two. The central disc represents the central fixed point of the building.

This layout allowed direct light to enter the relatively short corridors and stairwells. The steel frame construction was erected above a base volume with three basement levels. The outer sides are sheathed in aluminium and glass-suspended curtain wall. The narrow sides are clad in stainless steel sheeting.

1

2

Thyssenhaus Düsseldorf (originally Phoenix-Rheinrohr) | **Location** Düsseldorf, Germany | **Completion date** 1960 | **Architect** Professor Dr. Ing. Helmut Hentrich; Dipl.-Ing. Hubert Petschnigg | **Client** Phoenix-Rheinrohr AG | **Structural engineer** Prof. Dr.-Ing. E.H. Klöppel; Prof. Dr.-Ing. Fritz Leonhardt | **Mechanical engineer** Dipl.-Ing. O.H. Brandi | **Height** 94.66 m/310.6 ft | **Above-ground storeys** 25 | **Above-ground useable levels** 22 | **Basements** 3 | **Mechanical levels** 3 | **Use** Office | **Site area** 21,309 sq m/229,284 sq ft | **Gross floor area** 33,700 sq m/362,612 sq ft | **Structural materials** Steel, reinforced concrete, glass

3

1&2 *General view from Hofgarten*
3 *Front façade*
4 *Ground floor plan*

Photography: *Manfred Hanisch*

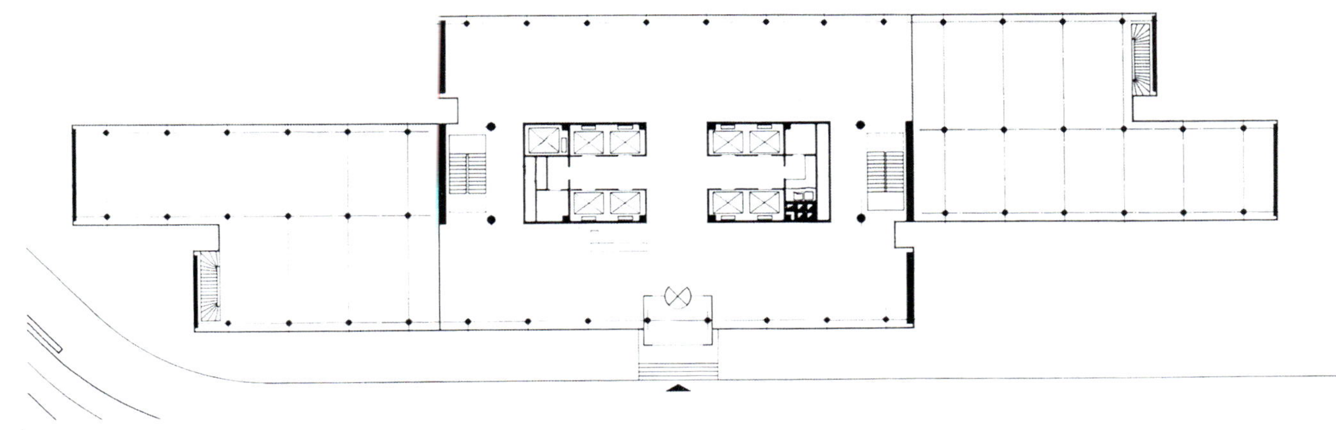

4

TORENGEBOUW (NOW KBC TOWER)

ANTWERP
BELGIUM

Built between 1928 and 1932 in the Art Deco style for the Algemeene Bankvereniging, the 'Torengebouw' or 'Boerentoren' is now the headquarters of the KBC Banking & Insurance company, and is also its emblem. Designed by architects Jan Vanhoenacker, Jos Smolderen and Emiel Van Averbeke, it was heightened by 10 metres during the transformation completed in 1971 by architects L Stynen and P De Meyer.

When originally completed in 1932, the 'Torengebouw', now KBC Tower, was the tallest high-rise building, and the first skyscraper, in Europe. It remained so until the 1950s. The building stands proudly at the end of the Meir, a major high-end retail boulevard in the centre of Antwerp. Built in a style reminiscent of the great early American skyscrapers, the tower comprised 24 storeys with an observatory deck open to the public built under the water tank.

Jan Vanhoenacker, who was Antwerp's City Architect-in-Chief and the tower's consulting architect, designed, at the time of the tower's completion, an overall masterplan for Antwerp's Linkeroever area. The plan comprised a series of tall buildings arranged along a main axis, but it was never built. Vanhoenacker also recommended the installation of the 230-cubic-metre water tank atop the building, to improve fire safety measures,

The building was hit by a V-bomb in January 1945, resulting in a hole several metres wide in the façade, but the building's steel skeleton withstood the explosion.

Although a series of residential tall buildings were built in the periphery of the city in the 1970s, very few other tall buildings have been completed in the city centre. The KBC Tower may well remain a major city landmark together with the Cathedral for many decades to come. At the turn of the third millennium, the KBC Tower remains one of the very few European tall buildings still reminiscent of famous early American examples.

1

2

3

1 *Torengebouw, now KBC Tower, seen in its early days*

2&3 *Façade details with window frames seen here after a recent renovation*

4 *KBC Tower today*

Photography: *Courtesy KBC Archives (1); Michael J Crosbie (2,3); Marc Detiffe; courtesy M.D. sprl (4)*

Torengebouw (now KBC Tower) | **Location** Antwerp, Belgium | **Completion date** 1932 | **Architects** Jan Robert Vanhoenacker, Jos Smolderen; Emiel Van Averbeke, stadshoofdbouwmeester Antwerp city chief architect, consultant | **Renovation architects** (1971) L Stynen and P De Meyer | **Client** Algemeene Bankvereeniging n.v. | **Height** 97 m/318 ft (originally 87.50 m/287 ft) | **Above-ground useable levels** 26 | **Use** Office | **Structural materials** Steel | **Other materials** Stone

4

COVENT GARDEN BRUSSELS BELGIUM

Located at the tip of downtown's Espace Nord area, Covent Garden is oriented towards the city. Its location against the railways and the botanical gardens will guarantee its long-term visibility as a new urban event. On the Place Rogier side, the low-rise building will recompose the urban fabric with scales equivalent to those of the neighbouring buildings. On the railway side, the tower will be enshrined in the urban fabric of the North Station business district, whose skyline will be extended.

The interior garden, covered by a 1300-square-metre glass roof, will be the natural extension of the park at the heart of Covent Garden. The oval-shaped main volume is pierced by a huge atrium extending to the 13th floor. The atrium is partly external, to allow natural ventilation. The upper levels are organised around a patio opening on to the city and a volume in recess. The interplay of the full and empty areas and the overlap reinforces the building's personality and gives it a human scale. The façade, comprised of non-reflective glass, features horizontal metal stringcourses at every second floor. At night, the illuminated roof will reinforce Covent Garden's role as a new downtown landmark.

The white architectural concrete mass of the low-rise building contrasts strongly with the tower. The building's volume will be aligned with the hotels located on the other side of the street. The overlapping of two low volumes forms Covent Garden's main entrance.

The glass-roofed interior landscaped garden connects the two buildings, allowing access to the lobby areas and to a possible restaurant at ground-floor level. The proposed Mediterranean-type garden, embellished with leisure areas and ponds, will form part of the wastewater treatment system designed specifically for the project.

Covent Garden will be equipped with a wastewater recovery process using advanced biological and bacteriological purification techniques. The objective is to treat all wastewater so that it can be recycled into the building's consumption cycle. Water is recovered at the end of the process and is stored in a pond of undrinkable water. It is recycled into the building for sanitary use and for building and garden maintenance.

1

2

3

1 *General view*
2 *Covent Garden at night*
3 *Covent Garden as seen from the Botanical Garden*
4 *High-rise floor plan, levels 20–24*
5 *Glass-covered landscape garden and promenade*

Digital renderings: *Détrois SA (1,3,5); Art & Build Architects (2)*

Covent Garden | **Location** Brussels, Belgium | **Completion date** 2006 | **Architect** Art & Build Architects; Montois Partners Architects | **Client** Immobilière du Royal Rogier sa | **Project manager** Buelens Real Estate nv | **Structural engineer** Bureau d'Etudes Greisch sa | **Mechanical engineer** JCD – STD jv | **Construction manager** Bopro | **Main contractors** Van Roey; Democo; Vooruitzicht | **Height** 99.13 m/325.23 ft | **Above-ground storeys** 27 | **Basements** 3 | **Above-ground useable levels** 27 | **Mechanical levels** 2 | **Use** Office, retail | **Area of above-ground building** 70,772 sq m/761,507 sq ft (typical floor 2282 sq m/24,554 sq ft) | **Parking spaces** 350 | **Structural materials** Reinforced concrete | **Other materials** Glass curtain wall

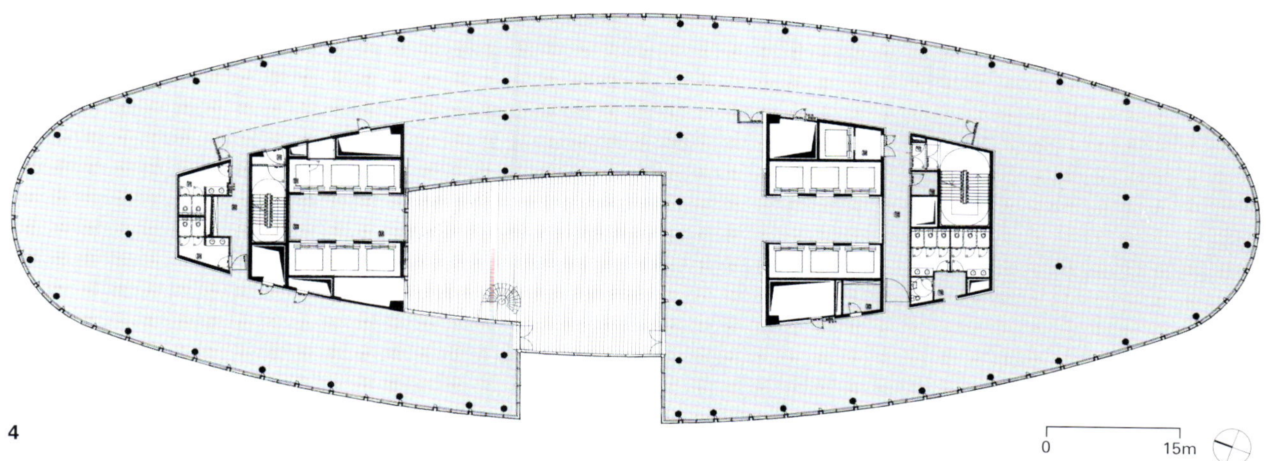

4

5

WESTHAFEN TOWER FRANKFURT GERMANY

Westhafen (West harbour) Tower marks one of the main entry points to the city as well as to the new Westhafen quarter. Its striking façade has already made it a new landmark on the skyline of Frankfurt. The tower, and the surrounding office buildings, are accessed via a central plaza. The plaza connects to the buildings, the street and the riverside walk.

The circular footprint of the tower makes maximum use of the floor area while minimising the area of the façade; the square-shaped floor plates inside the circle create optimum efficiency.

The superimposition of circle and square creates four-storey atrium spaces that serve as thermal buffer zones and allow the floors to be internally connected inside these interstitial spaces. Thus, a secondary circulation system can be established independent of the escape stairs located inside the core. Above ground, the building consists of a reception area on the ground floor, 28 office floors and a double-height technical floor. The central core holds all vertical circulation, services, sanitary, and meeting rooms and is surrounded by flexible office space that permits cellular as well as open plan office fit-out. Underground, the core of the building accommodates more services and storage space, and is surrounded by a spiralling parking garage.

Triangular, green-tinted glazed elements create the appearance of the façade. The cylindrical shape of the tower is clad with flat sheets of glass. In order to create as much curvature as possible with flat sheets (which means a polygonal division of the circular floor plate), the tips of the triangles are alternately tilted slightly inwards and outwards. Due to these minimal inclinations every sheet of glass reflects the light in a different angle, creating a stunning multifaceted effect that resembles a cut gem. The triangular windows can be opened to supply natural ventilation to the offices, either through the winter gardens, or directly through the façade. On the top office floor triangular cutouts perforate the tilted concrete ceiling, crowning the top of the building, and creating a spectacular effect at night.

1

2

1 *Westhafen Tower, Westhafen Brückengebäude and Westhafen Haus surround the central plaza*

2 *View from 28th floor*

3 *Central Westhafen plaza*

4 *Ground floor plan*

5 *Foyer, Westhafen Tower*

Photography: *Waltraud Krase (1); Jörg Hempel (2,3,5)*

Westhafen Tower | **Location** Frankfurt, Germany | **Completion date** 2003 | **Architect** schneider + schumacher Architekturgesellschaft mbH | **Developer** OFB Projektentwicklungs-GmbH; Max Baum Immobilien GmbH | **Structural engineer** SPI Schüsler-Plan Ingenieurgesellschaft | **Mechanical engineer** HL-Technik AG | **Façade consultant** IFFT Institut für Fassadenplanung Karlotto Schott, Frankfurt am Main | **Façade contractor** Josef Gartner GmbH & Co KG | **Height** 99.7 m/327 ft (+ technical roof levels) | **Above-ground storeys** 29 | **Basements** 5 | **Mechanical levels** 2 | **Use** Office | **Site area** 5021 sq m/54,026 sq ft | **Area of above-ground building** 4416 sq m/47,516 sq ft | **Structural materials** Reinforced concrete | **Other materials** Glass

3

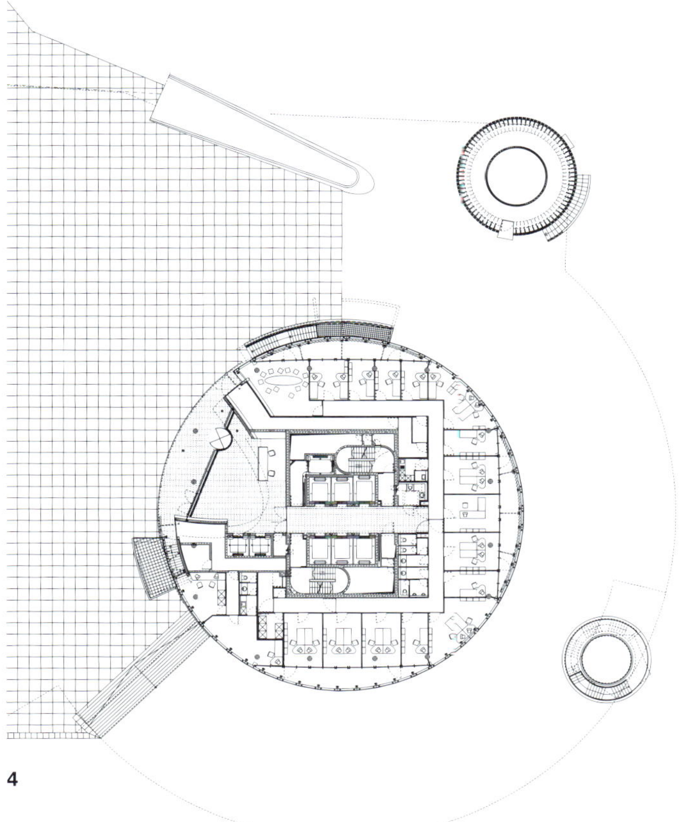

4

5

TORRE VELASCA MILAN ITALY

The late 1950s and early 1960s saw a series of mixed-use tall buildings built in Europe. These included the 30-storey Centre International Rogier in Brussels, built in 1961 but now demolished, and the Torre Velasca in Milan, which remains one of Europe's most intriguing towers.

From an urban standpoint, the tower is linked to the plaza. A two-level podium containing retail and services faces the main street. Because of the dense location in the center of the city, the architects chose a slender shaft for the office section of the building, surmounted by larger floors of apartments cantilevered out from the main structure. The top two levels comprise duplex apartments. The regular window grid of the lower levels expresses the feeling of the office levels while a more irregular window grid expresses the residential flavour of the upper levels.

Torre Velasca is reminiscent of Medieval Italian buildings such as the towers of Sforzesco Castle and is probably in its own way one of the early contextual towers, built at a time when Europe was assailed by a series of pure Modernist tall buildings.

1

2

Torre Velasca | **Location** Milan, Italy | **Completion date** 1958 | **Architect** B.B.P.R. (Gianluigi Banfi, Ludovico Barbiano di Belgiojoso, Enrico Peressutti and Ernesto Nathan Rogers) | **Client** Ricostruzione Comparti Edilizi Spa. | **Reinforced concrete structure** Arturo Danusso | **Height** 106 m/348 ft | **Above-ground storeys** 28 | **Basements** 2 | **Above-ground useable levels** 27 | **Mechanical levels** 1 | **Use** Office, residential, retail | **Structural materials** Reinforced concrete | **Other materials** Masonry

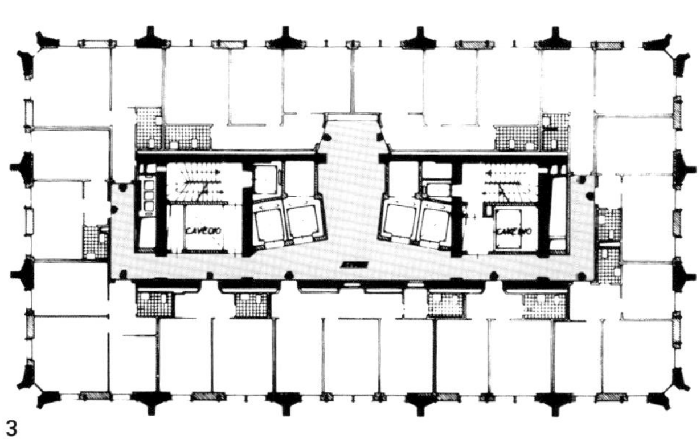

3

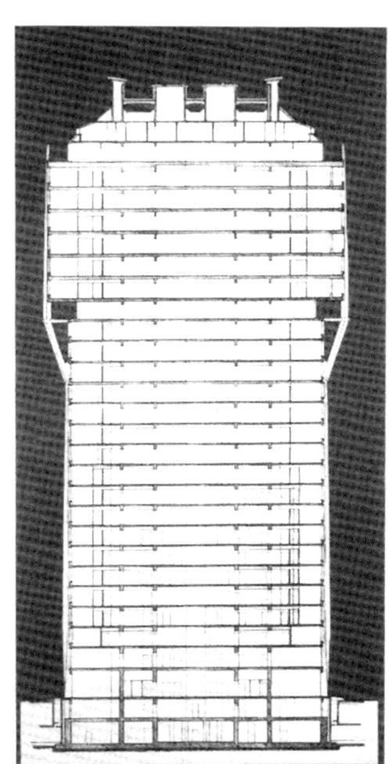

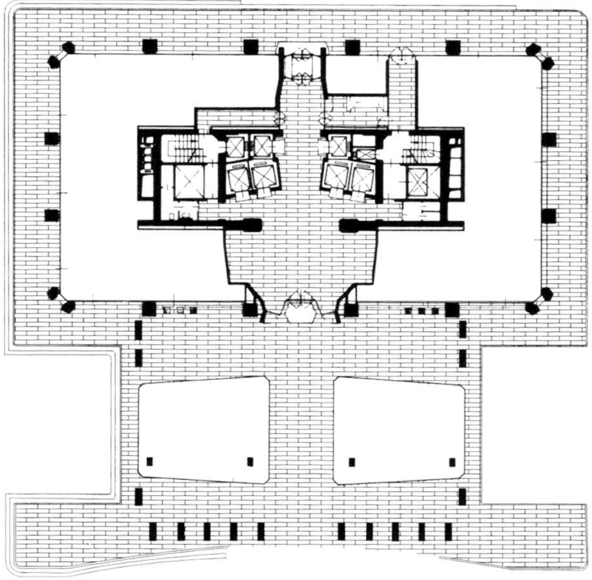

4

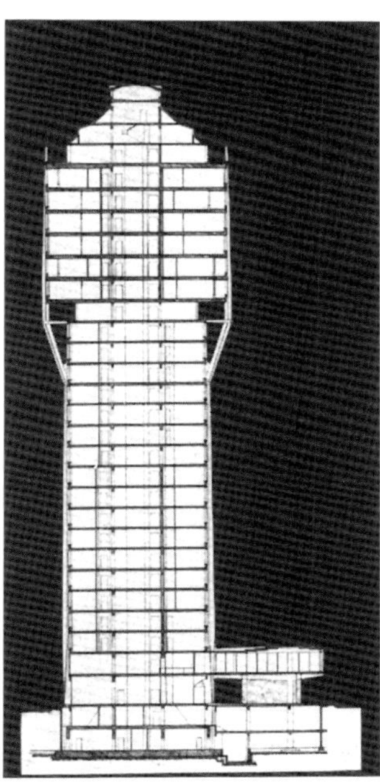

5

1 *Torre Velasca seen from Milan Dome*

2 *General view*

3 *Typical upper residential level floor plan*

4 *Ground floor plan*

5 *Sections*

Photography: *David Lucaccioni (1); G Binder, courtesy Buildings & Data SA (2)*

NORTH GALAXY BRUSSELS BELGIUM

North Galaxy is the most recent high-rise project completed in the 53-hectare Espace Nord area, a high-rise district located at the edge of the historical centre of Brussels. The area was first envisaged in the 1960s within the framework of an urban master plan designed by Groupe Structures, and North Galaxy is part of the original central eight-tower concept proposed in 1967. Five towers were completed – in 1973, 1975, 1983 and 1994 and eventually the twin towers of North Galaxy were completed in 2005.

The original overall scheme was composed of towers rising from platforms. It was proposed that pedestrians would walk from one tower to the next via sky-bridges and elevated platforms. Of this 1967 scheme, only the tower format remains (102 metres to the parapet x 50 metres x 30 metres) and its orthogonal plan has to be strictly adhered to in order to conform with Brussels' current urban guidelines for this particular intersection. North Galaxy was eventually designed to rise from the ground level without the originally planned platform base interrupting the high-rise effect.

The three-level, glass-enclosed, ovoid-shaped lobby has a spider glass double skin and acts as a link between the twin towers. The towers have been designed to function independently or as a whole, which is currently the case, as North Galaxy houses just one occupant, the Federal Finance administration.

The central boulevard, initially planned in 1967 as a freeway located underneath the pedestrian platform and connecting downtown Brussels to all major freeways and the airport, is now a landscaped promenade that features a series of sculptures designed by internationally acclaimed artists.
The Region of Brussels-Capital authorities, together with the owners of all the buildings located along the boulevard, have financed the landscaped promenade at the initiative of the Espace Nord's historical lead developer CDP, co-developer of North Galaxy.

With the completion of the North Galaxy towers, the Espace Nord now sees its central landmark crossroad (almost) complete, 30 years after the completion of the first Espace Nord building, the original bronze-tinted WTC twin towers developed by CDP. Together with La Défense in Paris, it is one of the few European examples of newly planned tall-building urban communities first envisioned in the 1950s and 1960s that have eventually been built.

1

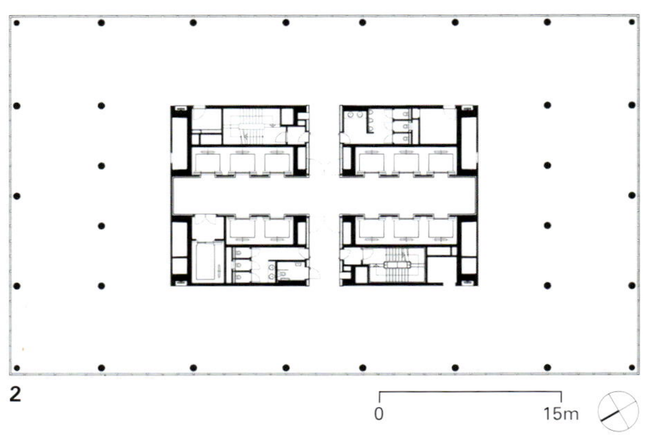

2

North Galaxy | **Location** Brussels, Belgium | **Completion date** 2005 | **Architect** Arch. Jaspers-Eyers & Partners; Montois Partners Architects; Art & Build Architects | **Client** North Galaxy SA: Atenor Group (47%), CDP Group (47%), Dexia (6%) | **Structural engineer** Bagon; Ingénieurs Associés | **Mechanical engineer** VK Engineering; Geocal | **Contractor** Galaxy SM: CIT Blaton, Interbuild, Van Laere, Willemen | **Height** 107.5 m/353 ft | **Above-ground storeys** 30 | **Basements** 4 | **Above-ground useable levels** 28 | **Mechanical levels** 2 | **Use** Office | **Site area** 12,000 sq m/129,120 sq ft | **Area of above-ground building** 108,576 sq m/1,168,278 sq ft; typical floor 1,538 sq m/16,549 sq ft | **Structural materials** Reinforced concrete | **Other materials** Dark structural glazing, natural stone, spider glass

3

1 *The North Galaxy twin towers with the glass-enclosed lobby in the foreground*

2 *Typical floor plan, 16th level: transfer level between low- and high-rise elevator banks*

3 *Three-level, ovoid lobby features double glass skin*

4 *North Galaxy (circled) is located at the end of the Espace Nord's landscaped promenade designed by Wirtz International*

5 *North Galaxy seen from the Boulevard du Roi Albert II*

Photography: *Marc Detiffe (1,3,5); Airprint (4)*

4

5

VICTORIA-HAUS DÜSSELDORF GERMANY

With a diameter of 34.4 metres and at 29 storeys, reaching a height of 108.8 metres, the VICTORIA-Haus is an unmistakable and dominant feature of the Düsseldorf skyline. It is a symbol of the capital city of the state of Nordrhein-Westfalen.

The tower is the pivotal point in the architectural and urban design of the open spaces of Düsseldorf's former Golzheimer cemetery and the denser, inner-city Fischerstrasse. To integrate the tower into the architectural concept, it is linked, from the second to the sixth storeys, to the office building that it abuts to the south. The street frontage along the Fischerstrasse has been designed as a building volume six storeys high and almost 100 metres long, corresponding specifically to the height of the buildings on the east side of Fischerstrasse. This part of the complex also provides protection from noise for the rest of the extension behind it.

The offices in the upper storeys are accessed via five passenger lifts, two fire brigade lifts (which double as goods lifts) and two stairways, one of which is external. At the very top of the tower, a large number of rooms have been created for use as meeting rooms, which have wonderful panoramic views over Düsseldorf. The tower is finished off with a floating steel canopy that incorporates photovoltaic equipment.

1

2

3

4

VICTORIA-Haus | **Location** Düsseldorf, Germany | **Completion date** 1998 | **Architect** HPP Hentrich-Petschnigg & Partner KG | **Client** VICTORIA Grundstücksverwaltungs-Gesellschaft GbR | **Structural engineer** Prinz & Pott Ing.-Büro für Tragswerksplanung VBI; LWS Lewer ton-Werner-Schwarz Ing.-Ges. für Tragwerksplanung GmbH | **Mechanical engineer** SRP Schmidt Reuter Partner Ingenieurgesellschaft mbH & Partner KG | **Landscape architect** Dipl.-Ing. Georg Penker | **Contractor** Wayss & Freytag AG; Strabag Hoch- und Ingenieurbau AG; Bilfinger + Berger Bauaktiengesellschaft; Philipp Holzmann AG | **Height** 108.8 m/357 ft | **Above-ground storeys** 29 | **Basements** 2 | **Use** Office | **Site area** 42,900 sq m/461,604 sq ft | **Gross floor area** 106,000 sq m/1,140560 sq ft | **Structural materials** Steel, reinforced concrete, glass

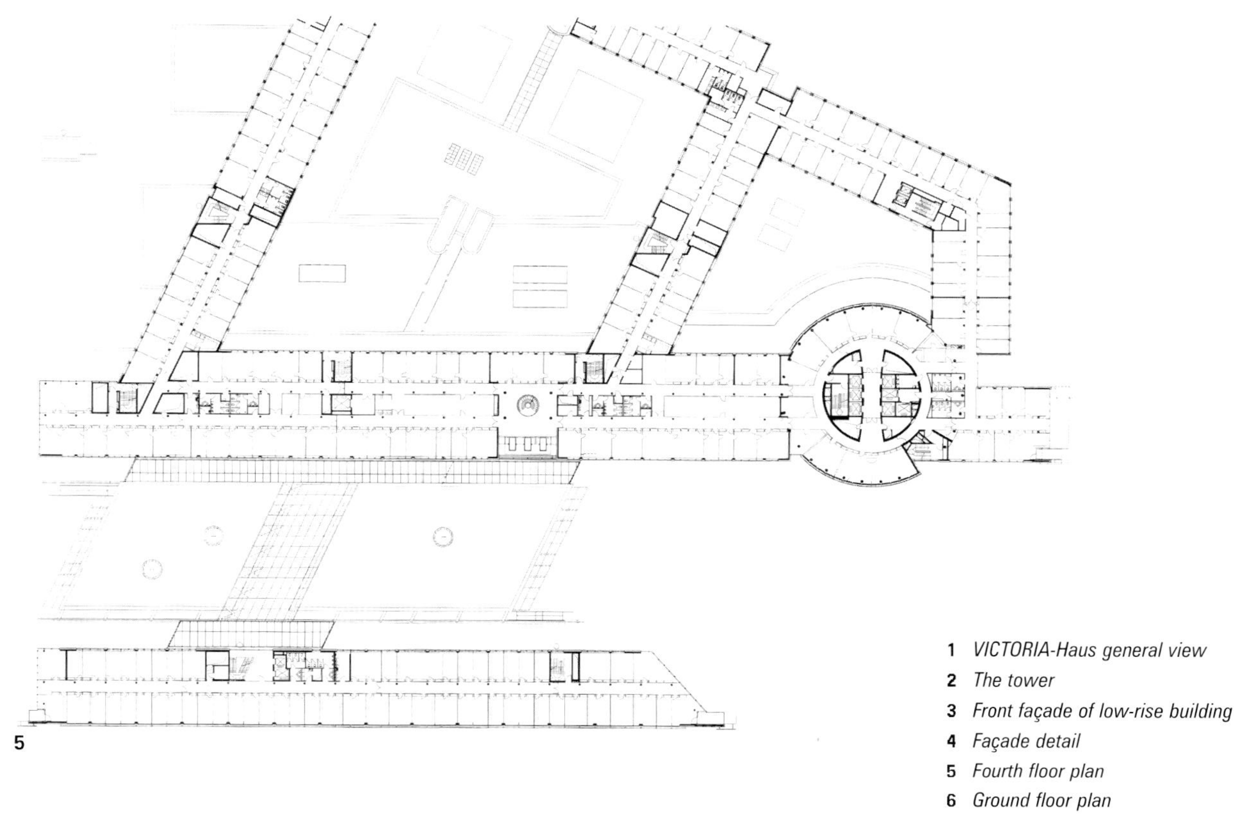

5

1 *VICTORIA-Haus general view*
2 *The tower*
3 *Front façade of low-rise building*
4 *Façade detail*
5 *Fourth floor plan*
6 *Ground floor plan*

Photography: *Manfred Hanisch*

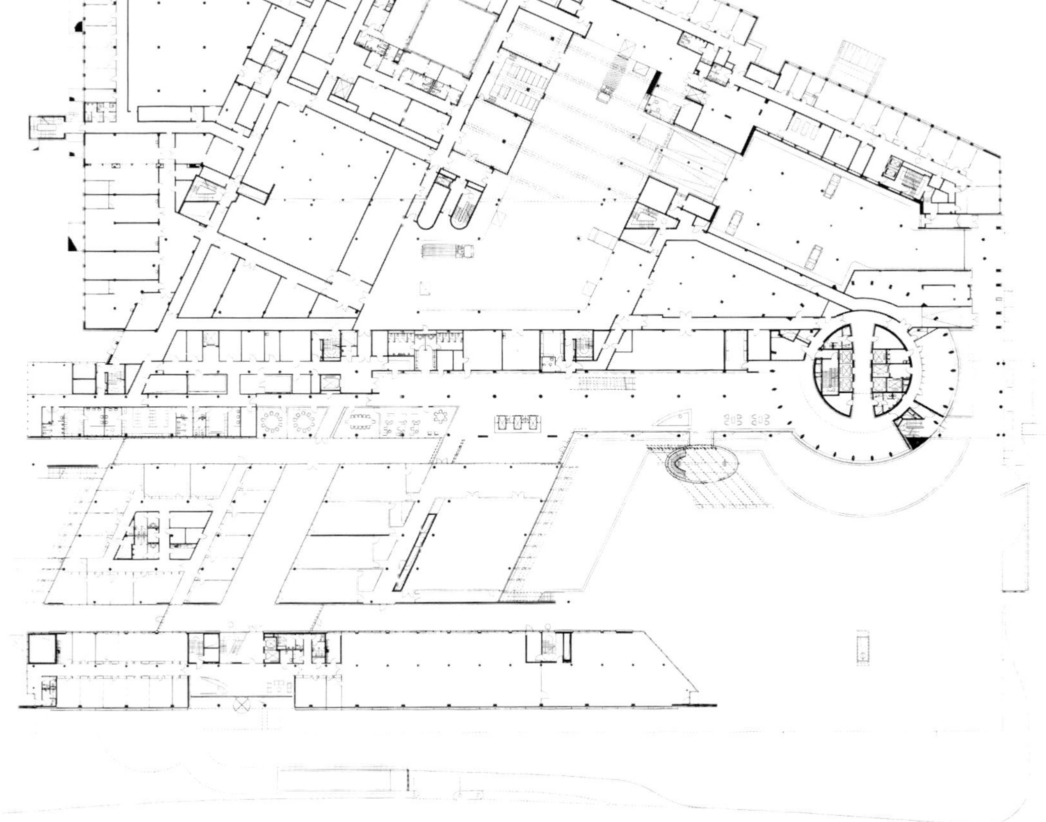

6

TOUR NOBEL (NOW TOUR INITIALE)

PARIS LA DÉFENSE
FRANCE

Thin and elegant, with rounded corners and skirted in copper, the Nobel Tower, now renamed Initiale, is illuminated once again after two years of construction – a giant lantern marking the entry to La Défense.

The first tower built at La Défense, designed as a collaboration between the engineer Jean Prouvé and architects de Mailly and Depussé, its renovation was both a restoration of an extremely inventive building and a contemporary reuse involving the reformulation of interior spaces based on lighting design.

With 1000-square-metre floor plates, under-ceiling heights of 2.8 metres, a curtain wall cleverly integrating dilatation, waterproofing and window cleaning, its technical innovations include curved double glazing, ventilated shadow boxes, ductwork integrated within the façade, building services incorporated within steel decking and a steel structure associated with a concrete core. The Tour Initiale represents a significant reference from the 1970s, both in terms of modern architecture and building technology.

The tower's safety updates, the elimination of asbestos (2000 tonnes removed) and exacting restoration provided the opportunity to re-examine the building's advanced design features.

The interior spaces are treated with lighting concepts inspired by Dan Flavin and James Turrell – contemporary sensibilities in harmony with the original design – and include backlit ceilings and opalescent coloured light wall panels.

After dark, slab edges and the central core are illuminated to create a chorus of light announcing the tower's revival and its uniqueness within the concert of towers comprising La Défense.

2

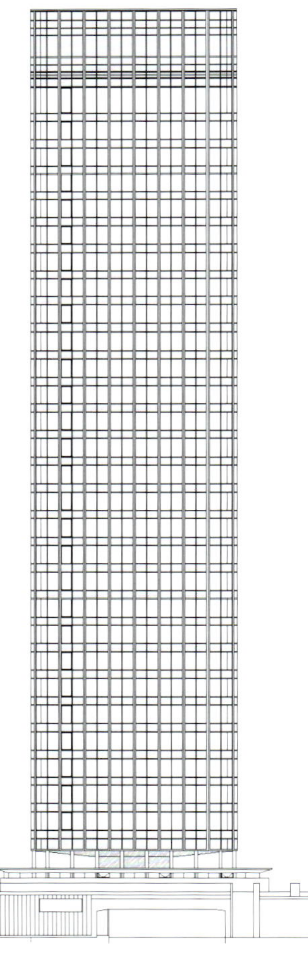

1

3

Tour Nobel (now Tour Initiale) | **Location** Paris La Défense, France | **Completion date** Initial construction 1966/renovation 2003 | **Architect** (1966) Jean de Mailly and Jacques Depussé, with Jean Prouvé, engineer | **Renovation architect** Valode & Pistre Architectes | **Client** Caisse de Depots CDC Ixis Immo | **Structural engineer** Negru | **Mechanical engineer** Cica | **Contractor** P.C.E. | **Height** 109 m/358 ft | **Above-ground storeys** 31 | **Basements** 3 | **Above-ground useable levels** 29 | **Mechanical levels** 1 | **Use** Offices, restaurants and conference facilities | **Site area** 7000 sq m/75,320 sq ft | **Area of above-ground building** 39,000 sq m/419,640 sq ft | **Structural materials** Concrete core, peripheral steel structure | **Other materials** Aluminium and glass curtain wall

4

5

1 *Section plan*
2 *Building before renovation*
3 *Tower as seen entering the La Défense district*
4 *Night lighting scheme*
5 *Typical floor plan*

Photography: *Georges Fessy*

WATERSTADTOREN AND HARBOUR VILLAGE

ROTTERDAM
THE NETHERLANDS

Rotterdam's Wijnhaveneiland is situated between Blaak and Boompjes. It was built between 1576 and 1616 by excavating new harbour basins and combining them to form a triangular island. Since the war it has been occupied mainly by offices, and from 1975 to 1995 it was something of a sleepy backwater.

In 1993 Kees Christiaanse produced an urban development plan designed to reinvigorate the area. He proposed a transformation based on its recent history and leaving the existing urban structure intact. He saw the area as a superb opportunity to put the municipality's policy – still current – of strengthening the city centre's residential function into practice. The whole idea of the plan is to create conditions that enable future development to be kept on the right track and minimise the disadvantages of unchecked high-rise building. Christiaanse's plan permits a host of variations.

It is in this context that HM Architekten has, since 1996, been developing a complex comprising 365 dwellings, underground car parks and commercial space in three towers on two substructures, following the outline of the original reconstruction plan along Jufferstraat, Bierstraat and Wijnbrugstraat, for De Wilgen Vastgoed in Rotterdam. The choice of materials for the towers is influenced by the location and orientation of the dwellings. The principal façades of the residential portion are fully glazed, to provide unimpeded views. The north and south walls are of brickwork. The glazed façades have an angled design, creating a lively aspect that changes depending on the light and the observer's position.

1

2

3

Waterstadtoren and Harbour Village | **Location** Rotterdam, The Netherlands | **Completion date** 2004 | **Architect** HM Architekten | **Client** De Wilgen Vastgoed | **Structural engineer** Corsmit Raadgevend Ingenieursbureau | **Mechanical engineer** Spindler Installatietechniek BV | **Contractor** Harbour Village: Bam Wilma; Waterstadtoren: Stam en de Koning | **Height** 71 m/233 ft; 85 m/279 ft; 109 m/358 ft | **Above-ground storeys** 25; 30; 37 | **Basements** 2 | **Above-ground useable levels** 25; 30; 37 | **Mechanical levels** 1 | **Use** Mixed-use | **Area of above-ground building** 55,000 sq m/591,800 sq ft | **Structural materials** Reinforced concrete | **Other materials** Brick, reinforced concrete

1 *The three towers, view from below*

2 *Left: Harbour Village; right: Waterstadtoren south façade*

3 *View from southwest, Scheepmakershaven Rotterdam*

4 *Waterstadtoren ground floor plan*

5 *Harbour Village ground floor plan*

Photography: *Luuk Kramer (Amsterdam)*

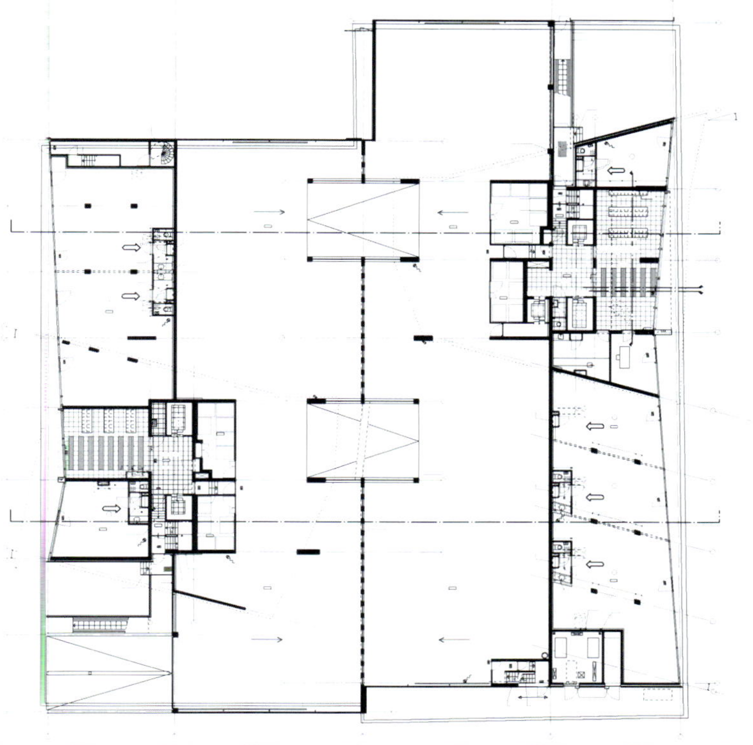

5

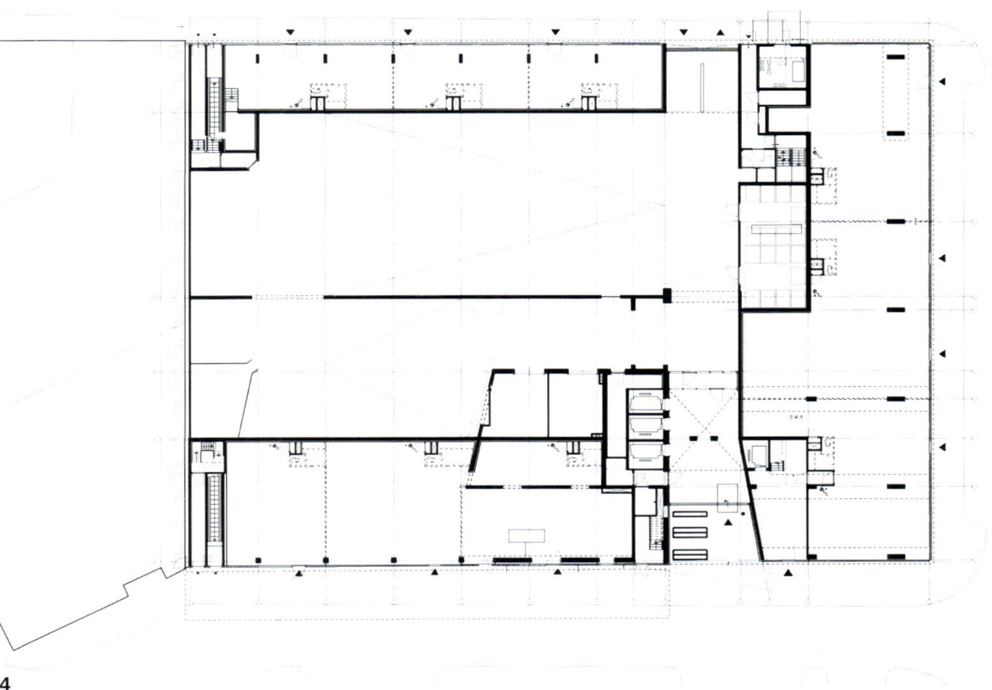

4

MONTE LAA PORR TOWERS

VIENNA
AUSTRIA

The Monte Laa area development is one of the most innovative urban initiatives underway now in Vienna. Hans Hollein was asked in 2000 to design the 110-metre-tall towers as a signal and landmark visible when entering Vienna and from the centre of the city. The project consists of two 90-metre towers, above which hovers a 30-metre horizontal structure, creating a second level and activity zone in the urban landscape.

This skyborne structure is designed to be a conference centre with a capacity of 750 and consists of four levels of different heights. Highly differentiated in shape, it protrudes beyond its footprint with far-reaching cantilevered structures. Resting on two slender tower buildings, this area of some 4000 square metres, interconnnected with glazed bridge constructions on two levels, forms a flexible multifunctional agglomeration of spaces.

Above the south tower, the reception area is reached by express lifts, one of which directly connects with a separate conference entrance on the ground floor. Arranged around the reception area are ample foyer zones, an inclined 170-seat auditorium, an exclusive restaurant with great vistas over the city and a spectacular bar floating in mid-sky.

Above the north tower is a 460-seat conference hall and additional seminar and meeting rooms with flexible partitioning. A press lounge on the top floor has views over Vienna, and a bridge connection to the south tower.

The towers below the conference centre are used as rentable office space. Centrally located between the towers on the ground floor, a 15-metre-high glazed hall connects the two core areas with a common reception lobby.

2

3

1

1 *Model view showing the top floor structures*
2 *View of south façade from express highway*
3 *Aerial view from north*
4 *26th floor plan*
5 *View of east façade*
6 *Conference floor plan*
7 *Site plan*

Renderings: *ARGE A Wimmer*
Photography: *Courtesy Studio Hollein/Arch. Sina Baniahmad*

Monte Laa PORR Towers | **Location** Monta Laa area, Vienna, Austria | **Design phase** | **Masterplan Monte Laa area** Alfred Wimmer | **Vienna Towers design phase** ARGE Hollein/Wimmmer; design architect Hans Hollein | **Client** PORR Immoprojekt | **Structural engineer** Alfred Strommer | **Landscape architect** Martha Schwartz Inc. | **Contractor** PORR AG, Dipl. Ing Erich Janda | **Height** 110 m/ 361 ft | **Above-ground storeys** 29 | **Use** Office, hotel, conference centre | **Site area** 1330 sq m/14,316 sq ft | **Area of above-ground building** 31,900 sq m/343,381 sq ft

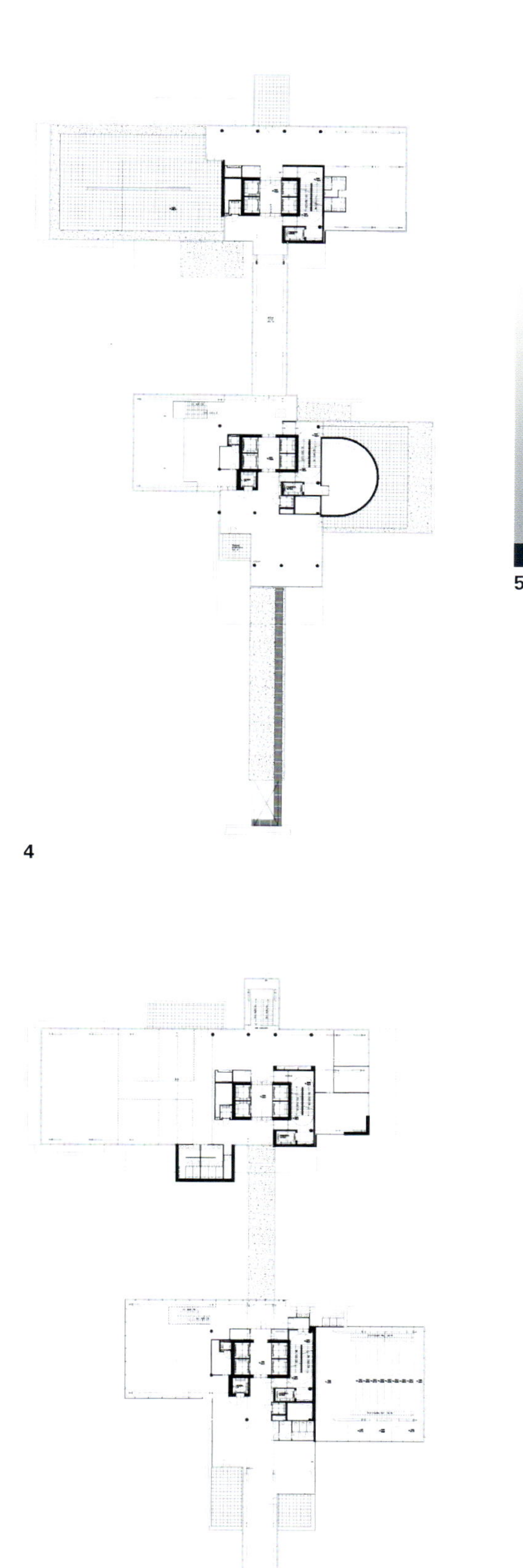

4

6

5

7

MISCHEK TOWER VIENNA AUSTRIA

A selected entry competition for residential buildings in Vienna's newly created Donau City was held in 1993. The prize winners developed an urban model that incorporated the Mischek Tower and Delugan Meissl was commissioned to design the exterior of the tower.

The skyscraper was deliberately designed as a slab with two different sides: a horizontal curve extends into the distance over the edge of the Donaupark; the vertical curve emerges from the ground and blends into the group of surrounding high-rises. The two sides complement each other like two folded hands, one directed upwards and the other horizontally. The two sides have been joined together so that the apartments located on the ends of each have light on three sides.

Approaching the Mischek Tower from the east, an extensive canopy of glass and metal dynamically defines the front, leading the visitor into the lobby of the tower where the canopy is continued as a metal ceiling. The walls and ceilings of the lobby are white meandering sculptural slabs in front of a background covered with high-sheen black paint. Black granite has been used as a floor covering, resulting in an unusual atmosphere for an apartment building.

The loggias along the side edges of the high-rise are equipped with frameless glass folding elements that can enclose the loggias to form outside rooms. To be able to offer this option for all apartments without compromising the design of the building, Delugan Meissl developed a 'façade interplay' with glass and aluminium elements that have been mounted facing each other so that no continuous rhythm is created optically. This way the façade retains its uniform appearance, even if the tenants later equip certain spots with glass elements that were designed by the architect for this purpose.

1

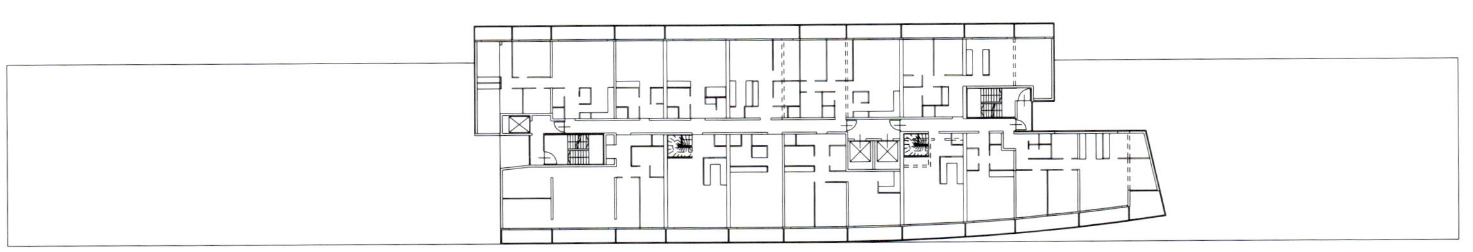

2

Mischek Tower | **Location** Vienna, Austria | **Completion date** 2000 | **Architect** Delugan Meissl Associated Architects | **Client** MISCHEK Wiener Heim Wohnbau GesmbH | **Structural consultant** Hochbau Consult (Mischek, Gerasdorf) | **Height** 110 m/361 ft | **Above-ground storeys** 35 | **Basements** 4 | **Use** Residential | **Site area** 6296 sq m/67,745 sq ft | **Area of above-ground building** 44,393 sq m/477,669 sq ft | **Structural materials** Concrete: 10,000 individual prefabricated construction pieces | **Cost** €64 M

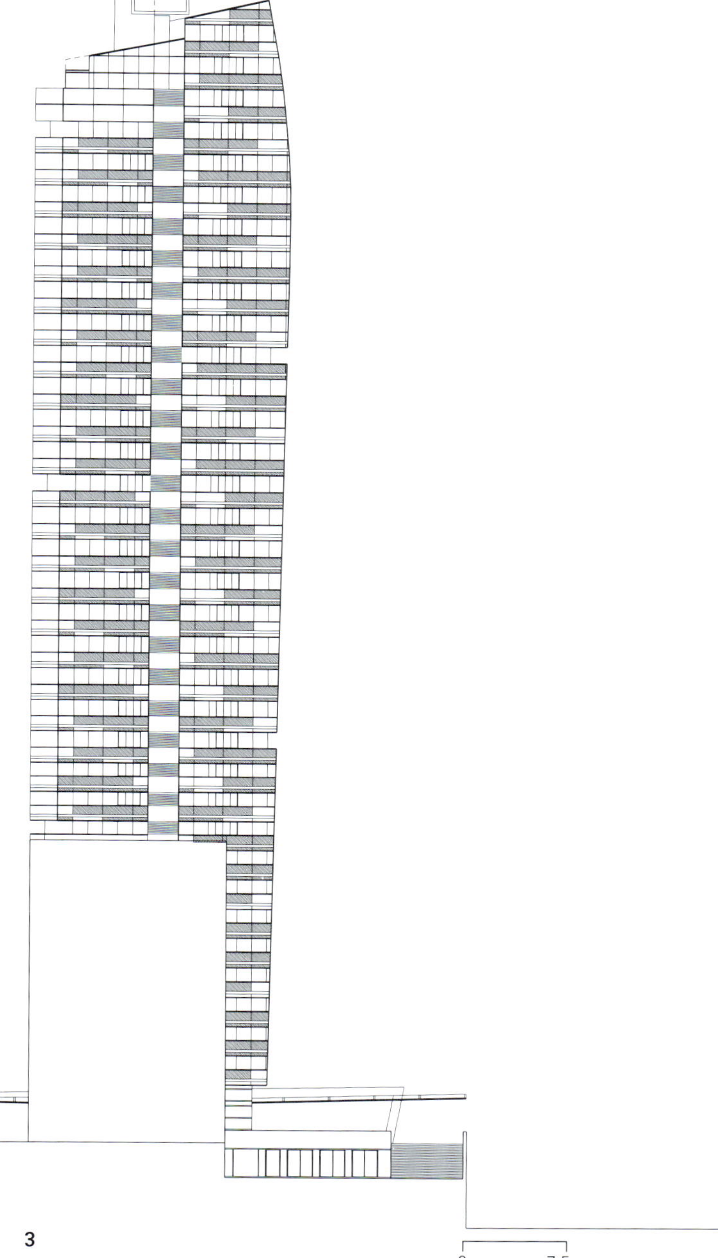

3

1 *North elevation*
2 *Typical floor plan*
3 *South elevation*
4 *Foyer*
5 *East elevation*

Photography: *Margherita Spiluttini*

4

5

NBS TOWER BRATISLAVA SLOVAKIA

This building is the head office and operational centre of the National Bank of Slovakia. It reflects the fusion of the urban structure of uniform-height blocks of housing on the east and northeast and the large spacious area of Sloboda square and Slovak technical university.

The basic architectural principal behind the design of the NBS building is the contrast of the horizontal base and the tower rising from it. The horizontal base houses the main daily operations of the NBS and its depositories while the tower contains the offices, including the directorate.

The horizontal base is designed to frame the central green atrium. The offices overlook the atrium, which is sheltered from the traffic on Mýtna Street. Planted with trees, the atrium provides a contrast with the material structure of the spacious office.

Parts of the entrance hall and the front office overlook the atrium. The entrance hall and lobby are located in the area where the tower rises from the horizontal base; this area is the centre of the material and spatial concept.

The layout of the stepped tower is designed as a skeleton construction, framing the concrete-core walls with metal and glass screening. The double climate screening of the interstitial space creates a unique optical effect.

The various materials and finishes relate to the purpose and role of the individual interior areas. Stone cladding and fine plaster are used in the entrance hall. Fine ground terrazzo flooring is used in the vestibules and hall floors.

The NBS head office is designed as an 'intelligent' building, incorporating the latest technology. The integral component of this project is the double skin façade screening, which creates the energetic climate zone and contributes to minimising running costs and improving office comfort by allowing direct ventilation.

1&2 *View of the NBS tower towards the Bratislava Castle*
3 *Section*
4 *Entrance lobby*
5 *First floor plan*
6 *Vestibule area with atrium*

Photography: *L Stacho*

1

2

4

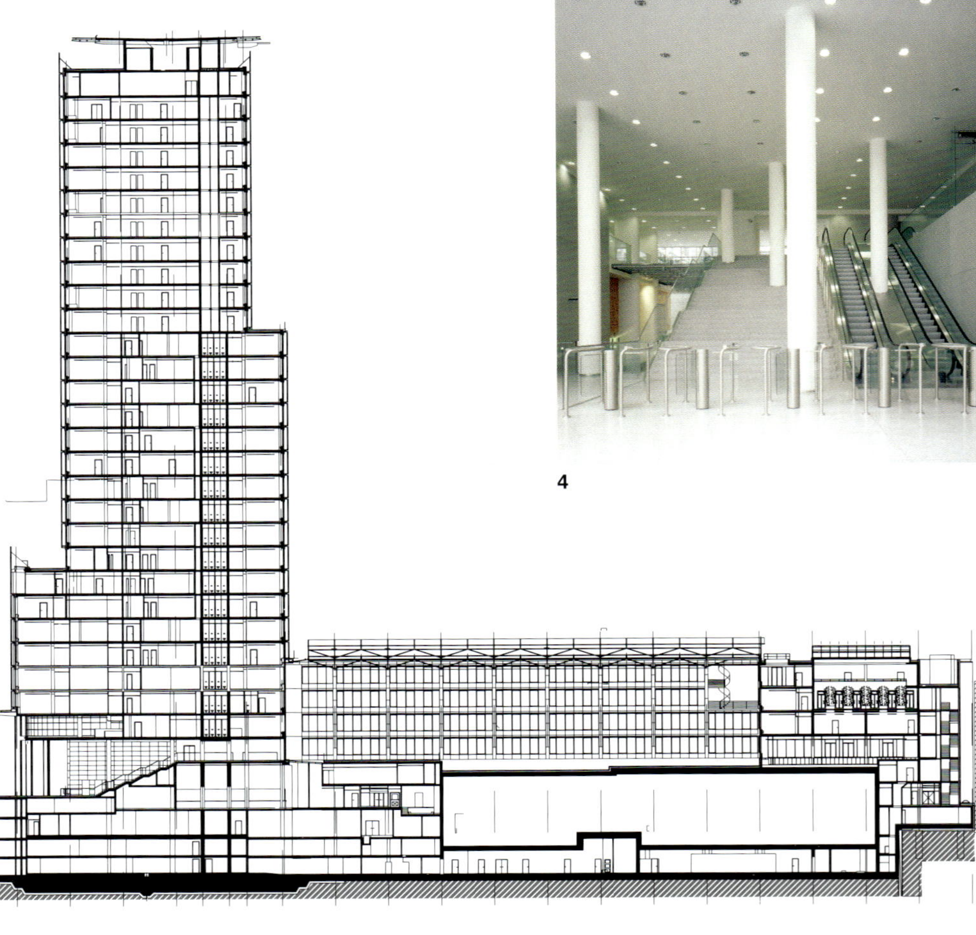

3

NBS Tower | **Location** Bratislava, Slovakia | **Completion date** 2002 | **Architect** Architekti BKPS | **Client** National Bank of Slovakia | **Structural engineer** L Tausinger; Z Czolle | **Mechanical engineer** J Forgac | **Contractor** Zipp Bratislava | **Height** 111 m/364 ft | **Above-ground storeys** 30 | **Basements** 3 | **Above-ground useable levels** 28 | **Mechanical levels** 2 | **Use** Office | **Site area** 6820 sq m/73,383 sq ft | **Area of above-ground building** 6270 sq m/67,465 sq ft | **Structural materials** Reinforced concrete | **Other materials** Stone cladding, aluminium façade, glass

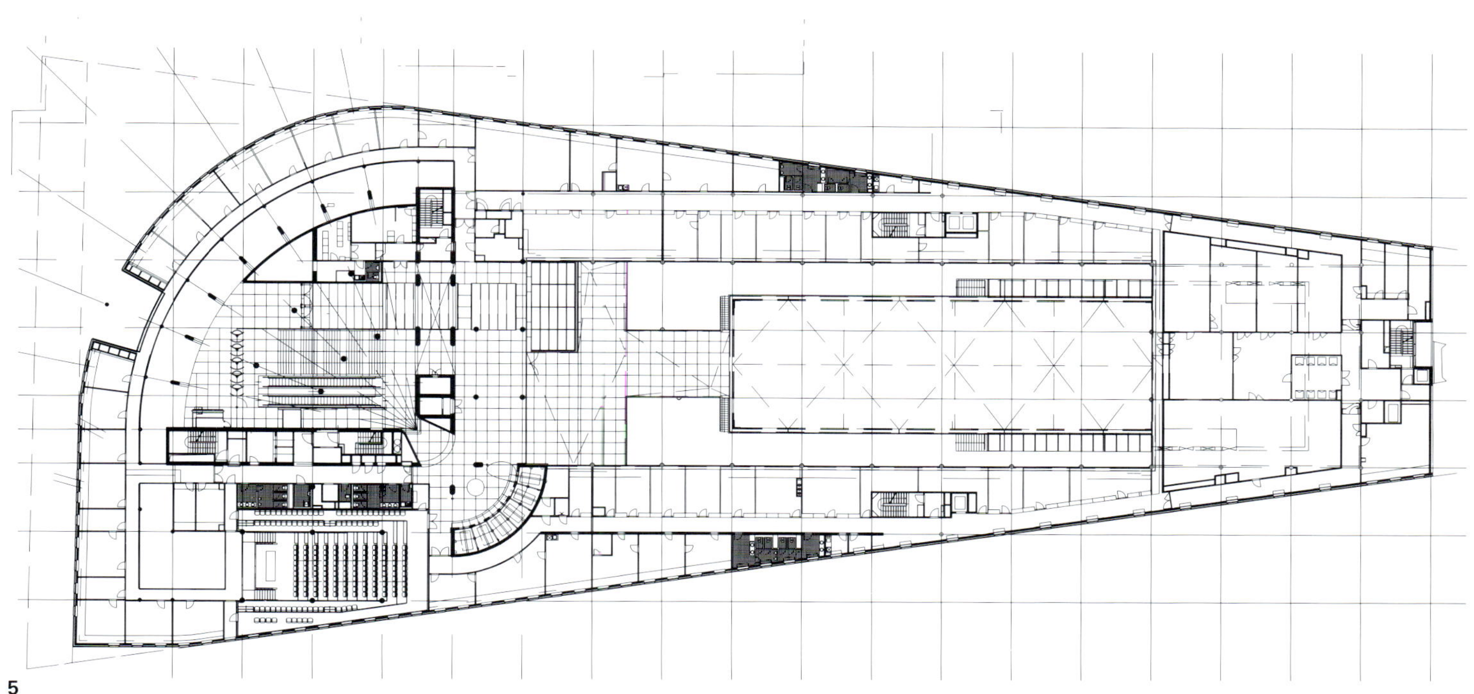
5

6

PUERTA DE EUROPA MADRID SPAIN

Puerta de Europa's unique design, comprising two 115-metre tall twin towers leaning at a 15-degree angle, has become a new urban symbol for Madrid.

Puerta de Europa is located on the Spanish capital's Plaza de Castilla, a focal point of the city, where the buildings tower over a major thoroughfare. Beneath the towers is one of the city's main transport interchanges with major subway lines, which meant that one of the towers could not be constructed along the natural street alignment. The leaning towers became a gesture that allowed the two towers to be closer and to form a major single contemporary city landmark.

The two skyscrapers are clad in dark tinted glass, framed by a grid of aluminium and decorative red strips emphasising the impressive structural elements of the building. The main frames are of stainless steel while the entrance lobby and elevators foyer are clad in luxury materials including wood, marble and polished stone.

1 *General view*
2 *East tower, level 17 floor plan*
3 *West tower, level 4 floor plan*

Photography: *Robert Royal*
Plans: *reproduced from original Puerta de Europa leasing brochure, collection G Binder/Buildings & Data SA*

1

Puerta de Europa | **Location** Madrid, Spain | **Completion date** 1996 | **Architect** John Burgee Architects, Philip Johnson Consultant, with Pedro Sentieri and Tomás Dominguez del Castillo y Juan Carlos Martin Baranda | **Client** KIO–Kuwait Investment Office | **Structural engineer** LERA–Leslie E. Robertson Associates | **Mechanical engineer** Goymar Inginieros Consultores | **Height** 115 m/377 ft | **Above-ground storeys** 28 | **Basements** 3 | **Above-ground useable levels** 26 | **Mechanical levels** 2 | **Use** Office | **Office area** 30,000 sq m/322,800 sq ft, per tower | **Structural materials** Steel | **Other materials** Dark-tinted glass and aluminium curtain wall, stainless steel

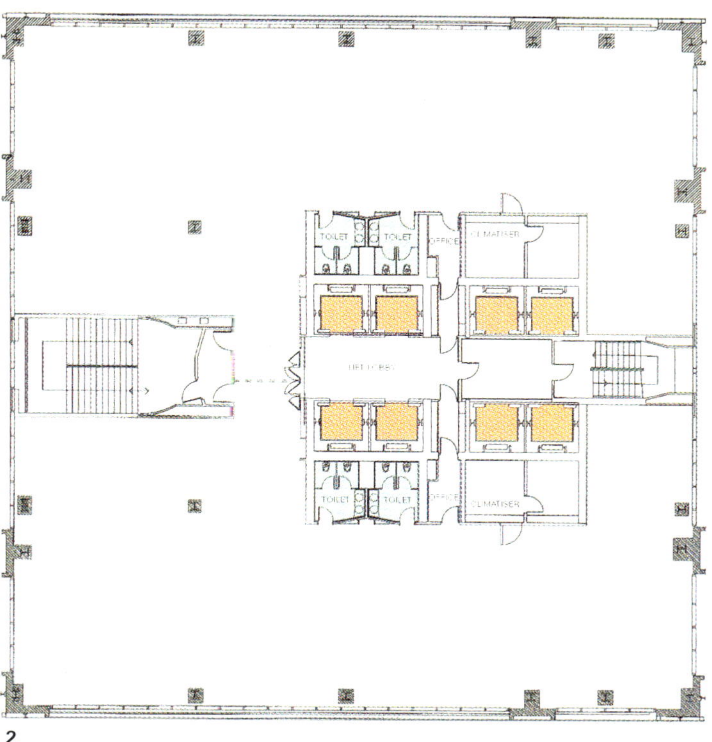

2

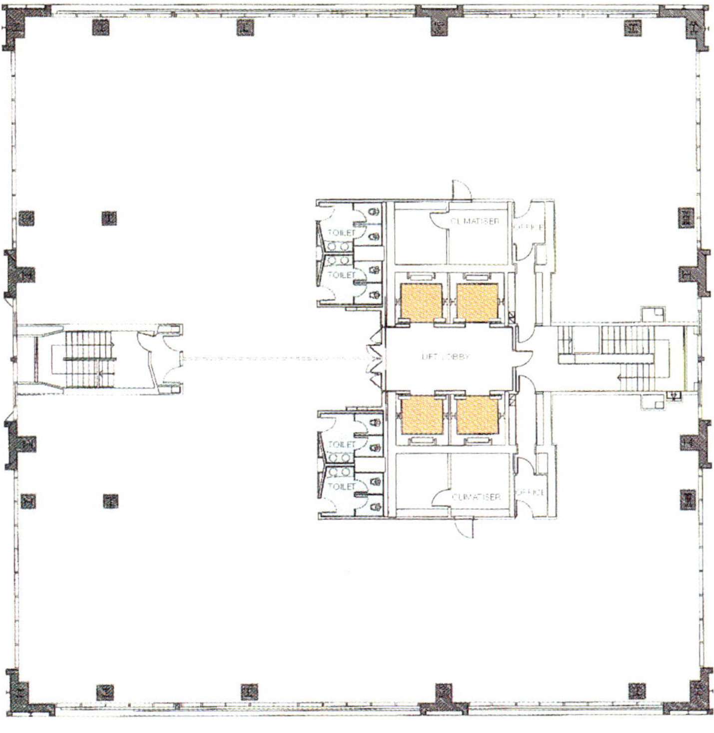

3

CASABLANCA TWIN CENTER

CASABLANCA MOROCCO

Casablanca Twin Center, a landmark in the heart of the city, is at present the most representative building of modern, enterprising Casablanca. The source of inspiration for the two 115-metre-high towers that constitute the building's nucleus was traditional Moorish architecture, which influences both the volumetrics and façade composition.

The towers accommodate offices, dwellings and commercial establishments, including 300 shops. A monumental stairway from the street leads to an open-air plaza on the fifth floor with a terrace café and entrance to an auditorium. Terraces, bars and restaurants occupy the top floor. Three basement car parks complete the programme.

The entire structure is composed of reinforced concrete and the towers are the tallest in Morocco.

1 *Typical floor plan*
2 *View at sunset*
3 *Building detail*
4 *Commercial center, interior view*
5 *General view of buildings*

Photography: *Carlos Casariego*

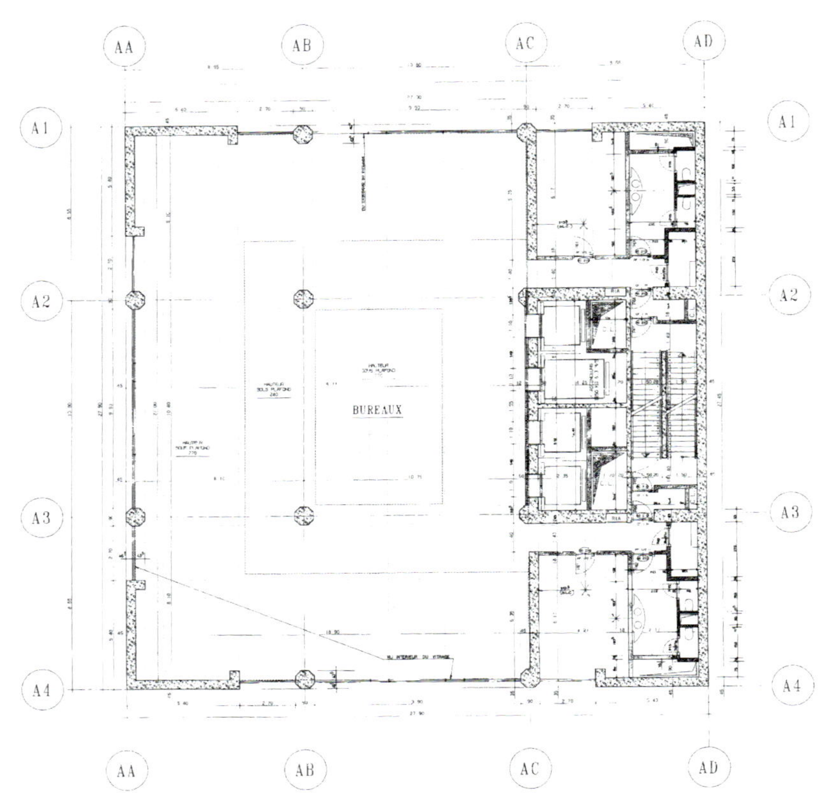

1

2

3

4

Casablanca Twin Center | **Location** Casablanca, Morocco | **Completion date** 1999 | **Architect** Ricardo Bofill Taller de Arquitectura | **Associate architect** Elie Mouyal | **Client** ONA | **Structural engineer** Oger International | **Mechanical engineer** Oger International | **Contractor** SCII | **Height** 115 m/377 ft per tower | **Above-ground storeys** 30 | **Basements** 5 | **Mechanical levels** 1 | **Use** Office, retail | **Area of above-ground building** 93,000 sq m/1,000,680 sq ft | **Structural materials** Reinforced concrete

5

TOUR DU CRÉDIT LYONNAIS LILLE FRANCE

The tower is an inhabited bridge that spans a railway station. As part of Rem Koolhaas's master plan for Euralille, the Crédit Lyonnais office tower is part of an alignment of large buildings that were to be set within a single theoretical grid. This tower straddles the new railways station in the manner of a bridge with no intermediate structural supports.

The architect created the powerful image as a formal response to an extremely demanding brief, with many constraints and technical difficulties that made it necessary to circumvent functional and commercial specifications. The constraints addressed by the project include:

- a bridge structure above a 70-metre-long railway station, attaining a height of at least 100 metres, with a surface not exceeding 14,600 square metres
- orienting a maximum of offices towards the city and not the railway lines
- setting the entire building on narrow foundations between the underground network, the railway and the undergound car park
- keeping within the budgetary limit of FRF 162 M.

The result is a forceful, generous, sheer form, both bridge and tower, tapered and oriented to the south – a right-angle floating above its base.

1

2

1 *Typical floor, interior view*

2 *General view*

3 *Side elevation view*

4 *Main elevation view*

5 *From bottom to top: lower, mid- and high-rise typical floor plans*

Photography: *Nicolas Borel*
Plans: *Atelier Christian de Portzamparc*

Tour du Crédit Lyonnais | **Location** Lille, France | **Completion date** 1995 | **Architect** Atelier Christian de Portzamparc | **Client** Crédit Lyonnais | **Developer** Euralille | **Investor** Férinel Industries, Groupe George V | **Structural engineer** Seer | **Mechanical engineer** Serete; Férinel Industries | **Façade engineering** Ceef | **Contractor** Caroni | **Height** 116.74 m/383 ft | **Above-ground storeys** 25 | **Use** Office | **Area of above-ground building** 18,135 sq m/195,133 sq ft | **Structural materials** Reinforced concrete, extra-reinforced concrete bridge structure | **Other materials** Powder-coated aluminium cases, limestone and granite

3

4

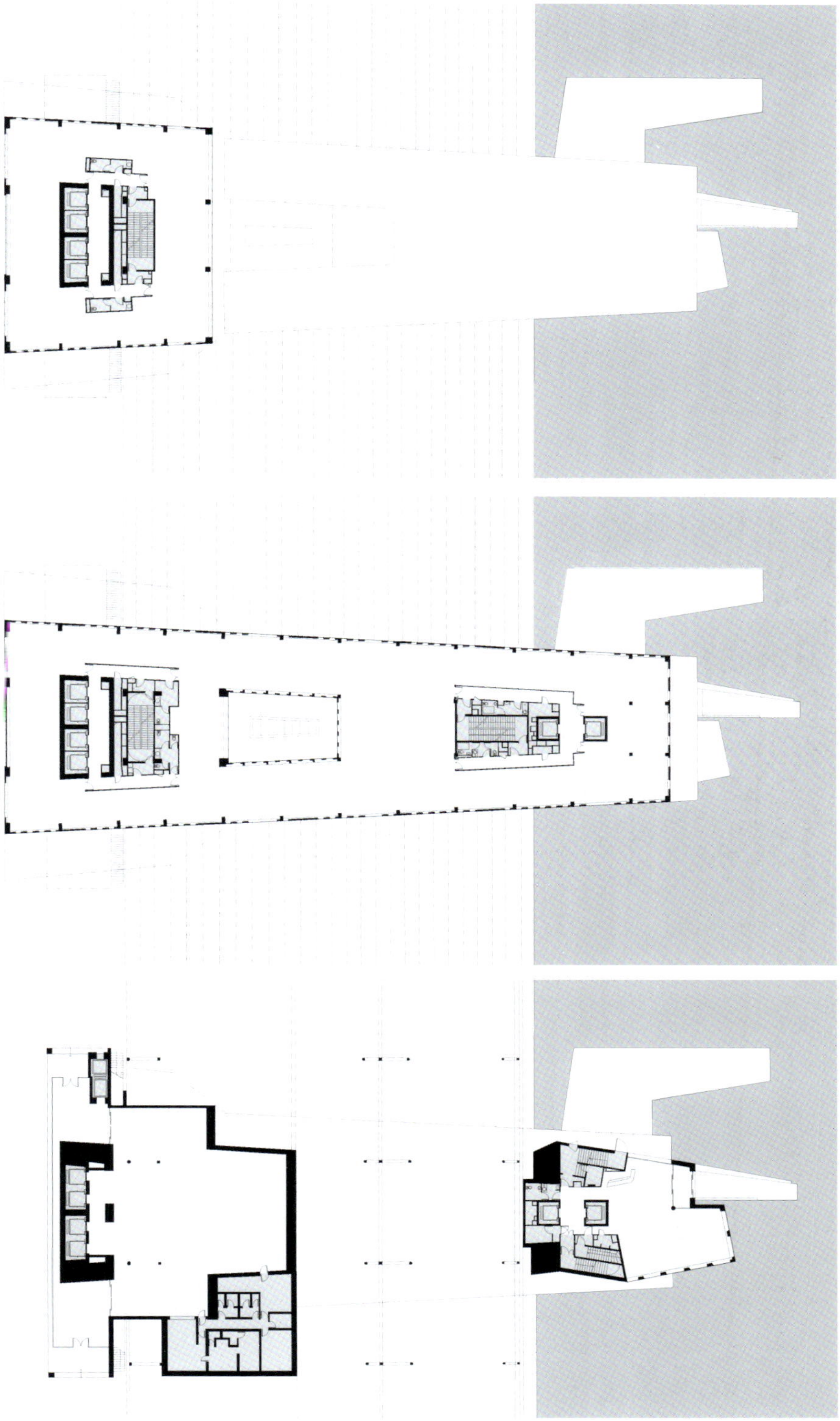

5

MADOU PLAZA BRUSSELS BELGIUM

Originally completed in 1965, Madou Plaza is the tallest building in the Brussels CBD. Its renovation is probably one of the most ambitious of its kind ever undertaken in the city. Completely rethought in terms of its function, circulation routes and relationship to its surroundings, the 34-level, 120-metre-high building has been entirely rebuilt around its original structure.

Some 8000 square metres of new construction at the base have created a podium for the 32,000-square-metre existing tower. This 13-level podium is organised around an atrium, the tallest in Brussels. Madou Plaza now includes a conference centre equipped with an auditorium and business services facilities.

The 'glazed promontory' located in the façade underlines the design of the new entrance to the tower; the micro-climate of the plaza is improved by both this feature and the design of the curved façades.

A semi-reflective double-skin type façade and cold ceilings provide the occupants with the highest standard of comfort. The entire ceiling surface acts as a cooling radiator thanks to the circuit of chilled water in tiny tubes circulating behind the perforated metal panels of the ceiling.

At ground level, a large area along a retail street has been allocated to shops. A new street flanked by housing has been created at the rear of the tower while an esplanade has been laid out at the front. Madou Plaza now constitutes a genuine plaza, which, for the past 20 years, has existed in name only.

1

2

Madou Plaza | **Location** Brussels, Belgium | **Completion date** 2006 (renovation and addition) | **Architect** ASSAR (lead architect, concept and master plan); Archi 2000 | **Client** IVG Real Estate Belgium | **Project coordinator** Cetim | **Structural engineer** Waterman TCA | **Mechanical engineer** Tractebel Development Engineering | **Landscape architect** ASSAR; Archi 2000; JNC International | **Contractor** Herpain; Strabag | **Height** 119.7 m/392.7 ft in 2005; 112 m/367 ft in 1965 | **Above-ground storeys** 34 | **Basements** 4 | **Above-ground useable levels** 34 | **Use** Office, retail, auditorium | **Site area** 3440 sq m/37,014 sq ft | **Area of above-ground building** 40,000 sq m/430,400 sq ft | **Structural materials** Reinforced concrete, steel | **Other materials** Active double skin clear glass wall, white metal cases, grey granite, polished black Chinese granite

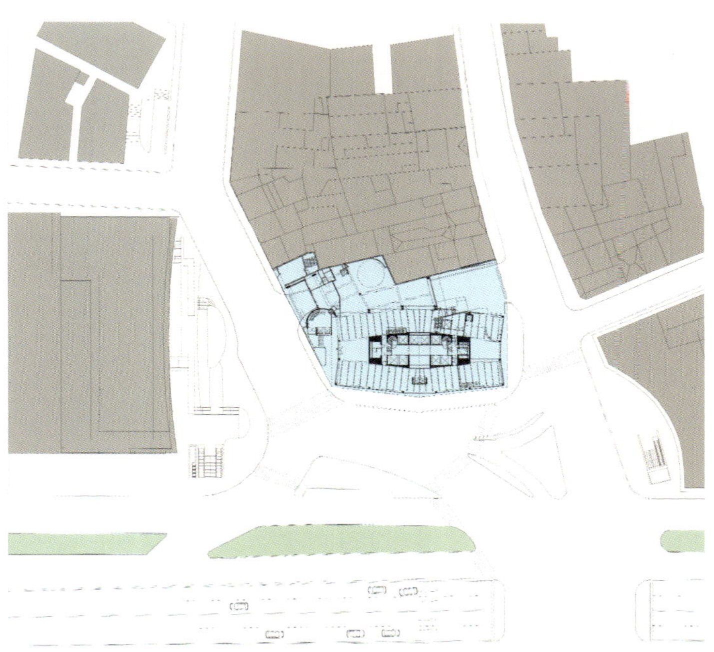

3

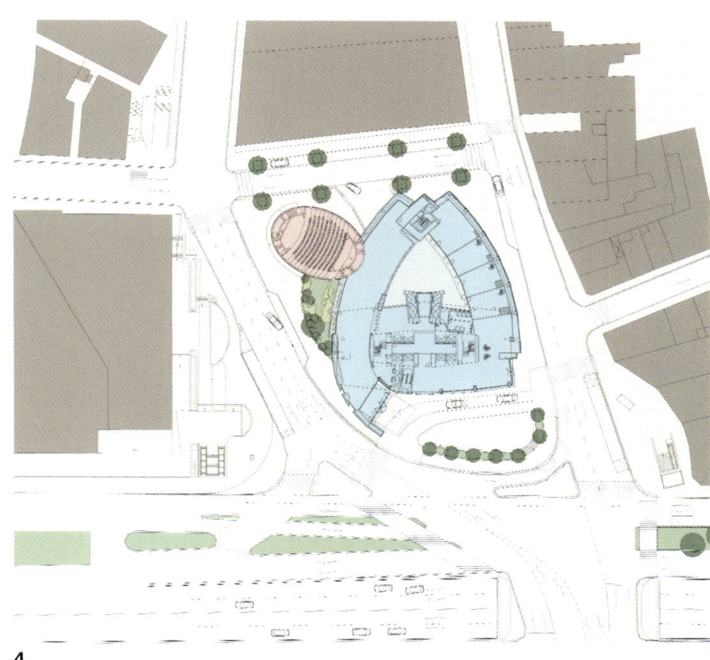

4

1 *Madou Plaza, before its renovation. Originally named Tour Madou, the 1965 tower, then 112 metres (367 feet) high, was designed by Robert Goffaux*

2 *General view from the Boulevard du Régent*

3 *Site plan before renovation*

4 *Site plan after renovation*

5 *General view from the Boulevard Bischoffsheim*

6 *North elevation with the 13-storey atrium located at the rear of the tower*

7 *Atrium*

Photography: *Marc Detiffe (1,5,6); ASSAR (2,7)*
Plans: *ASSAR*

5

6

7

HEADQUARTERS OF REGIONE PIEMONTE

TURIN ITALY

This project is a new landmark for Turin, a symbolic building, easily recognised, and the central element of a vast and complex system. The programme includes offices, an exhibition centre and an auditorium. The new Headquarters of the Region of Piemonte not only creates a dialogue with its adjacent buildings but with its context at a regional scale. With its orientation based on the cardinal points, the building establishes relationships with the surrounding natural elements: the mountains, the plains, the river, and the hills.

The intervention is anchored within a proposal to redefine the site and its key feature: the termination of a central axis.

The complex is composed of two elements: the tower, which houses the offices of the Region and a lower building containing the congress centre and other services for the city. The interface between the two is the 'great void', representing the unifying space of the entire complex and functioning as an atrium for the offices as well as for the congress centre and its adjoining public spaces. Celebrative in scale, it remains transparent and permeable, a lively filter through which the building encounters the city and the city enters into the building.

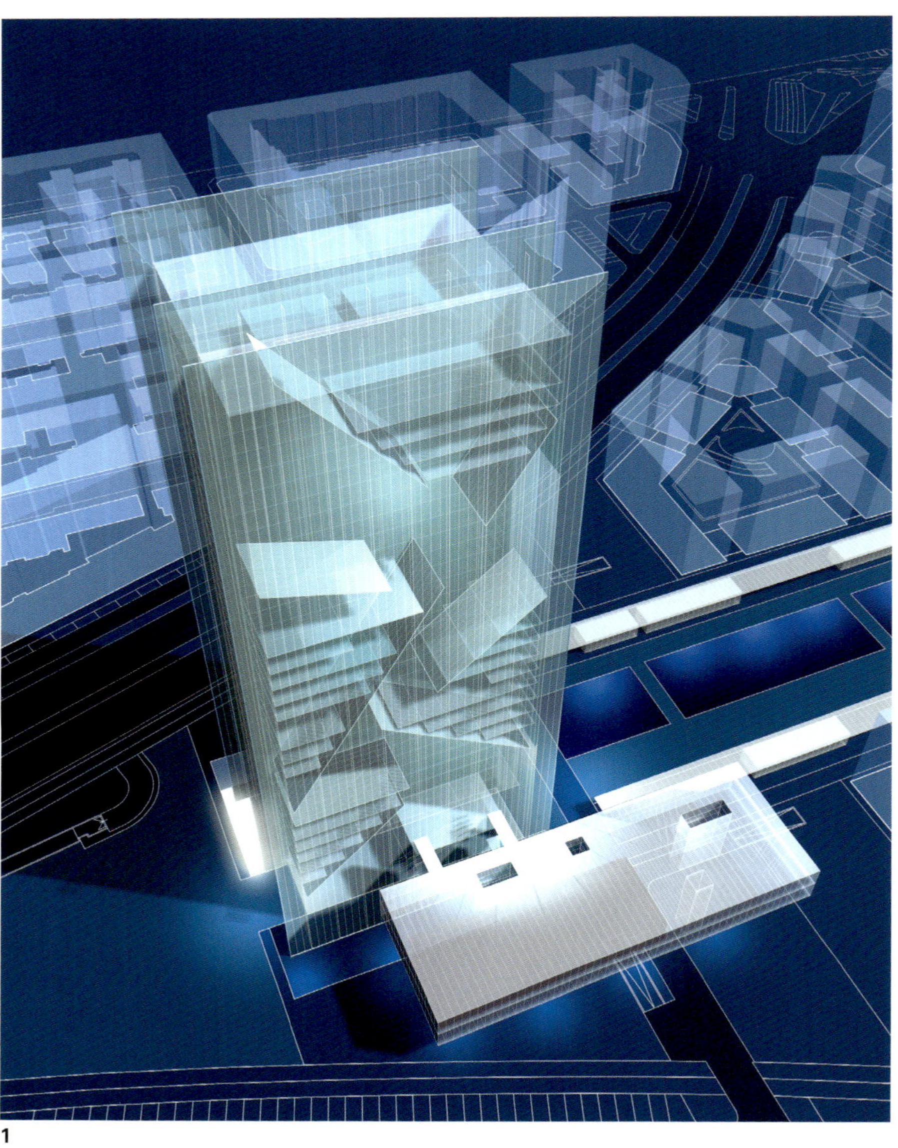

1

2

Headquarters of Regione Piemonte | **Location** Turin, Italy | **Design phase** | **Architect** Massimiliano Fuksas Architetto | **Client** Regione Piemonte | **Structural engineer** A.I. Engineering | **Mechanical engineer** A.I. Engineering | **Height** 120 m/394 ft | **Above-ground storeys** 30 | **Basements** 3 | **Mechanical levels** 2 | **Use** Office | **Area of above-ground building** 35,000 sq m/376,600 sq ft | **Structural materials** Concrete, steel | **Other materials** Glass | **Cost** €88 M

3

1–3 *Perspectives of proposed building*

4 *Sections*

Photography: *Courtesy Fuksas archives*

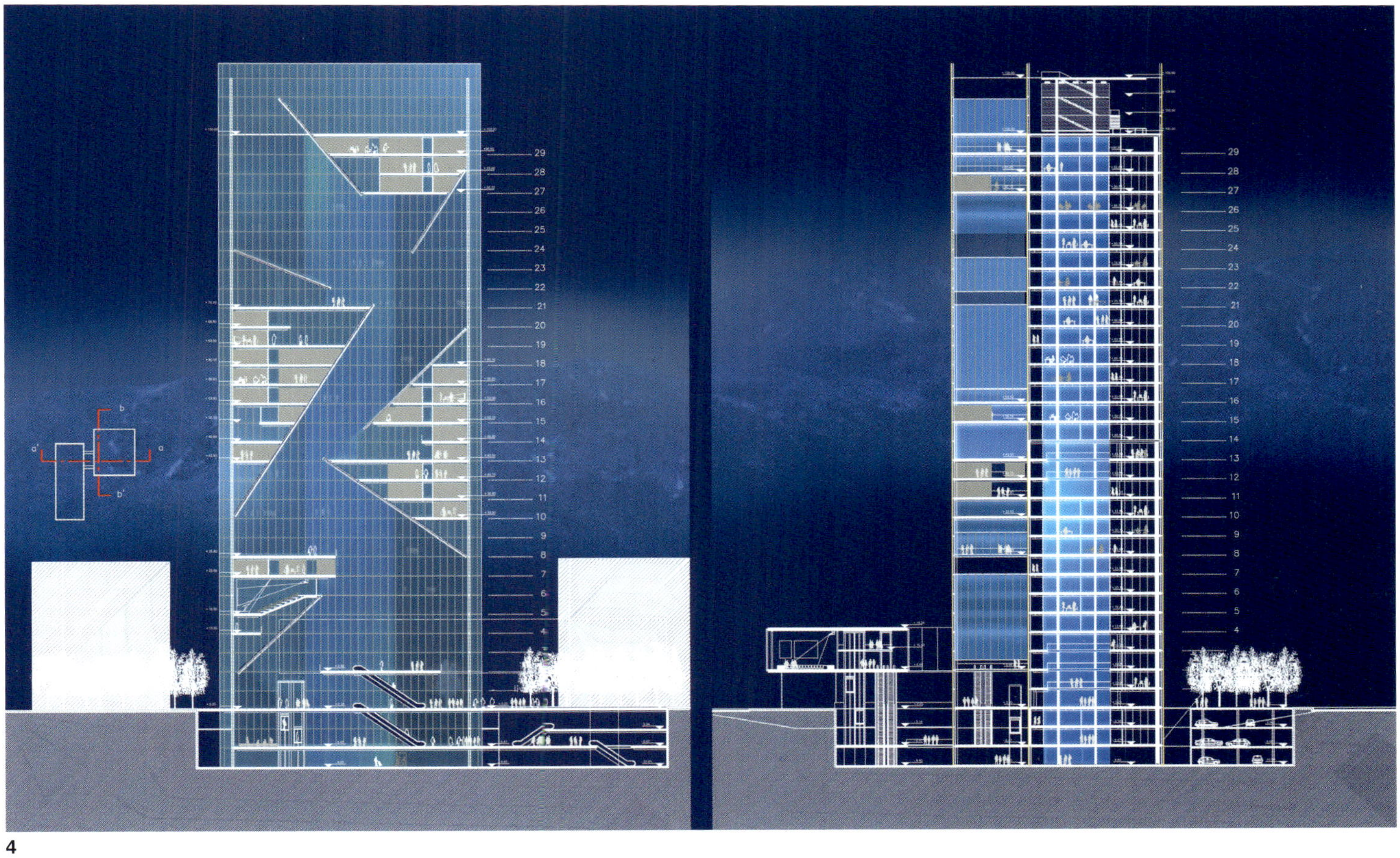

4

TSAMERET TOWERS TEL AVIV ISRAEL

This is an exclusive residential complex situated on a 30,000-square-metre site in the north-central area of Tel Aviv. The complex contains around 400 apartments in three 37-storey towers. The three towers rise from a green carpet and create an urban park of almost 21,000 square metres on three levels, following the natural topography of the site.

The upper level of the park is a public garden that connects the complex to the residential neighbourhood to the south and serves both the neighbourhood and the project itself. The intermediate level is an enclosed private garden for the project's tenants where they can enjoy a spa, the swimming pool and other luxurious amenities. The lower level of the park connects to the street and creates an urban plaza. The height difference between the levels creates a three-storey-high entrance lobby for each tower that opens to the street plaza. The three towers are connected by a retaining wall clad in natural stone from the site itself.

The architectural language of the towers is inspired by the white, modern spirit of Tel Aviv's architectural heritage. The tension between the vertical proportions and the horizontal cantilevered balconies creates an internal rhythm that evolves into a composition that at first glance looks arbitrary but on the scale of the whole building is well calculated and organised. The building materials are a combination of light-coloured flamed granite and glass curtain walls, which give the building an airy look.

The organisation of the apartments around the central service core enables a flexible division of the floors in a variety of configurations. The living rooms in most of the apartments are located in the corners and allows panoramic views of the city from almost every apartment on every floor.

1

1 *General view from northwest*
2 *Detail of west façade*
3 *View of first tower from the south*
4 *15th floor plan*
5 *11th floor plan*

Photography: *Yaki Assayag*

Tsameret Towers | **Location** Tel Aviv, Israel | **Completion date** 2005 | **Architect** Yasky & Partners Architects – A Yasky, J Sivan; associate architect Rachel Feller | **Client** Alrov (Israel) Ltd. | **Structural engineer** S Ben Avraham Engineers Ltd. | **Mechanical engineer** Doron-Shahar consulting engineers (air conditioning); D Bar Akiva consulting engineer (electrical) | **Landscape architect** Dan Zur | **Contractor** A Dori | **Height** 122 m/400 ft | **Above-ground storeys** 37 | **Basements** 2 | **Above-ground useable levels** 35 | **Mechanical levels** 2 | **Use** Residential | **Site area** approx 30,000 sq m/ 322,800 sq ft | **Area of above-ground building** 94,600 sq m/1,017,896 sq ft | **Structural materials** Reinforced concrete | **Other materials** External walls: granite, aluminium and glass curtain wall; internal walls: wood veneer, granite, stucco, plasterboard

2

3

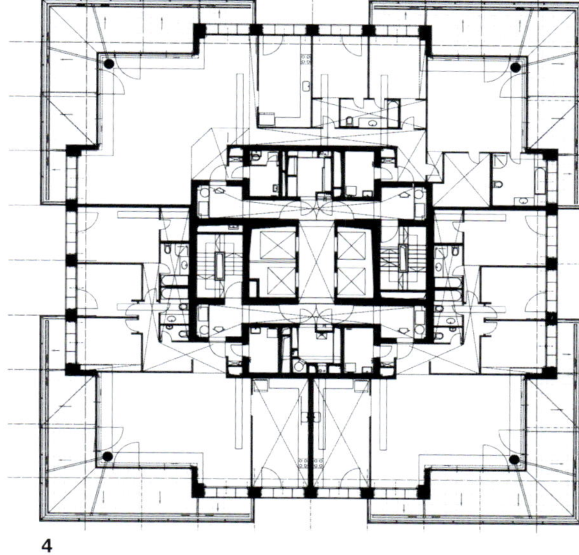

4

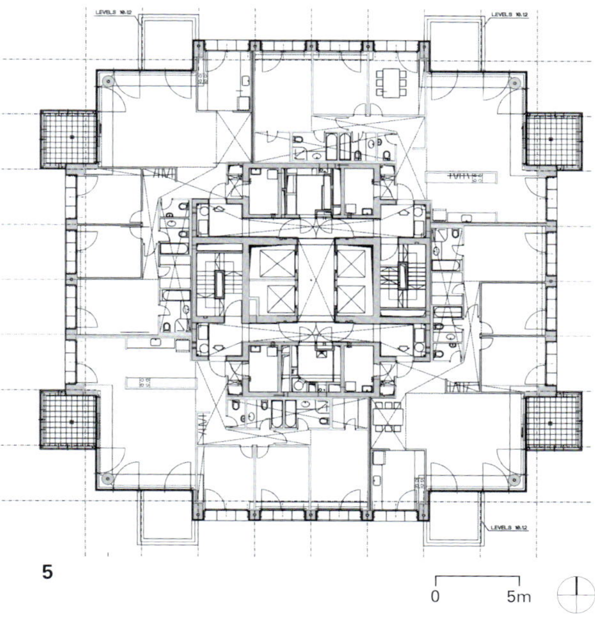

5

HIGHLIGHT MUNICH BUSINESS TOWERS

MUNICH
GERMANY

The project evolved from an invited competition from which Murphy/Jahn emerged with a first and second prize. The buildings were developed with a series of models that led to the winning scheme that incorporates the topology of the proposed surrounding Parkstadt Schwabing. The scheme consists of two towers that are shifted against each other and two base buildings. The base buildings at the north and south are separated from the towers. Because of the building's small footprint, most of the site could be left open, allowing landscape architect Peter Walker to create a quality outside space with his characteristic geometric forms.

The two towers are connected by bridges, intended as 'clip on elements', that can be added or taken away wherever needed. Together with the exposed elevators and the stairs, they provide the building with a dynamic image. The transparency of the buildings allows organisation, components and materials to read like a clear and simple diagram.

The single-layer façade for the building was developed to reduce construction costs and energy consumption. The façade also re-examines the nature of the high-rise enclosure, addressing shading, daylighting, natural ventilation, increased vision and visual control of the tower façades. The typical 1.35-metre façade module consists of a narrow operable window behind vertical panels of stainless steel and a glass portion of high-performance triple-glazed insulating glass. A selective interior shade reduces vision and daylight. The perforated stainless steel panels in front of the operable windows also serve as sun, wind, rain and safety protection. From the inside, the stainless steel panels give an interesting modulation to the views; on the outside, they reinforce the verticality. Mechanical assistance is provided by fan coil units in the floor, which distribute the air as displacement systems. Cooled or heated ceilings, or integral piping in the concrete structure, use the efficiency of water as an energy carrier and concrete for thermal mass to optimise the efficiency of the mechanical systems.

1

2

3

1,2,5 *General views*
3 *Night lighting in entrance court*
4 *Typical floor plan*
6 *Two-level bridge at night*
7 *Façade detail*

***Photography**: Ranier Viertlboeck*

Highlight Munich Business Towers | **Location** Munich, Germany | **Completion date** 2004 | **Architect** Murphy/Jahn, Inc | **Client** Bürozentrum Parkstadt München-Schwabing KG | **Structural engineer** Werner Sobek Ingenieure GmbH | **Mechanical engineer** Transsolar Energietechnik GmbH; ENCO Energie-Consulting GmbH | **Landscape architect** Peter Walker & Partners; Prof. Rainer Schmidt | **Contractor** STRABAG KG | **Height** 113 m/370.7 ft and 126 m/413 ft | **Above-ground useable levels** 28 and 33 | **Basements** 3 | **Mechanical levels** 2 (in elevator tower) | **Site area** 14,570 sq m/156,800 sq ft | **Area of above-ground building** 74,198 sq m/798,700 sq ft

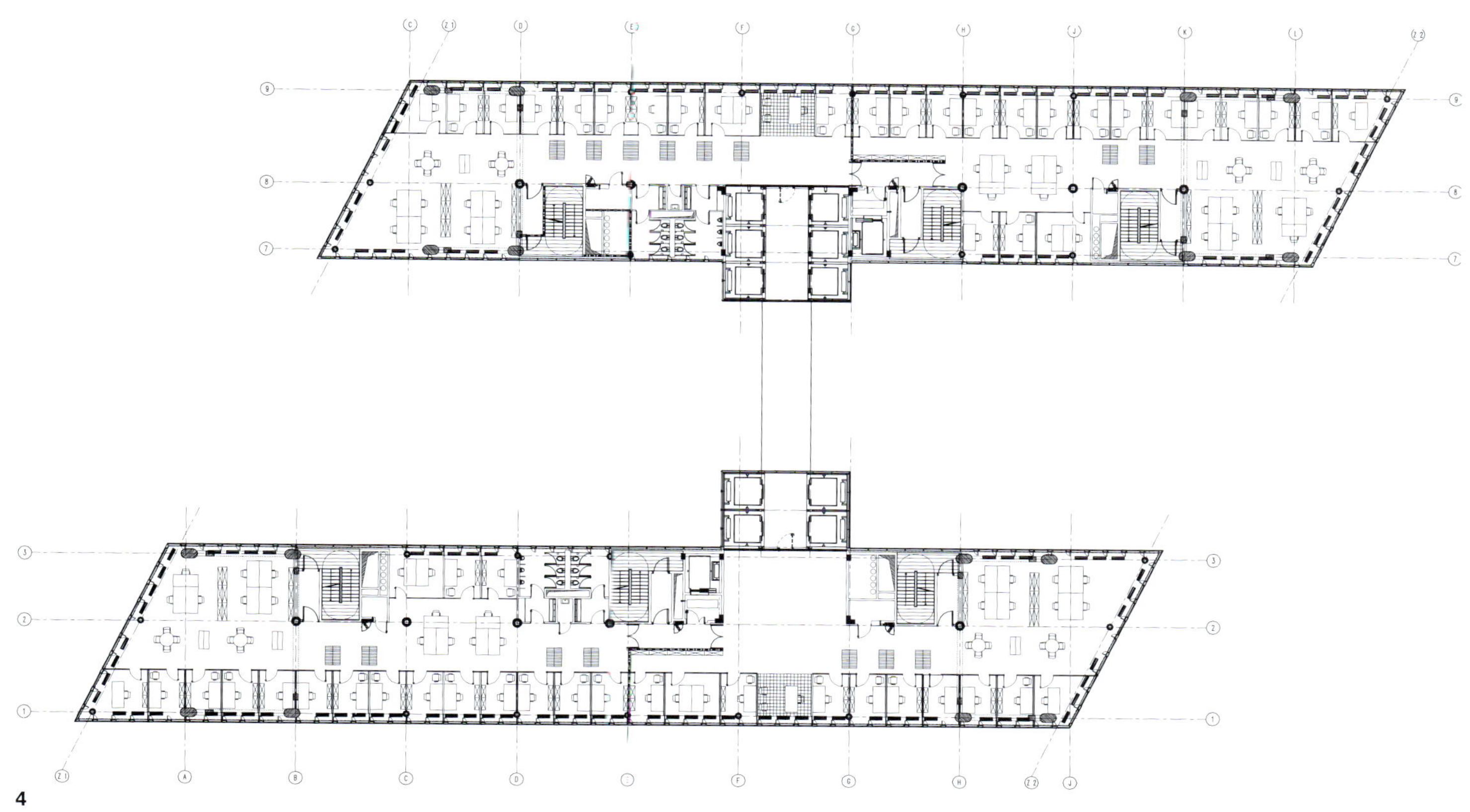

4

5

6

7

CLIFFORD CHANCE HEADQUARTERS

LONDON
UNITED KINGDOM

This 33-storey headquarters tower for the international law firm Clifford Chance commands a central position at Heron Quay, the second phase of development at Canary Wharf. The project overlooks Jubilee Park to the west and the south docks to the east and south. A six-storey low-rise podium is linked to the tower by a five-storey atrium facing the park. The glass and anodised aluminium curtainwall provides floor-to-ceiling views of the park, the buildings of Canary Wharf, the river Thames and the London skyline.

The building is fully attuned to the program and technology demands of the headquarters of an international law firm. The complex includes below-grade parking, a ground-floor auditorium, two floors of conference rooms, a cafeteria and dining area, a fitness centre with a skylit swimming pool overlooking the water, and a roof terrace with a tented outdoor reception space. A number of public amenities connect the office facility to the Canary Wharf neighbourhood, including a waterfront promenade with retail space, an underground shopping mall, and a link to the Jubilee Line.

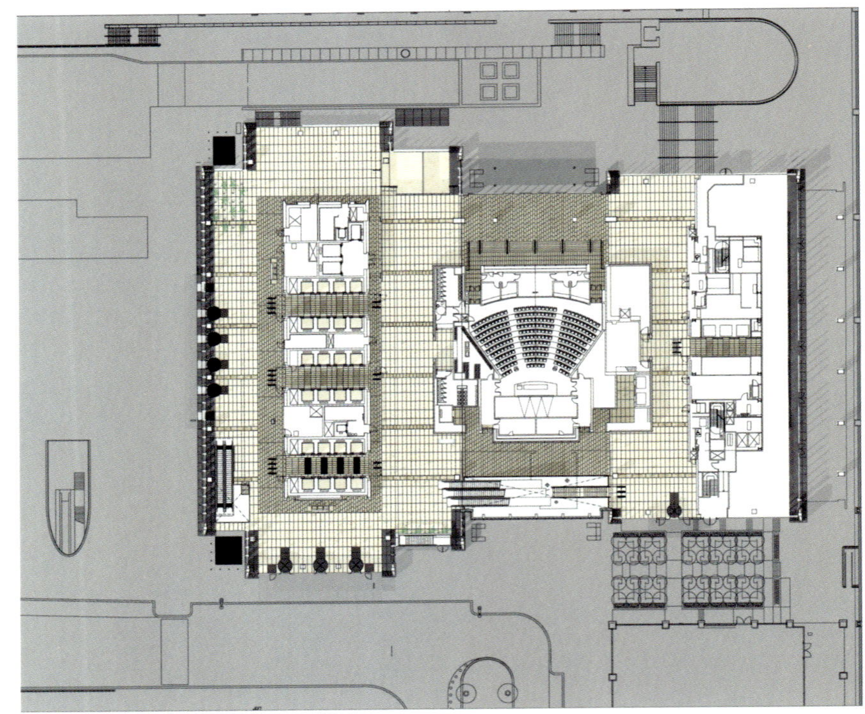

1

2

3

4

1 *Ground floor plan*
2 *West elevation*
3 *South elevation*
4 *West elevation atrium*
Opposite *View from southeast*

Photography: *Peter Murray (2); HG Esch (3,4,opposite)*

Clifford Chance Headquarters | **Location** London, United Kingdom | **Completion date** 2002 | **Architect** Kohn Pedersen Fox Associates | **Associate architect** Adamson Associates Architects | **Client** Canary Wharf Limited | **Structural engineer** Yolles Partnership | **Mechanical engineer** HH Angus & Associates Limited | **Contractor** Canary Wharf Contractors | **Height** 137 m/449.5 ft | **Above-ground storeys** 33 | **Basements** 4 | **Above-ground useable levels** 31 | **Mechanical levels** 2 | **Use** Office | **Site area** 9476 sq m/102,000 sq ft | **Area of above-ground building** 169,100 sq m/1,820,000 sq ft | **Structural materials** Steel structure, concrete core | **Other materials** Glass, aluminium, stone

DE ROTTERDAM

ROTTERDAM
THE NETHERLANDS

The site for De Rotterdam is on the former harbour waterfront between the KPN tower and Café Rotterdam at Kop van Zuid. The different programs are organised into different blocks – essentially shell and core – that provide the individual users with great flexibility. The clustering of these blocks into a functioning ensemble creates a seemingly random composition that allows the building to blend into its context and yet maintain a distinctive look.

The multi-use complex accommodates offices, 200 residences, a 196-room hotel and congress centre, a 7-screen cinema, fitness rooms, shops and restaurants, and a 750-car garage. Three access cores serve the different parts of the building and provide access for each program.

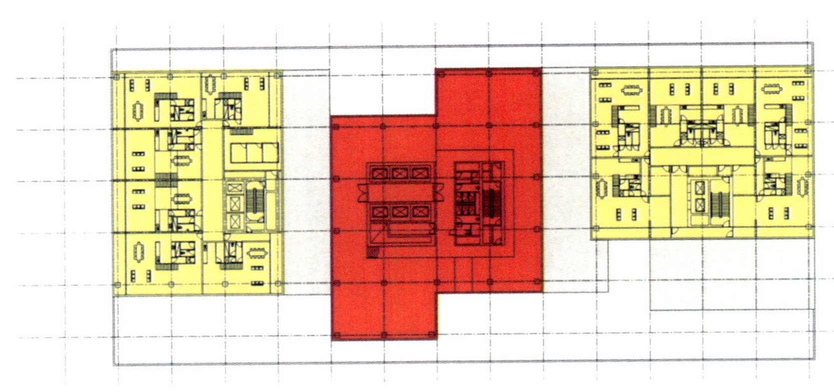

1

2

3

4

5

1 *High-rise typical floor plan*
2–5 *General views*
6 *Section showing different building uses*

Photography: *Hectic Pictures*

De Rotterdam | **Location** Rotterdam, The Netherlands | **Design phase** | **Architect** OMA Office for Metropolitan Architecture | **Associate architect** ABT Bouwkunde | **Client** MAB bv, The Hague | **Structural engineer** Arup, London/Corsmit | **Height** 138 m/453 ft | **Above-ground storeys** 38 | **Basements** 2 | **Above-ground useable levels** 36 | **Use** Office, apartments, hotel, cinema, commercial, restaurants | **Area of above-ground building** 125,750 sq m/1,354,000 sq ft

6

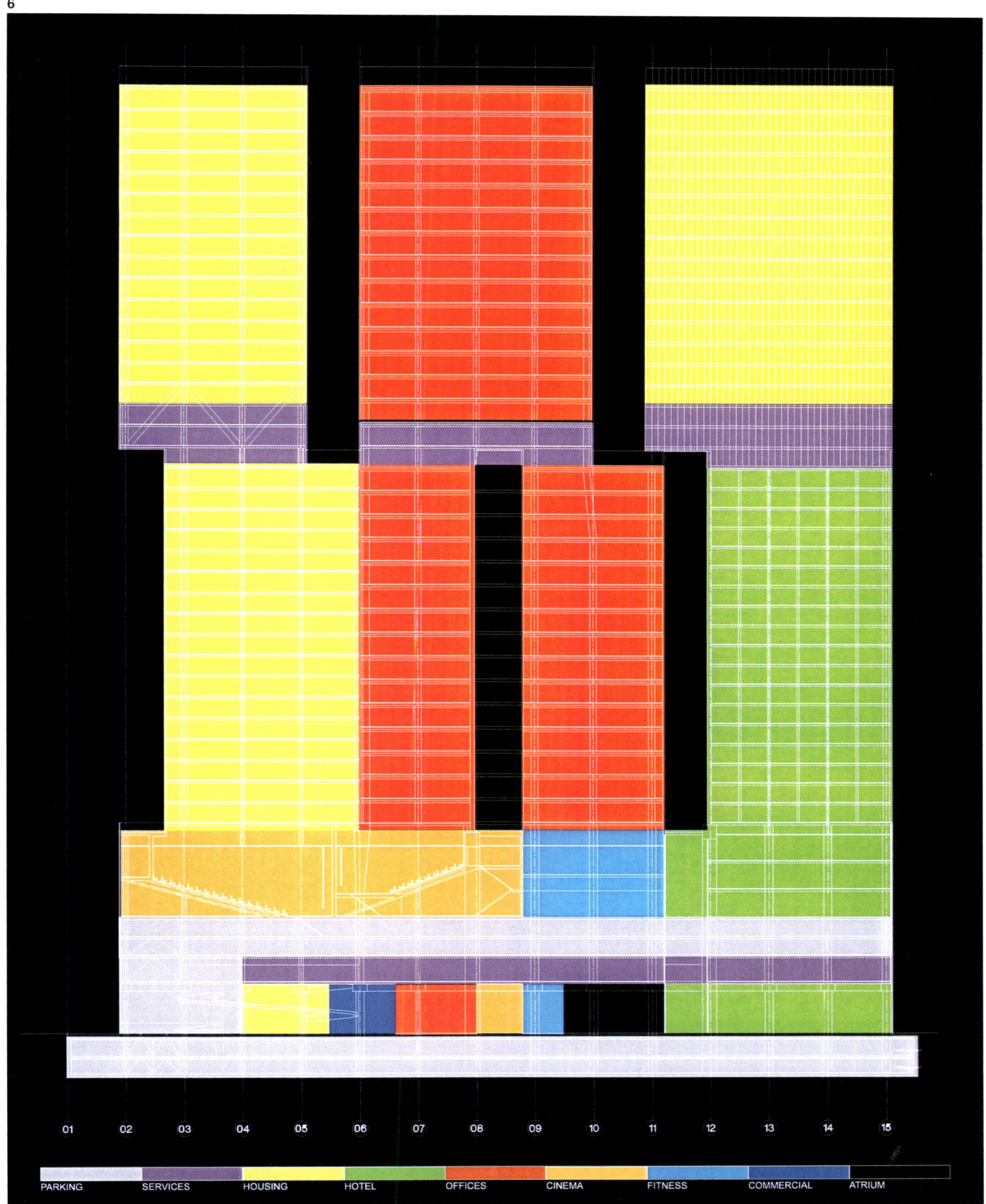

STANDARD BANK CENTRE JOHANNESBURG SOUTH AFRICA

The Standard Bank Centre, headquarters of the Standard Bank of South Africa Limited, is located at the heart of Johannesburg's financial district. The fundamental planning idea was to devise a design solution for a building in the densely built up area of inner Johannesburg, which would be accessible via a generously proportioned plaza. Minimising the massing at plaza level consequently led to the design of a hanging structure. The 139-metre-high building is organised into three hanging volumes of nine office floors each. The floors above, with 5.4-metre-high cantilevers, house the air-conditioning plants, a cooling plant and the transformer station.

The building is constructed from precast concrete parts. The exception is the core with its four shafts, which was erected using slipforming. The prefabricated parts are characterised by a vertical surface structure created by moulded plastic formwork. The parapet beams are 1.5 metres high and 24.6 metres long. With a specially constructed rotary tower crane, it was possible to install a quarter of a floor level with one single lifting action.

The building has 35 storeys above ground and 5 levels below ground. The first two basements house the computer centre, including the open-plan evaluation department with 300 employees. On the basement levels a double-skin safe tower is linked directly with the banking hall. The safe tower runs through all basement levels with access and delivery located in the lowest garage level. The building does not have a window cleaning system. Access and cleaning is carried out via the 60-centimetre-wide window parapet. The 9.7-metre-deep office floors are column-free. The building has tinted, sun-absorbent laminated double glazing with internal vertical sunshading louvres. The air volumes required for ventilation are distributed via the vertical air ducts located in the façade corners. The project was executed in cooperation with Prof. EWN Mallows and Stucke, Harrison, Ritchie and Partner, Johannesburg.

1 *General view*
2 *General view at night*
3 *Mechanical floor plan*
4 *Typical floor plan*
5 *Main lobby*
6 *Ground floor plan*

Photography: *Manfred Hanisch*

1

Standard Bank Centre | **Location** Johannesburg, South Africa | **Completion date** 970 | **Architect** HPP Hentrich-Petschnigg & Partner KG | **Client** The Standard Bank of South Africa Limited | **Structural engineer** Ove Arup & Partners, London – Johannesburg | **Mechanical engineer** Everitt, de Kock & Partners, Pretoria | **Contractor** LCB Consortium (Pty) Limited: LTA Building & Manufacturing Company Limited; Concor-Grinaker (Pty) Limited; Bondcrete (Pty) Limited | **Height** 139 m/456 ft | **Above-ground storeys** 35 | **Basements** 5 | **Above-ground useable levels** 28 | **Use** Office | **Gross floor area** 30,000 sq m/322,800 sq ft | **Structural materials** Steel, reinforced concrete, glass

2

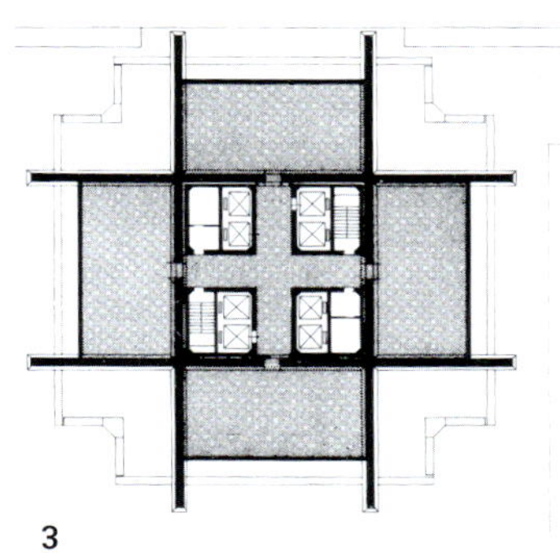

3

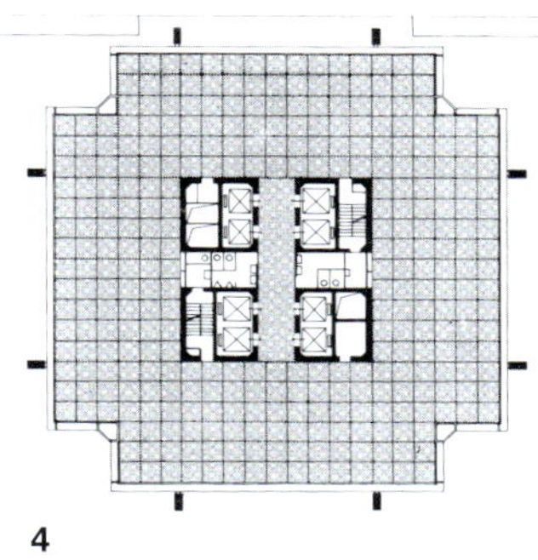

4

5

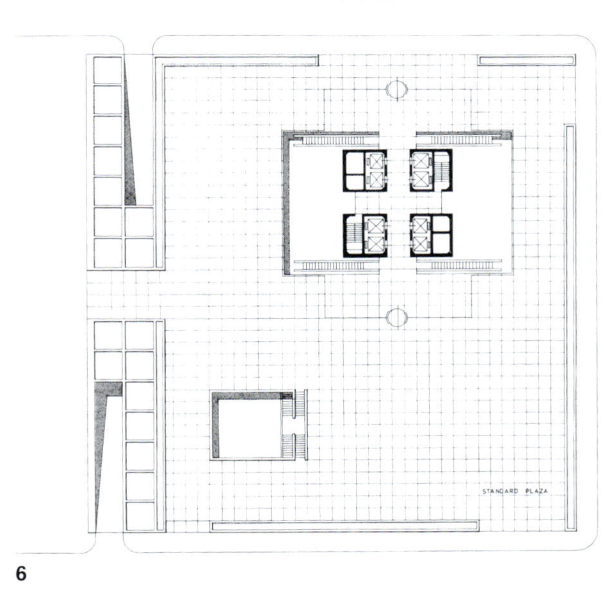

6

TORRE AGBAR BARCELONA SPAIN

This is not a tower. It is not a skyscraper in the American sense of the expression: it is a unique growth in the middle of this rather calm city. But it is not the slender, nervous verticality of the spires and bell towers that often punctuate horizontal cities. Instead, it is a fluid mass that has perforated the ground – a geyser under a permanent calculated pressure.

The surface of this construction evokes water: smooth and continuous, but also vibrating and transparent because it manifests itself in coloured depths – uncertain, luminous and nuanced. This architecture comes from the earth but does not have the weight of stone. It could even be the faraway echo of old formal Catalan obsessions, carried by a mysterious wind from the coast of Montserrat.

The uncertainties of matter and light make the campanile of Agbar vibrate in the skyline of Barcelona, like a faraway mirage day and night – a precise marker to the entry of the new diagonal that starts at Plaça de las Glorias. This singular object becomes a new symbol for an international city.

Jean Nouvel

1

2

3

4

5

1 *Exterior view*
2 *View from interior*
3 *General view*
4 *Building under construction*
5 *Façade under construction*
6 *Level 25 floor plan, executive level*
7 *Typical floor plan*

Photography: *Rafael Vargas*
Renderings: *Courtesy Ateliers Jean Nouvel*

Torre Agbar | **Location** Barcelona, Spain | **Completion date** 2005 | **Architect** Ateliers Jean Nouvel | **Associate architect** b720 Arquitectos | **Client** Layetana Inmuebles | **Structural Engineers** Obiol, Moya y Asociados, S.L. (OMA) & Robert Brufau i Associats, S.A. (RBA) | **MEP engineers** Gepro & Ibering | **Contractor** Dragados y Construciones, S.A. | **Height** 141.5 m/464.3 ft | **Above-ground storeys** 35 | **Basements** 4 | **Above-ground useable levels** 32 | **Mechanical levels** 3 | **Use** Office | **Area of above-ground building** 30,000 sq m/322,800 sq ft | **Structural materials** Concrete | **Other materials** Glass

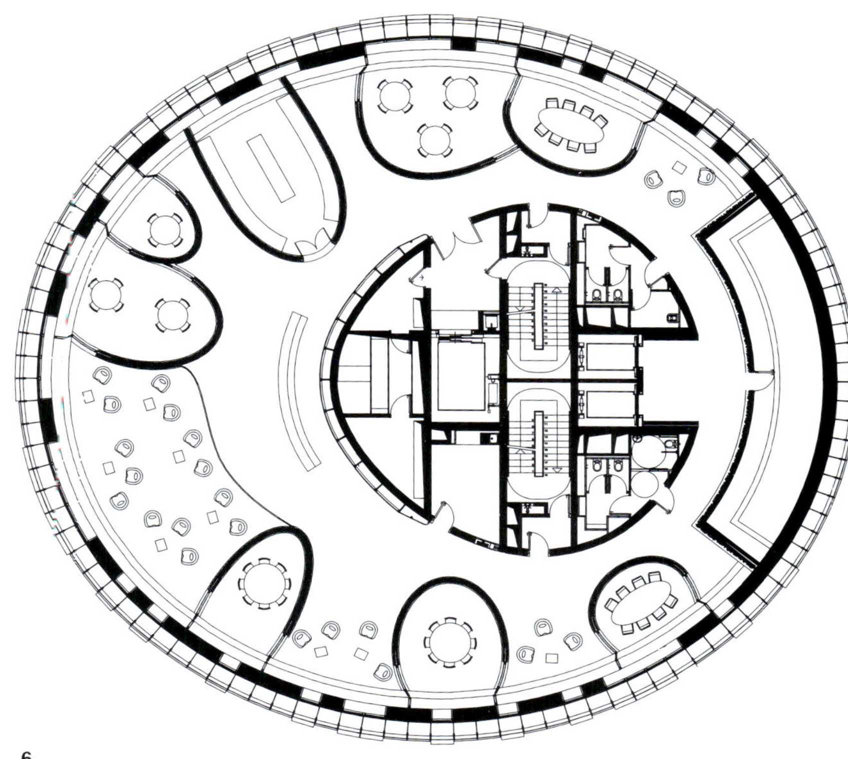

6

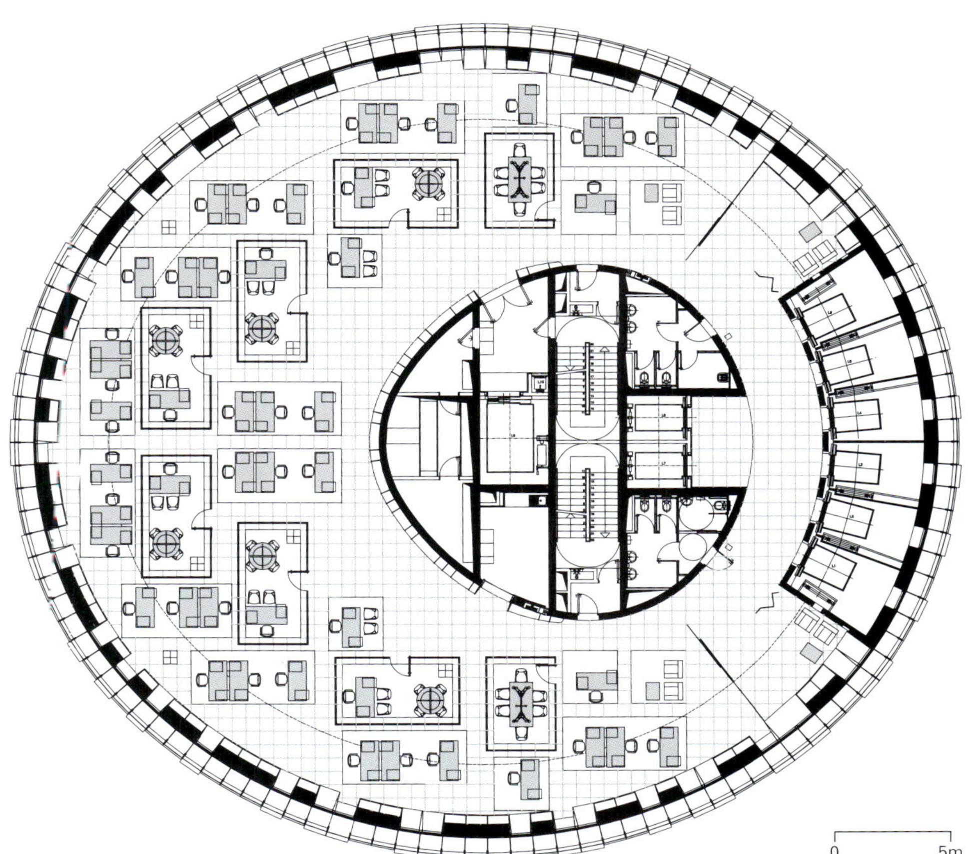

7

TOUR CBX PARIS LA DÉFENSE FRANCE

The design for the CBX Tower is driven by a concern for the delicate context of this prominent site located along the major east–west thoroughfare linking old Paris to the modern commercial district of La Défense. Spatial constraints and view corridor restrictions influenced the design for this project. Rather than occupy the entire site, the building takes an asymmetrical blade form that changes dynamically according to the viewer's orientation.

The tower's sculptural form stands at the gateway between the verticality of La Défense and the dominant low-rise character of central Paris. The curved face of the tower addresses the north–south axis. The blades at either end of the curved façade run parallel to the Boulevard Circulaire in a gesture that connects old Paris to the modern landscape of La Défense.

The apparent weightlessness of the tower contrasts with the weighty masses of neighbouring buildings. The glass and metal curtainwall has been delicately handled to provide an elegant addition to La Défense. The tower's dramatic profile provides a distinctive backdrop to the Parisian skyline.

Thirty-four floors and a double-height plaza level rest on a four-storey podium that houses public and service spaces for the building. The ground floor contains a lobby/drop off, loading facilities and mechanical areas. A cafeteria and kitchen occupy the second floor. These levels are served by two banks of six elevators, as well as an escalator connecting the ground floor to the plaza.

Twenty-seven floors of office space float above an elevated plaza level that contains a double-height main lobby space and provides a view to the skylit cafeteria below. This open space meets with the mandated view corridor requirements. Two banks of six elevators as well as a dedicated service elevator allow access to the office tower.

1

1 *General view*
2 *Low-rise typical floor plan*
3 *Podium*

Renderings: *Courtesy Kohn Pedersen Fox Associates*

Tour CBX | **Location** Paris La Défense, France | **Completion date** 2006 | **Architect** Kohn Pedersen Fox Associates | **Associate architect** SRA Architectes | **Client** Tishman Speyer Properties LP | **Structural engineer** Setec TPI, Thornton-Tomasetti Engineers | **Mechanical engineer** Flack & Kurtz Consulting Engineers | **Contractor** BESIX | **Height** 142 m/466 ft | **Above-ground storeys** 34 | **Basements** 4 | **Above-ground useable levels** 32 | **Mechanical levels** 2 | **Use** Office | **Site area** 15,169 sq m/163,218 sq ft | **Area of above-ground building** 43,800 sq m/471,288 sq ft | **Structural materials** Concrete | **Other materials** Glass, aluminium, stone, aluminium panels

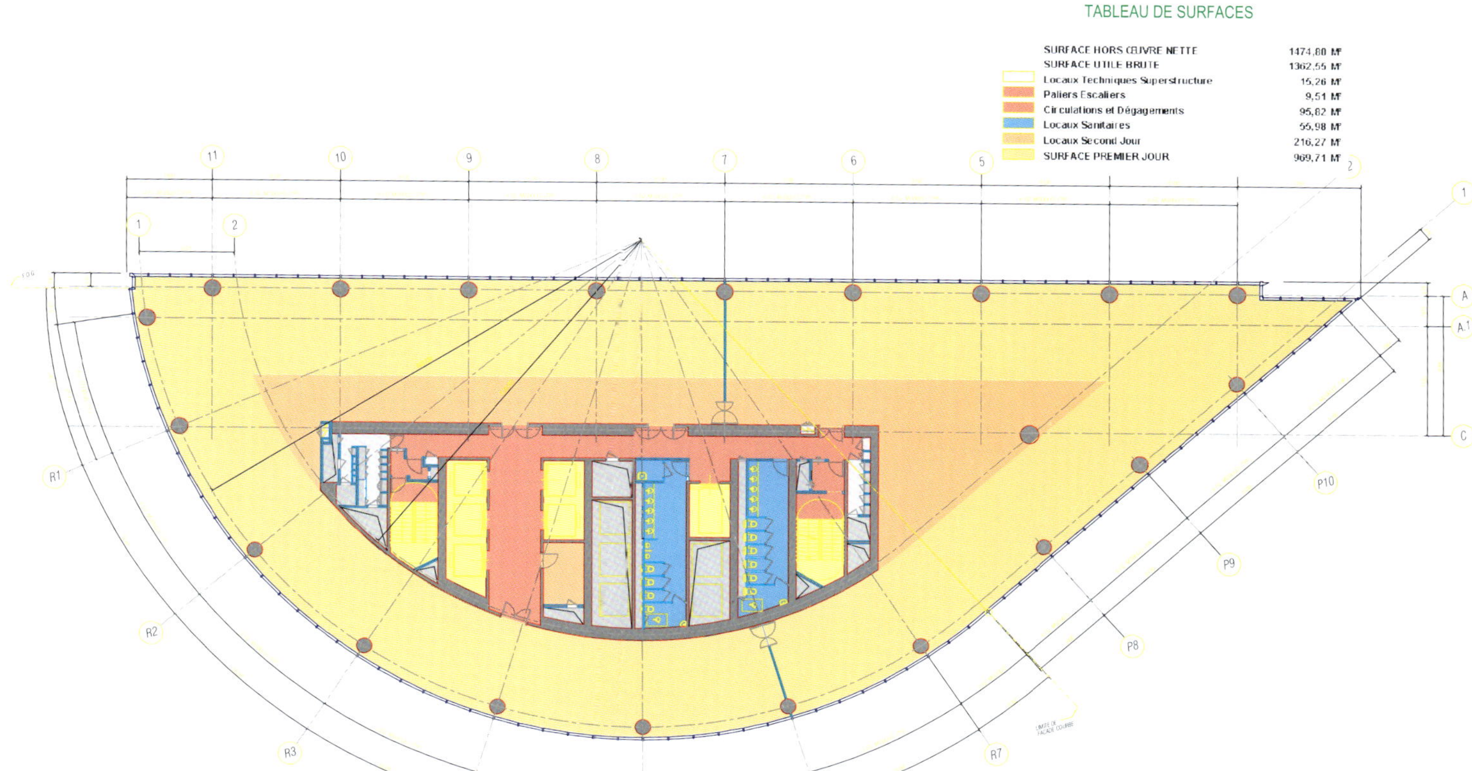

2

3

NILE CITY CAIRO EGYPT

When fully complete, Nile City will comprise two 143-metre, 35-storey towers and one 100-metre, 25-storey, V-shaped hotel tower. They are located in the heart of the Egyptian capital, opposite the island of Zamalek, and form part of a group of high-rise buildings designed to add character to the business district. The architects had no qualms about accentuating the ensemble's verticality, nor about emphasising the features that indicate a strong link with traditional Levantine architecture. Visual interest has been provided and the various functions of the building are made easily readable through the use of massive bases, decorative pillars and monumental porticoes at ground level, and pergolas or golden cupolas at the top of the towers, along with pilasters, cornices, banding, balconies and coloured stone. The base is common to all three towers and houses the separate entrances to the offices, the shopping galleries and the five-star Fairmont Cairo hotel scheduled for completion in 2007. Glass roofs, monumental porticoes and access ramps provide each entrance with an appropriate layout below a colossal order.

The two office towers feature strong vertical divisions, and large glazed panels. The horizontal divisions of the elevation are also emphasised by powerful cornices, and the highest floors are set back and crowned with picturesque, gleaming cupolas. The most difficult aspect of the scheme was establishing a successful balance between the size of the different towers – they have been designed to not stand directly opposite each other and to create interesting relationships with the surrounding area, while also maximising views towards the pyramids, which can be glimpsed on the horizon.

1

2

3

4

Nile City | **Location** Cairo, Egypt | **Completion date** Office towers 2003; Fairmont Cairo hotel 2007 | **Design and architectural design follow-up** Atelier d'Art Urbain, Architects | **Architect of record** Etienne Watelet; I.D.S. Limited and Partners | **Client** Nile City Investments | **Structural engineer** Hamza Associates; BESIX Engineering Department | **Mechanical engineer** Shaker Consultancy Group | **Contractor** BESIX – Orascom jv | **Height** 143 m/ 469 ft (offices); 100 m/328 ft (hotel) | **Above-ground storeys** 35 | **Basements** 1 | **Above-ground useable levels** 34 | **Mechanical levels** 1 | **Use** Office, Fairmont hotel, retail | **Area of above-ground building** 192,590 sq m/2,073,023 sq ft | **Structural materials** Reinforced concrete | **Other materials** Glass reinforced concrete

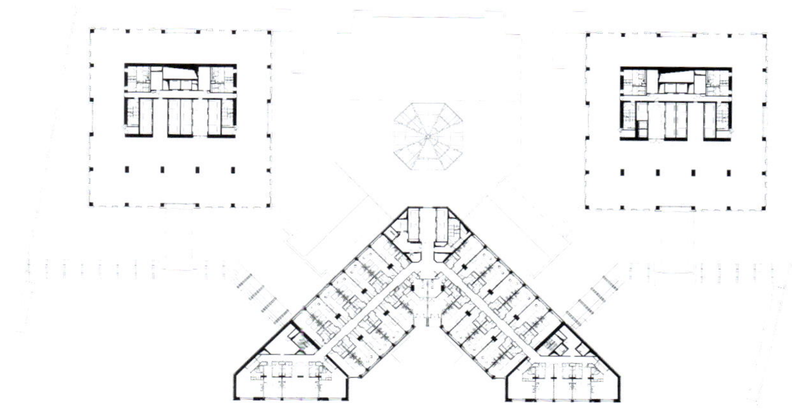

5

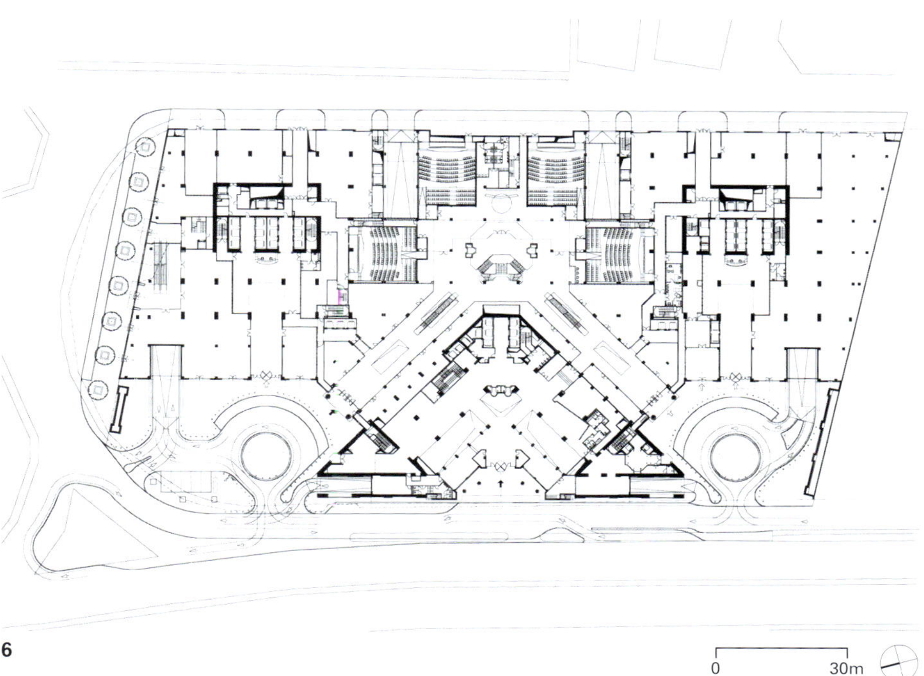

6

7

1 Perspective
2 Office tower upper level elevation
3 General view
4 Cornice detail
5 Typical floor plan
6 Ground floor plan
7 Model

Rendering: *Patrick Van Der Stricht (1)*
Photography: *Sherif Sonbol (2); courtesy BESIX (3); Atelier d'Art Urbain (4); Fabien de Cugnac (7)*
Model: *Tetraedre (7)*

UPTOWN MÜNCHEN

MUNICH
GERMANY

Uptown München is located in northwest Munich, along the city's central ring road, opposite the Olympic Park. The project, offering 84,000 square metres of office space, consists of a 146-metre high-rise and four, seven-storey campus buildings with curved roofs, connecting the buildings alongside the wide pedestrian boulevard. The horizontal form of the campus buildings stands in contrast to the distinct high-rise and at the same time complements the project. With its distinct architecture, the project has an impact on Munich's skyline.

The tower's single-shell curtain wall with storey-high glazing incorporates operable circular windows, which open parallel to the façade and act as individual elements, providing additional natural ventilation.

The high-rise, with its gallery on the top floor, and the spacious roof terraces at the top of each campus building, offer unique views of the Alps.

A man-made landscape has been created for Uptown München. The landscaped grounds with spacious green areas have been planned on an elevated ground level, creating an individual site. The site will be planted with 3000 square metres of pine wood, creating a pleasant atmosphere. Parking for 790 vehicles is offered on two levels below ground.

With its distinctive architecture, Uptown München will be a landmark neighbour to the prominent four-cylinder BMW building as well as the Olympic Stadium. Munich is gaining a bold new landmark, enriching the skyline of the city.

1

2

3

Uptown München | **Location** Munich, Germany | **Completion date** 2004 | **Architect** Ingenhoven und Partner Architekten, Düsseldorf; ATP Architects and Engineers | **Client** Hines | **Structural engineer** Burggraf, Weichinger und Partner | **Mechanical engineer** Ingenieur Consult, HL-Technik | **Landscape architect** Prof. Gustav Lange | **Contractors** Wayss & Freytag AG, Lindner AG, MCE Anlagenbau Germany GmbH, Josef Gartner GmbH & Co KG, BUG-Alu Technik AG | **Height** 146 m/479 ft | **Above-ground storeys** 38 | **Basements** 3 | **Above-ground useable levels** 37 | **Mechanical levels** 1 | **Use** Office | **Site area** 36,666 sq m/394,700 sq ft | **Area of above-ground building** 84,000 sq m/904,200 sq ft | **Structural materials** Reinforced concrete, single shell curtainwall façade | **Cost** Approx €350 M

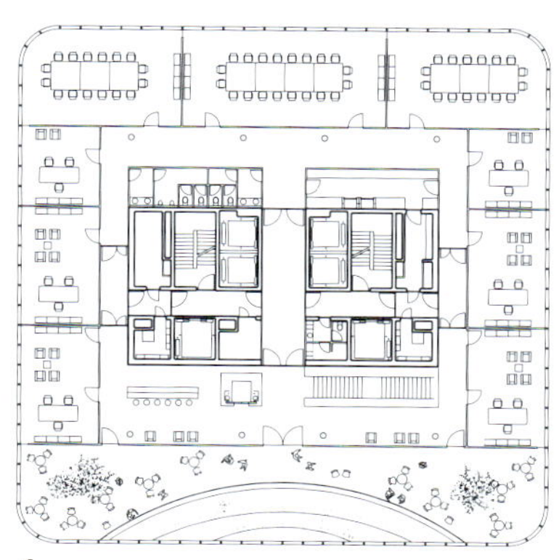
4

1 *The tallest building in Munich is situated on the Mittlerer Ring, near the Olympic stadium*
2 *The high-rise and the campus-type buildings are supplemented by a large new garden with pine trees that are more than 30 years old*
3 *General view*
4 *Level 36 floor plan*
5 *Levels 29–35 floor plan*
6 *Levels 17–28 floor plan*
7 *Levels 1–16 floor plan*
8 *The glazed and rounded corners typical of the high-rise*
9&10 *The characteristic feature is the single-layer glass façade with curved, electrically controlled awning windows for natural ventilation*

***Photography**: HG Esch*

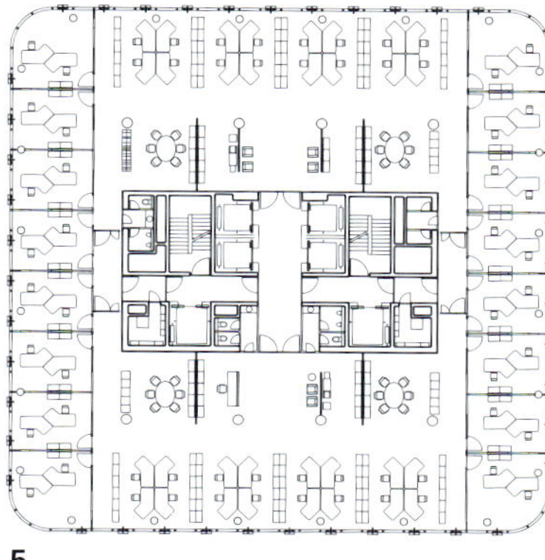
5

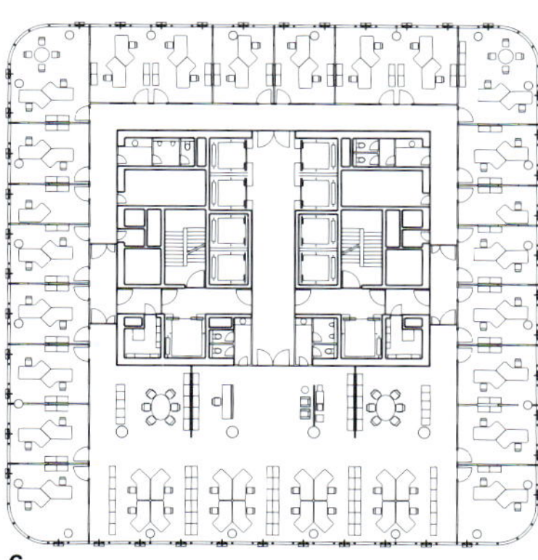
6

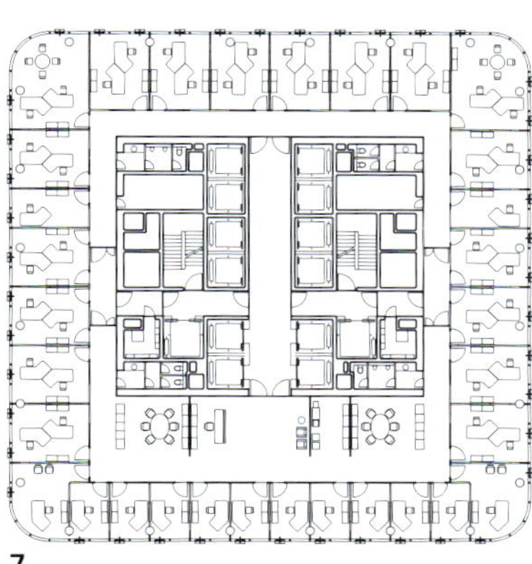
7

8

9

10

NEGURI GANE BENIDORM SPAIN

At 148 metres, the Neguri Gane tower is a reference point in the skyline of the tourist resort of Benidorm, on the shores of the Mediterranean. Located in the high part of the town in an area that has been laid out applying new environmental criteria, it shares a block with two other buildings designed by the same architect: the Cibeles Tower and the Neptuno Tower.

The Neguri Gane, rising up like an enormous lighthouse and re-creating the movement of the waves in curvilinear façades and balconies, proclaims the nearness of the sea. The structure, which has the shape of a starfish, is crowned with a golden canopy that the architect calls a *txapela* (a Basque word meaning 'beret'). With a pillar as its centrepiece, it has a series of screen walls running the height of the building, linked by a reticular slab, which contains the communication core.

The building includes two recreational/meeting points: one on the ground floor, with gardens and a recreational area, and the other on the 26th floor, consisting of a solarium, heated swimming pool, and outside terrace with panoramic views. The layouts for the floors vary as one moves up the building, resulting in an overall impression of diversity. Floors 1 to 25 have two or three apartments each, whereas the upper floors have just one apartment per floor. All the apartments are equipped with state-of-the art technological and telecommunications installations.

1

2

Neguri Gane | **Location** Benidorm, Spain | **Completion date** 2002 | **Architect** Pérez-Guerras Ingenieros & Arquitectos Asociados S.L | **Client** Negur 2000 Promociones S.A. | **Structural engineer** CYPE Ingenieros | **Landscape architect** Consuelo Arana | **Contractor** ECISA | **Height** 148 m/486 ft | **Above-ground storeys** 43 | **Basements** 2 | **Above-ground useable levels** 41 | **Mechanical levels** 2 | **Use** Residential | **Site area** 5805 sq m/62,480 sq ft | **Area of above-ground building** 5153 sq m/55,470 sq ft | **Structural materials** Reinforced concrete

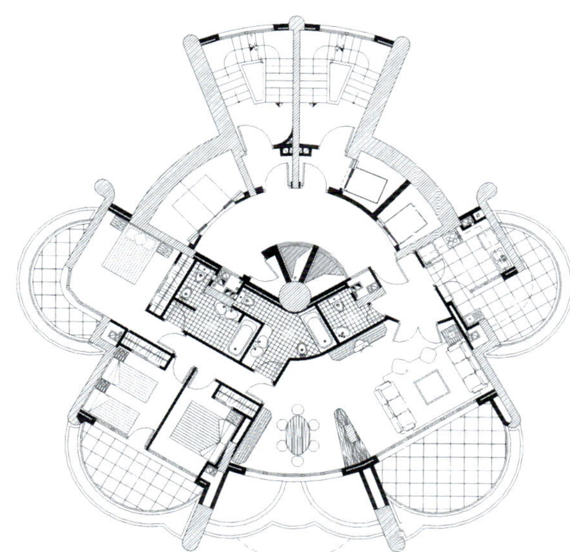

3

4

6

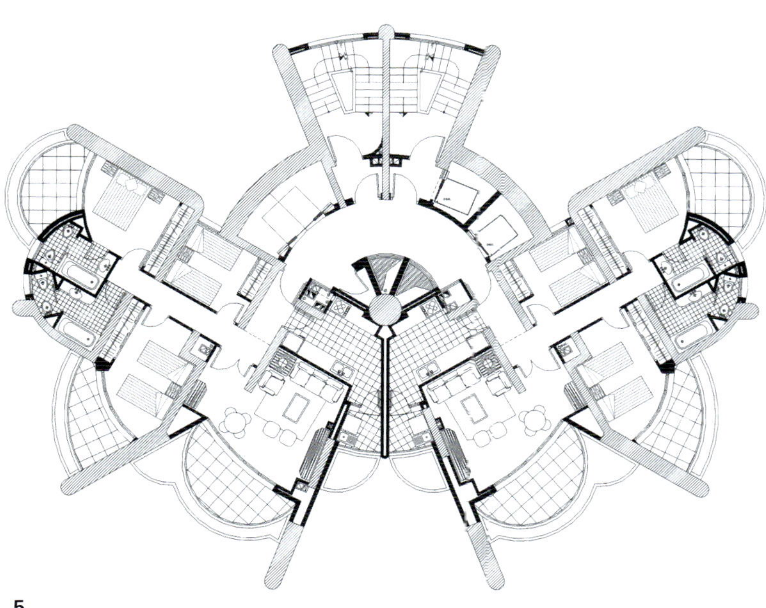

5

1 *View of Neguri context*
2 *General view*
3 *35th level floor plan*
4 *Panoramic view from the canopy*
5 *11th level floor plan*
6 *Solarium and heated swimming pool on the 26th floor*

Photography: *Joan Roig, 2004*

THE GREEN EMERALD AT FIERA MILANO

MILAN
ITALY

Daniel Libeskind, in collaboration with Zaha Hadid, Arata Isozaki and Pier Paolo Maggiora, was the winner of the Fiera Milano redevelopment 2004 competition. The Fiera Milano site has always represented excellence in Italian design, furniture, fashion and technology and deserves nothing less than a visionary, yet practical urban scheme.

The proposal provides a seamless connectivity into the existing city fabric. It creates a new neighbourhood around a central park and a new public piazza within a beautiful high-rise skyline. The proposal is a series of archipelagos, each one placed within the park, with each one proposing a variety of scales. The housing units, ranging from villas to apartment blocks, are carefully sited on the perimeter and are of a scale that resonates within the existing context.

The scheme carefully places essential cultural buildings and prominent retail amenities within the site. A central part of the scheme is the restoration and reconstruction of the historical Palazzo della Sport into a unique wellness, recreational and ecological centre. The facility is an indoor greenhouse, which is emblematic of the sustainability and ecological power of this plan.

Close to the centre of the new grand central park are three iconic commercial high-rise buildings. This component of the site is deliberately concentrated in order to maximise space for a grand park, a grand piazza and the other public and private spaces. Each high-rise building has an individual expression, yet all three are combined in a cohesive arrangement to create the grand public piazza. These skyscrapers have been engineered with state-of-the art technology and are environmentally sound and sustainable. The towers have been carefully positioned to provide appropriate shade, maximum light and a pleasant atmosphere at the pedestrian level. This allows the new piazza to be a substantial amenity for both the residents of the new housing and the workers in the office complexes.

Buildings on the site designed specifically by Daniel Libeskind include an office tower, a housing development, and a museum. Studio Daniel Libeskind is also responsible for the design of the park, along with the Piazza Domodossola.

1

1&5 *Rendering and model view of the three Fiera Milano Towers designed by Zaha Hadid (left), Daniel Libeskind (centre) and Arata Isozaki (right)*

2 *Ground floor plan*

3 *Level 10 floor plan*

4 *Level 20 floor plan*

6 *Section*

***Digital renderings:** Stack!*
***Plans:** © Studio Daniel Libeskind*

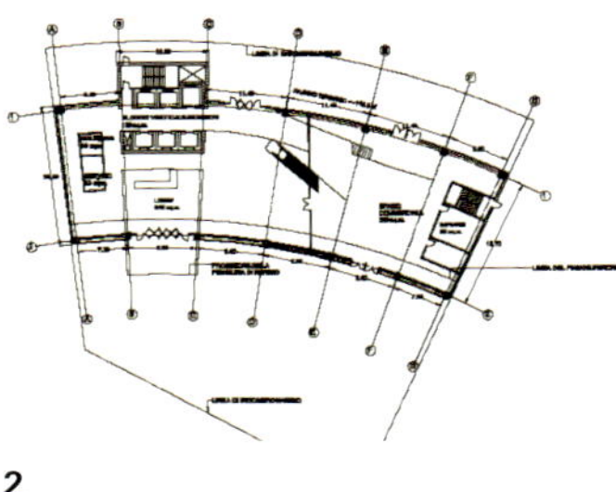

2

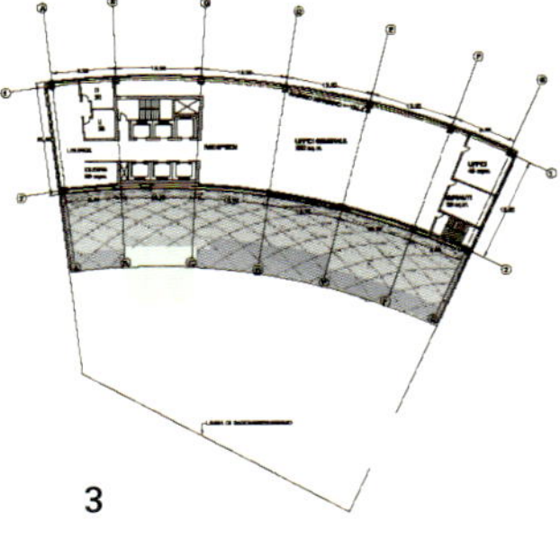

3

The Green Emerald at Fiera Milano | **Location** Milan, Italy | **Scheduled completion date** 2012 | **Architect** Studio Daniel Libeskind | **Client** CityLife | **Height** 150 m/492 ft | **Above-ground storeys** 34 | **Basements** 2 | **Above-ground useable levels** 33 | **Mechanical levels** 1 | **Use** Office | **Area of above-ground building** 34,000 sq m/365,840 sq ft | **Structural materials** Composite steel and concrete | **Other materials** Glass

5

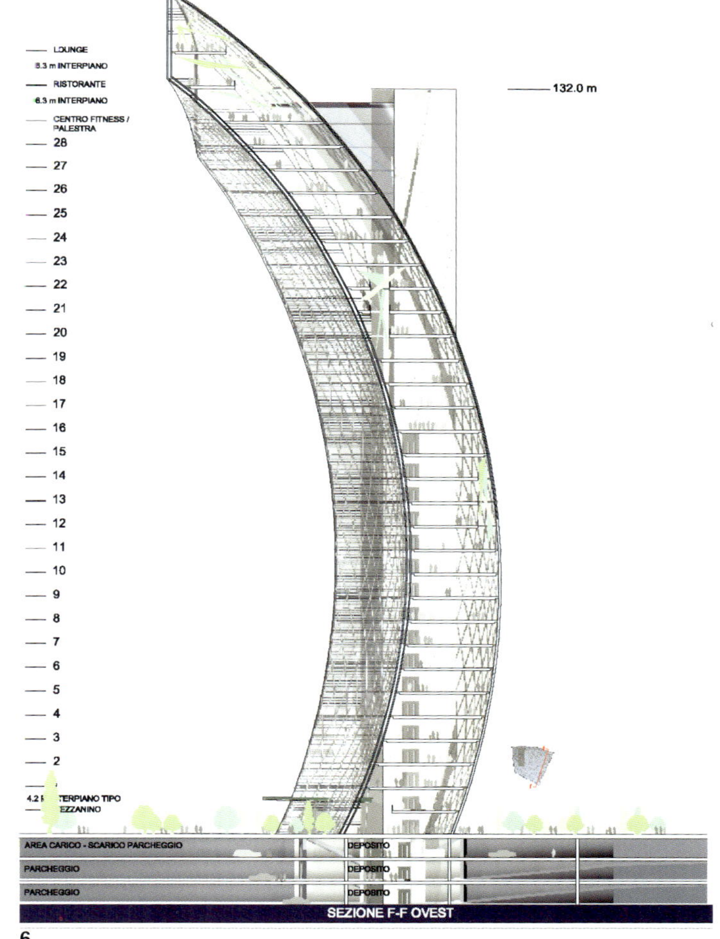

6

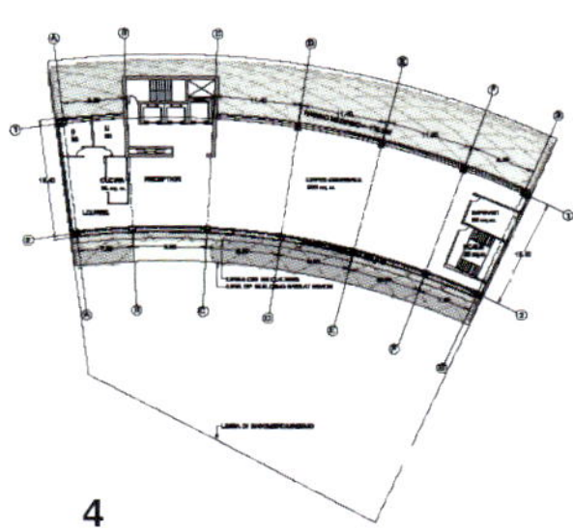

4

MONTEVIDEO

ROTTERDAM
THE NETHERLANDS

Montevideo is currently the highest residential and office tower block in The Netherlands. The name Montevideo refers to the old warehouses of the Holland-America line that were situated on the peninsula in the River Maas and named after exotic places from all over the world. Most of the warehouses have been demolished and the Wilhelmina Pier, part of the Kop van Zuid, is being redeveloped on the basis of an urban plan drawn up by Mecanoo. Montevideo is the first building on the south quay and serves as a prototype for the new buildings on this side of the pier.

Montevideo also refers to the feeling that the site evokes: the place where ocean steamers and cruise ships made the crossing from Rotterdam to New York. The basic development programme has been elaborated in a high-quality residential concept: a mixture of living, working, service and leisure, brought together in a vertical city. Not only will there be offices, shops and restaurants in the skyscraper, but the residents can also make use of a communal health club with swimming pool, sauna and fitness centre. Other service facilities include shopping, catering, cleaning, maintenance, mail, and laundry services. The four types of luxury apartments, with splendid views over the Maas, the Rijnhaven or the city, have high ceilings, large living rooms and spacious sun lounges or loggias, depending on their position in the building. The entrance foyers have the atmosphere and aura of a hotel lobby. A concierge is stationed at the entrance and coordinates the services.

The construction up to the first floor of the tower is a combination of concrete and steel, a so-called hybrid construction. The 2nd to 27th floors consist of concrete. From the 28th floor, the structure continues in steel, so that the floors of the apartments are easily divisible.

1

2

1 *Southeast façade*

2 *Bird's-eye view of location, including Wilhelmina Pier, River Maas and Erasmus Bridge*

3 *5th floor plan*

4 *Ground floor plan*

Photography: *Rob 't Hart*

Montevideo | **Location** Rotterdam, The Netherlands | **Completion date** 2005 | **Architect** Mecanoo architecten bv, Delft | **Client** ING Real Estate, the Hague | **Structural engineer** ABT adviesbureau voor bouwtechniek bv, Delft | **Mechanical engineer** Schreuder Groep, Heerhugowaard | **Contractor** BESIX, Brussels | **Height** 152.32 m/499.76 ft | **Above-ground storeys** 45 | **Basements** 2 | **Above-ground useable levels** 43 | **Mechanical levels** 2 | **Use** Residential, office | **Area of above-ground building** 57,530 sq m/619,023 sq ft | **Structural materials** Concrete, steel

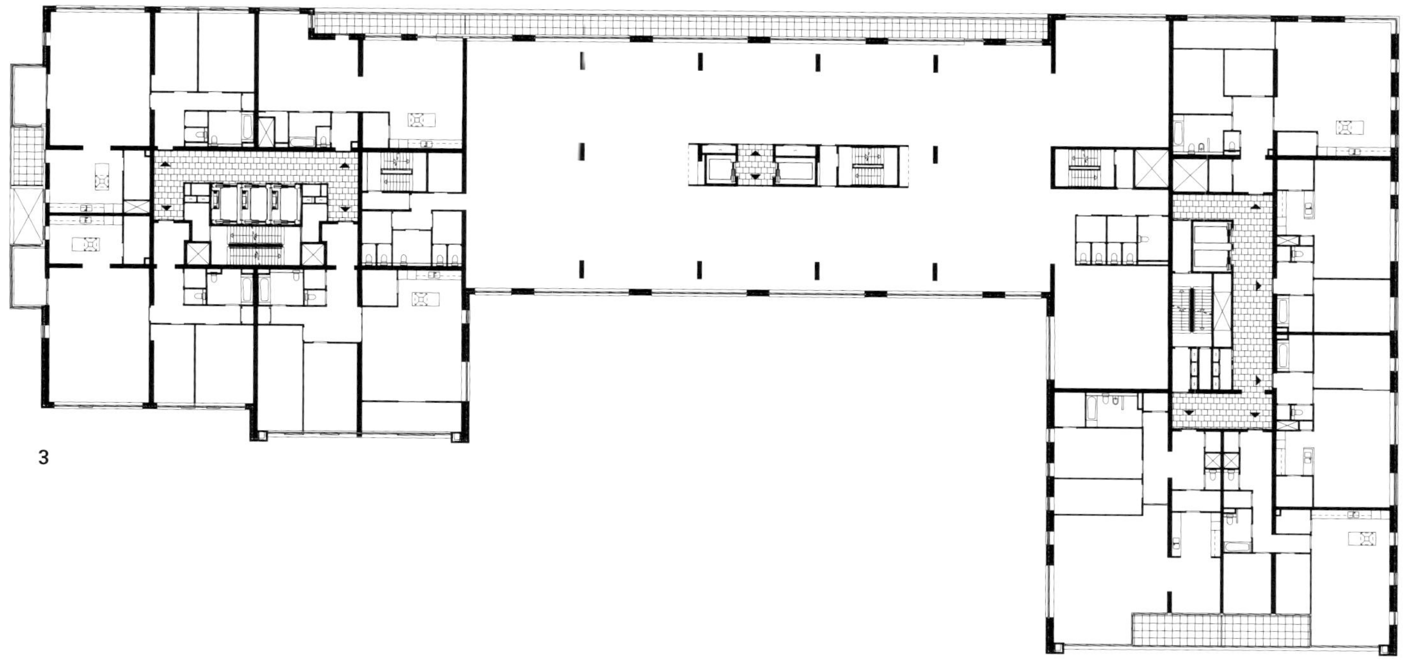

3

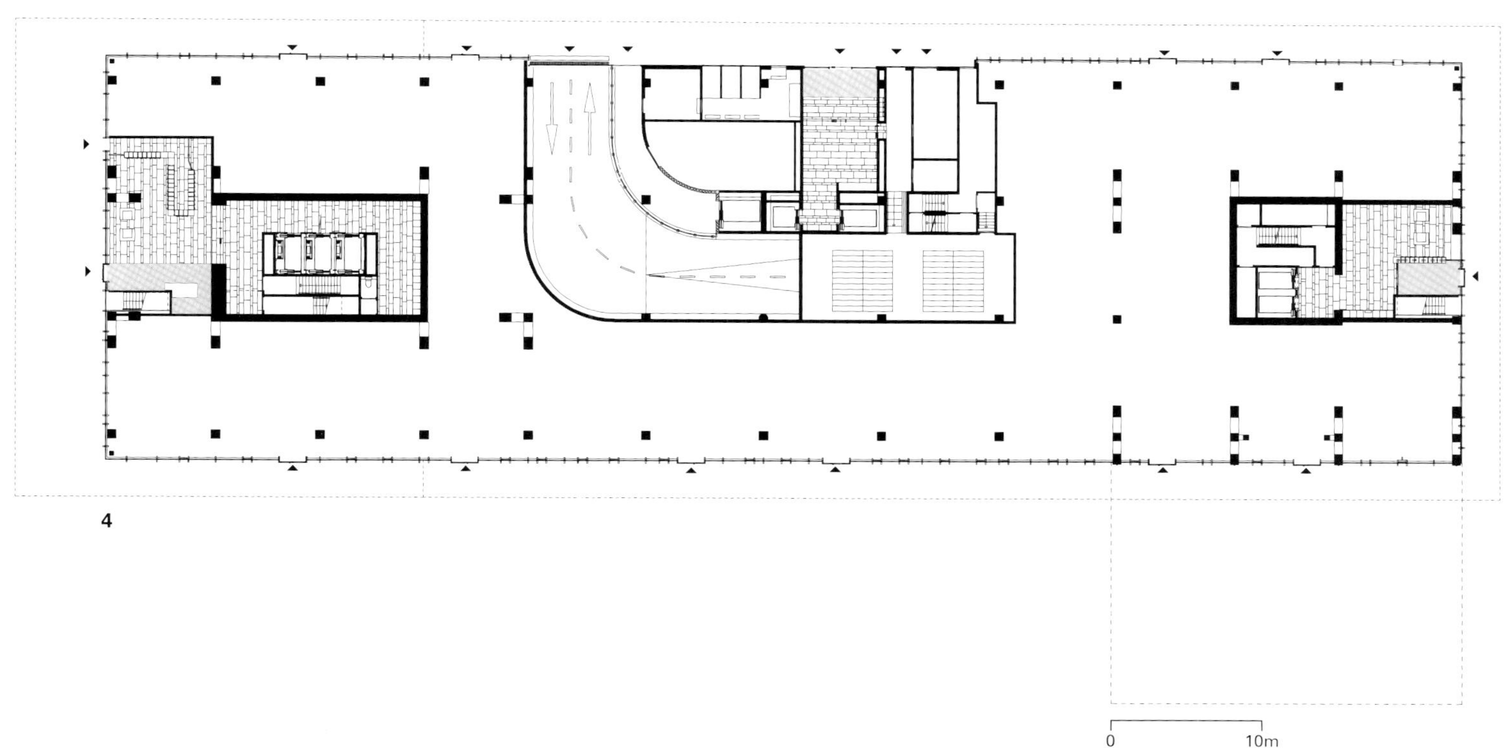

4

THE FAIRMONT DUBAI

DUBAI
UNITED ARAB EMIRATES

The Fairmont Dubai, situated on Sheikh Zayed Road is a mixed-use development containing a hotel, offices and apartments in a 36-storey tower over a basement and ground floor base structure.

The basement contains the nightclub, main kitchen and stores, hotel staff amenities and MEP services. The ground floor accommodates the main entrance, reception lobby, front office, central atrium, lounge, retail outlets, coffee shop, and an access lobby for the office and apartment floors. The second floor accommodates the business centre, bars, and meeting rooms and the fourth floor houses hotel administration and rentable office space.

The swimming pool, health club, gymnasium, aerobics and exercise rooms and landscaped roof garden are situated on the ninth floor.

Floors 10 to 32 offer 115 two- and three-bedroom apartments on the rear side while floors 10 to 20 comprise 110 hotel rooms and suites on the front side. An additional 220 hotel rooms are located over floors 21 to 30. Within the tower block, floors 31 to 35 comprise ethnic-style guest rooms, executive suites and royal/imperial/presidential suites. The top floor includes an attractive roof garden combined with a deluxe penthouse suite.

A multistorey car park for 665 cars is included in the design. It also contains water tanks, boiler rooms, pump rooms and electrical services at basement and ground floor levels. The roof of the car park block is reserved for AC chiller units and a chilled water pump room.

1

2

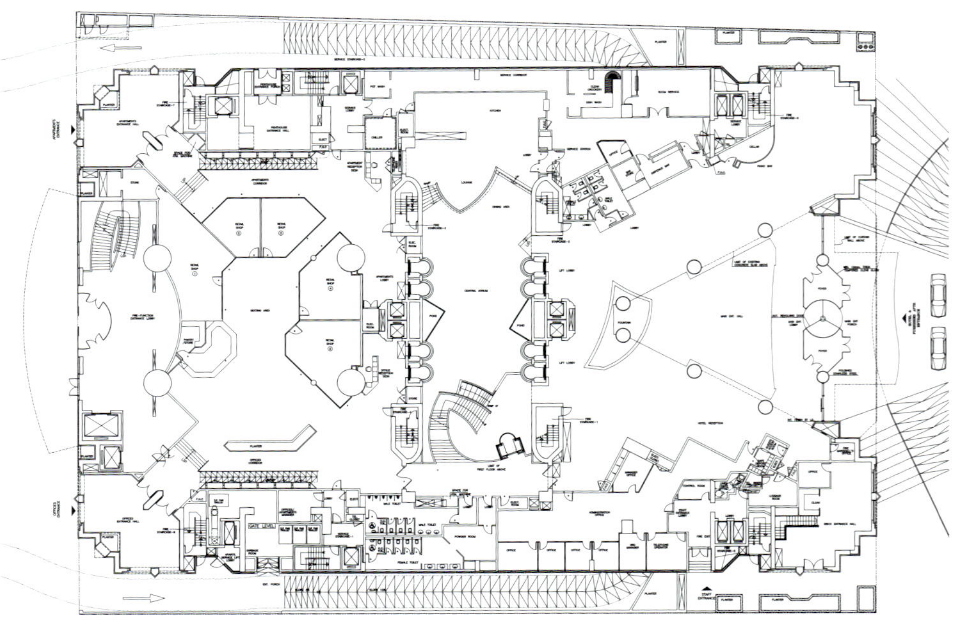

3

The Fairmont Dubai | **Location** Dubai, United Arab Emirates | **Completion date** 2002 | **Architect** Khatib & Alami C.E.C | **Client** H. E. Sh. Sultan Bin Khalifa Bin Zayed Al Nahayan | **Structural engineer** Khatib & Alami C.E.C. | **Mechanical engineer** Khatib & Alami C.E.C. | **Landscape architect** Desert Landscaping | **Contractor** Arabtic & Dubai Contracting Co. | **Height** 152.75 m/501 ft | **Above-ground storeys** 36 | **Basements** 1 | **Above-ground useable levels** 34 | **Mechanical levels** 2 | **Use** Hotel, residential, office | **Area of above-ground building** Tower 120,000 sq m/1,292,000 sq ft; car park 26,000 sq m/ 279,900 sq ft | **Structural materials** Concrete | **Other materials** Granite | **Cost** US$149.5 M

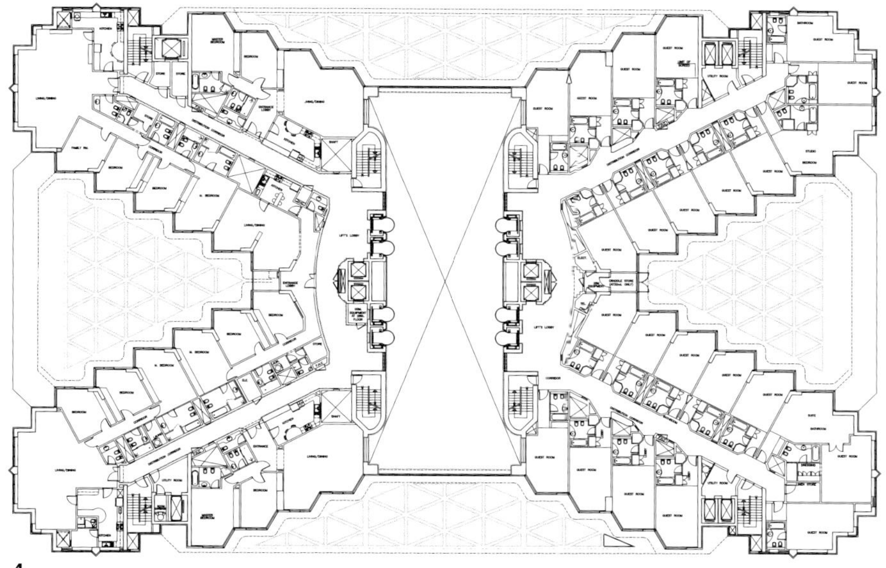
4

1&2 *General views*
3 *Ground floor plan*
4 *Typical hotel and residential floor plan*
5 *Fourth floor plan*

Photography: *Courtesy Khatib & Alami C.E.C*

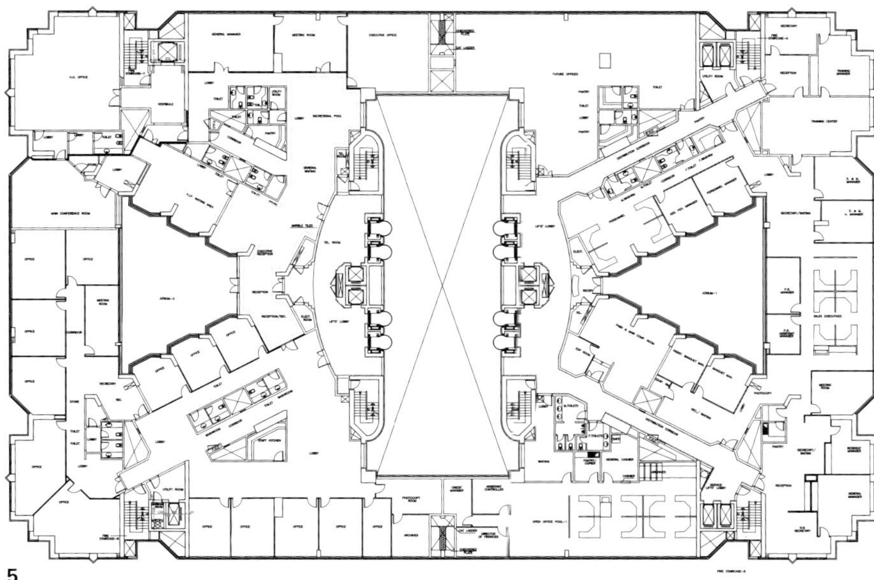
5

HOTEL ARTS BARCELONA

BARCELONA
SPAIN

Vila Olimpica, a 110,000-square-metre multi-use complex, with a five-star Ritz-Carlton hotel, a village-like retail centre and first-class office facilities, provides a rich focus of interest and activity within a defined waterfront environment. Located along the coast of the Mediterranean Sea, a 15-minute walk from the Ramblas, the complex was envisioned as a timely opportunity and a bold vision to bring the city to the sea and create a powerful sense of place.

The 482-room hotel complex combines all the amenities of a world-class business hotel with outstanding resort-like facilities. Restaurants and lounges, ballroom facilities, and a health club with a swimming pool afford the opportunity to mix business with relaxation and exercise. The hotel tower provides 58 suites and 27 apartments, which are accessed from their own private lobby. The office building, located directly across the Francisco de Aranda from the hotel and retail complex, is ideally situated for meetings with business travellers, and offers convenient access to the city. The five-storey structure is wrapped around a raised plaza and provides 13,000 square metres of office space, allowing for open floor plans and flexibility in interior planning.

1

2

Hotel Arts Barcelona at Vila Olimpica | **Location** Barcelona, Spain | **Completion date** 1992 (soft opening); 1994 (grand opening) | **Architect** Bruce Graham, FAIA, Design Partner, Skidmore, Owings & Merrill LLP, in association with Brufau, Obiol, Moya & Ass., SL (BOMA) | **Client** Travelstead Group | **Structural engineer** Skidmore, Owings & Merrill LLP, in association with BOMA | **Mechanical engineer** Skidmore, Owings & Merrill LLP, in association with Projectes | **Contractor** Bovis International (to June 1992); Shimizu | **Height** 154 m/505 ft | **Above-ground storeys** 45 | **Basements** 2 | **Above-ground useable levels** 45 | **Use** Hotel | **Area of above-ground building** 52,000 sq m/559,520 sq ft | **Structural materials** Steel, reinforced concrete | **Other materials** Aluminium, glass

3

1 *General view from marina*
2 *Exterior looking west*
3 *Porte-cochère at entry to building*
4 *Monumental fish sculpture by Frank Gehry*
5 *Tower at ground level reflecting pool*

Photography: *James Morris*

4

5

TOUR EDF PARIS LA DÉFENSE FRANCE

In 2001, Hines France delivered the 41-storey, 63,000-square-metre office tower in the La Défense high-rise business district just west of the city of Paris. The building, which stands 155 metres above street level is the result of a limited competition organised by Hines in 1995.

Henry N Cobb from New York-based Pei Cobb Freed & Partners designed the elliptical tower with a 93.5-metre conical shape carved into its base up to level 26. The distinctive tower blends elegantly with its surroundings; its position and form are calculated to respect the Louvre–La Défense axis while complementing its main counterparts on the esplanade: la Grande Arche and the CNIT. The entrance to the tower is situated on the axis perpendicular to the centre of the Grande Arche.

The EDF Tower's façade is clad in alternating bands of stainless steel and non-reflective glass to optimise natural daylight. A circular floating entrance canopy, 23 metres wide, creates a comforting sense of arrival from the plaza.

Inside the tower, raised floors allow for technologically advanced communications, with average floor plates of 1350 square metres and a floor-to-ceiling height of 2.7 metres.

Initiated by Hines in the mid 1990s, at a time when the La Défense area was in a state of depression, the success of the project has created a new dynamic for the whole area.

2

3

1

1 *North façade and cradle*
2 *The Tour EDT mirrored in a fountain by Agam*
3 *Lobby, detail*
4 *View from the La Défense statue*
5 *Main entrance seen from beneath the canopy*
6 *Lobby and restaurant access*
7 *Level 23 floor plan*

Photography: *GD Morand, courtesy Hines France*

Tour EDF | **Location** Paris La Défense, France | **Completion date** 2001 | **Architect** Pei Cobb Freed & Partners; SRA-Architectes | **Client** EDF (50%); Caisse des Dépôts et des Consignations (Ecureuil-Vie 25%, CNP 25%) | **Developer** Hines France | **Structural engineer** Setec | **Mechanical engineer** Trouvin | **Contractor** Bateg | **Height** 155 m/509 ft above street level; 148 m/486 ft above La Défense Esplanade | **Above-ground storeys** 41 | **Basements** 4 | **Above-ground useable levels** 40 | **Mechanical levels** 1 | **Use** Office | **Site area** 3700 sq m/39,812 sq ft | **Area of above-ground building** 63,000 sq m/677,880 sq ft; typical floor area 1315 sq m/14,139 sq ft | **Structural materials** Concrete | **Other materials** Stainless steel, non-reflective glass

4

5

6

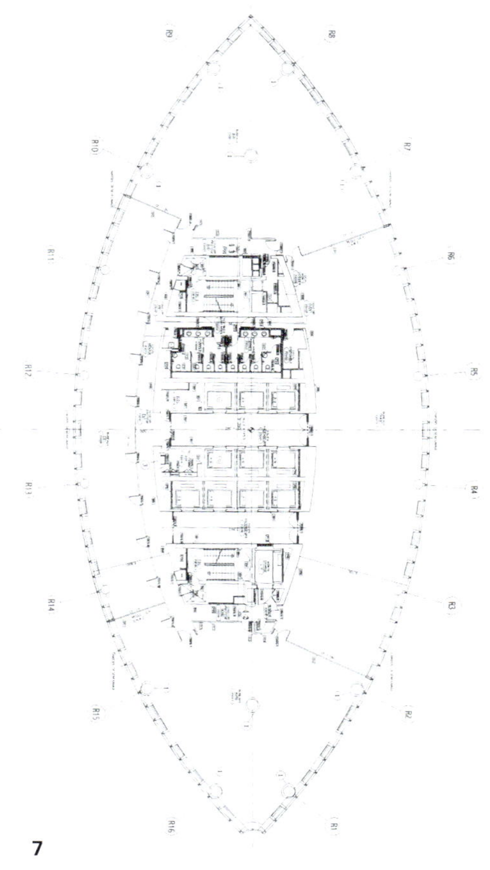

7

COEUR DÉFENSE PARIS LA DÉFENSE FRANCE

This is the largest corporate project built in Europe in recent decades, encompassing 350,000 square metres of floor space. It stands in the heart of La Défense, beside the historic east–west axis of Paris that runs from the Louvre to the Grand Arch.

The two 180-metre-high towers are linked by an 'inter-tower', and three low buildings (eight levels), all connected by a large atrium that rises to 44 metres and covers more than one hectare of floor area. The typology chosen shuns the model of thick towers, preferring thin streamlined volumes that generate work spaces near glazed façades, and are thus open to daylight.

The atrium is a complex space sitting on a three-level base, the highest of which connects to the Charles de Gaulle esplanade and provides access to all the buildings, restaurants, services and conference centre. This huge space accommodates 10,000 people. Under the atrium are physical plant rooms, archives, delivery bays, kitchens, taxi stands and five levels of parking space containing 3000 slots. The project meets the latest 'high quality environment' standards.

Together, the five buildings create an impression of lightness and modernity, smooth and white, in the manner of the Grand Arch.

1

1 *General view from Esplanade Charles de Gaulle*
2 *Model showing view over atrium*
3 *General side view with the Arche de la Défense behind and looking towards Paris*
4 *Original sketch by Jean-Paul Viguier*
5 *Typical floor plan, lower floors*
6 *Typical floor plan, upper floors*

Photography: *Nicolas Borel*
Model: *Alain Hugon*

2

3

Coeur Défense | **Location** Paris La Défense, France | **Completion date** 2001 | **Architect** Jean-Paul Viguier SA d' Architecture | **Client** Tanagra – Unibail Paris | **Structural engineer** Setec, AR&C (structural glazing), Interface (façade) | **Mechanical engineer** Sfica Capri Acoustique | **Contractor** Bouygues | **Height** 161 m/528 ft | **Above-ground storeys** 40 | **Basements** 5 | **Above-ground useable levels** 39 | **Mechanical levels** 1 | **Use** Office | **Area of above-ground building** 199,500 sq m/2,147,000 sq ft | **Structural materials** Reinforced concrete, curtain wall, structural glazing and metal (atrium) | **Cost** €372 M (budget)

4

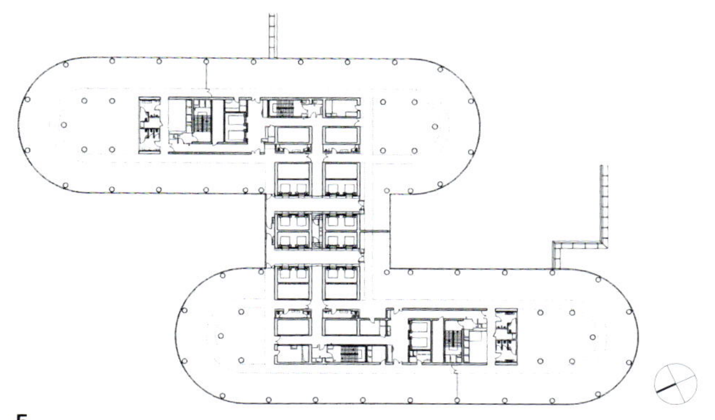

5

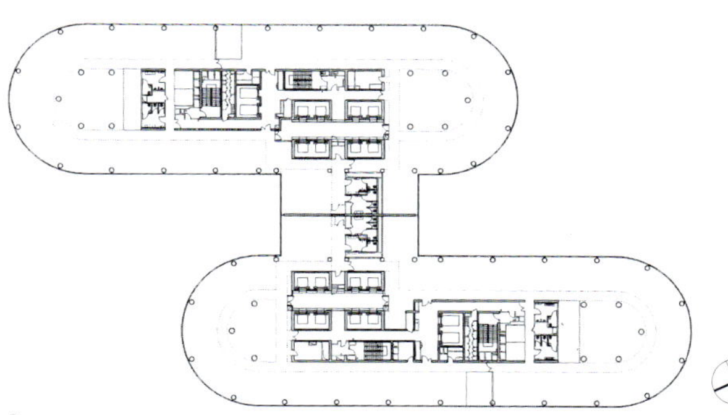

6

HEADQUARTERS RWE AG ESSEN GERMANY

The Ruhr area is striving in numerous ways to evolve into a modern economic region less dependant on the traditional heavy industries. Rheinisch-Westfälische Energie AG (RWE) is one of the pioneers of this change. The new RWE glass tower at the main railway station in Essen is a visible symbol of the transformation of an energy conglomerate into a modern service enterprise.

The approach to the cylindrical highrise leads through an urban loggia of aluminium louvres on delicate columns and covered in photovoltaic cells. The elegant, spacious lobby in fair-faced concrete features a curving staircase, which leads to the garden level, and a creatively designed ceiling with indirect lighting, which transfers the central loads of the highrise above to the surrounding columns.

The highrise is divided into base, shaft and capital like a Greek column. The conical base on the garden side is invisible from the entrance due to the slope of the site. The office floors were designed according to criteria for modern and flexible workstations. The employees can control the internal climate at the workstations via individual panels installed in each office, and the floor-height glass façades offer fascinating vistas across the entire Ruhr area. The rooms for the board of directors and the executives are located at the top of the tower.

The uniqueness of the high-rise capital stems from a pillared disk above the roof, which was originally slated for use as a heliport. When this plan was abandoned, the disk was transformed into an emblem. Equipped with louvres, it now serves as a shading component and a platform for the façade maintenance system. The crown of the high-rise is topped by an antenna, bringing the total height of the building to 162 metres.

The RWE highrise is widely regarded as a prime example of a pragmatic solution for a complex building task. The shimmering cylinder has become a new symbol of responsible energy management.

1

2

3

Headquarters RWE AG | **Location** Essen, Germany | **Completion date** 1996 | **Architect** Ingenhoven Overdiek und Partner | **Client** Hochtief Projektentwicklung GmbH & Co. | **Structural engineer** Hochtief AG, Happold Consulting Engineers Ltd. | **Mechanical engineer** Happold Consulting Engineers Ltd. | **Landscape architect** Weber Klein Maas, Ingenhoven Overdiek und Partner | **Contractor** Hochtief AG | **Height** 127 m/417 ft; 162 m/531.5 ft with antenna | **Above-ground storeys** 31 | **Basements** 2 | **Above-ground useable levels** 29 | **Mechanical levels** 2 | **Use** Office | **Site area** 4800 sq m/51,648 sq ft | **Area of above-ground building** 25,200 sq m/271,152 sq ft

1–3 *General views*
4 *Roof plan, 1:750*
5 *Conference level plan, 1:750*
6 *Façade detail*
7 *Conference room plan, 1:750*
8 *Typical floor plan, 1:750*
9 *Penthouse roof garden*
10 *Ground floor elevator lobby*

Photography: *HG Esch, Holger Knauf, courtesy Ingenhoven und Partner Architekten*

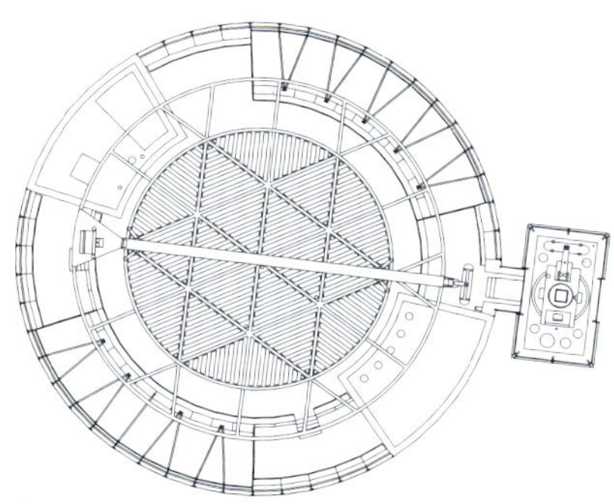

4

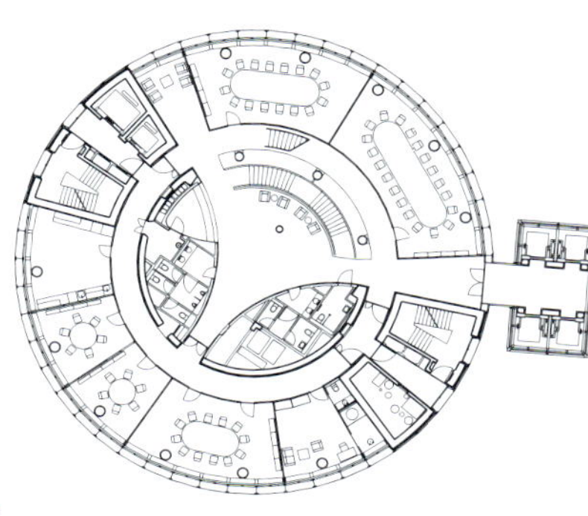

5

6

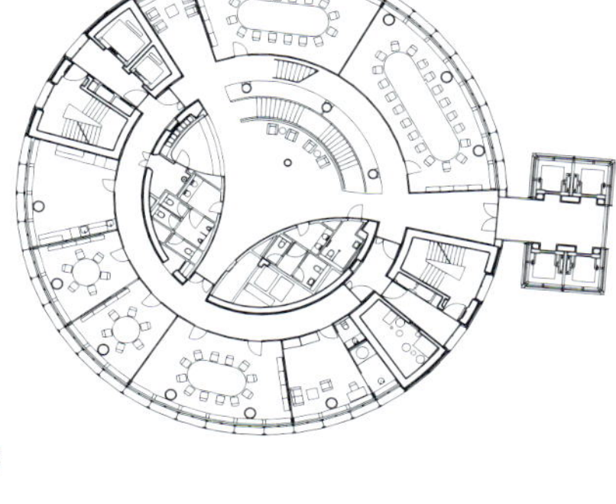

7

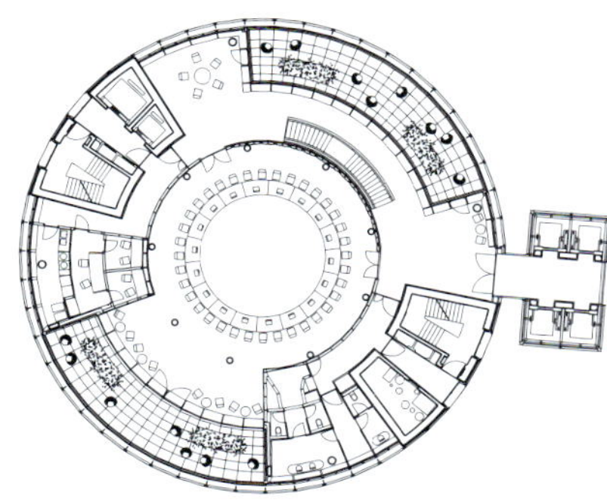

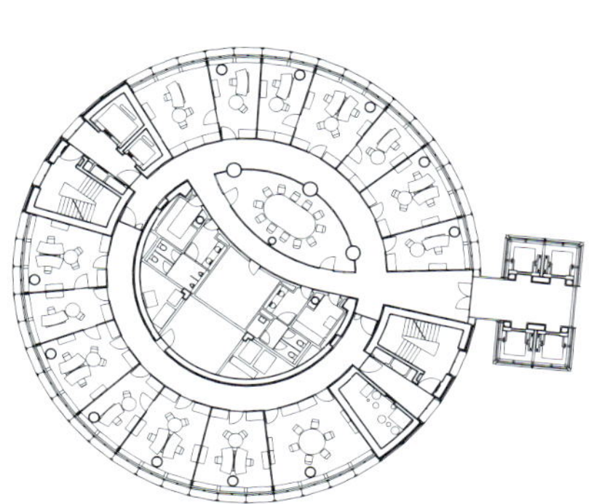

8

9

10

POST TOWER BONN GERMANY

The Post Tower represents a new typology for an office tower. The north and south half shells are separated by 7.2-metre-wide spaces, which are divided by glass floors into nine-storey skygardens. At the top, a two-storey space and a penthouse with a screened roof terrace define the executive areas. Two groups of glass lifts serve all floors and allow dramatic views of the city and the landscape.

The structure and façade display advanced and innovative solutions: for example, the structural reinforced concrete slabs not only act as load-bearing elements, they contain an integrated piping system for heating and cooling, and are coffered to minimise dead weight. The curved surfaces of the coffers also act as light reflectors. Many other parts of the structure are similarly multifunctional.

The interior follows the typical German standard of a systematic office layout. A special glass partition system fulfills the goals of visual openness and transparency, achieved through clear and translucent surfaces, and also meets the occupants' need for privacy. Lighting and lighting art are integral parts of the architecture. The functional office lighting and the façade lighting vary with the occupancy of the building and result in dynamic colour variations.

'Breathing in the wind' describes the balanced airflow through the different façade layers and spaces, based on the twin-shell façade concept. The building is ventilated year-round through the air space between the shells without using the central mechanical system. The comfort and energy concept is controlled by the individual user with regards to the room temperature, air quality and office lighting.

With the building envelope, building structure and building environmental system working together, the energy demand of this building is predicted to be less than 100 kWh/m^2 per year for heating, ventilation, cooling and artificial lighting.

1

2

3

4

Post Tower | **Location** Bonn, Germany | **Completion date** 2003 | **Architect** Murphy/Jahn, Inc. | **Client** Deutsche Post Bauen GmbH | **Structural engineer** Werner Sobek Ingenieure GmbH | **Mechanical engineer** Brandi Consult GmbH | **Landscape architect** Peter Walker & Partners | **Height** (tower) Glass façade: 162 m/533 ft; Roof level: 152 m/499 ft | **Above-ground storeys** 45 | **Basements** 5 | **Use** Office | **Area of above-ground building** (tower) 65,323 sq m/703,100 sq ft | **Structural materials** Concrete, steel | **Other materials** Glass, steel

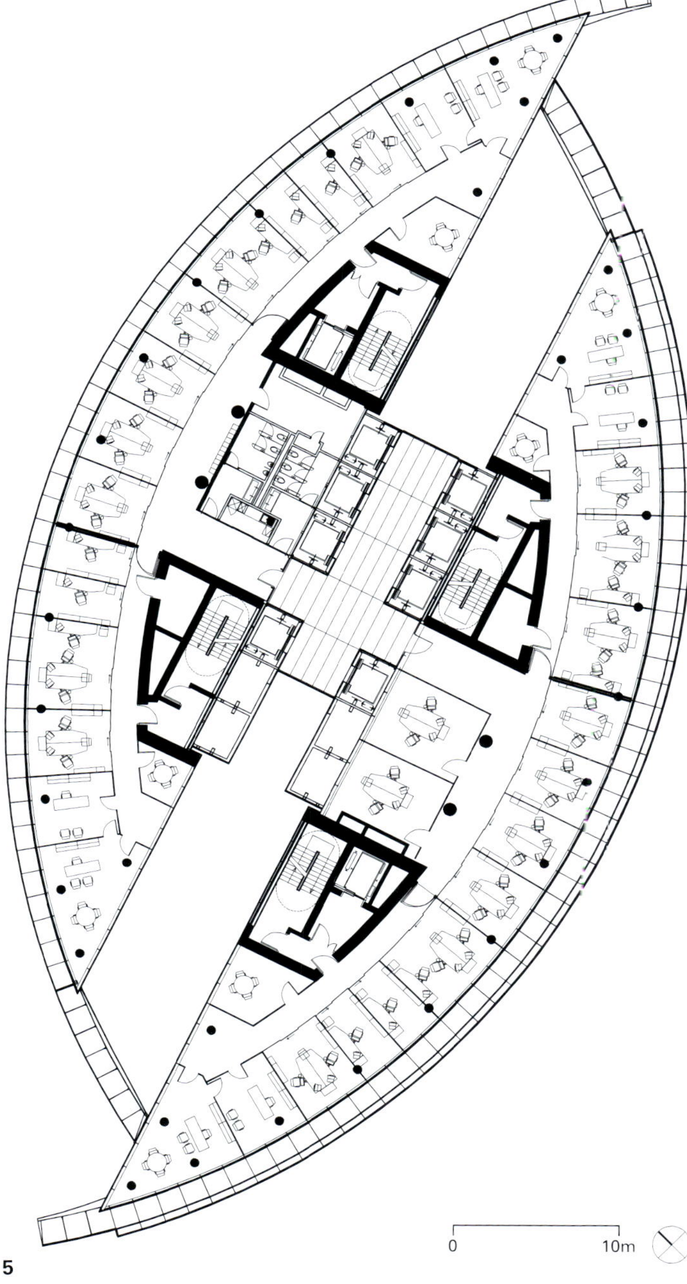

5

6

7

8

9

1,7 *General view*
2 *Entrance detail*
3 *Lobby*
4 *Skylobby*
5 *Typical floor plan*
6 *Façade detail*
8 *View from skylobby*
9 *Dual wall façade*

Photography: *Andreas Keller (1,4,8–9); HG Esch (2,7); Atelier Altenkirch (3); Josef Gartner & Co. (6)*

LA TOUR CRÉDIT LYONNAIS

LYON
FRANCE

Since the Gallo-Romans first founded the fortified city of Lugdunum, Old Lyon grew through the Middle Ages along the steep hillside and the banks of the River Saône. In the 15th century, with the construction of bridges over the river, the peninsula formed by the confluence of the Rhône and the Saône opened up a new area for the expansion of the constricted city where for several centuries thereafter life and activities of the Lyonnais remained concentrated.

Industrialisation and overcrowding of the peninsula in the 19th and 20th centuries left the city no choice but to reach out east, into the plain of Brotteaux, offering almost limitless expansion for the vision of a greater Lyon. There, the Renewal Authority of the Part-Dieu planned and created a new, regional transportation hub, symbolised by its most visible and recognisable landmark, the Crédit Lyonnais tower.

In 1972 at its conception, the fundamental focus was not only on the architecture of the tower; it also aimed to bring to the nascent metropolis a new, individual and unique image.

The cylindrical shape of the Crédit Lyonnais tower responds to this need. The vertical triangular notch facing west interrupts the circular façade from top to bottom, and by its orientation pays homage to the Old City. The elegance of its proportions is further accentuated by the glass pyramid crowning the tower. The deeply recessed glass of 2900 precast window units enlivens the curved surface of the façade by the ever-changing play of light and shadow. The soft red colour produced by polishing the cast stone units, made up of granite aggregates and sands, harmonises with the ochres, browns and pinks of the traditional Lyonnais tile rooftops and extends the city skyward.

1

2

La Tour Crédit Lyonnais | **Location** Lyon, France | **Completion date** 1977 | **Architect** Cossutta & Associates, Architects PC | **Client** S.C.C. (Société des Centres Commerciaux); Crédit Lyonnais; Chaîne Hôtelière Frantel | **Structural engineer** Weiskopf & Pickworth, New York; B.E.T. Jean L. Sarf, Paris | **Mechanical engineer** Cosentini Associates, New York; AGIP Technique, France; BETSE/Cabinet Martin, France | **Construction manager** CO.TE.BA | **Contractor** Thinet et Cie, Boulogne s/Seine, France | **Height** 164 m/537 ft | **Above-ground storeys** 42 | **Basements** 3 | **Above-ground useable levels** 42 | **Use** Office, Radisson SAS Hotel | **Site area** 5627 sq m/60,568 sq ft | **Area of above-ground building** 63,853 sq m/687,327 sq ft | **Structural materials** Reinforced concrete | **Cost** US$40.83 M

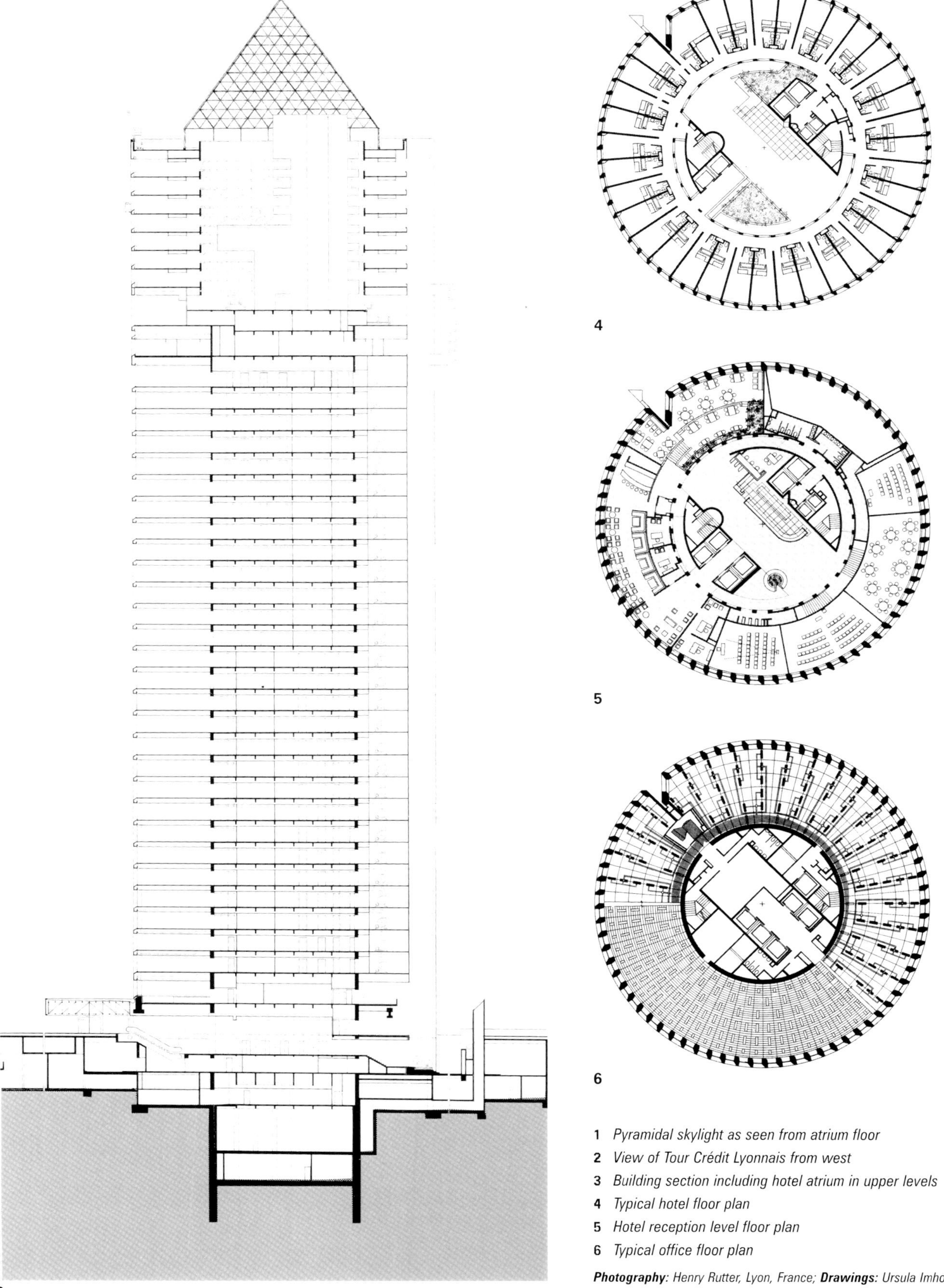

3

4

5

6

1 *Pyramidal skylight as seen from atrium floor*
2 *View of Tour Crédit Lyonnais from west*
3 *Building section including hotel atrium in upper levels*
4 *Typical hotel floor plan*
5 *Hotel reception level floor plan*
6 *Typical office floor plan*

Photography: *Henry Rutter, Lyon, France;* ***Drawings:*** *Ursula Imhof*

INTERCONTINENTAL WARSZAWA

WARSAW
POLAND

The five-star InterContinental Warszawa is the tallest hotel in Poland. Located in the heart of Warsaw, it has 326 guest rooms and 75 residence suites.

The building's unique feature is a concrete pillar that spans 16 storeys between the 5-storey pedestal base and the 24-storey section above. More than merely an architectural gesture, its function is to allow sunlight to penetrate through the 'cut-out' section of the building to the apartment block behind the tower. When illuminated at night, it adds an exciting component to the Warsaw skyline.

The structure is of steel-reinforced concrete, perforated with windows and stiffed by a concrete core of lifts and staircases. The façade blends in with those of other high-rise buildings in Warsaw. The double glass-aluminium panels create an animated skin of screen-printed glass, which changes its appearance depending on the time of day and the quality of light.

The pedestal of the building is suspended from beams below the cut-away section, allowing a column-free lobby and reception areas filled with natural daylight. It provides unobstructed space for the hotel's public areas such as the ballroom, ten conference rooms and themed bars and restaurants.

The 43rd and 44th floors of the hotel house the wellness centre with its main attraction – a 6 x 18-metre swimming pool, the highest indoor pool in Europe. It provides spectacular views of Warsaw, from the Old Town in the north to the Vistula River in the south.

1

1 *View from the entrance to the Congress Hall*
2 *View from the East side – central Park Garden*
3 *View from the Palace of Culture and Science*
4 *View from the hotel pool to the Palace of Culture and Science tower*
5 *Ground floor plan*
6 *Typical floor plan, residence suites*

Photography: *Wojciech Krynski (1,4); Wojciech Poplawski (2,3)*

InterContinental Warszawa | **Location** Warsaw, Poland | **Completion date** 2004 | **Architect** Tadeusz Spychala; associate architects: Wojciech Poplawski, Willibald Fürst | **Client** InterContinental Hotels Group; Warimpex Finanz und Beteiligungs AG; UBM | **Structural engineer** Projektierungsbüro GmbH | **Interior architects** Jestico & Whiles; InterContinental Hotels Group; Projektierungsbüro GmbH | **Contractor** PORR Projekt und Hochbau AG | **Height** 164 m/538 ft | **Above-ground storeys** 46 | **Basements** 5 | **Above-ground useable levels** 45 | **Mechanical levels** 1 | **Use** Hotel, including guest rooms, residence suites, conference centre, wellness centre, bars and restaurants | **Site area** 1900 sq m/20,444 sq ft | **Area of above-ground building** 43,800 sq m/471,288 sq ft | **Structural materials** Reinforced concrete, curtain wall, steel | **Other materials** Natural stone, glass, stainless steel, aluminium | **Cost** €113 M

2

3

4

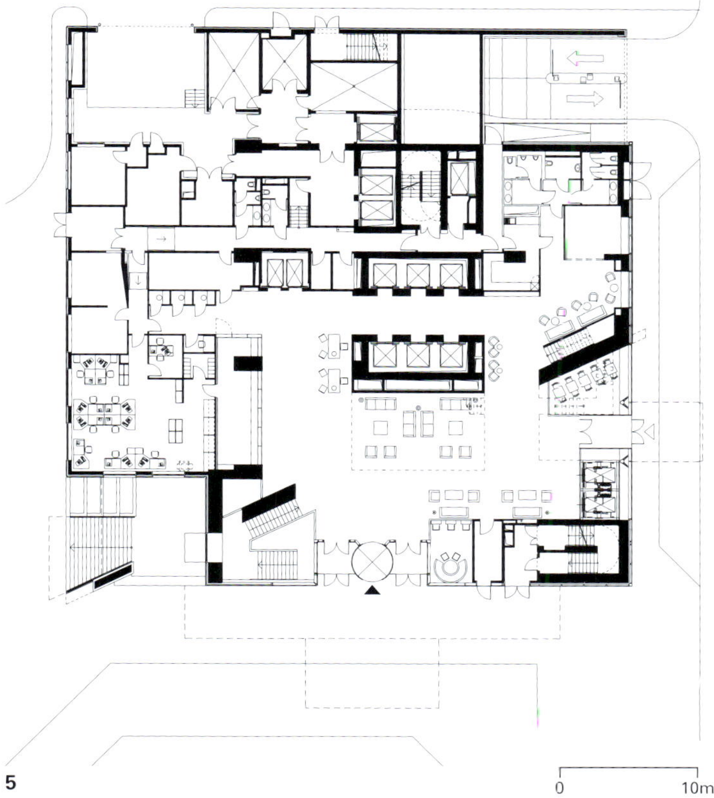

5

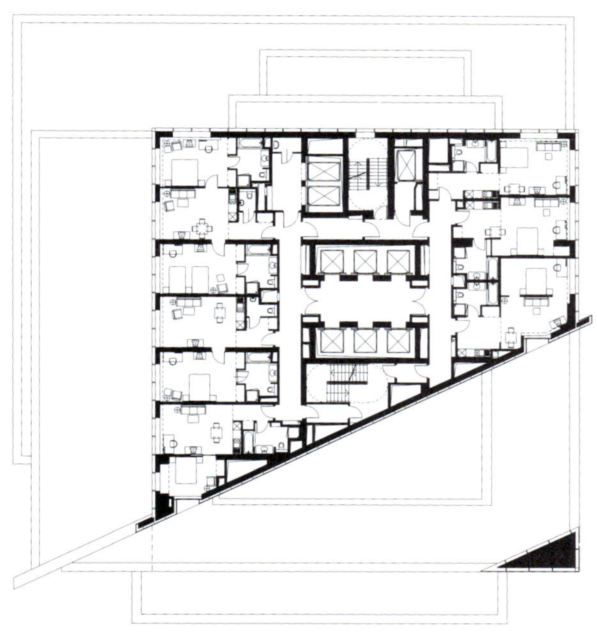
6

BEETHAM TOWER

MANCHESTER
UNITED KINGDOM

The developer's initial brief was for a substantial mixed-use development of exceptional design quality, incorporating residential apartments, a Hilton hotel and a commercial office building. Combined with Manchester City Council's aspirations for a landmark building at a gateway location, this provided the opportunity to create an elegant and beautiful tower that will contain the highest living space in the United Kingdom.

The development is split into three elements: a 169-metre-tall tower containing guest bedrooms and residential apartments; a lower, 'podium' element containing the hotel public areas; and a stand-alone office building.

The narrow floorplates required for residential accommodation allowed the creation of an elegant tower with a very high slenderness (height-to-width) ratio. A dramatic cantilever at level 23, the floor occupied by the hotel's destination (sky) bar, articulates the separation between hotel and residential.

The tower envelope will be a fully sealed, unitised curtain walling system. The façade design will emphasise the verticality of the building. Elements such as the projecting, shading fins and the perforated, anodised aluminium panels, which conceal opening lights and ventilation terminals, are aligned vertically so that they run across a number of floors.

The residential apartments on the south-facing elevation are protected by a glazed 'buffer' zone, a semi-external space formed between the double-glazed inner skin and glass-louvred outer skin of the unitised cladding. This buffer zone provides an extension to the living accommodation with spectacular views across the city and the surrounding countryside.

While the lower levels of the building create new public spaces for people to enjoy, the top is light and appears to challenge gravity. The glazed skin of the buffer zone to the south façade cantilevers above roof level to form a crystalline 'blade', which blurs the distinction between the building and the sky and dematerialises the crown of the building.

1

1–3 *General views*
4 *Typical floor plan*

Renderings: *Courtesy Ian Simpson Architects*

Beetham Tower | **Location** Manchester, United Kingdom | **Completion date** 2006 | **Architect** Ian Simpson Architects | **Client** Beetham Organization Limited | **Structural engineer** Cantor Seinuk | **Mechanical engineer** WSP | **Contractor** Carillion plc | **Height** 169 m/554 ft | **Above-ground storeys** 48 | **Basements** 2 | **Above-ground useable levels** 48 | **Mechanical levels** 2 | **Use** Hotel, residential, commercial | **Site area** 4645 sq m/50,000 sq ft | **Area of above-ground building** 45,428 sq m/489,000 sq ft (Phase 1) | **Structural materials** Post-tensioned concrete structure to the tower, steel structure to the podium | **Other materials** Fully glazed, unitised curtain walling system to the tower, polished precast concrete cladding to the podium | **Cost** £55 M

2

3

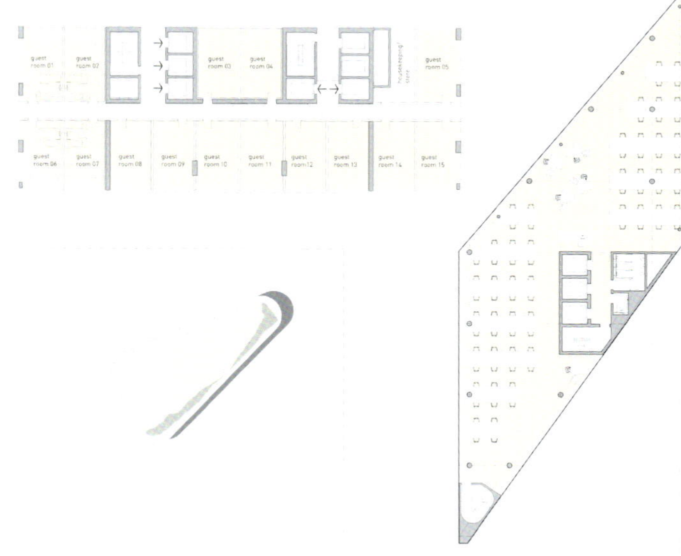

4

ALYE PARUSA MOSCOW RUSSIA

Alye Parusa ('scarlet sails') is located in a scenic corner to the northwest of Moscow, on the banks of the Moscow River.

Building design in the first section offers remarkably high ceilings (up to 3.2 metres), panoramic windows and spacious balconies. In the second section, apartment space is not quite as large and more efficiently organised. The floor-to-ceiling corner glazing design in the apartments offers panoramic views of the Moscow River, the Strogino floodlands and the Silver Pine Woods. Each building is crowned with penthouses with spacious terraces and winter gardens. Moscow's largest penthouse, which tops the 175.6-metre-high Building IV, features a helicopter pad and a swimming pool. An important detail of the Alye Parusa design is a system of overhead galleries that provide indoor connections between the buildings.

The estate's two-level promenade embankment includes cascade fountains, a rotunda, moorings for boats, and an operating lighthouse. The yacht club is situated on the embankment's lower level, on the water line, and its interior imitates the hull of a real yacht: even the floors in the club are made of teak wood, like a boat deck. The club's windows look over the embankment where mooring areas have been constructed and furnished with the latest Marinetek equipment to berth up to 35 boats at a time. The yacht club includes a working lighthouse of red-pink bricks, trimmed with travertine stone. Forged-iron dragons support a viewing platform that houses the navigation light.

Alye Parusa provides residents with many choices for recreation. Building I houses a water park, an artificial surf swimming pool, and a 6-lane, 25-metre swimming pool with a diving tower. The Spa Zone includes three Finnish saunas, three Turkish baths, an ice-water pool, Austrian low-temperature baths and a fitness gymnasium. Building II houses a seven-lane bowling alley and Building III includes two tennis courts for adults and one for children. The professional soccer field on the estate has special grass carpeting used for golf courses. A running track surrounds the perimeter. The vast territory of the Alye Parusa estate also includes an apple orchard with a fountain, an alpine-style garden with exotic plants, and playgrounds for children.

1

2

1 *General view*
2 *Promenade*
3,5,6,8 *Penthouse level floor plans, levels 45, 46, 47, 48*
4 *Penthouse exterior detail*
7 *Entrance*
9 *Penthouse levels 45–48, detail*

Photography: *Courtesy DON-Stroy*

Alye Parusa | **Location** Moscow, Russia | **Completion date** 2006 | **Architect** TROMOS | **Client** DON-Stroy | **Structural engineer** SMU-1 | **Mechanical engineer** SMU-1 | **General contractor** SMU-1 construction department | **Height** 175.6 m/576 ft | **Above-ground storeys** Tower IV 48 | **Basements** 2 | **Mechanical levels** 2 | **Use** Residential, office, entertainment | **Site area** approx 6 ha/14.8 acres | **Building area** 60,300 sq m/648,828 sq ft, including 49,208 sq m/529,478 sq ft of residential area | **Materials** Natural stone, brick, steel, iron

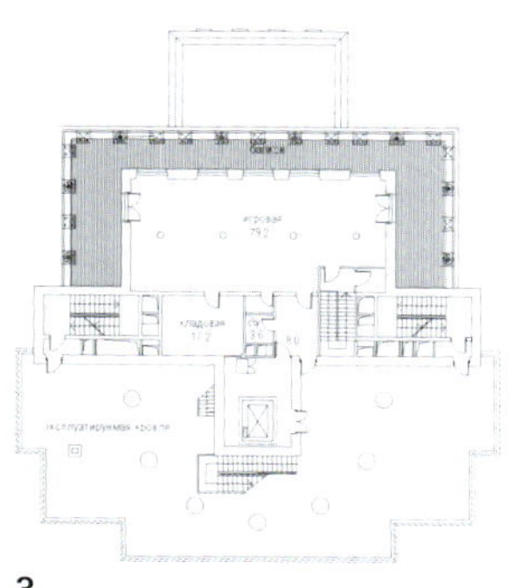

3

4

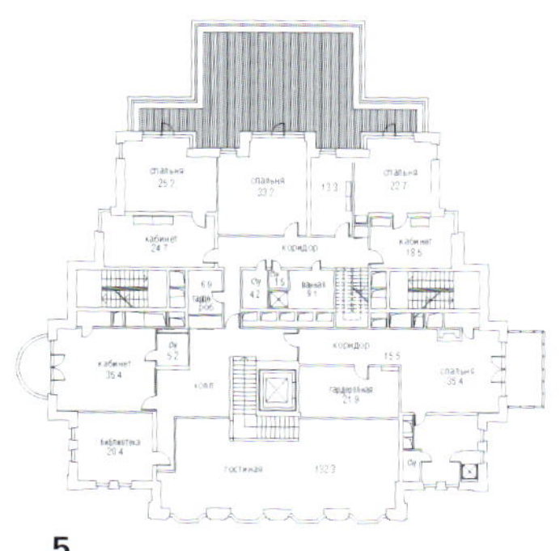

5

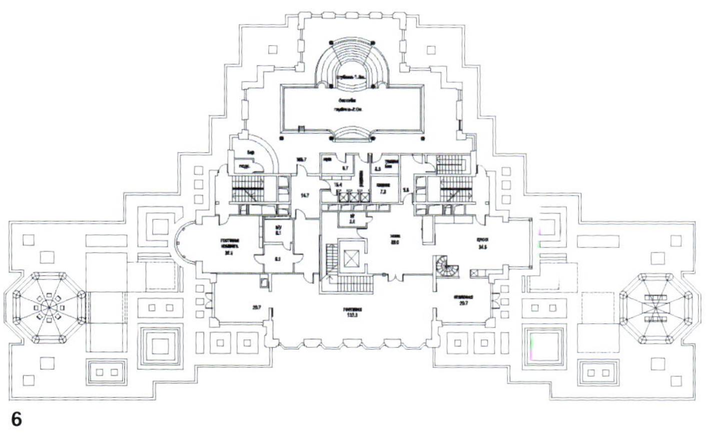

6

7

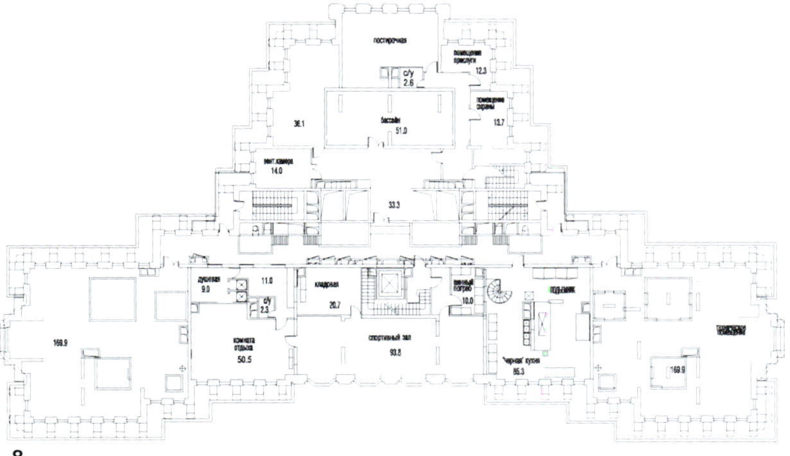

8

9

JUMEIRAH BEACH RESIDENCE

DUBAI
UNITED ARAB EMIRATES

The first major mass residential development in the Middle East, the Jumeirah Beach Residence will overlook The Palm Jumeirah, one of the three man-made 'Palm Islands' off the coast of Dubai. Overlooking this magnificent site, the residences will embody luxury, comfort and style, attracting both regional and international attention.

The 36 high-rise towers range in size and scope, but they all adhere to equally superior quality, fantastic views over the Palm Islands development and global prestige. Each tower will be serviced and decorated to the highest standard.

The Jumeirah Beach Residence shows the innovative, dynamic and sympathetic character of one of the world's fastest growing tourist destinations, and is a signature design statement that sets a new standard for residential developments.

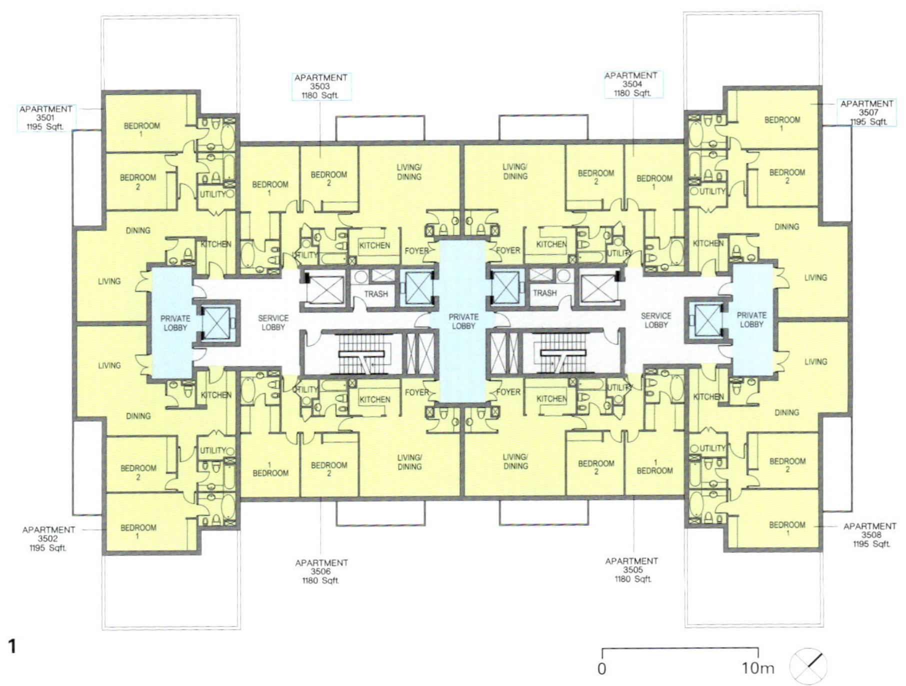

1

2

Jumeirah Beach Residence | **Location** Dubai, United Arab Emirates | **Completion** 2007 | **Design architect** Wimberly Allison Tong & Goo (WATG) | **Client** Dubai Properties (formerly Tecom) | **Structural engineer** BG and E | **Mechanical engineer** Roberts and Partners | **Landscape architect** Al Khatib Cracknel | **Height** 177 m/581 ft (tallest building) | **Above-ground storeys** 55 | **Above-ground useable levels** 55 | **Use** Residential, office, retail, entertainment, recreation | **Site area** 1.3 million sq m/14 million sq ft | **Structural materials** Reinforced concrete | **Cost** DHS 5.2 billion

3

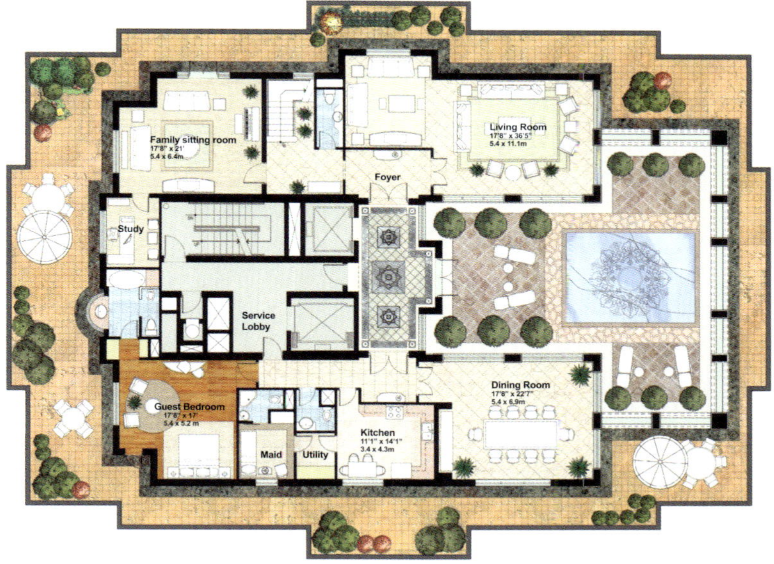

4

1 *Tower A series, 35th level*

2 *Night view, rendering*

3 *Tower A series, penthouse apartment (upper level)*

4 *Tower A series, penthouse apartment (lower level)*

5 *Rendering of 1.7-kilometre-long project, seen from the sea*

Renderings: *Courtesy Wimberly Allison Tong & Goo*

5

VOROBYOVY HILLS MOSCOW RUSSIA

Vorobyovy Hills is one of Moscow's most elevated residential estates, commanding panoramic views over the Russian capital. All seven Vorobyovy Hills buildings rest on a single five-level stylobate, the roof of which is an extremely complex technical structure, and Moscow's largest at the time of completion. The stylobate guard walls are protected by railings of high-tensile triplex laminated glass. The design of the stylobate integrates a natural elevation drop of 20 metres, while connecting design elements with the terrain and resolving functional problems.

The original civil engineering design addressed the problem of constructing the foundations of the project in complex soil conditions. Approximately 4000 piles, each 30 metres long and with 80 tonnes bearing capacity, were used to lay a 1.5-metre-thick reinforced concrete monolith foundation plate. Ventilated façades are decorated with coloured panels, ceramic granite, and natural rock. The colour spectrum is a combination of blue shades with ivory tones. Natural stone and wood is used for the entrance halls and elevator halls.

Apartment layouts are highly variable. Apartments of the high-rise buildings have rounded walls, while those in the lower buildings use corner glazing and bay windows. The top level of each building is cascade-roofed with terraced apartments and penthouses. A glass gallery-type passageway links all seven Vorobyovy Hills buildings.

Infrastructure includes recreation and sports amenities that range from a supermarket located in the stylobate to tennis courts. The highlight of the estate is a 10,000-square-metre water park. A green zone on the stylobate includes large groves of conifers, a fruit orchard, shrubs and bushes.

When the Setun estate construction is completed, the two estates will become a single 15-hectare entity, sharing the same infrastructure and premises. An elevated passage gallery will connect one building of the Setun estate with the stylobate of the Vorobyovy Hills estate, so the residents of both estates will have immediate access to the embankment over the lake.

1

Vorobyovy Hills | **Location** Moscow, Russia | **Completion date** 2005 | **Architect** TROMOS | **Client** DON-Stroy | **Structural engineer** SMU-2 | **Mechanical engineer** SMU-2 | **General contractor** SMU-2 | **Height** 161 m/528 ft (buildings 1 and 3); 178 m/584 ft (building 2) | **Above-ground storeys** 43 (buildings 1 and 3); 48 (building 2); 23 (building 4); 20 (building 5); 18 (building 6); 16 (building 7) | **Basements** 5 | **Mechanical levels** 5 | **Use** Residential, office, entertainment facilities, retail | **Site area** 4.7 ha/11.6 acres | **Building area** 286,253 sq m/3,080,082 sq ft including 191,000 sq m/2,055,160 sq ft housing area | **Materials** Natural stone, brick, ceramic, steel, iron, concrete

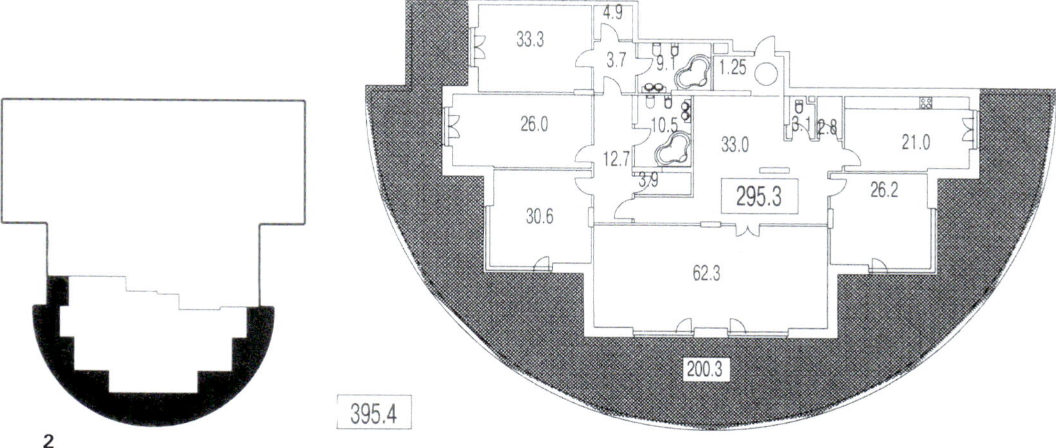

2

3

4

1,3,4 *General views*

2 *Penthouse apartment, building 1, level 36 floor plan*

***Photography**: courtesy DON-Stroy*

30 ST MARY AXE – SWISS RE HEADQUARTERS

LONDON
UNITED KINGDOM

30 St Mary Axe is London's first environmental skyscraper. A comprehensive range of sustainable measures mean that the building will use 50 percent less energy than a traditional prestige office building. Fresh air is drawn up through the spiralling light-wells to naturally ventilate the office interiors and minimise reliance on artificial cooling and heating. The light-wells and the shape of the building maximise natural daylight, moderate the use of artificial lighting and allow views out from deep within the building.

The tower's circular plan is tapered at the base and the crown to improve connections to the surrounding streets and allow the maximum amount of sunlight to the plaza level. The building's smooth shape directs air movement around the building and minimises the amount of wind at plaza level to improve pedestrian comfort. The external diagonal steel structure is, by virtue of its triangulated geometry, inherently strong and light, permitting a flexible column-free interior space.

The exterior cladding consists of 5500 flat triangular and diamond-shaped glass panels, which vary at each level. The glazing to the office areas consists of a double-glazed outer layer and a single-glazed inner screen that sandwich a central ventilated cavity. The cavities act as buffer zones to reduce the need for additional heating and cooling and are ventilated by exhaust air that is drawn from the offices.

The design of the entrance lobby connects the outside experience to the interior scheme. Seven-metre-high panels of extruded aluminium flow from the plaza into the heart of the lobby in one continuous sweep. The dining areas have a spectacular western view of St Paul's Cathedral and the bar offers a unique 360-degree panoramic view from the City's highest occupied viewpoint.

1

2

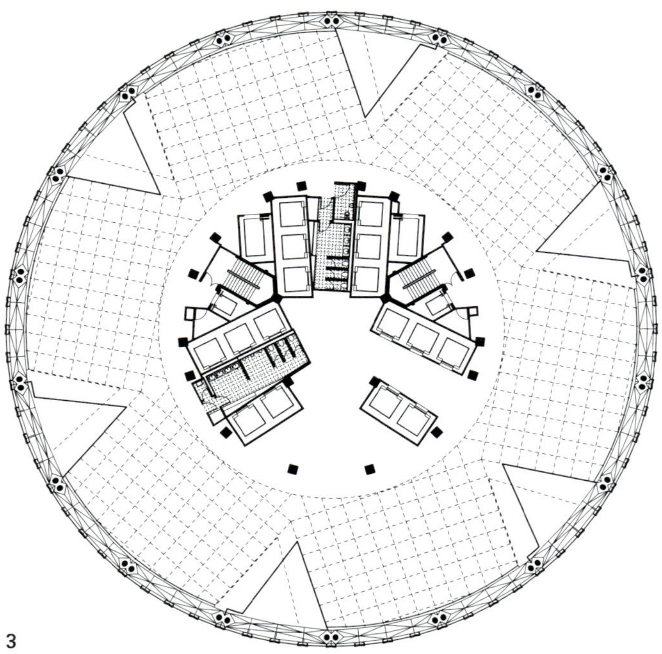

3

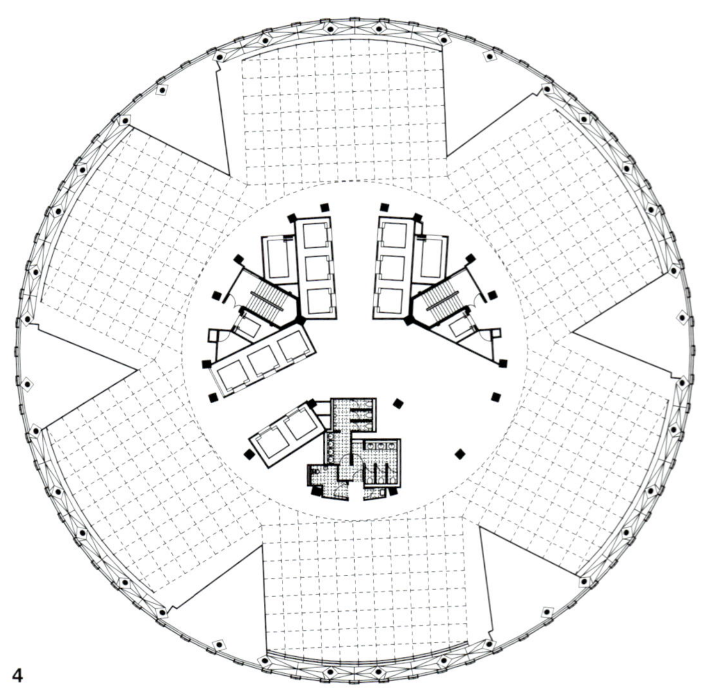

4

30 St Mary Axe Swiss – Re Headquarters | **Location** London, United Kingdom | **Completion date** 2003 | **Architect** Foster and Partners | **Client** Swiss Re | **Structural engineer** Arup Waterman Partnership | **Mechanical engineer** Hilson Moran Partnership Ltd | **Landscape architect** Derek Lovejoy Partnership | **Contractor** Skanska Construction UK Ltd | **Height** 180 m/590 ft | **Above-ground storeys** 41 | **Basements** 1 | **Use** Office | **Site area** 0.57 ha/1.4 acres | **Area of above-ground building** 47,844 sq m/515,000 sq ft | **Structural materials** Concrete, steel, glass, aluminium

1 *General view*
2 *Level 40 bar has 360-degree panoramic view over London*
3 *Level 6 floor plan*
4 *Level 21 floor plan*
5 *View from street level*
6 *Level 33 floor plan*
7 *Level 39, restaurant for private functions*
8 *Level 40, bar for private functions*

Photography: *Nigel Young/Foster and Partners*

5

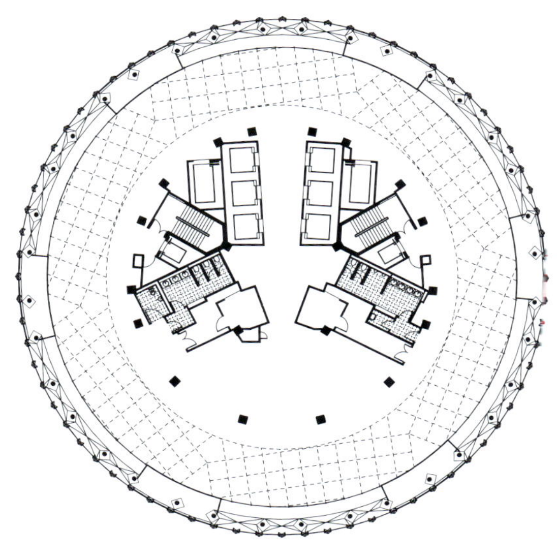

6

7

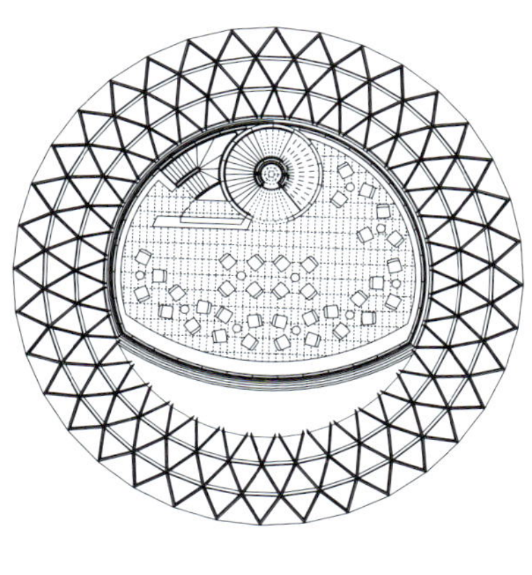

8

EUROPEAN CENTRAL BANK

FRANKFURT GERMANY

The new European Central Bank Headquarters in Frankfurt 'Ostend' is destined to become a new, visible icon for the Frankfurt skyline.

The 180-metre-high towers create a strong, solitary figure with enhanced proportions from all important views of downtown Frankfurt and along the river Main. On the local urban context, the double horizontal structures connect with the vertical diagonal cut of the atrium of the towers, creating a vertical city and connecting the ECB with the larger urban network of the Frankfurt skyline.

The combination of the horizontal structure and the verticality of the double towers express the functional program of the ECB. The Grossmarkthalle contains the entrance lobby and all public and semi-public functions, such as an exhibition space, visitor centre, library and auditorium. The 'groundscraper', which is the horizontal connection to the office towers, accommodates the conference centre with an internal lobby, restaurant and office areas over two levels. The towers provide the majority of office space.

A sculptural transformation of torsion and bending applied to an economical double slab high-rise typology created a number of differentiated office spaces through slight variance in floor plan development and views. It also resulted in the dynamic shaping of the atrium space between the tower slabs. The two large connecting platforms connect the two office towers in the lower third of the atrium and form a heavily frequented marketplace with recreational hanging gardens, cafeteria and lounges for informal meetings. Daylight reflectors bring light and green into the atrium.

Numerous 'short circuit' elevators and ramps connect the various office floor levels across the atrium, providing the opportunity for larger floor plates by connecting space functionally across the atrium. These stairs and ramps act as streets and passages within the 'vertical city', offering short and direct connections.

1

2

1–3 *General model views*
4 *Ground floor plan*

Photography: *Markus Pillhofer (1,2); Robert Metsch (3)*

ECB – European Central Bank | **Location** Frankfurt, Germany | **Expected completion date** 2011 | **Architect** COOP HIMMELB(L)AU; local architect revision phase Albert Speer & Partner GmbH | **Client** ECB – European Central Bank, Frankfurt/M, Germany | **Structural engineer** Bollinger + Grohmann | **Mechanical engineer** Arup (Germany) | **Landscape architect** (revision phase) Agence Ter.de, Karlsruhe | **Height** 180 m/591 ft (proposed) | **Above-ground storeys** 48 | **Use** Office | **Site area** 120,000 sq m/1,292,000 sq ft | **Area of above-ground building** 180,000 sq m/1,937,504 sq ft | **Floor area** 115,000 sq m/1,237,850 sq ft | **Structural materials** Reinforced concrete ribbed slats with encased composite columns

3

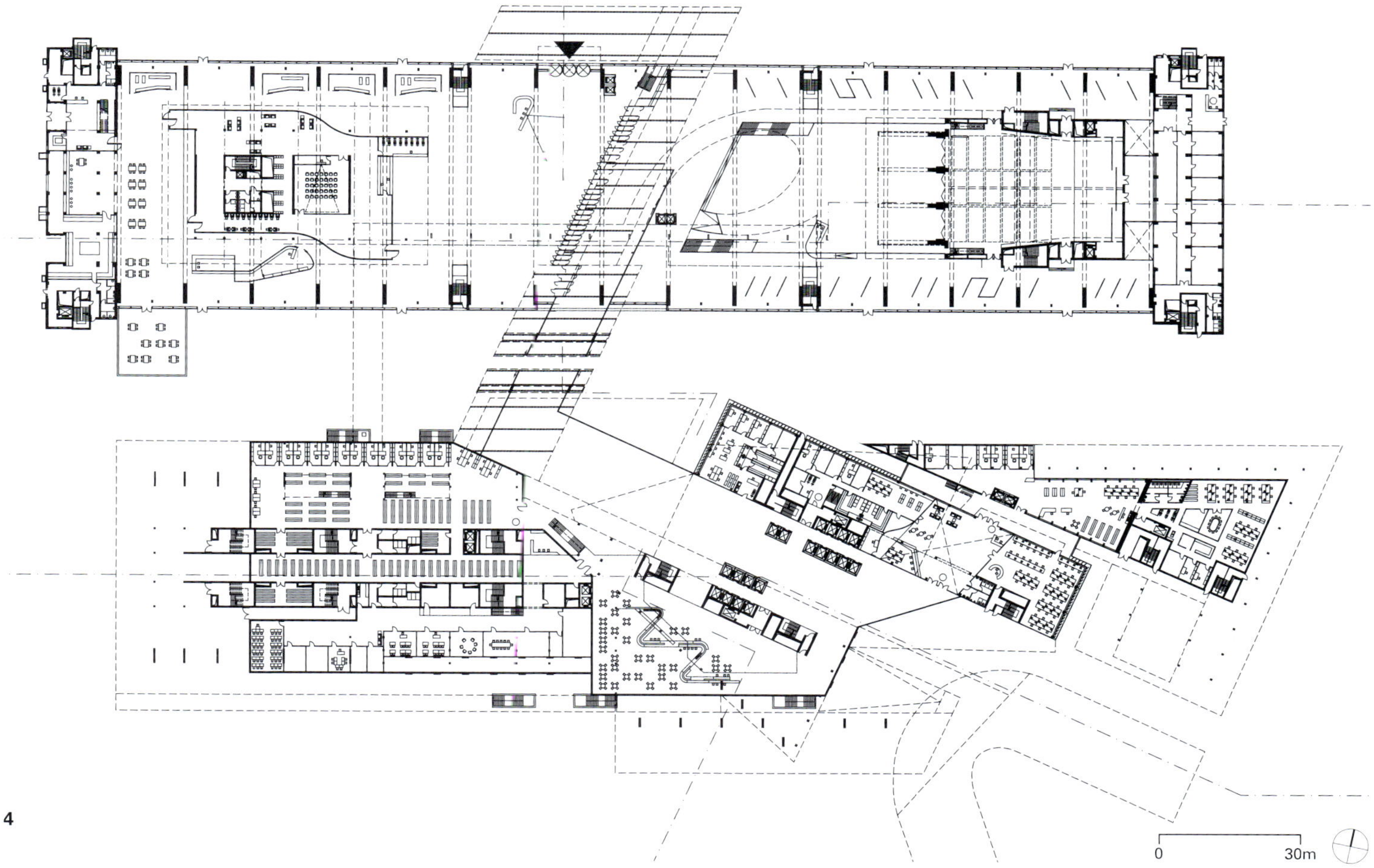

4

T1 TOWER PARIS LA DÉFENSE FRANCE

The T1 Tower is conceived as a folded glass plate, 185 metres high, cut by an arc on its north face. The distinctive profile changes according to one's vantage point and assures the tower's insertion within the surrounding context.

Seen from the south, the tower appears as a ship's bow, a vertical element and complement to the skyline of the Paris La Défense business district.

Seen from the east and west, T1 is perceived as a large sail, its curving form providing transition to the lower scale of the adjoining neighbourhood. The image created by the north façade is one of a tall staircase, climbing to the sky and disappearing as the façade curves out of view.

The tower's configuration allows for large floor plates and panoramic views, providing spatial quality, efficiency and the latest building services.

1

2

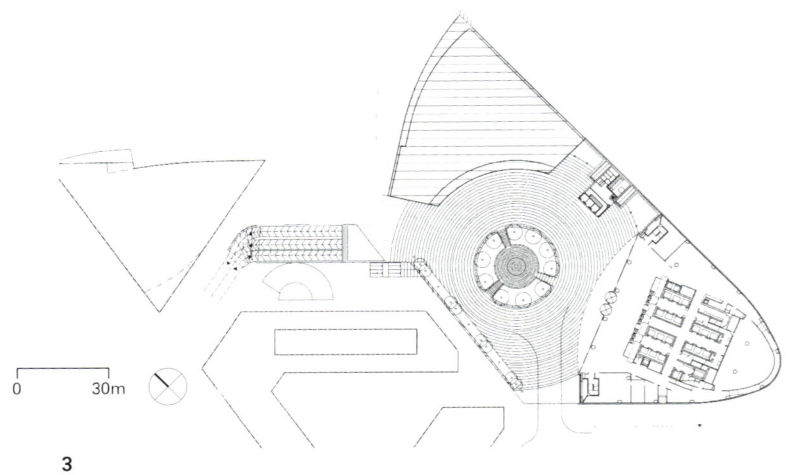

3

T1 Tower | **Location** Paris La Défense, France | **Completion date** 2007 | **Architect** Valode et Pistre Architectes | **Client** Colony Capital and the Caisse de Depots du Quebec | **Structural engineer** Terrell Rooke and VP Green | **Mechanical engineer** Ciec Engineering; Coteba Ingenierie; Lerch Bates & Associates | **Contractor** Bouygues | **Height** 185 m/607 ft | **Above-ground storeys** 39 | **Basements** 8 | **Above-ground useable levels** 37 | **Mechanical levels** 2 | **Use** Office, restaurants, fitness and conference facilities | **Site area** 17,000 sq m/182,920 sq ft | **Area of above-ground building** 70,000 sq m/753,200 sq ft | **Structural materials** Concrete, steel | **Other materials** Aluminium curtain wall incorporating clear, back-painted and fretted glazing. Steel parapet structure and granite-clad base. | **Cost** €150 M

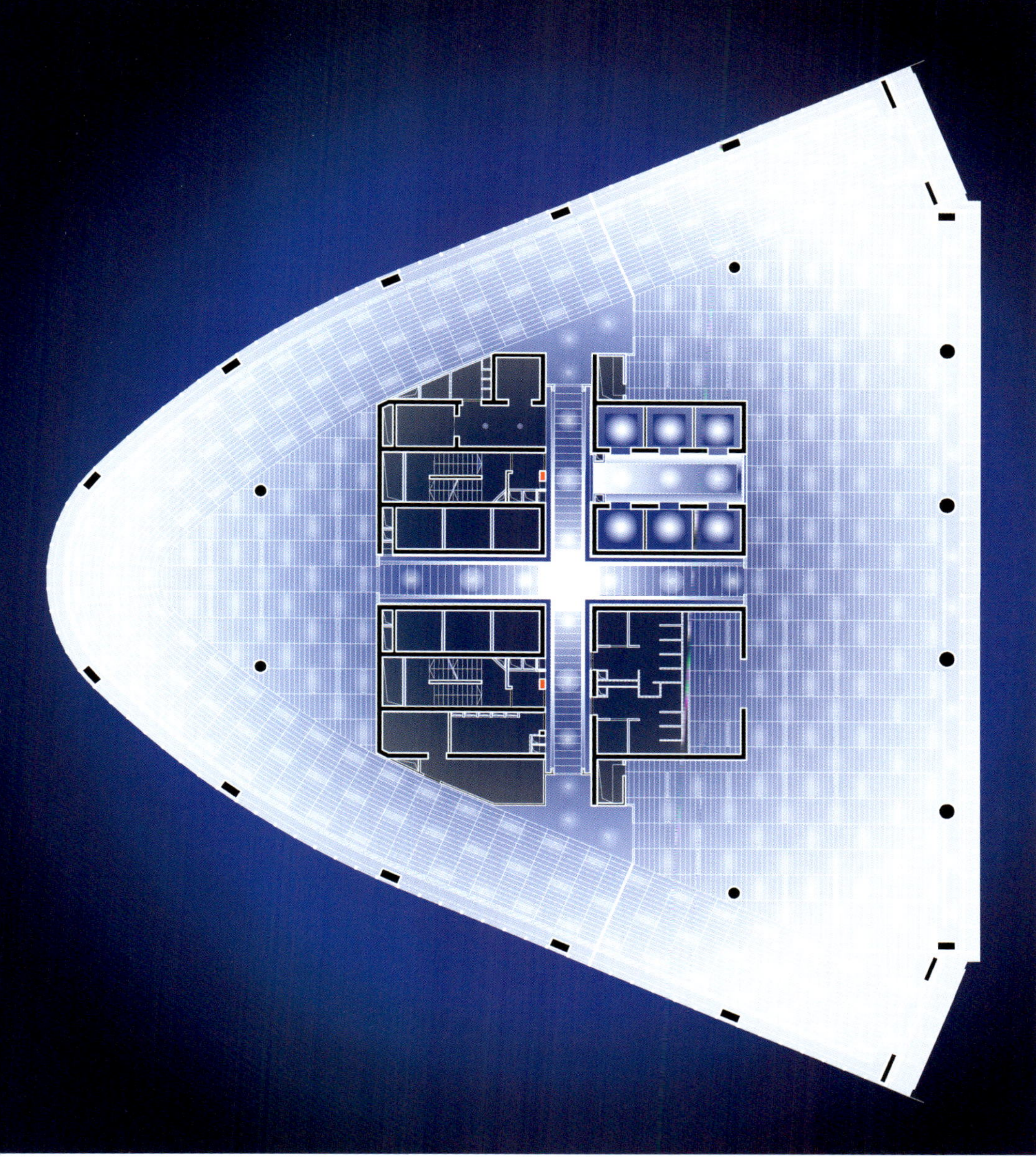

4

5

1 *View from the La Défense esplanade*
2 *General view*
3 *Ground floor plan*
4 *Typical floor plan*
5 *The tower as 'lighthouse'*
6 *Tapered building profile*

Renderings: *Courtesy Valode et Pistre Architectes*

6

ADIA HEADQUARTERS

ABU DHABI
UNITED ARAB EMIRATES

The headquarters building for the Abu Dhabi Investment Authority draws on KPF's renowned expertise in the design of tall buildings. The building features wings of office space flanked by central, full-height atria. The curvaceous form made of a single 'wrapping' façade fabric of glass provides ADIA with a single silhouette.

Response to urban context is a significant theme in the ADIA project. The site is a green waterfront fringe of the city, away from the historic centre, where new office and associated developments have taken place in recent years. Some of the new buildings here have a distinctly anodyne character. However, the aim at ADIA, which was designed for a major government agency, was to reconnect to the city and to echo, if subtly, themes found in traditional Islamic architecture. But the new building had equally to express the dynamism of 21st-century Abu Dhabi and its role in the international business community.

The origins of Abu Dhabi were, in fact, on the seafront, where the ancient fort was established, but the city has subsequently become relatively detached from the sea. The building expresses the tension between city and waterfront in its bifurcated form. The north wing follows the grain of the city grid, the south opens to the water and the wider world. The landscaping is intended to further root the building to its site and to reinforce the image of Abu Dhabi as 'the garden of the Gulf'.

The building has been compared to a giant dhow, about to set sail, yet its form is far from capricious and reflects a strong response to the operational brief. Relatively straightforward office floors, containing both open-plan and cellular spaces, were needed, together with central zones for interaction and meetings. The latter are located within the central atrium space, with a series of sky gardens, in the Islamic tradition of planted spaces within buildings, punctuating the office floors.

ADIA represents a progressive approach to energy use. KPF's low-energy double wall is incorporated into an environmental programme for ventilating and cooling the building. The central atrium acts as a thermal chimney for the extraction of stale air.

1

ADIA Headquarters | **Location** Abu Dhabi, United Arab Emirates | **Completion date** 2006 | **Architect** Kohn Pedersen Fox Associates | **Client** Abu Dhabi Investment Authority | **Structural engineer** Buro Happold | **Mechanical engineer** Buro Happold | **Landscape architect** EDAW Ltd. | **Contractor** Samsung Engineering & Construction Co. | **Height** 190 m/623 ft | **Above-ground storeys** 38 | **Basements** 2 | **Above-ground useable levels** 37 | **Mechanical levels** 2 | **Use** Office | **Site area** 14,800 sq m/159,300 sq ft | **Area of above-ground building** 83,235 sq m/895900 sq ft | **Structural materials** Concrete frame | **Other materials** Aluminium, glass

2

3

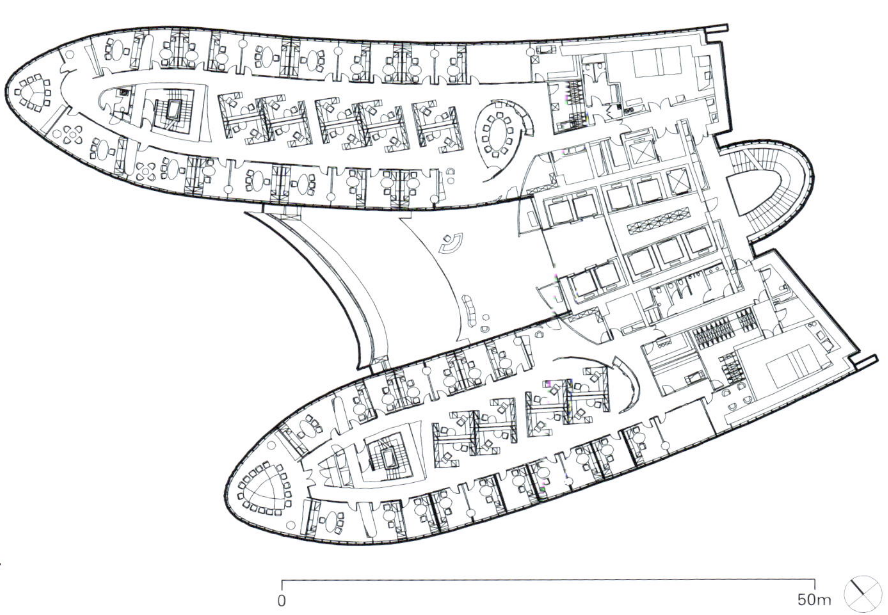

4

5

1 *Model view of tower on corniche and sea*

2 *View of back stair enclosure*

3 *Main elevation view*

4 *Typical floor plan*

5 *View looking down interior atrium during construction*

Photography: *Courtesy Kohn Pedersen Fox Associates (2,3,5)*
Model: *Eamonn O'Mahony*

CAPRICORN TOWER DUBAI UNITED ARAB EMIRATES

This project was based on the geometries and treatments of light found in traditional Islamic architecture. Planning began with the square parcel of land measuring 30.48 x 30.48 metres. The square and the cube, central to Islamic culture in symbology and geometry, informed the design.

The structure was based on four corner pillars, which rise to the fifth-floor level in the striking atrium. The atrium becomes an important great hall, which leads to the tower access.

The façade includes panels of curtainwall and aluminium cladding, which diffuse natural light both into and out of the building. The curtainwall panels are a melange of azure blue and clear glass units in a sheer expression of modernity, combining the ethereal and the transparent. The façade that faces the desert sun is protected by a 'moucharabie' that serves as a sunshade, reminiscent of the Islamic wooden latticework gratings through which inhabitants can see out without being seen. The slender figure of the tower stands out with its lateral white façades that resemble the traditional white clothing of Dubai.

The tower is crowned by a canopy that points the building towards the city flow and the Gulf development. The building becomes part of the Islamic culture with a contemporary shape, an expression of the symbiosis between tradition and modernity.

1

1 *View of tower from Zayed Road*
2 *Corner pillar*
3 *Side façade*
4 *View of tower from the future Dubai Financial City*
5 *Base of building with connecting bridge*
6 *Base floor plan*
7 *Apartment floor plan*

Photography: *Sebastián di Girolamo*

2

3

Capricorn Tower | **Location** Dubai, United Arab Emirates | **Completion date** 2003 | **Architect** Borja Huidobro + A4 Architects | **Client** Abdul Hamied Seddiqi | **Structural engineer** Samir Abdul Ghani | **Consulting engineer** Schuster Pachtold & Partners | **Contractor** Dubai Contracting Company | **Height** 190 m/623 ft | **Above-ground storeys** 48 | **Basements** 1 | **Above-ground useable levels** 45 | **Mechanical levels** 2 | **Use** Office, residential | **Site area** 929 sq m/9996 sq ft | **Area of above-ground building** 32,918 sq m/354,198 sq ft | **Structural materials** Concrete | **Other materials** Aluminium composite, curtainwall

4

5

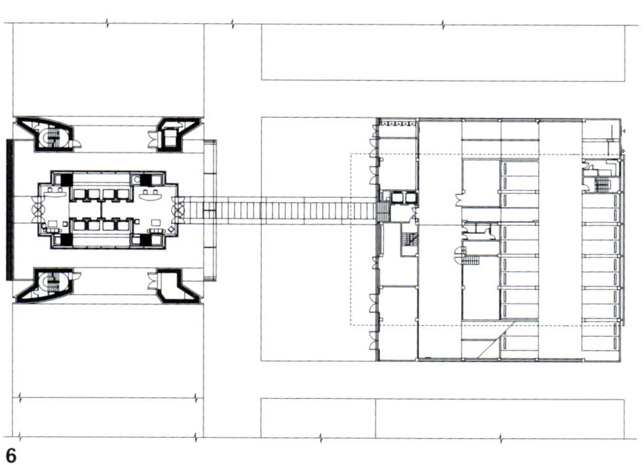

6

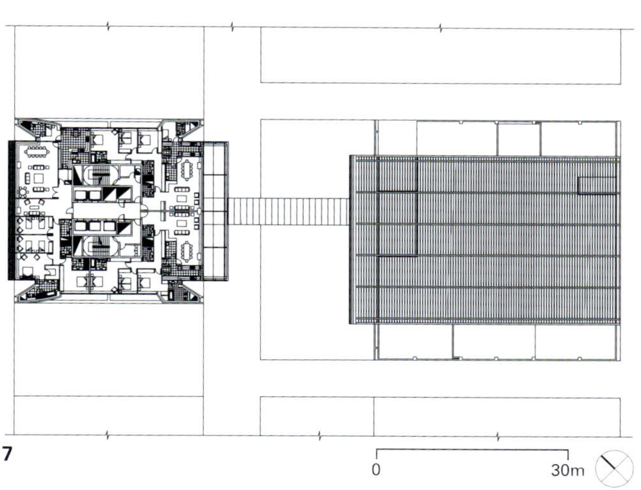

7

HSB TURNING TORSO

MALMÖ
SWEDEN

HSB Turning Torso climbs to 190 metres above sea level and consists of nine cubes with five storeys in each individual cube. The area between cubes three and nine will accommodate 147 apartments. There are 54 floors, including the intermediate floors, and each will have approximately 400 square metres of floor space. Each floor consists of an almost square area around the centre core, and a triangular section reinforced by an external steel support. The entire construction twists 90 degrees on its way up to the top storey.

The total apartment area is about 15,000 square metres, spread between the third and ninth cubes while the total commercial space is approximately 4200 square metres in the lower two cubes. The commercial area has its own entrance and service for efficient heating, cooling and IT systems. Three elevators service the apartments while the commercial area is served by two separate elevators.

Each level of HSB Turning Torso will be separated into several apartments, each with a different approach to modern living. There is also the opportunity for residents to combine a home with a separate private office or business space.

HSB Turning Torso provides a unique service, offering a wide range of different facilities. The 43rd level houses an array of high-end facilities including three fully equipped guest rooms, two sauna sections and a fitness centre. A large meeting room with a capacity for 20 people is located on the 43rd and 49th floors while a function suite is located on the 7th floor with seating capacity for up to 30 people. There are also eight fully equipped office modules on the first floor that can be rented by the residents. The 53rd and 54th floors, known as 'HSB Turning Torso Meetings', comprise one of the Nordic region's most exclusive meeting places, featuring panoramic views and inspiring interiors designed by architect Santiago Calatrava.

HSB Turning Torso's reception is staffed 24 hours a day. A concierge is always available to greet and provide assistance.

1

2

1,2,5 *General views*
3 *Typical floor plan*
4 *Model*

Photography: *© HSB Turning Torso, Pierre Mens*
Floor plan: *Samark*

HSB Turning Torso | **Location** Malmö, Sweden | **Completion date** 2005 | **Architect** Santiago Calatrava, Zürich, Switzerland | **Associate architect** Samark Arkitektur & Design, Malmö and Stockholm (apartment design) | **Client** HSB-Malmö | **Structural engineer** Santiago Calatrava | **Mechanical engineer** NCC Teknik, Malmö; Bengt Dahlgren AB, Gothenburg | **Height** 190 m/623 ft | **Above-ground storeys** 54 | **Basements** 2 | **Above-ground useable levels** 50 | **Mechanical levels** 4 | **Use** Residential, office | **Site area** 2500 sq m/26,900 sq ft | **Area of above-ground building** 15,000 sq m/161,400 sq ft (housing); 4200 sq m/45,192 sq ft (offices) | **Structural materials** Circular reinforced concrete structural core; steel truss exoskeleton; floor structure: reinforced concrete | **Other materials** Concrete, steel

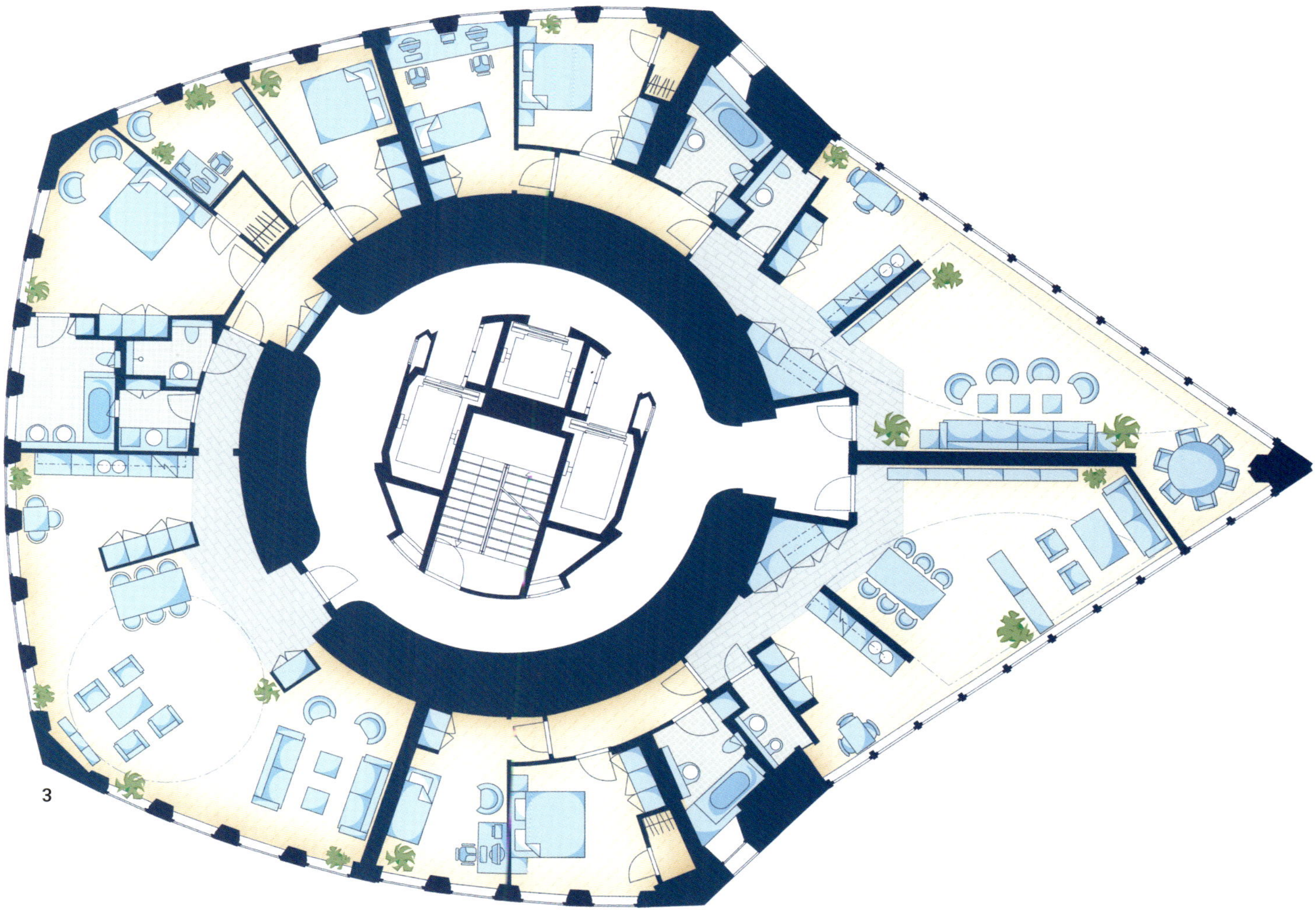

3

4

5

RONDO 1 WARSAW POLAND

In early 2001, the London office of Skidmore, Owings & Merrill (SOM) was commissioned by Hochtief Project Development Polska to design the Rondo 1 tower.

The Rondo 1 complex consists of two buildings on a 5832-square-metre site located in Warsaw's city centre: a 40-storey tower (158.4 metres) and a 10-storey low-rise building (40.2 metres).

It is located close to one of Warsaw's largest and most prestigious building complexes, the Sciana Zachodnia (West Wall), and is classified as one of special importance, designated only for high-quality, city-shaping development. The Rondo 1 complex forms a gateway to the Sciana Zachodnia, complementing existing development while re-creating the delicate pattern of the city centre's historic quarters.

The architectural design has been developed to create an attractive and efficient work environment of the highest standard. The tower provides a landmark building comprising office spaces suited to financial, corporate, and professional service organisations. The complex is also characterised by flexibility of use. The design fulfils the client's functional requirements as well as aesthetic aspirations, while the architectural style and expression create a new and strong accent to the cityscape. The virtually uninterrupted office floor plate allows Class A fit-out, appropriate to tenants from the United States, United Kingdom and Europe. It is also possible to lease each floor to multiple tenants, or to lease an entire floor or few floors to a single tenant.

With the design of the Rondo 1 tower, SOM has aimed to present and inspire the concept of cutting-edge integrated architectural–engineering practice, particularly enabling a new architectural vision through the practical introduction and application of the most advanced technologies, materials and methods.

1

1 *General view at night*
2 *General view*
3 *Atrium*
4 *Typical floor plan*

Images: *Courtesy Skidmore, Owings & Merrill LLP*

Rondo 1 | **Location** Warsaw, Poland | **Completion date** 2005 | **Architect** Skidmore Owings & Merrill Inc. London; Epstein Spólka z oo; AZO Sp. z oo | **Client** Hochtief Project Development, Polska | **Structural engineer** SOM (Chicago); associate structural engineer BWL Project (Warsaw) | **Mechanical engineer** POL-CON Consulting (Warsaw) | **Contractor** Hochtief Polska Budokor | **Height** 158.4 m/520 ft; 194 m/636.5 ft with antenna | **Above-ground storeys** 40 | **Basements** 2 | **Above-ground useable levels** 40 | **Mechanical levels** 1 | **Use** Office and retail | **Site area** 5832 sq m/ 62,752 sq ft | **Area of above-ground building** 90,742 sq m/972,754 sq ft | **Structural materials** Steel, curtain wall, aluminium, reinforced concrete, glass | **Other materials** Stone | **Cost** €200 M

2

3

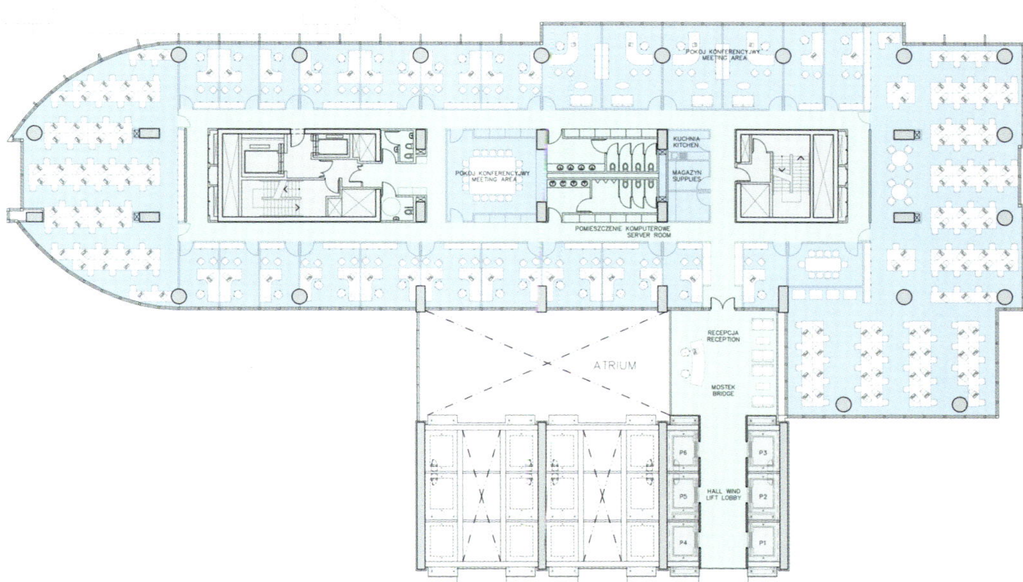

4

HSBC HEADQUARTERS LONDON UNITED KINGDOM

In 1979 the Hongkong and Shanghai Bank (HSBC) presented a brief for its Hong Kong headquarters that allowed the practice to rewrite the rules of tall office building design. Twenty-eight years later the Bank offered a very different challenge: to design a London headquarters in Canary Wharf.

As the owner-occupier of the Hong Kong building, the Bank was able to encourage formal and technical experimentation to an unprecedented degree. In London, however, the Bank decided to follow a commercially led path: although it initially leased the entire building, later it may wish to sublet part or all of the accommodation. The developer-led solution therefore had to work within tight cost limits and meet market expectations for high-quality, flexible office space.

This meant providing an air-conditioned building with a central core, to maximise the development potential of the site and optimise net-to-gross floor ratios. The challenge was not simply to meet market expectations, but to raise values in every area, from materials to ecological performance, thereby setting new standards.

All main facilities are configured within the core, allowing open-plan floors throughout. Rapid transit to the 39 office floors is provided by a sophisticated multi-tier elevator system. Three interchange levels allow easy movement between elevator groups and contain meeting rooms, shops, cafés, catering and medical facilities. Three double-height trading floors are accessible by escalator from the entrance lobby. Below ground there is a direct link to Canary Wharf Underground station, together with three levels of car-parking.

The 200-metre-high tower is given elegant, minimal expression through its sheer glass surface treatment. Curved corners soften the form and the tower's transparent shaft is capped with an illuminated 'halo'.

1

3

2

4

1 *Exterior view*
2 *Floor plan*
3 *Exterior view at night*
4 *Art work in the 28-metre-high entrance lobby*
5 *Interior circulation*

Photography: *Nigel Young/Foster and Partners*

HSBC Headquarters | **Location** London, United Kingdom | **Completion date** 2003 | **Architect** Foster and Partners | **Client** Canary Wharf Contractor (DS-2) Ltd; HSBC Holdings plc | **Consultants** Davis Langdon & Everest; Lerch Bates Associates Ltd; Ove Arup & Partners | **Height** 200 m/656 ft | **Above-ground useable levels** 41 | **Basements** 4 | **Mechanical levels** 3 | **Use** Office | **Area of above-ground building** 160,000 sq m/1,721,600 sq ft | **Structural materials** Concrete, steel, glass

5

25 CANADA SQUARE AT CANARY WHARF

LONDON
UNITED KINGDOM

This 42-storey, 200-metre-high, headquarters tower adjoins the 17-storey Citibank building. The corporate and investment banking businesses of Citigroup, including Salomon Smith Barney and Citibank, occupy 600,000 square feet of the building, creating a combined Citigroup complex of 1.16 million square feet for 6000 Citigroup staff plus the capacity for potential future expansion. The tower faces two parks, one with the Jubilee Line Station to the south and Canada Square Park, with its shopping mall below, to the north.

The tower has a centric composition that gently tapers towards the top. A tracery of stainless steel modulates the curtain wall, which is clad in energy efficient neutral glass, optimising natural light and views. The stainless steel super-grid on the curtain wall enhances the tower's formal order and aligns with the super-grid of the adjacent Citibank building designed by Norman Foster and Partners to form a common building base. The tower top is crystalline and transparent, offering a crowning gesture when lit at night.

The tower joins the 50-storey landmark One Canada Square, also designed by Cesar Pelli & Associates, and the 42-storey HSBC tower designed by Foster and Partners. The three towers, together with the retail area and park connecting them, all as originally masterplanned, will aggregate more than three and a half million square feet net commercial space.

1&3 *General views*
2 *Typical Citigroup lower floor plan (GF–9)*
4 *Upper level façade and roof detail*

Photography: *Courtesy Canary Wharf Group Plc.*

1

25 Canada Square at Canary Wharf | **Location** London, United Kingdom | **Completion date** 2001 | **Architect** Cesar Pelli & Associates | **Architect of record** Adamson Associates | **Client** Canary Wharf Contractors Ltd | **Structural engineer** Yolles Partnership Ltd | **Mechanical engineer** The Mitchell Partnership & Donald Smith | **Electrical engineer** HH Angus & Associates Ltd | **Height** 200 m/656 ft | **Above-ground storeys** 42 | **Basements** 4 | **Use** Office | **Area of above-ground building** 148,610 sq m/1,800,000 sq ft | **Structural materials** Curtainwall, glass, aluminium, stainless steel

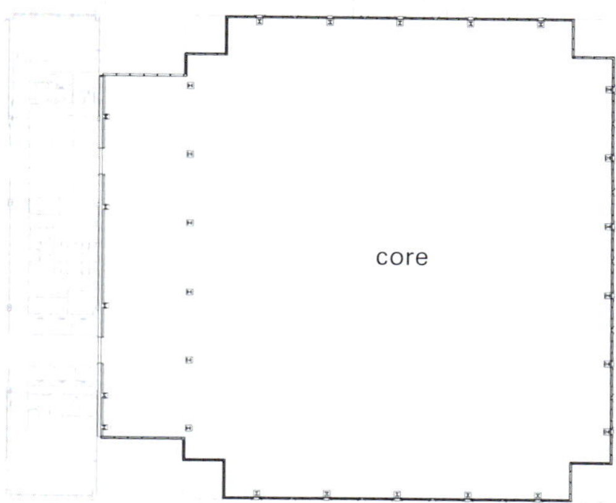

2

3

4

MAIN TOWER

FRANKFURT
GERMANY

The international competition for the Hessische Landesbank was won in 1991 with an innovative concept and the striking idea of breaking the shaft up into a square and a circle to create duality on the park and city side. On the base floors, the listed sandstone façade of the existing historical buildings was integrated, and structurally complemented by the new section. The square part of the tower has a bronze façade, which will acquire a patina over the years and which contrasts with the glazed openness of the round part of the tower. The novel concept of the single-sheet glass façade with opening windows is perfectly implemented. A restaurant, a public viewing platform and a radio studio offer a fantastic panorama of the city centre and the surrounding area from the top of the round tower, the highest publicly accessible viewing point in Frankfurt.

The MAIN TOWER has both high utility and aesthetic value, and fits in well with its environment. The specific qualities of the location are conveyed by the duality of the building. The square section is solid and static, and reflects the urban space, whereas the round tower suggests the panoramic view. One section of the building stands for stability, the other for lightness and flexibility. As a result the Main Tower appears delicate and slender compared to other high-rise buildings in the city.

The MAIN TOWER is optimally equipped for the 21st century with some outstanding technical features. These include an innovative lighting system, a state-of-the-art fire alarm system, a powerful security system, and windows that open and close automatically, centrally if needed, dependent on weather and wind conditions. The use of innovative technology makes this a low-energy building with an annual energy consumption of less than 75 kWh per square metre.

1

2

MAIN TOWER | **Location** Frankfurt, Germany | **Completion date** 1999 | **Architect** Architekten Schweger + Partner: Prof. Peter P. Schweger, Harmut Reifenstein, Bernhard Kohl, Wolfgang Schneider, Prof. Wilhelm Meyer | **Client** Helicon OHG; Verwaltungs GmbH & Co. Immobilien OHG | **Structural engineer** Ingenieurbüro Förster, Sennwald, Linse; Ingenieurbüro Burggraf, Weichinger + Partner | **Contractor** Arge Main Tower c/o Hochtief AG Niederlassung Frankfurt | **Height** 200 m/656 ft | **Above-ground storeys** 56 | **Basements** 5 | **Above-ground useable levels** 56 | **Use** Office, restaurant, TV studio | **Area of above-ground building** 85,000 sq m/914,600 sq ft | **Structural materials** Reinforced concrete | **Other materials** Bronze (façade) | **Cost** Approx €190 M

3

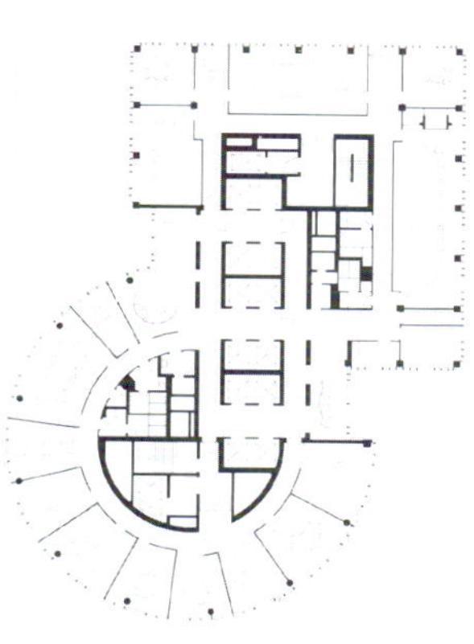

4

5

6

1 *General view*

2 *View from west*

3 *Level 53 restaurant*

4 *Level 38 plan: sky lobby, changeover floor with conference areas*

5 *Façade detail showing manually operable windows*

6 *Ground floor plan*

Photography: *Bernhard Kroll*

MILLENNIUM TOWER VIENNA AUSTRIA

The 202-metre-high Millennium Tower is the new symbol and focus of the Handelskai city quarter, about two kilometres from the heart of Vienna. With 60,000 square metres of retail space, 50,000 square metres of offices and 480 apartments, the 'Millennium City' promotes a new urban way of life on the banks of the Danube. The 50-storey tower – Austria's highest – rises from a base containing a two-storey shopping centre with four levels of underground parking, together with four storeys of apartments. Around 2000 parking places and above- and below-ground train connections guarantee integration into the city. The entire concept was completed between 1996 and 2001, and the construction of the tower from commencement above ground to fitting out was achieved in just ten months. ATP, whose full service role encompassed responsibility for detailed design, project organisation, site supervision and technical monitoring, was able to complete construction to a record minimum programme and budget, all within the constraints of the planning permits obtained for the original outline design, setting cost and quality benchmarks.

1

Innovations in reinforced concrete technology developed in partnership with the Technical University of Innsbruck allowed the construction of the tower to advance at two storeys per week, while many further constructional elements – façades, raised floors, ceilings and plant – could be stored storey-by-storey, ready for swift installation. Similarly, the question of tolerance – crucial for a tower which descends into a six-storey base – was solved by an innovative pre-stressed piling system that reduced the tolerance from the expected 16 centimetres to just 2 centimetres. The optimisation of the core design – which included a decentralised ventilating plant for each group of three self-sufficient floors – led to considerable improvements in the lettable floor ratios.

2

1 *View of tower from the Donauinsel*
2 *View of tower façade from pedestrian bridge over the Handelskai*
3 *Typical floor plan (18th floor)*
4 *View from plaza towards the pedestrian bridge (first floor)*
5 *View from plaza towards the tower façade (first floor)*

Photography: *courtesy ATP Achammer-Tritthart & Partner*

Millennium Tower | **Location** Vienna, Austria | **Completion date** 1999 | **Architect** ATP Architects and Engineers; Peichl, Podrecca, Weber | **Client** OSMIN Projekt AG/Stumpf Immobilien | **Structural engineer** Kollitsch und Stanek | **Mechanical engineer** ATP Architects and Engineers | **Contractor** ARGE MCE – Habau | **Height** 202 m/663 ft | **Above-ground storeys** 50 | **Basements** 4 | **Above-ground useable levels** 50 | **Mechanical levels** 0 | **Use** Office, retail, residential | **Site area** 13,000 sq m/139,900 sq ft | **Area of above-ground building** 171,000 sq m/1,841,000 sq ft | **Structural materials** Reinforced concrete, steel, curtainwall | **Other materials** Granite, stainless steel, glass | **Cost** €107 M

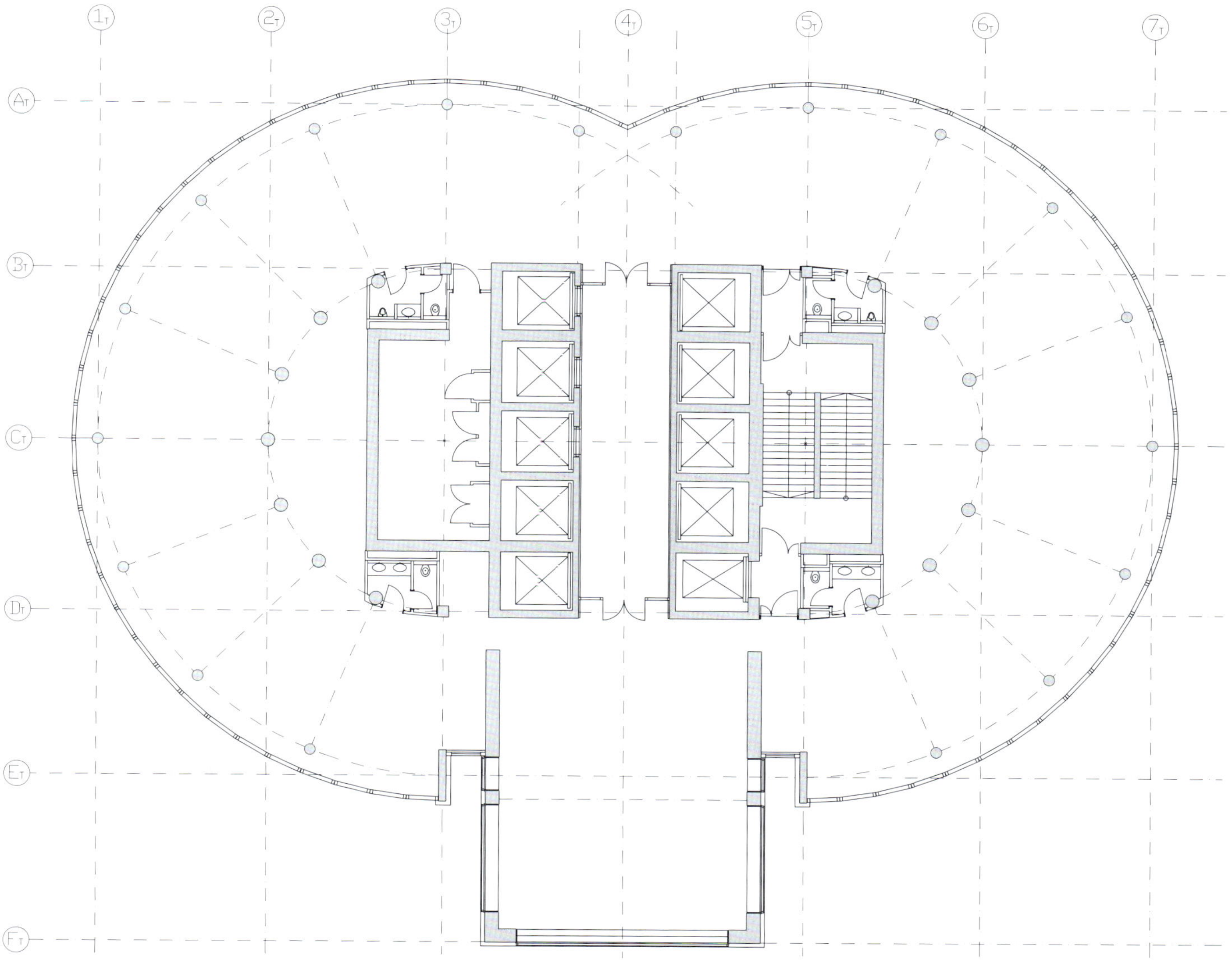

3

4

5

DZ BANK HEADQUARTERS FRANKFURT GERMANY

The headquarters of DZ Bank (formerly known as DG Bank) is situated on the major business artery, Mainzer Landstrasse, in the midst of Frankfurt's banking centre, and adjacent to the prestigious Westend residential district. It is designed as an enlarged civic version of the great European palm courts, or crystal palaces, and creates a new central focus for the Westend community. This office complex includes retail at ground level, a public wintergarden, apartments, and three levels of below-grade parking with approximately 600 parking spaces.

The 52-storey tower contains 41,000 square metres of office space for the bank. Together with a perimeter building which varies between 8 and 16 floors, the complex totals 77,000 square metres above grade. The tower and the perimeter building maintain the existing street lines and envelop a public wintergarden built of steel and glass, inspired by European train stations and conservatories of the 19th century. Twelve majestic palm trees add a natural element to the structural rigor of the space, making it both 'green' and urban. Shops and restaurants spill out from adjacent buildings to enliven the public hall.

The building mediates between the scale of the office towers in the city's banking quarter and the residential scale of the Westend. For this reason, the building complex has strong setbacks at 22 and 60 metres relating to the traditional heights of Westend residences and the first generation of high-rise buildings along Mainzer Landstrasse. At 150 metres, the tower sets back again, in reference to the traditional height of the second generation of Frankfurt towers, rising in a curved glass and metal shaft that culminates at 200 metres in a dramatic cantilevered crown of steel, the project's signature on Frankfurt's skyline. The curved shaft and crown are oriented towards the historic fortified city centre.

1

DZ Bank Headquarters | **Location** Frankfurt, Germany | **Completion date** 1993 | **Architect** Kohn Pedersen Fox Associates | **Associate architect** NHT Nägele Hoffmann Tiedemann und Partner | **Client** AGIMA; DG Immobilien Anlagegesellschaft mbH | **Structural engineer** Ingenieursczietät BGS | **Mechanical engineer** P & A Pettersson Ahrens | **Landscape architect** Büro Heinz Eckebrecht | **Contractor** Hochtief AG | **Height** 208 m/682 ft | **Above-ground storeys** 52 | **Basements** 4 | **Above-ground useable levels** 50 | **Use** Office, retail, residential, wintergarden | **Site area** 2508 sq m/ 27,000 sq ft | **Area of above-ground building** 77,000 sq m/828,520 sq ft (gross); 54,000 sq m/581,040 sq ft (net) | **Structural materials** Reinforced concrete | **Other materials** Glass, painted aluminium, painted steel, celtic grey flamed and honed granite

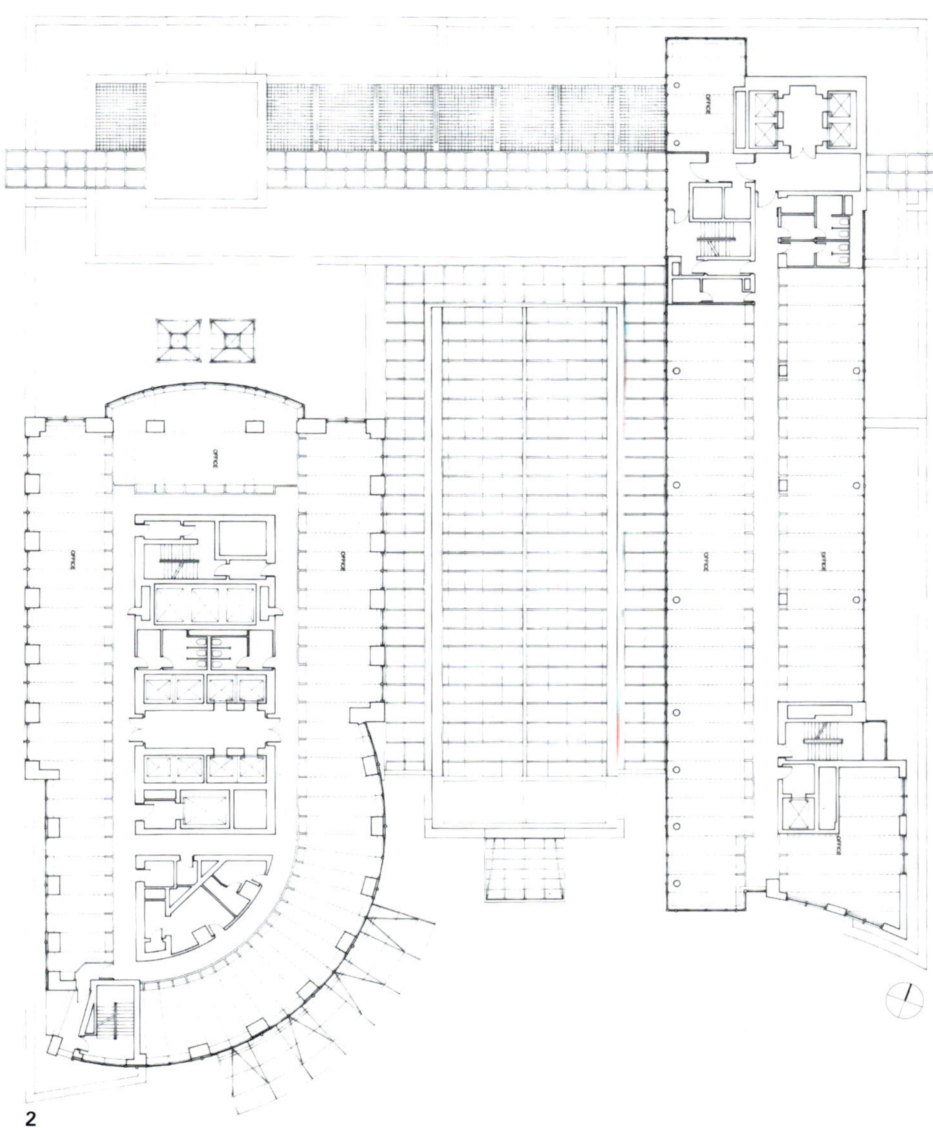
2

3

4

1 *Northeast view from Westend residential district*
2 *Typical low-rise floor plan*
3 *Entrance to the wintergarden*
4 *West façade*

Photography: *Dennis Gilbert*

TOUR MONTPARNASSE PARIS FRANCE

Approved in principle in 1956, the Tour Montparnasse (also known as Tour Maine-Montparnasse) was eventually completed in 1973 after years of difficult discussions and debates. It became the tallest skyscraper in Western Europe until the completion of the 63-storey MesseTurm in Frankfurt in 1990. The Tour Montparnasse forms part of a much larger town-planning project known as Opération Maine-Montparnasse, which was undertaken on the initiative of the SNCF – the French National Railway Company, and the City of Paris.

The original 8-hectare Montparnasse area masterplan dates from 1956 and includes the scheduled demolition and relocation of the former Montparnasse Railway Station where the Tour Montparnasse now stands. The project was planned by a public-private joint venture and executed by two developers, the American Wylie F.L. Tuttle and Frenchman Jean-Claude Aaron.

The vast completed ensemble comprises the tower, another 12-storey cubic building and the vast podium, which is located next to the tower. These characteristics distinguish the skyscraper from many of the lookalike projects of the time.

Standing next to the rebuilt Montparnasse Railway Station, the tower forms a major axis in the city with the Eiffel Tower and the La Défense district. Much debated at the time for its supposed dullness and height, the almond-shaped building brought, with its curved façades, some innovative design among the ubiquitous square boxes of its time. With its large plaza around the building, the Tour Montparnasse epitomises the urban ideas of the 1950s and the 1960s that were put into reality in the early 1970s all over Europe. Today, more than 30 years after its completion, the building remains the tallest in France.

1

2

1 *General view*

2 *Rendering, general view*
3 *Aerial view*
4 *Typical floor plan*
5 *Axonometric showing vertical transportation*

Photography: *Michael Hierner (1); courtesy Tour Montparnasse 56 (3)*
Rendering, plan and axonometric: *OTIS brochure, collection G Binder/ Buildings & Data SA*

Tour Montparnasse | **Location** Paris, France | **Completion date** 1973 | **Architect** Agence d'architecture de l'Opération Maine-Montparnasse (Eugène Beaudouin, Urbain Cassan, Louis de Hoym de Marien, Jean Saubot) | **Consulting architect** A Epstein and Sons | **Client** Société Civile Immobilière de la Tour Maine-Montparnasse 1; Société d'Economie Mixte pour l'Aménagement du Secteur Maine-Montparnasse | **Developer** Collins Tuttle and Company; SEFRI-Société d'Etudes Financières et de Réalisations Immobilières | **Consultant engineer** Carl A Morse, Inc. | **Contractor** Campenon Bernard | **Height** 209 m/686 ft | **Above-ground storeys** 58 | **Basements** 6 | **Above-ground useable levels** 54 | **Mechanical levels** 4 | **Use** Offices, observation deck, retail | **Site area** 23,647 sq m/254,442 sq ft | **Area of above-ground building** 112,000 sq m/1,206,000 sq ft | **Structural materials** Reinforced concrete central core; peripheral metal frame structure with concrete slabs | **Other materials** Bronze coloured anodised aluminium and glass curtain wall

3

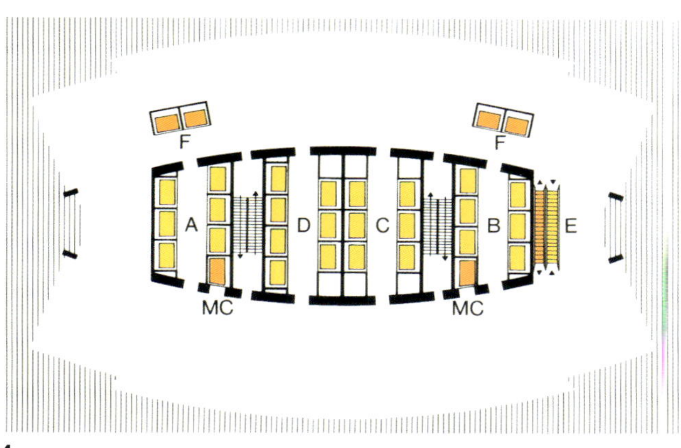

4

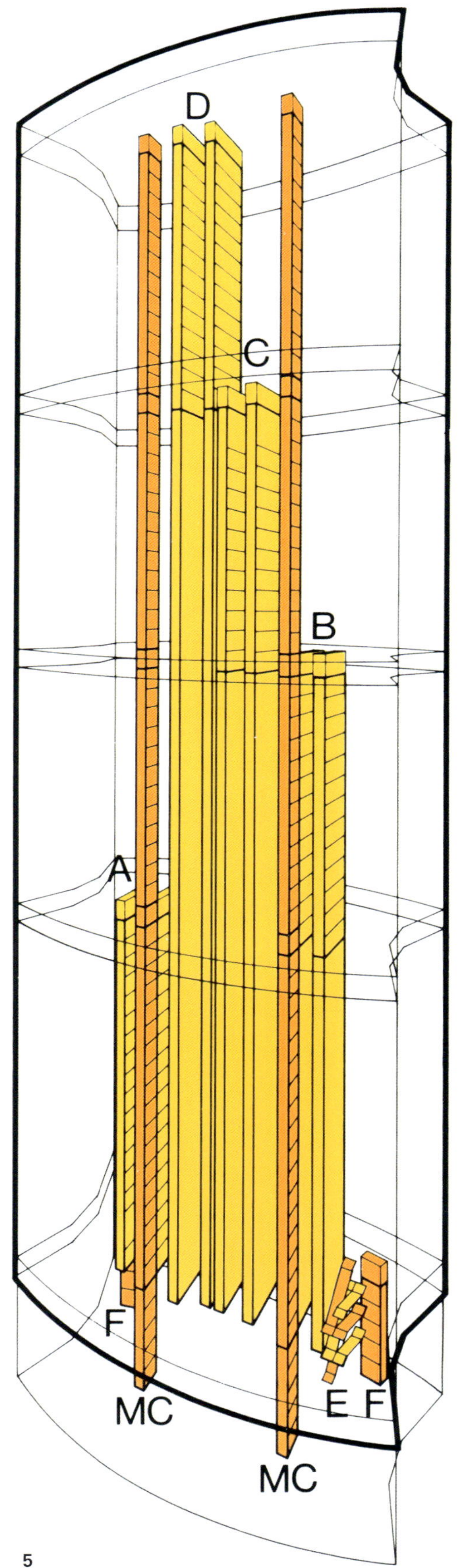

5

COOLSINGEL TOWER ROTTERDAM THE NETHERLANDS

The Coolsingel project consists of a 700-seat theatre, a 51-storey mixed-use high-rise tower, and a landmark building. The project is part of the rejuvenation process in Rotterdam that began in 1945.

The complex is a result of Rotterdam's vision to realise high-rise buildings along important avenues in the downtown area. Wytze Patijn, appointed by the city to oversee the project, was instrumental in shaping the vision for this area of Rotterdam. Discussions and workshops between Wytze Patijn and architect Rene Steevensz of PPKS resulted in the final design of the Coolsingel Tower.

The most visible component of the project is the high-rise tower, an all-steel building with a perimeter cross-bracing system to ensure the stability of the tower. The exterior wall system is 'interactive', allowing the building to be almost completely transparent, while meeting all the stringent energy codes of The Netherlands.

The combination of the exterior wall and structure allows for the creation of different functions within the tower in the future. For example, the structural system gives the option of removing three floors to create an auditorium, without violating the integrity of the structural system.

The theatre is located on a significant corner of Kruiskade and Coolsingel. At street level, the theatre and restaurant allow for interaction with city life. The atrium provides for a semi-private urban space connecting the theatre and 'Generale Bank' buildings. As it is the only place where one can experience the tower meeting the ground level, a frail skin of stainless tension rods and glass has been designed to optimise the visibility of the tower beyond the atrium.

2

3

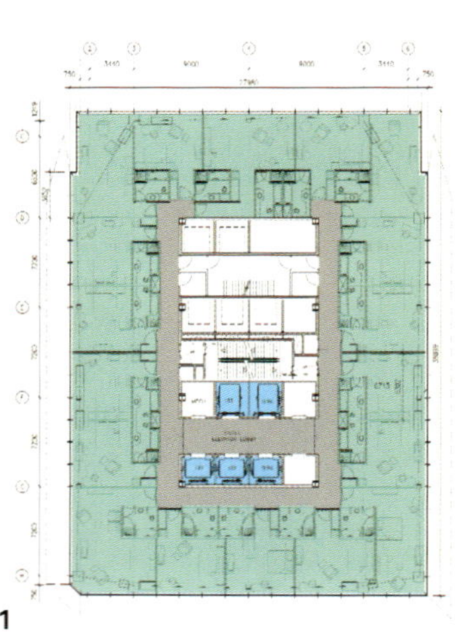

1

1 *Hotel floor plan*
2&3 *General views*
4 *Aerial view*
5 *Atrium*
6 *Apartment floor plan*
7 *Office floor plan*

Renderings: *Courtesy PPKS Architects Ltd.*

Coolsingel Tower | **Location** Rotterdam, the Netherlands | **Construction documents phase** | **Architect** PPKS Architects, Ltd | **Client** BPF Bouwinvest; Bouwfonds MAB; Willemsen Minderman | **Structural engineer** Ingenieursbureau Zonneveld BV | **Mechanical engineer** Techiplan Adviseurs BV | **Building physics** Cauberg Huygen | **Height** 215 m/705 ft (including antenna) | **Above-ground storeys** 51 | **Basements** 5 | **Above-ground useable levels** 48 | **Mechanical levels** 3 (levels 16, 32 and roof) | **Use** Mixed: office, residential, hotel | **Site area** 5300 sq m/57,050 sq ft | **Area of above-ground building** 55,000 sq m/592,000 sq ft (tower only) | **Structural materials** Steel | **Other materials** Glass, aluminium

4

5

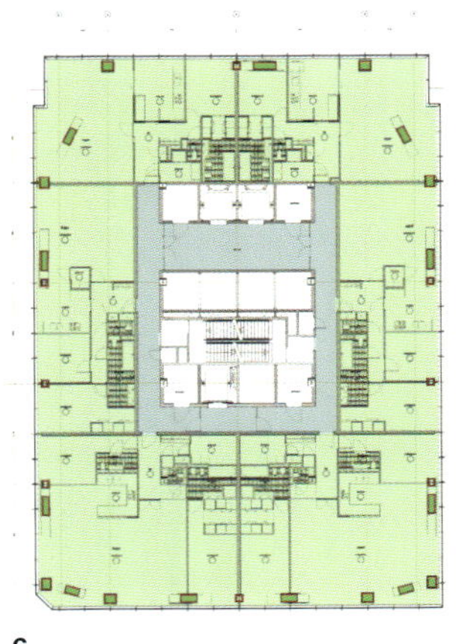

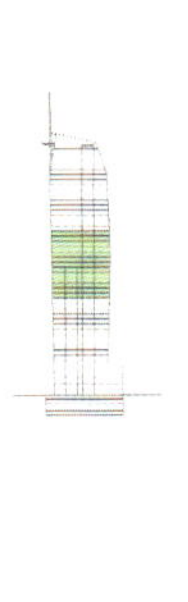

6

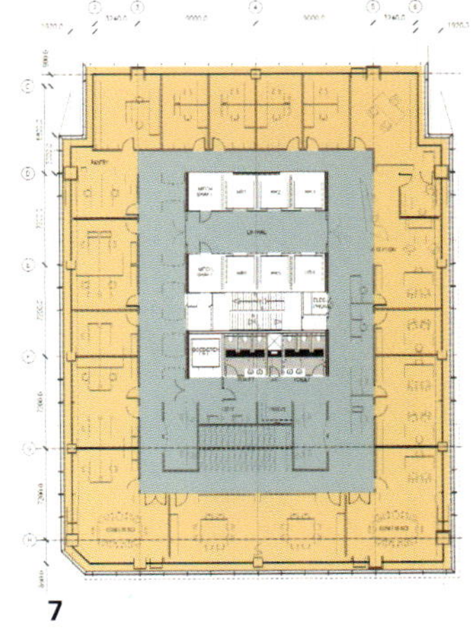

7

DOHA HIGH-RISE OFFICE BUILDING

DOHA
QATAR

Development in Qatar has taken a unique turn in putting significant emphasis on culture with the declared goal to make Qatar at large, and the city of Doha in particular, the cultural heart of the Gulf region.

The National Council for Culture, Arts and Heritage, under the chairmanship of Sheikh Saud Bin Mohammed Bin Ali Al-Thani, is planning a large scheme featuring cultural buildings such as museums and libraries. This scheme will redefine the skyline of the Doha bay through landscaping the Cornice and the design of a series of remarkable buildings, intended as landmarks, along the shore. This high-rise building by Ateliers Jean Nouvel is located between the new city centre and the Cornice on the north side of the bay.

The Doha high-rise tower is cylindrical, measuring about 45 metres in diameter. It is capped by a dome and topped by a lightning conductor at 231.5 metres. The steel and concrete structure is on a lozenge grid, bending upon the virtual surface of the cylinder. The façade is composed of a double cladding. The exterior, which evokes the geometric complexity of the oriental moucharabieh and acts as solar protection, is composed of four 'butterfly' aluminium elements of different scales. Its overall pattern is different according to its orientation and differing requirements for protection: 25 percent towards the north, 40 percent towards the south and 60 percent to the east and west. The inside layer is a slightly reflective glass skin that complements the solar protection. Finally, a system of roller blinds can be used if required. Each floor offers panoramic views towards the Gulf to the east, the port to the south, the city to the west and the coast and desert to the north.

Access to the tower is through a planted garden that slopes gently towards the large lobby. A glass canopy surrounds the building and suggests that the tower is deeply rooted in the earth. Vegetation and the glass canopy overlap, blurring the limits between nature and the man-made environment. A huge atrium rises up to level 27 at a height of 112 metres. Tall and slim, glittering in its silvery, laced silhouette against the skyline, the tower is destined to become a landmark on the Doha Cornice.

1

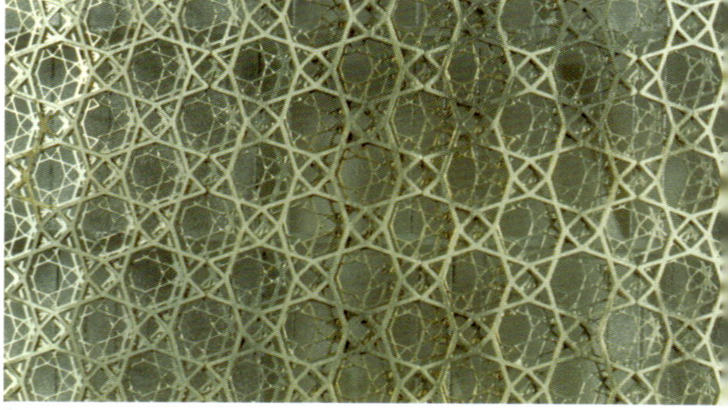

2

1 *General view*
2 *Façade detail*
3 *Level 37 plan*
4 *Ground floor plan*

Renderings: *Courtesy Ateliers Jean Nouvel*

Doha High-Rise Office Building | **Location** Doha, Qatar | **Completion date** 2007 | **Architect** Ateliers Jean Nouvel | **Local architect** Arab Engineering Bureau | **Client** H.E. Sheikh Saud Al-Thani | **Structural and mechanical engineers** Terrell International | **Landscape architect** Hardy Ingénieurs et Paysages | **Façade consultant** BCS s.a. | **Height** 204 m/669 ft; 231.5 m/759.5 ft with spire | **Above-ground storeys** 44 | **Basements** 3 | **Use** Office | **Gross building area** 100,000 sq m/1,076,000 sq ft | **Structural materials** Steel, concrete | **Other materials** Aluminium, glass

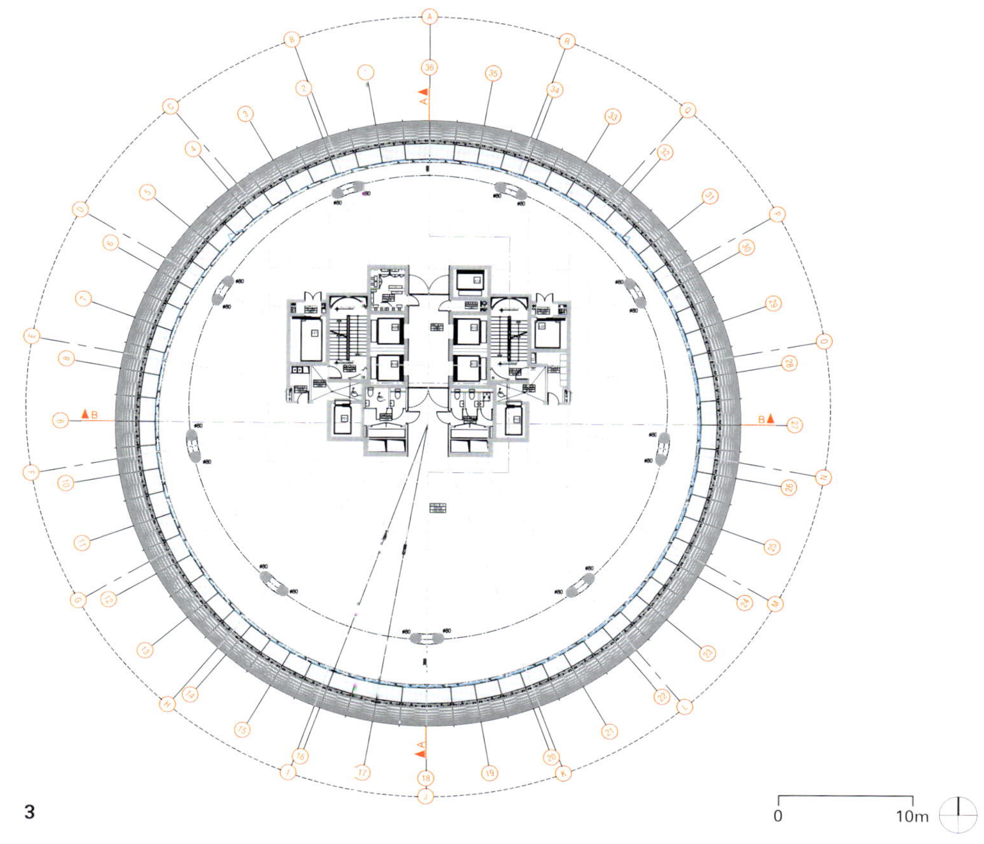

3

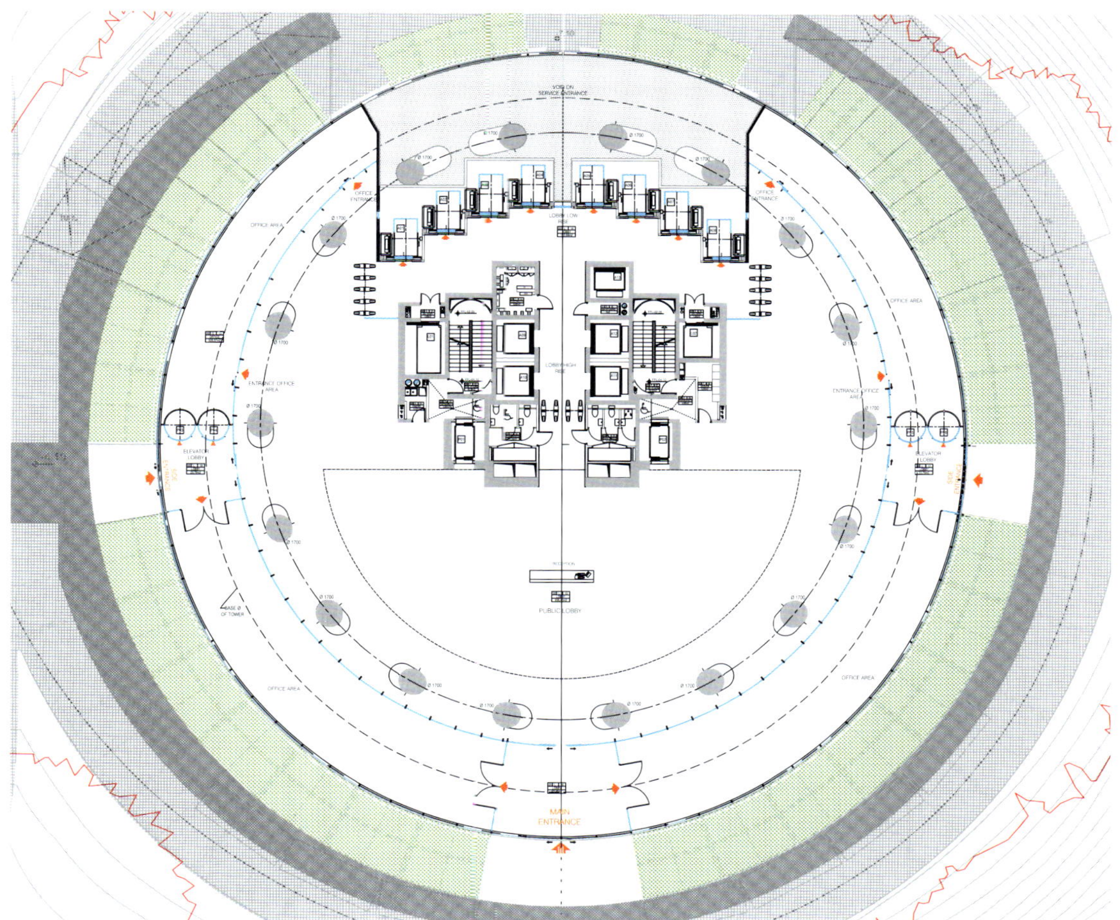

4

MOSHE AVIV TOWER RAMAT GAN ISRAEL

The Moshe Aviv Tower is located in the diamond exchange area of Ramat Gan, close to the main traffic arteries of metropolitan Tel-Aviv.

The building has two main entrances, with an elegant residential lobby and an office lobby. Its 69 upper floors are divided into a commercial floor, entrance lobby, office floors up to the 54th floor, apartments up to the 66th floor, a three-storey technical floor and helipad on the roof. The third floor contains a synagogue, and floors four and five house a luxurious spa with a swimming pool.

At the main entrance to the building is a 2500-square-metre plaza with cafés and restaurants, cascades of water and a series of podiums and stairs providing seating. The lobby is a continuation of the entrance plaza and the impressive entrance is covered by a canopy suspended from the stone columns that rise above it.

The façade of the rectangular block was designed for the most part in granite, with an emphasis on its corners and verticality. The circular wing, 'supported' by the rectangular wing, was designed as a glass and aluminium cylinder, rising up to the full height of the building and topped by a crown that forms part of the helipad.

The residential floors occupy the top 13 storeys of the circular wing. The larger windows on these floors required a special design for the upper floors in the rectangular wing, which enriched the design of the building as a whole.

The Moshe Aviv Tower, as a very tall reinforced concrete building, posed unique challenges that required the use of innovative construction techniques. The engineering approach involved the creation of a rigid frame, so that the core that stabilises the building in practice is an external concrete frame with a much higher degree of rigidity relative to the core.

1

2

3

1 *General view*
2 *Façade detail*
3 *Residential upper levels*
4 *Main elevation*
5 *Typical office floor plan*
6 *Upper residential floor plan*

Photography: *Ronna Vatash (1,3); Ran Erde (2)*

Moshe Aviv Tower | **Location** Ramat-Gan, Israel | **Completion date** 2003 | **Architect** A Niv, A Schwartz Architects – Amav Planning | **Client** Aviv & Co Ltd; Ocif Investment & Development Ltd | **Structural engineer** Y David Engineer Ltd | **Contractor** Aviv & Co Ltd | **Height** 235 m/771 ft | **Above-ground storeys** 68 | **Basements** 5 | **Above-ground useable levels** 63 | **Mechanical levels** 5 | **Use** Office, residential | **Site area** 8373 sq m/90,093 sq ft | **Structural materials** Reinforced concrete, glass and stone curtainwall | **Other materials** Aluminium, glass, stone | **Cost** US$100 M

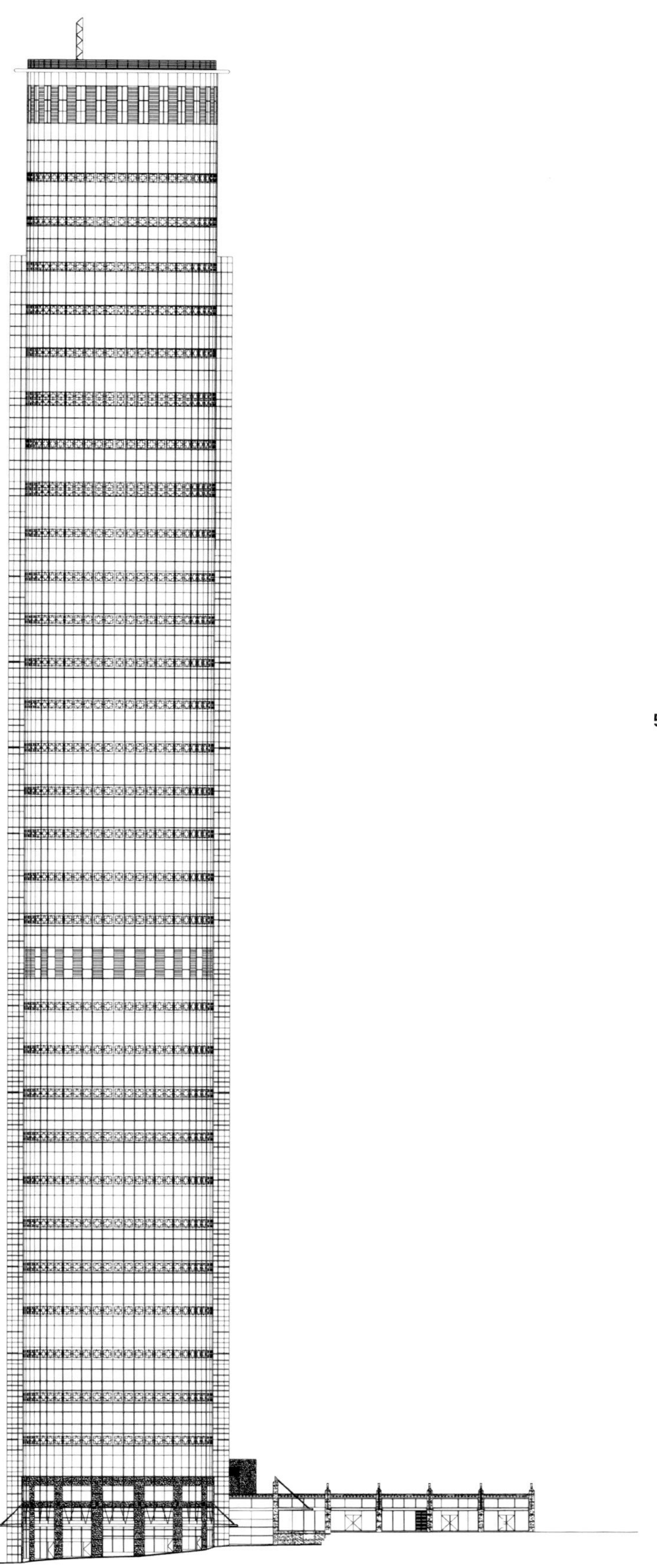

4

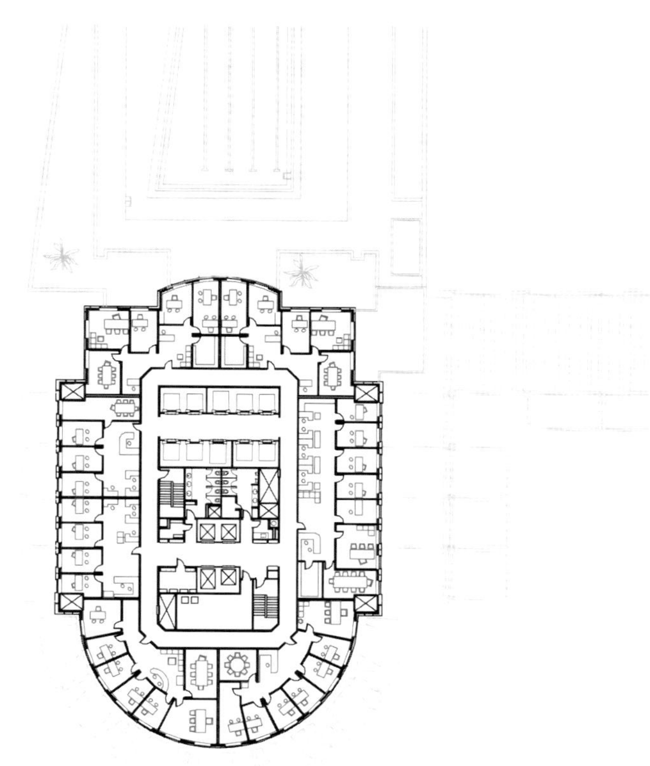

5

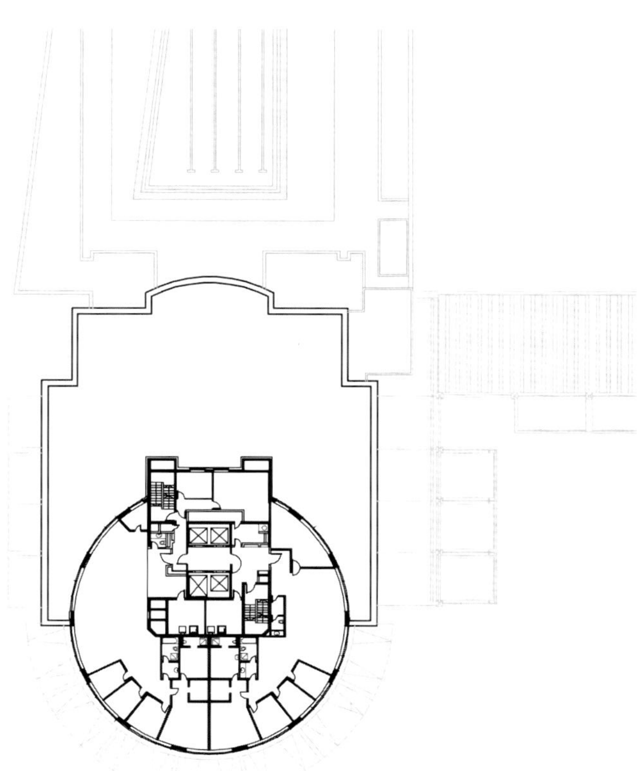

6

ONE CANADA SQUARE AT CANARY WHARF

LONDON
UNITED KINGDOM

The One Canada Square tower embodies the spirit of London's economic future, its bold form marking the entire Canary Wharf complex on the London skyline. At 236.2 metres and 48 storeys, the building, a tall square prism with indented corners that culminate in a square pyramid against the sky, is considered England's first true skyscraper.

Designed as a connection with the future – a building for the 21st century – the tower's exterior walls and pyramidal roof are stainless steel surfaces that reflect changes in the light and colour of the sky. The tower appears to softly gleam in the grey and misty London days. The highlights on the ribbing of the walls create a thin tracery of vertical lines that reflect the sunlight. The corners are indented to reduce the apparent girth of the tower and emphasise its height. The articulated corners also allow natural light to illuminate the interior and reach the inner ring of corridors on every floor.

1 *Aerial view*
2,4,5 *General views*
3 *Site plan*

Photography: *Courtesy Canary Wharf Group Plc.*

1

2

One Canada Square at Canary Wharf | **Location** London, United Kingdom | **Completion date** 1991 | **Architect** Cesar Pellli & Associates | **Architect of record** Adamson Associates | **Client** Olympia & York Canary Wharf Limited | **Structural engineer** WS Atkins Transportation Engineering, Epsom, Surrey; M.S. Yolles & Partners, Toronto; M.S. Yolles & Partners Ltd., London | **Transportation engineer** MS Yolles & Partners, Toronto and London | **Mechanical engineer** The Mitchell Partnership | **Height** 236.2 m/775 ft | **Above-ground storeys** 48 | **Use** Office | **Area of office space** 162,575 sq m/ 1,750,000 sq ft | **Structural materials** Curtainwall, glass, aluminium, stainless steel

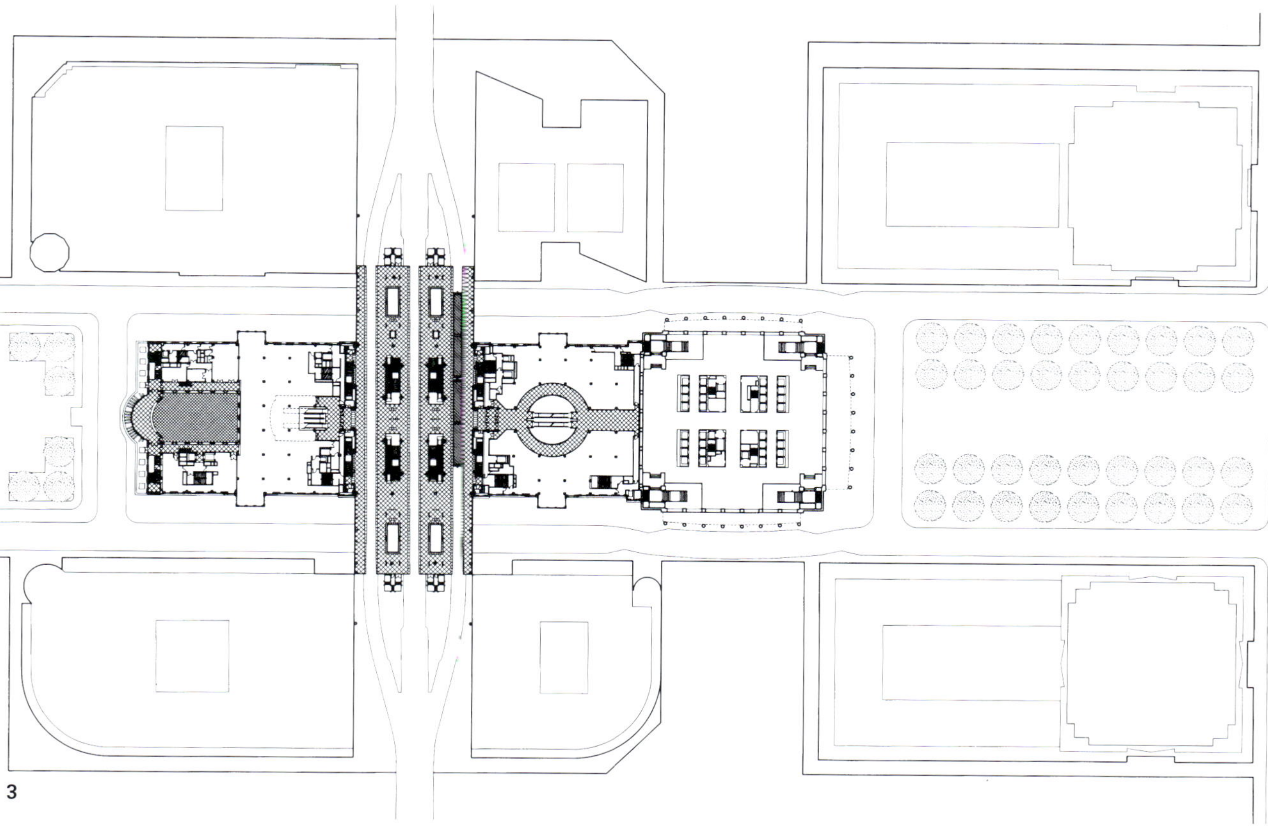

3

4

5

MOSCOW STATE UNIVERSITY

MOSCOW
RUSSIA

A fact not widely known is that the Moscow State University was the tallest building in Europe (with its spire included in the overall height) until 1990, when it was surpassed by Frankfurt's MesseTurm.

The university building was the tallest of eight high-rise projects planned in Moscow in the late 1940s according to a plan supported by Stalin. Those high-rise structures were not to imitate the tall buildings seen in other countries. Eventually, only seven of the eight scheduled high-rise buildings were completed, in the 1950s. The series of tall buildings include the 170-metre, 27-storey Ministry of Foreign Affairs completed in 1954 by architects V Gelfreikh and M Minkus; the 1955 Leningrad Hotel by architects A Boretsky and L Polyakov; and the 198-metre Hotel Ukraine by architects A Mordvinov with V Kalish and V Oltarzhevskii, also completed in 1957. The 264-metre, 57-storey Triumph-Palace recently completed by DON-Stroy was designed in the spirit of those early Russian tall buildings, and is the first building in Moscow to be taller than the Moscow State University.

The university rises higher above the city than any other Moscow skyscaper, and occupies a dominant position on the Vorobyovy Hills; the others accentuate the concentric radial design of the city's plan of expansion. The high-rise central part of the project with two symmetrical wings was to accommodate the chemistry and physics faculties.

Those Russian skyscrapers added life to the city skyline and interestingly accommodated a variety of different building uses such as apartments, offices, hotels and academic quarters when at the time, most of the American tall buildings were used as office buildings.

1

1 *Main elevation*
2 *General view*
3 *Spire detail*

Photography: *Airprint; courtesy Airprint Business Communication, Brussels*

Moscow State University | **Location** Moscow, Russia | **Completion date** 1953 | **Architect** Lev Rudnev, Sergei Tchernitchev, Pavel Abrosimov, Alexander Khriakov | **Client** Moscow University | **Engineer** Vsevolod Nasonov | **Height** 240 m/787 ft | **Above-ground storeys** 36 | **Basements** 4 | **Use** Academic | **Area of above-ground building** 100,000 sq m/1,076,000 sq ft

2

3

BAHRAIN WORLD TRADE CENTER

MANAMA
KINGDOM OF BAHRAIN

The Bahrain World Trade Center site is prestigiously located on the main King Faisal Highway in Manama, Bahrain. Offering unobstructed views over the Arabian Gulf, more than half its area is currently developed, and comprises the Bahrain Sheraton Hotel, the associated single-storey luxury shopping mall, an office tower, car parking, services and landscaped areas.

The masterplan for the new development will provide additional twin office towers, a new shopping mall with anchor tenant, garden court and food outlets. Overall, the entire complex will include improvements designed to rejuvenate and breathe new life into the existing mall and hotel development.

Two triangular shaped towers tapering to a height of 240 metres sit above a sculpted three-storey podium, each providing 34 floors of office space and an exclusive 42nd floor viewing deck. Borrowing from a distinctly nautical theme, each tower is visually anchored to the ground by a concertina of curved, sail-like forms that progressively peel back to reveal a dramatic form that resembles a shard of blue glass.

Unique to this building and rising to the challenge of incorporating renewable energy solutions with sustainable architecture, the design provides for three 29-metre-diameter wind turbines horizontally supported between the towers. In plan, the sail profiles of the two towers funnel the onshore breeze between them as well as creating lift behind, thus further accelerating the wind velocity between the twin structures. The turbines are expected to produce between 11 and 15 percent of the total electrical consumption of the building.

The podium accommodates a single-storey extension to the existing shopping mall and reflects the already established modular, axial and spatial parameters. Three levels of covered car parking are available within the podium with further extensive parking and service areas provided in the basement.

1

1 *General view*

2 *16th floor plan of the Bahrain World Trade Center*

3 *The BWTC has the potential to become an iconic building*

4 *The twin towers face the Arabian Gulf*

5 *Three horizontally supported wind turbines are located between the towers*

Photography and renderings: *Courtesy Atkins*

Bahrain World Trade Center | **Location** Manama, Kingdom of Bahrain | **Completion date** 2006 | **Architect** Atkins | **Client** Awal Hoteling Company SPC | **Structural engineer** Atkins | **Mechanical engineer** Atkins | **Landscape architect** Shankland Cox Limited | **Contractor** Nass-Murray & Roberts (JV) | **Height** 240 m/787 ft | **Above-ground storeys** 45 | **Basements** 1 | **Above-ground useable levels** 37 + 1 (parking) | **Mechanical levels** 7 | **Use** Mixed use | **Site area** 88,617 sq m/953,900 sq ft | **Area of above-ground building** 708,936 sq m/7,631,000 sq ft | **Structural materials** Steel, block work, curtain wall, reinforced concrete | **Other materials** Stone cladding, aluminium

2

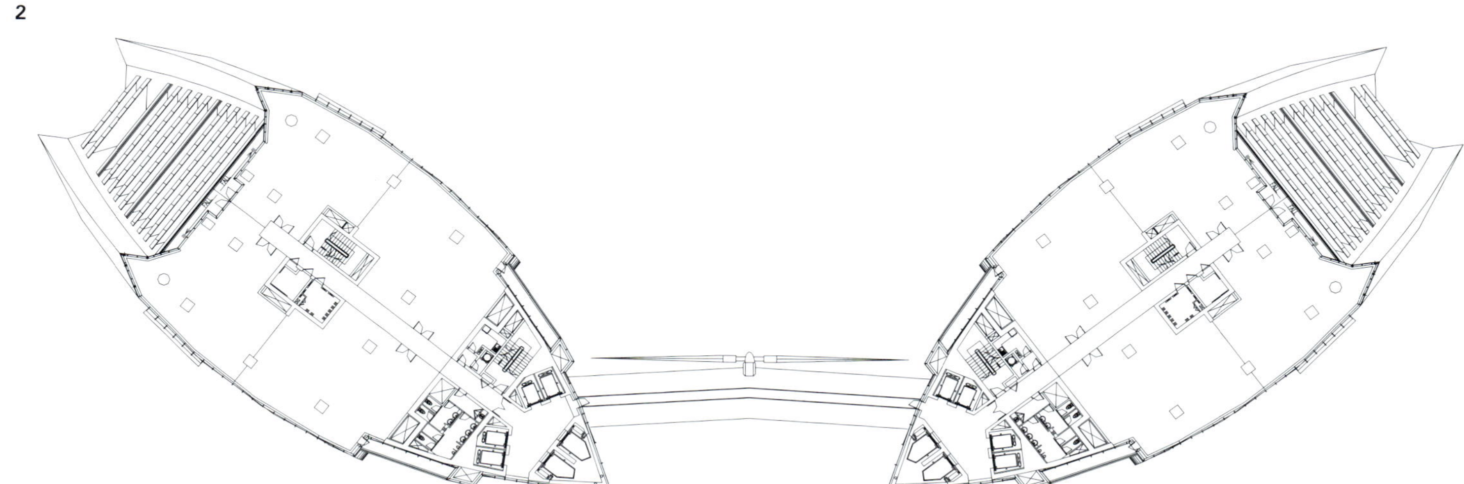

3

4

5

HERON TOWER LONDON UNITED KINGDOM

Heron Tower synthesises urban concerns with innovative technology and environmental responsibility. Set within the City cluster on a prominent site at the junction of Bishopsgate and Camomile Street, the building will provide the highly flexible work space demanded by the latest generation of City occupiers. Responding to both the technical and social demands of the modern workplace, the building is organised around a series of office 'villages'. At the heart of each is a triple-height atrium.

Unlike the earlier generation of tall buildings in the City whose monolithic forms are mute within their urban context, Heron Tower will be a transparent and articulate structure. To the south, a slender lift core is animated by the movement of glazed lift cars, two of which provide access to the new public restaurant at roof level. The face of the building reveals the internal organisation of office villages. Its richly textured northern elevation displays the internal organisation of stacked atria. To the east and west, a bio-climatic ventilated façade provides an energy efficient and highly transparent enclosure.

The proposed building will offer significant improvements through the pedestrianisation of the section of Houndsditch to the north of the site. An arcade along Bishopsgate provides a generous footpath to this busy street.

For its user, the building will set a new standard of accommodation in the City. For London, Heron Tower will be the first bespoke multi-tenant high-rise, providing a powerful magnet for attracting foreign tenants. The public will benefit from the quality of the enhanced civic realm with its new retail and restaurant facilities at the base and top of the building.

Heron Tower challenges the conventional typology of the highrise to provide a unique addition to London's architecture.

1

1 *View from London Wall looking west*
2 *Bishopsgate, looking south*
3 *Typical floor plan. The deep plan floor at the base of the village can accommodate a variety of tenant fitouts.*

Renderings: *Hayes Davidson*

Heron Tower | **Location** London, UK | **Completion date** 2010 | **Architect** Kohn Pedersen Fox Associates | **Client** Heron Corporation | **Structural engineer** ARUP | **Mechanical and electrical engineer** Foreman Roberts | **Landscape architect** Charles Funke Associates | **Height** 242 m/794 ft (above ground to top of mast) | **Above-ground storeys** Ground + 46 | **Basements** 3 | **Above-ground useable levels** 41 | **Mechanical levels** 6 | **Use** Office, restaurant, retail | **Site area** 1920 sq m/20,659 sq ft | **Area of above-ground building** 63,000 sq m/677,880 sq ft | **Structural materials** Steel frame | **Other materials** Glass, stainless steel cladding

2

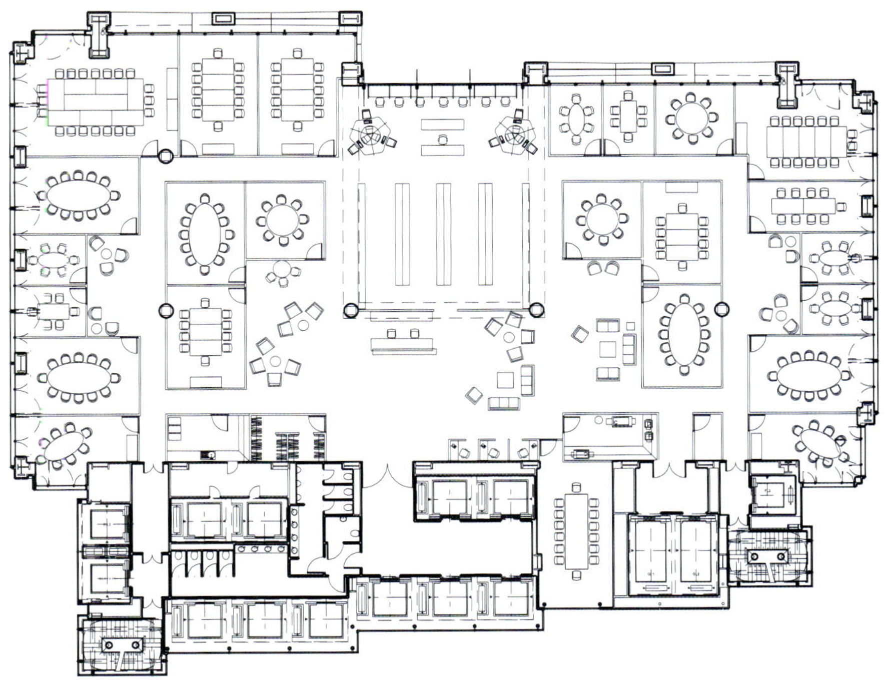

3

THE TOWER DUBAI
UNITED ARAB EMIRATES

The Tower is a landmark, high-rise residential project located on Sheikh Zayed Road in Dubai. It consists of a 54-storey superstructure that rises to 248 metres above grade level.

The basement level houses MEP service rooms. The ground floor contains the main entrance hall and reception for apartments as well as building administration offices, a coffee shop and circulation spaces. Floors 2 to 31, accessible from the multistorey car park, offer a total of 180 three-bedroom apartments. Floors 34 to 49 accommodate 192 one-bedroom apartments. Certain floors within the tower block are designated as mechanical floors and have been devoted to MEP system installation. The roof level comprises additional building services and has been covered in elevation by a glazed pyramid-style crown feature combined with metal fins that impart a distinctive, stylish look to this slender skyscraper. External treatment consists of metal panel wall cladding with a high-performance, double-glazed, curtain wall system.

An eight-storey car park building annexed to the tower provides parking for 350 vehicles and offers a health club and swimming pool. Structural design of the project is based on precast reinforced concrete floor slabs over composite steel beams resting onto universal steel columns and RCC central vertical core element. The lateral force-resisting system at floors 32 and 50 connects the perimeter structural columns to the central core.

1

2

1&2 *General view*
3 *Floors 6 to 31 offer 6 3-bedroom apartments per floor*
4 *Ground floor plan*
5 *Elevation*

Photography: *Courtesy Khatib & Alami (1); courtesy Union Properties (2)*

The Tower | **Location** Dubai, United Arab Emirates | **Completion** 2002 | **Architect** Khatib & Alami C.E.C. | **Client** M/s Union Properties PJSL, Dubai | **Structural engineer** Khatib & Alami C.E.C. | **Mechanical engineer** Khatib & Alami C.E.C. | **Landscape architect** Khatib & Alami C.E.C. | **Contractor** Nasa Multiplet | **Height** 248 m/814 ft | **Above-ground storeys** 51 | **Basements** 1 | **Above-ground useable levels** 47 | **Mechanical levels** 4 | **Use** Residential | **Structural materials** Steel | **Other materials** Aluminum cladding | **Cost** US$63.8 M

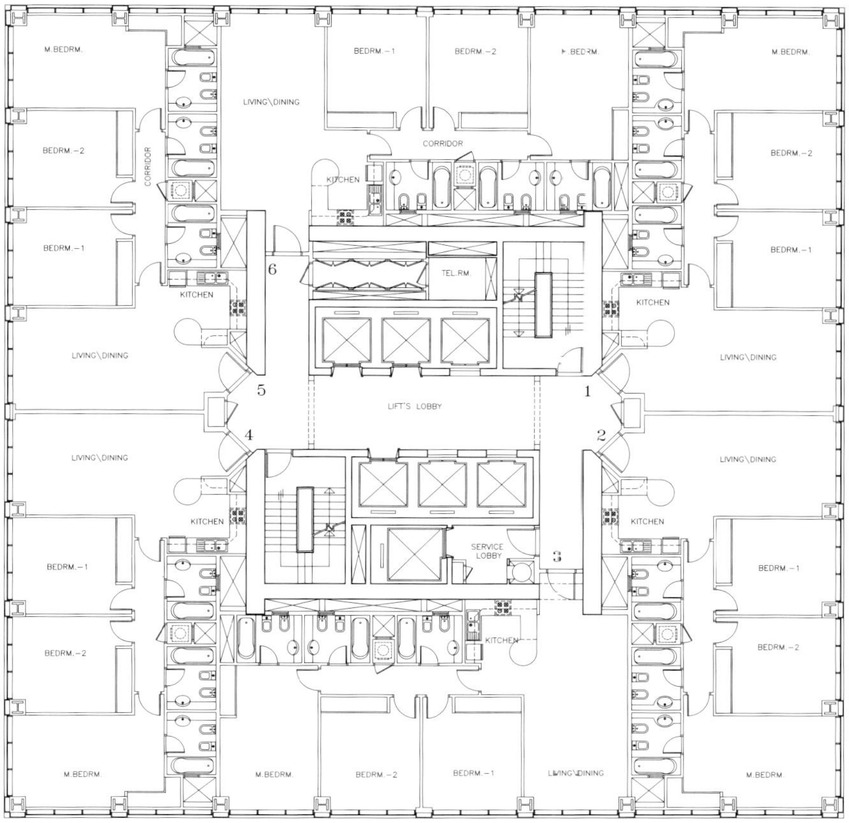

3

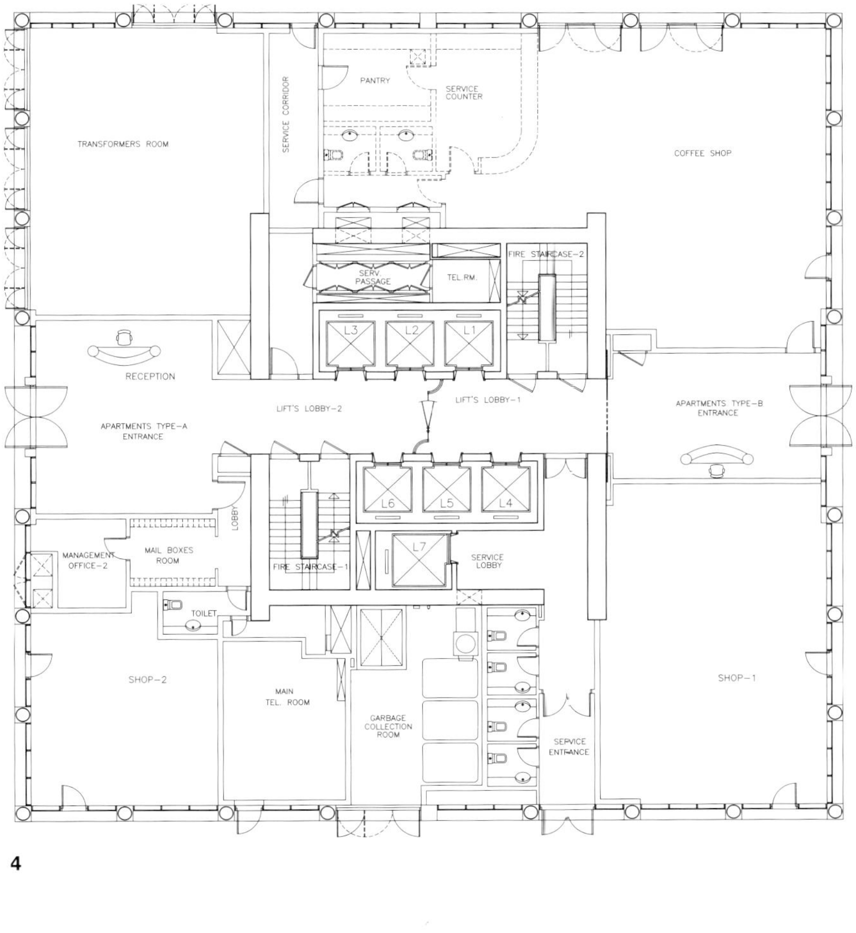

4

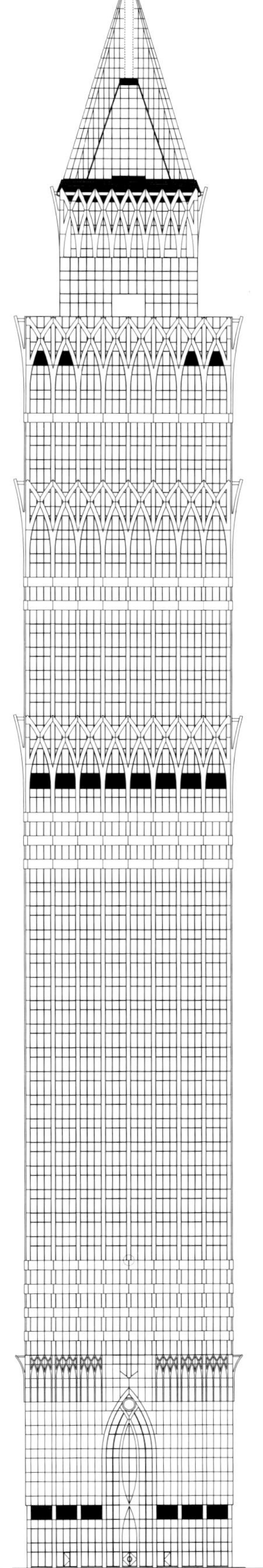

5

TORRE DE CRISTAL MADRID SPAIN

The four towers of Ciudad Deportiva will constitute a group of the most recent and important buildings in Madrid (and in all Spain). Although the towers form a group, they can still be identified as individual vertical sculptures against the sky.

The design of the Torre de Cristal expresses the optimism and the dynamism of the new Madrid. The tower will appear like a sculpture chiseled out of a great block of crystal, its facets capturing the light of the sky as if it were a carved diamond. As a result of the variety of facet angles, some of them will always reflect the light of the sky more strongly, giving life and movement to the total form.

The shape of the tower has a very old lineage that perhaps begins with the obelisks of Egypt but, at the same time, has a contemporary presence, full of life. The tower seems to arise from the earth with great force and aim towards the sky, accentuating its verticality. The Torre de Cristal's top is completed with sloping facets in a gesture of reverence towards the sky. It will immediately be a recognisable and unforgettable form in the skyline of Madrid.

The winter garden, at the top of the tower, will also communicate the message of the ecological aspirations and sustainability of the building. At night, the winter garden will become an immense source of light that will be visible all along the Paseo de la Castellana and from the north area of Madrid.

1

1 *General view*

2 *Level 45 floor plan, the top-most occupied floor with its sky garden*

3 *Ground floor plan*

Rendering: *Dieguez Fridman Architectos*
Plans: *Courtesy Pelli Clarke Pelli Architects*

Torre de Cristal | **Location** Madrid, Spain | **Expected completion date** 2007 | **Architect** Pelli Clarke Pelli Architects; Ortiz León Architectos | **Client** Mutual Madrileña Automovilista | **Structural engineer** Otep International SA | **Height** 250 m/820 ft | **Above-ground storeys** 45 office floors + 1 restaurant level | **Basements** 6 below-grade parking levels | **Mechanical levels** 6 | **Use** Office | **Area of above-ground building** 77,000 sq m/828,520 sq ft | **Structural materials** Aluminium and glass curtain wall

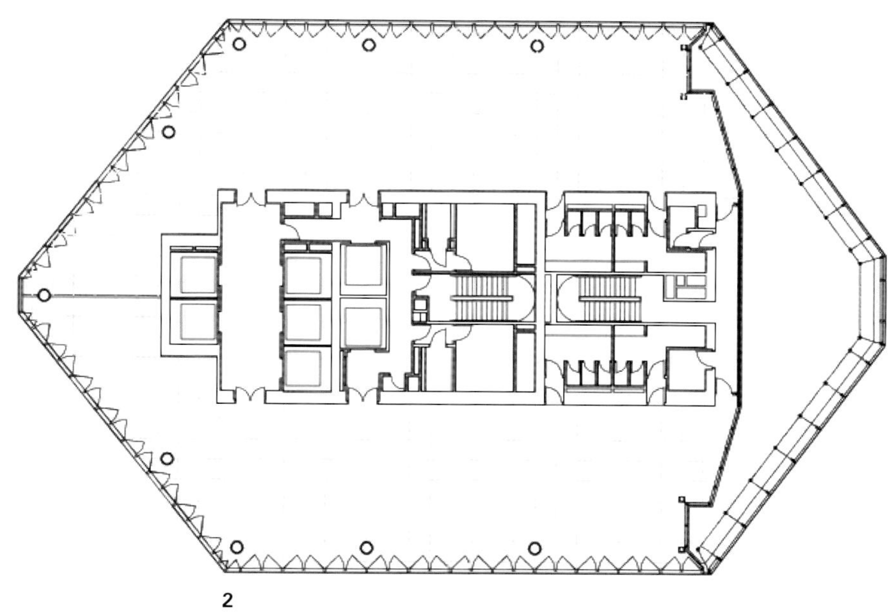

2

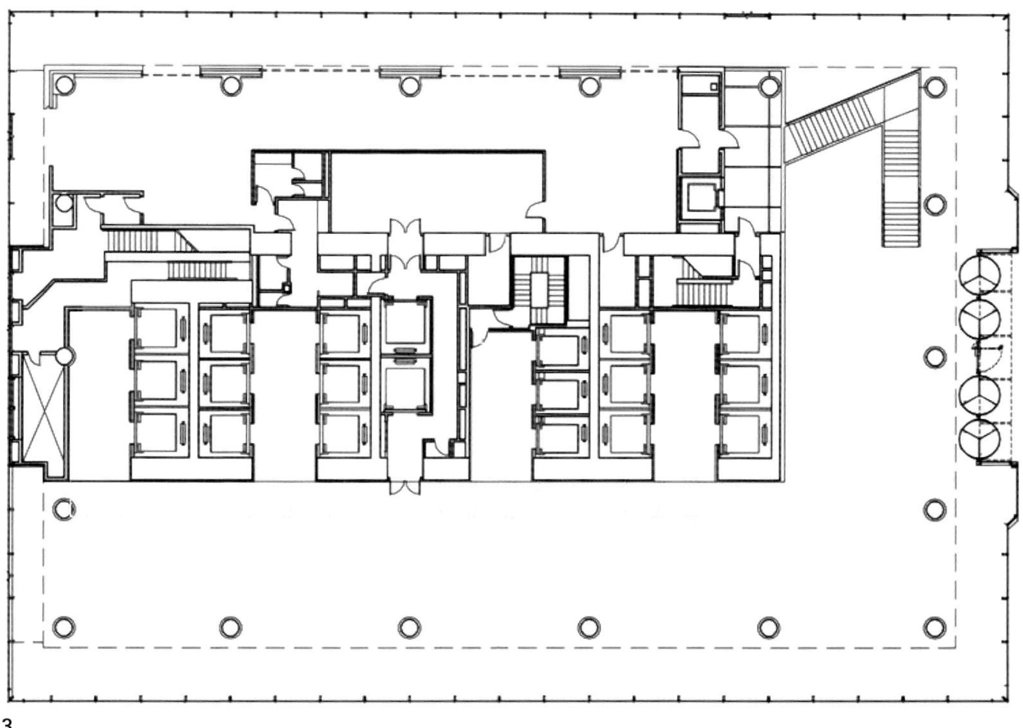

3

METRO TOWER AT CITY OF ARABIA

DUBAI
UNITED ARAB EMIRATES

City of Arabia is situated in a new suburb in the heart of Dubailand, developed by Ilyas and Mustafa Galadari Group. The project is a 40.4-million-square-foot development on a 20-million-square-foot parcel of land about 18 kilometres from Dubai International Airport. The main features of the City of Arabia development include the huge Mall of Arabia, the largest retail facility in the region and one of the largest in the world, with more than 1000 retail outlets and a wide range of attractions designed to make it a renowned shopping resort; the Restless Planet dinosaur theme park, developed in collaboration with the Natural History Museum of London, with the aim of blending a little science and education with a large dose of excitement; a canal flowing between apartment buildings, and lined with shady walkways, cafés, restaurants, convenience stores and places to relax; and finally, 34 elegant towers. The aim of the project is to build a community and create a desirable new suburb of Dubai.

The 53-storey Metro Tower is situated on a prominent site in the City of Arabia, facing towards the Emirates Road. The tower overlooks the new leisure and entertainment suburb of Dubailand to the north and is connected to the Wadi houses and covered walkways that line both sides of the flowing canal to the south.

The elegant metal-clad tower accommodates 16 office storeys in its lower portion and 28 residential storeys in the upper part, divided by the club house and sky garden. The façade of uniform punch-hole windows and white metal cladding extends from the very bottom to the highest tip of the building, successfully unifying the two different uses. The edges of the tower are streamlined by subtle curves. The floor plates of the building diminish as the tower rises, tapering from the maximum office floor of 19,500 square feet to the luxury sky-high duplexes at its crown.

This prestigious tower accommodates more than 200 luxurious one- to three-bedroom apartments, ranging in size from 600 to 2400 square feet.

1

1 *General view*
2 *Ground floor site plan*
3 *Typical residential floor (high zone)*
4 *Typical office floor (low zone)*
5 *Aerial model view of City of Arabia*

Renderings: *P & T Architects and Engineers Ltd.*

Metro Tower at City of Arabia | **Location** Dubai, United Arab Emirates | **Completion date** 2008 | **Architect** P & T Architects and Engineers Ltd. | **Client** Ilyas and Mustafa Galadari Group | **Structural and mechanical engineer** WSP Middle East Ltd. | **Height** 250 m/820 ft | **Above-ground storeys** 53 | **Basements** 1 | **Above-ground useable levels** 50 | **Mechanical levels** 2 | **Use** Office, residential | **Site area** 6359 sq m/68,450 sq ft | **Area of above-ground building** 62,708 sq m/675,000 sq ft | **Structural materials** Reinforced concrete | **Other materials** Metal cladding and reflective/tinted glass

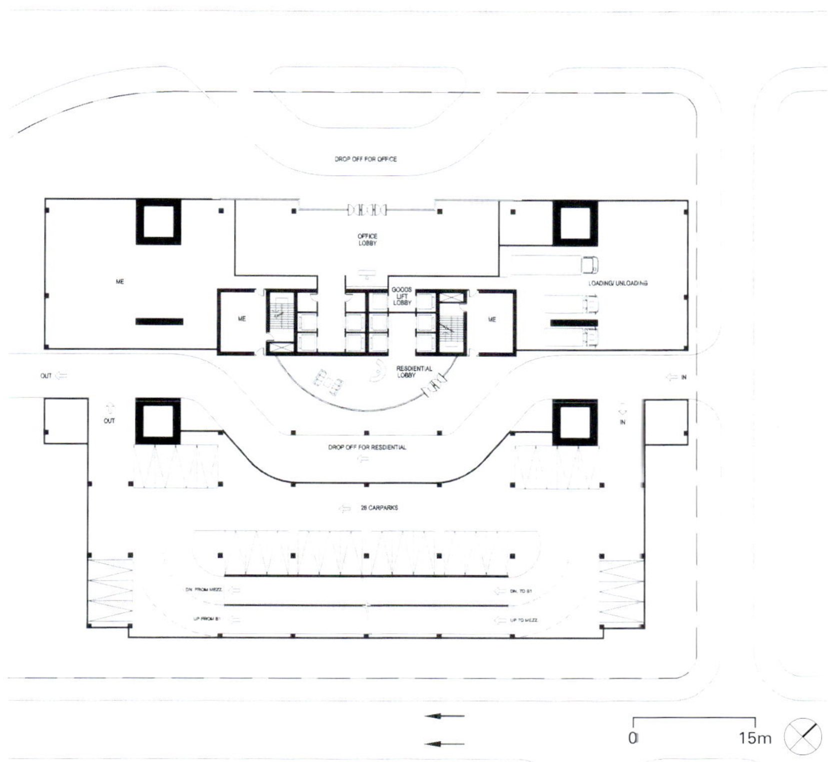

2

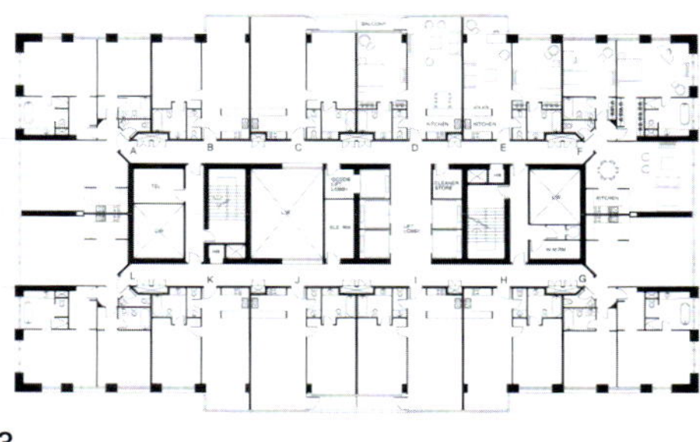

3

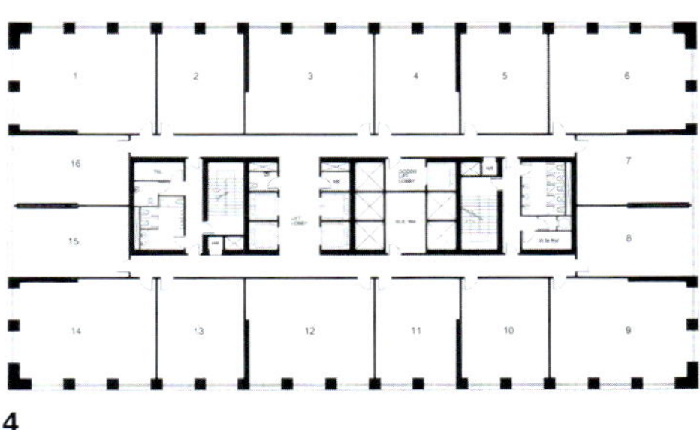

4

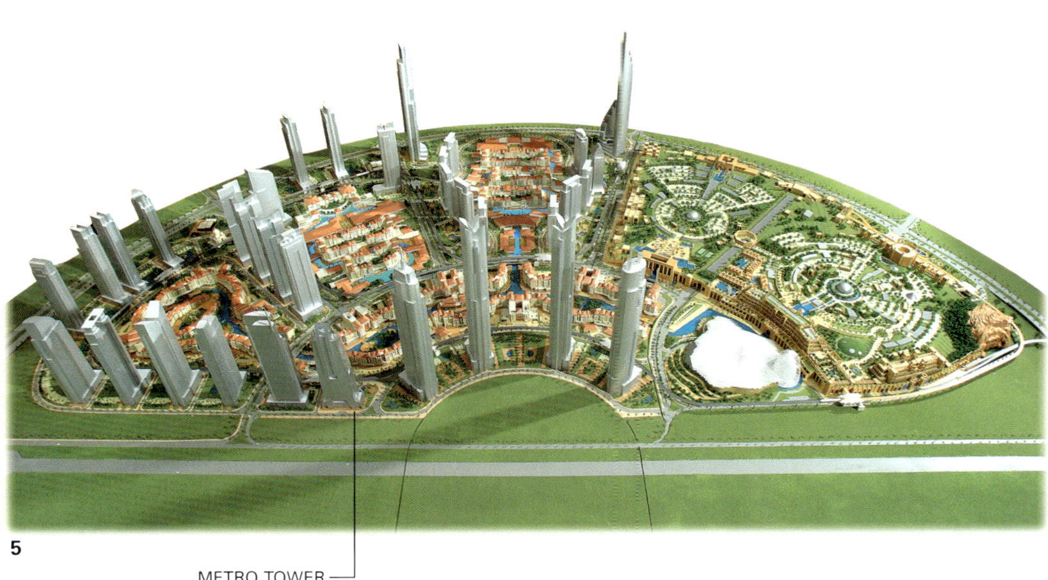

5

TORRE REPSOL YPF MADRID SPAIN

This new headquarters building for Repsol – the Spanish oil and gas company – continues Foster and Partners' investigations into the sustainable workplace that can be traced through a family of recent office towers, most notably for Swiss Re and Commerzbank. With this new headquarters, Repsol – for whom the firm also designed new service stations and roadside identity – will be able for the first time to consolidate its 3600-strong team in one location in Madrid in a building that communicates the company's core values.

The 53-storey building is located on the site of the former Real Madrid training grounds, where the city council has assigned sites for four new towers by international architects. It marks a curve in the wide boulevard of the Paseo de la Castellana – the 'backbone' of Madrid – and is carefully positioned to maximise the exceptional qualities of its site. Compositionally, the building can be thought of as a tall arch, the services and circulation cores framing the open office floors. At ground level, a 22-metre glazed atrium provides the transition from the street, and accommodates a 'floating' glass-walled auditorium set into a mezzanine. At the top of the building, the void space beneath the uppermost section of the 'portal' frame is designed to house wind turbines capable of providing a significant proportion of the building's power supply. This is an innovation that both signals Repsol's commitment to environmental sustainability, and indicates the company's progressive investigations into potential alternative energy sources.

Although the building is conceived as a corporate headquarters, it also has the flexibility to be partly sub-let, enabling Repsol to expand or contract its accommodation easily in the future as required. This degree of flexibility results in part from pushing the service cores to the edges of the plan – a strategy first used in the design of the Hongkong Bank – to create uninterrupted 1200-square-metre floor plates. Vertical circulation routes occupy minimal space as a result of an intelligent lift system that requires fewer lift cars than conventional systems. The cores are strategically positioned so as to block west–east direct sunlight, a move that has the added benefit of framing spectacular views of the hills of Sierra de Guadarrama to the north and the centre of Madrid to the south.

1

2

3

1 *Elevation*
2 *Visualisation from street level*
3 *Visualisation from street level at night*
4 *Plaza plan*
5 *Visualisation of entrance lobby*

Photography: *Courtesy Foster and Partners*

Torre Repsol YPF | **Location** Madrid, Spain | **Expected completion date** 2008 | **Architect** Foster and Partners | **Associate architect** Reid Fenwick Asociados | **Client** Repsol YPF | **Structural engineer** SGS Tecnos SA | **Mechanical engineer** Aguilera Ingenieros SA | **Height** 250 m/820 ft | **Above-ground storeys** 53 | **Basements** 5 | **Above-ground useable levels** 34 office levels | **Use** Office | **Site area** 7500 sq m/80,700 sq ft | **Area of above-ground building** 56,250 sq m/605,250 sq ft

4

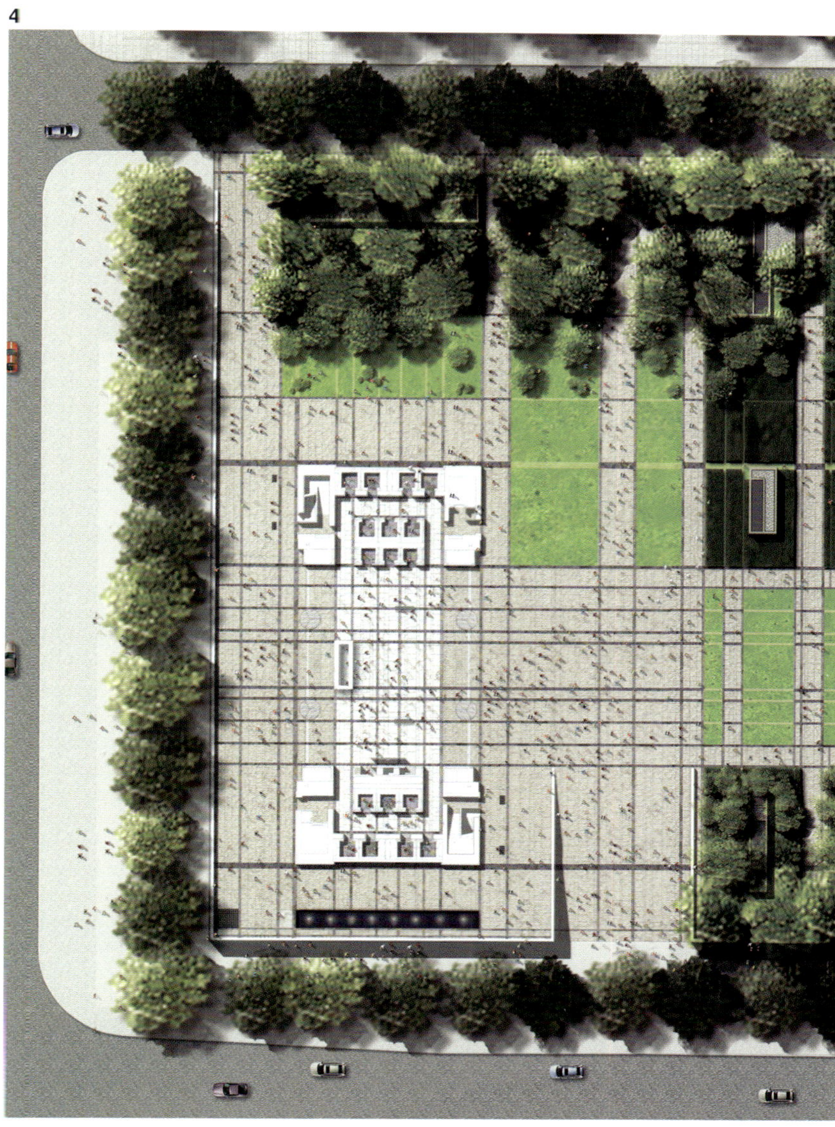

5

CHELSEA TOWER DUBAI UNITED ARAB EMIRATES

With its boldly sculpted white diagonal spine that encapsulates the building from ground to apex, the Chelsea Tower rises majestically above its neighbours, offering both aesthetic and spatial relief to a congested section of urban development. The tower is prominently located on a prime business plot on Sheikh Zayed Road within Dubai's 'skyscraper mile'. The building comprises a ground-plus-50-storey residential tower and an associated multistorey car park.

Atkins' scope of services includes the conceptual design, detailed architectural, structural, landscaping and electromechanical designs as well as full site supervision.

The tower comprises 86 two-bedroom apartments and 172 three-bedroom apartments on 46 typical floors. The three lower floors will accommodate 24 one-bedroom apartments and retail space on the ground floor. The building services are accommodated on the 19th, 35th and 49th floors. The car park building consists of nine floors with a capacity of 347 parking bays. A 25-metre swimming pool, gymnasium, squash courts and changing rooms are accommodated on the roof of the car park building. Total built up area of the project is 65,920 square metres.

The most striking feature of the building is the white diagonal spine, which stretches from the ground to its apex at a height of 230 metres. At this point, the white spine connects, forming a perfect square opening that frames the sky. A 40-metre-high needle is suspended at the centre of the opening, increasing the overall height to 251 metres.

1

2

3

Chelsea Tower | **Location** Dubai, United Arab Emirates | **Completion date** 2005 | **Architect** Atkins | **Client** Abdulsalam Alrafi Group | **Structural engineer** Atkins | **Mechanical engineer** Atkins | **Landscape architect** Atkins | **Contractor** Dubai Contracting Company | **Height** 251 m/824 ft | **Above-ground storeys** 51 | **Basements** 1 | **Above-ground useable levels** 51 | **Mechanical levels** 3 | **Use** Residential | **Site area** 929 sq m/10,000 sq ft | **Area of above-ground building** 51,042 sq m/549,400 sq ft | **Structural materials** Reinforced concrete | **Other materials** Reflective grey and blue glass and aluminium panel cladding

4

5

1 *Visual of the elegant tower*
2 *Entrance lobby*
3 *Roof top swimming pool*
4 *Apex of building seen from the pool deck*
5 *Typical floor plan*

Photography: *Nick Otty (1); Atkins (2,3,4)*

MESSETURM FRANKFURT GERMANY

At the time of construction, the MesseTurm, with a height of 256.5 metres (842 feet), was the tallest building in Europe. This height was the result of several factors, including the German workplace requirement that an office worker must be in the immediate vicinity of a window. This requirement reduced the size of the floor space surrounding the core of the building. The 'gate', which the tower forms at the street level, and the pyramid top, which is occupied by the cooling towers, also adds to the height.

Architecturally, the tower is derived from the great American skyscrapers of the 1920s and 1930s, rather than the modern buildings that compose the Frankfurt skyline today. The rigorous geometry that governs its shape begins in plan with a granite-clad, 41.8-metre square. This square is inscribed around a circle that is clad in glass. The circle, a cylinder in volume, is visible above the 'gate', at the notched corners and near the top, where the granite-clad square recedes. The glass cylinder steps back twice below the top pyramid and is articulated there by rhythmically alternating window recesses. Over the top rises a pyramid, stepping three times. The corners of the pyramid are centred on the sides of the tower where triangular bay windows rise from the apex of the gate to the top.

The entrance lobby is a clear glass cylinder and is surrounded by powerful columns supporting the core. The entrance lobby contains six shuttle lifts in an open frame leading to the sky lobby from which twelve lifts bring the occupants to their respective floors.

The building is constructed in concrete with a façade of polished red granite columns laced with flamed stripes and profiled aluminium bands at every floor. The glass is silver reflective glass. The mullion and window frame colour is metallic silver-beige baked-on paint.

1

1 *General view*
2 *Main entrance elevation*
3 *Lobby*
4 *Floor plan, level 57 to topmost office floor*
5 *Floor plan, levels 48–56*
6 *Floor plan, levels 9–28*
7 *Ground floor plan*

Photography: *Roland Halbe*

MesseTurm | **Location** Frankfurt, Germany | **Completion date** 1990 | **Architect** Murphy/Jahn, Inc. | **Client** Messe Frankfurt GmbH | **Developer** Tishman Speyer Properties | **Structural engineer** Dr.-Ing. Fritz Noetzold | **Mechanical engineer** Brendel Ingenieure GmbH | **General contractor** Hochtief | **Height** 256.5 m/842 ft | **Above-ground storeys** 63 | **Basements** 2 | **Above-ground useable levels** 60 | **Mechanical levels** 3 | **Use** Office | **Area of above-ground building** 85,000 sq m/915,000 sq ft | **Structural materials** Concrete | **Other materials** Granite, aluminium, glass

2

3

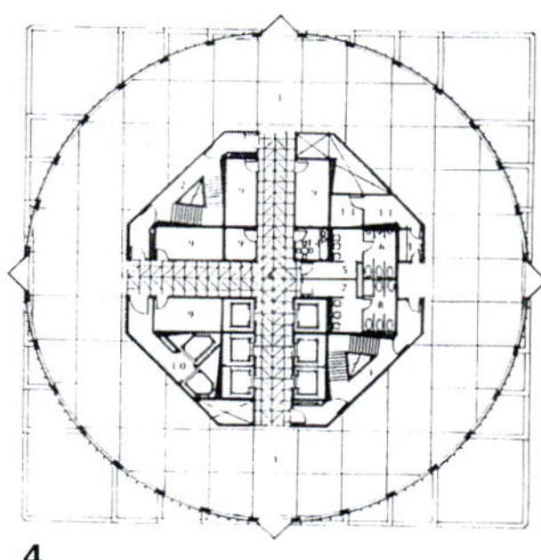
4

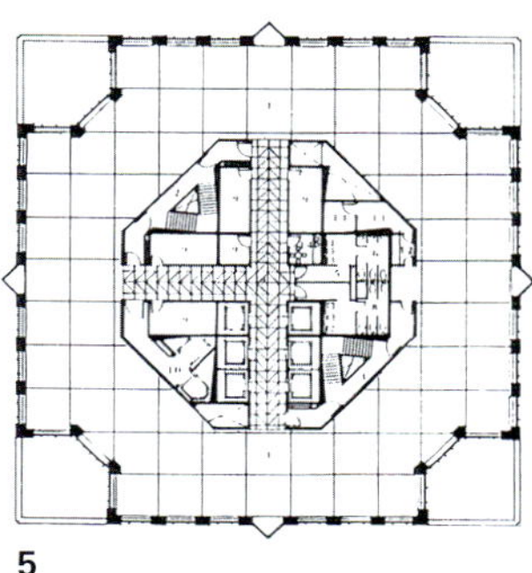
5

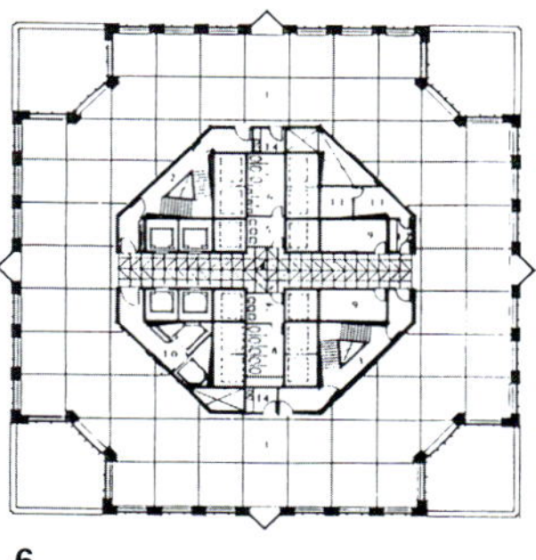
6

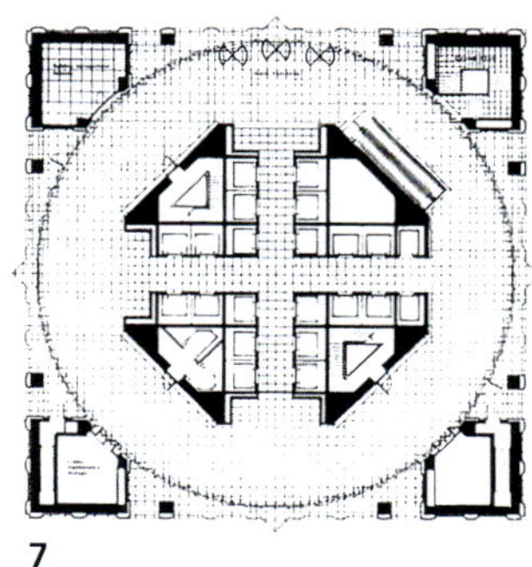
7

DUAL TOWERS AT BAHRAIN FINANCIAL HARBOUR

MANAMA
KINGDOM OF BAHRAIN

The US$270-million, phase one Financial Centre consists of three components: the Dual Towers (two 57-level buildings), the Financial Mall and the Harbour House.

At an imposing 57 levels, the uniquely designed Dual Towers will become the most visible and striking buildings on Manama's skyline. Offering beautiful panoramic views, the towers will provide office and commercial space for the financial sector. The Dual Towers will offer an expansive and efficient interior, with a balance of form, function and flexibility adaptable to the needs of its occupiers and will provide a high-tech, sophisticated environment for regional and international financial firms, offering the best IT installation opportunities and all the security and failsafe setup needed.

Spread across more than 74,000 square metres, the Financial Mall is a nine-level building. It takes the concept of a modern shopping mall and applies it to finance and ancillary activities and will offer an array of finance-related activities and services under one roof. The Financial Mall will house the Bahrain Stock Exchange and a retail environment for finance and investment services firms such as stockbrokers, market makers, proprietary investment firms, futures commission merchants and options brokers. It will also accommodate exclusive retail outlets and a state-of-the-art health club and spa.

Directly linked to the Financial Mall via a suspended bridge, the Harbour House is a 12-level building that is roughly circular, with an approximate diameter of 28 metres for a typical office floor. The building has primarily been set up for media and marketing enterprises that will benefit from the financial-based businesses of Bahrain Financial Harbour.

1

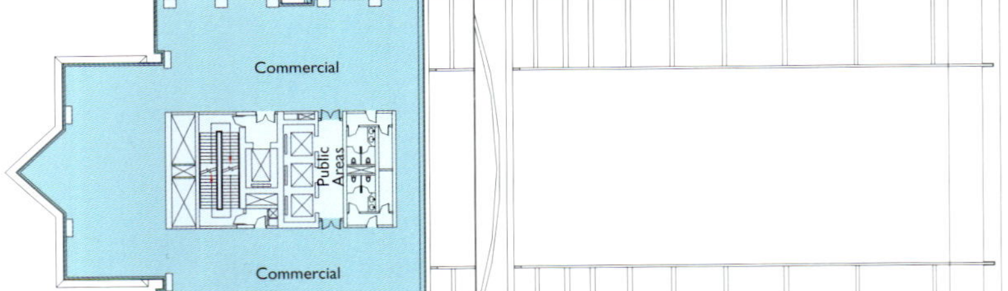

2

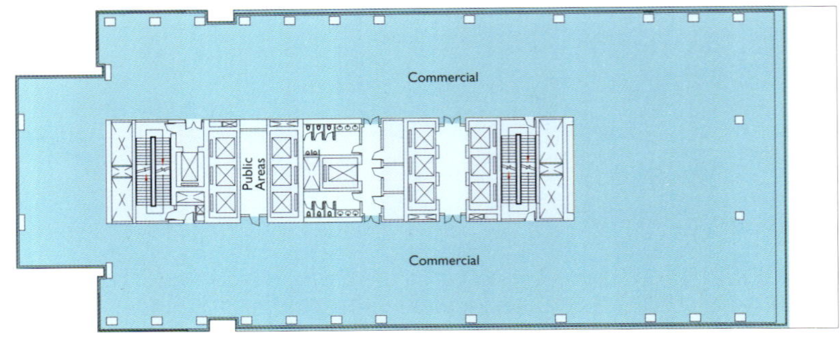

3

1 *Dual Towers – east and west towers*
2 *High-rise floor plan*
3 *Low-rise floor plan*
4&5 *Bahrain Financial Harbour general views*

Renderings: *Courtesy Bahrain Financial Harbour Holding Company B.S.C. (c)*

Dual Towers at Bahrain Financial Harbour | **Location** Manama, Kingdom of Bahrain **Completion date** 2006 (Phase 1) | **Architect** Ahmed Janahi Architects S.P.C. | **Client** Bahrain Financial Harbour Holding Company B.S.C. (c) | **Contractor** (Phase 1) Al Hamad Construction and Development Company | **Height** 260 m/853 ft (Dual towers) | **Above-ground storeys** 57 | **Basements** 1 | **Above-ground useable levels** 55 | **Mechanical levels** 2 | **Use** Office, retail, restaurants, leisure | **Area of above-ground building** 74,000 sq m/796,240 sq ft, per tower | **Structural materials** Reinforced concrete | **Other materials** Granite, aluminium panels and semi-reflective green glass

Bahrain Financial Harbour (BFH) is a US$1.3-billion development, to be completed in several phases and will cover 380,000 square metres of reclaimed land on a prime, north-facing section of the Manama corniche, near the historic Bab Al-Bahrain gateway to the capital. Designed and developed by the team responsible for the Dual Towers, this project is situated on the Kingdom's main island, just 10 minutes away from Bahrain International Airport, and 15 minutes from the King Fahad Causeway that links the country to Saudi Arabia. The waterfront development consists of 10 projects comprising 30 individual development parcels including the Financial Centre, office towers, upmarket residences, retail and dining outlets, Bahrain Performance Centre, which will house the Bahrain Royal Opera House, seafront walkways and promenades and marinas. When completed in early 2009, BFH will provide approximately 198,000 square metres of residential space, 210,000 square metres of office space and 130,300 square metres of retail, dining and leisure space.

4

5

TRIUMPH-PALACE MOSCOW RUSSIA

At 264.1 metres (including its spire), Triumph-Palace is Europe's tallest residential building. Located in the prestigious historical borough of Sokol, Triumph-Palace commands impressive views of downtown Moscow, Leningrad Avenue, and surrounding parks and recreation zones. The design of Triumph-Palace continues the glorious tradition of the monumental architectural style of the Russian capital's seven high-rise buildings built in the late 1940s.

All nine building sections are integrated into a single composition by a five-storey stylobate. The central building is the dominant element of the composition, with its proportionate vertical sections that gradually decrease as the building climbs higher. The front entrance of the central building is accessed from Chapayevski Park, though each building also has an independent entrance. The façades are panelled with light-toned natural stone and ceramic tiles of warm brown shades. The building has a Eurofox ventilated façade system. Vertical stained glass windows are a striking detail on the façades. Stained-glass corner glazing systems provide more natural light for the living quarters.

All apartments, each of which can accommodate a winter garden, include floor-to-ceiling corner glazing, bay windows, and French-style balconies protected by strong multi-layer triplex glass. Each section has two terraced apartments on the 25th level. Twelve unique penthouses, with panoramic windows and spacious terraces, crown the eight sections of the estate.

The infrastructure of the estate is oriented to an active lifestyle: the 5000-square-metre fitness centre includes a 25-metre swimming pool, Finnish saunas and Turkish baths, aerobics gymnasiums and sports halls.

The construction phase was completed by a unique technical operation to install a spire on the central building. Eight structural components, each weighing 4 to 8 tons, were transported to the building and each was installed in 5 to 10 minutes, while six days were required to assemble the spire as a whole. Using an original technique, an active lightning conductor on the spire attracts lightning and deflects it away from the building. The spire rests on an octagonal, three-storey-deep foundation, and special stairs inside the foundation access maintenance areas. The highest public viewing platform is at the foot of this foundation octagon, at the 200-metre point. The spire is coated with 700 square metres of stainless steel.

1

1 *General view*

2 *Penthouse apartment with terrace, rendering*

3&4 *Façade details*

Photography: *Courtesy DON-Stroy*

Triumph-Palace | **Location** Moscow, Russia | **Completion date** 2005 | **Architect** TROMOS | **Client** DON-Stroy | **Structural engineer** SMU-1 | **Mechanical engineer** SMU-1 | **General Contractor** SMU-1 | **Height** 264.1 m/866.5 ft | **Above-ground storeys** 57 | **Basements** 2 | **Mechanical levels** 4 | **Use** Residential, office, entertainment facilities, retail | **Site area** 6 ha/14.8 acres | **Area of building** 276,033 sq m/2,970,115 sq ft, including 168,633 sq m/1,814,491 sq ft of residential area | **Materials** Natural stone, brick, steel, iron

2

3

4

AL FAISALIAH COMPLEX

RIYADH
KINGDOM OF SAUDI ARABIA

The 240,000-square-metre complex includes a distinctive 267-metre-high office tower alongside a five-star hotel, a banqueting and conference centre, luxury apartments and a three-storey retail mall.

The office tower is square in plan, designed around a compact central core, and tapers to a point, with four main corner columns defining its unique silhouette. Observation decks at stages up the building correspond with giant K-braces, which transfer loads to the corner columns. The building is clad in silver-anodised aluminium panels with cantilevered sunshading devices that minimise glare, allowing the use of non-reflective, energy-efficient glass. These layered façades provide maximum control over the internal environment.

Above its 30 floors of office space, the tower houses the highest restaurant in Saudi Arabia, set within a golden glass sphere 200 metres above ground level. The observation deck below the globe provides a breathtaking panorama of Riyadh and the surrounding landscape. At its pinnacle, the tower narrows to a brightly lit lantern, topped by a stainless-steel finial.

The tower is set back from the King Fahd Highway to create a landscaped plaza. Beneath this is a banqueting hall, which can accommodate activities ranging from Islamic wedding ceremonies for up to 2000 people to conferences for up to 3400. A high degree of flexibility is achieved by a unique long-span arch system, which provides a column-free space 57 metres wide and 81 metres long, with a moveable partition system that can divide the hall into a maximum of 16 separate rooms.

A five-storey lobby at the tower's base forms a link between the hotel to the north and the apartments and shopping mall to the south. A spectacular coloured-glass wall in the lobby by the artist Brian Clarke has a desert theme interspersed with images representing natural regional and environmental features.

1

3

2

Al-Faisaliah Complex | **Location** Riyahd, Kingdom of Saudi Arabia | **Completion date** 2000 | **Architect** Foster and Partners | **Client** King Faisal Foundation | **Structural engineer** Buro Happold | **Contractor** Saudi Bin Ladin Group (SBG) | **Height** 267 m/876 ft | **Above-ground storeys** 30 office floors plus restaurant and viewing platform | **Use** Office (tower), retail mall, hotel, apartments | **Site area** 55,000 sq m/591,800 sq ft | **Area of above-ground building** 240,000 sq m/2,582,400 sq ft | **Structural materials** Concrete, steel, glass

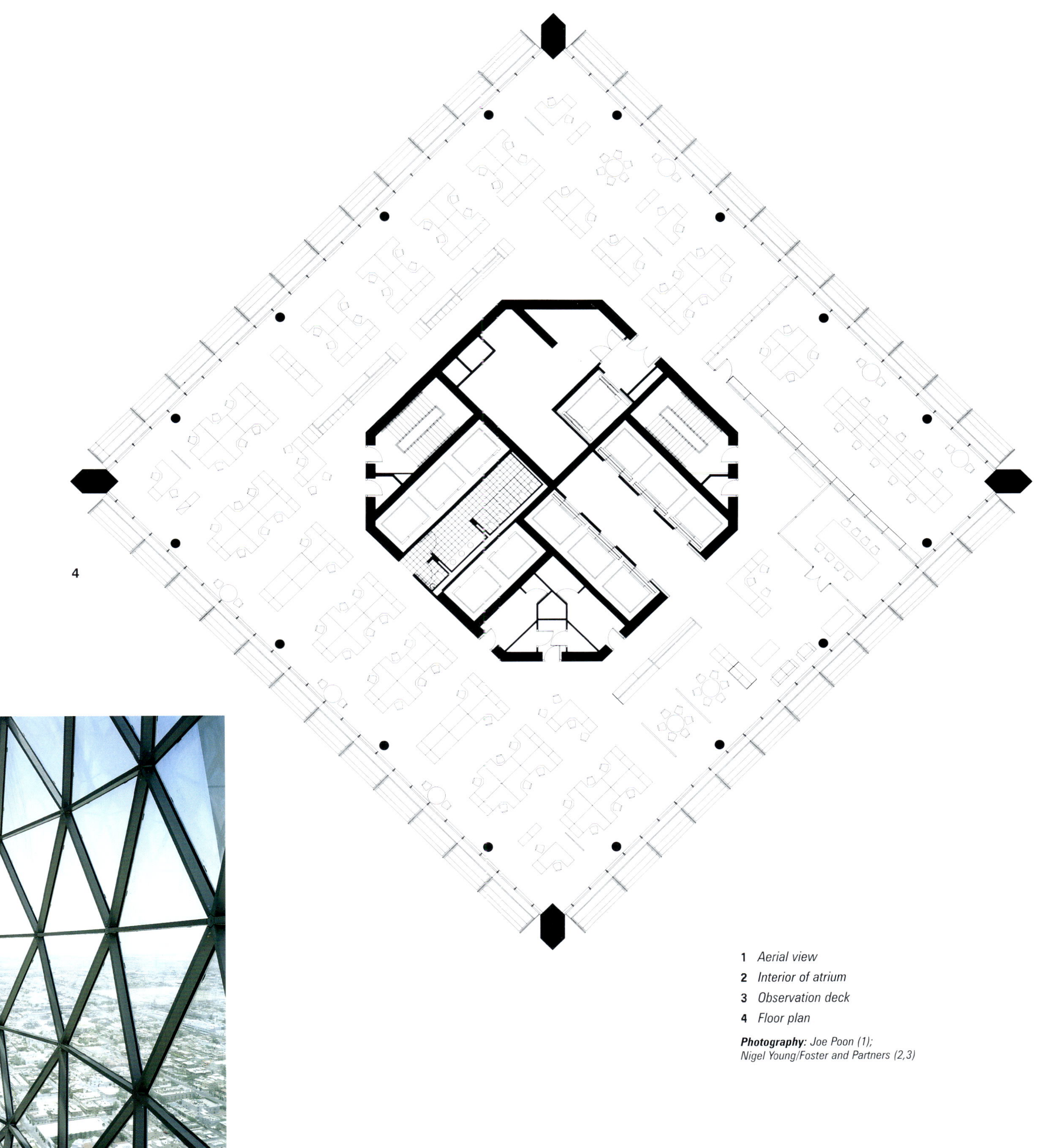

4

1 *Aerial view*

2 *Interior of atrium*

3 *Observation deck*

4 *Floor plan*

Photography: *Joe Poon (1); Nigel Young/Foster and Partners (2,3)*

21ST CENTURY TOWER DUBAI UNITED ARAB EMIRATES

The visually distinctive and modern 21st Century Tower was acclaimed as the tallest residential building in the world at the time of its completion in 2003. At 270 metres, it occupies a pre-eminent position on the Sheikh Zayed Road and adds a new sense of prominence with its simple clean lines and elegant form, complementing Dubai's contemporary urban landscape.

Atkins was appointed as lead consultant for architecture, interior design, structural, mechanical and electrical engineering design, construction supervision and project management.

The client's desire was for a signature tower with a modern design. The original design concept was derived from elements of the client's logo of overlapping birds in flight. A need to use durable external materials, capable of maintaining the building's appearance in the long term, was also expressed.

The concept reflects these aspects of the brief, and the front elevation features a curved silver aluminium and glass winged or 'feather' element that represents flight, grace and strength. This is complemented by the back elevation, which is a simple, symmetrically balanced façade that does not compete with the dynamic movement of the front elevation.

The initial massing of the tower was borne out of the site constraints, in terms of maximizing both its footprint and the height restriction. The result is a ground plus 53-level residential tower and adjoining multi-storey car park, with a total built up area of 86,000 square metres. The residential tower comprises 300 three-bedroom apartments and 100 two-bedroom apartments on 50 typical floors. The tower also accommodates retail space on the ground and mezzanine floors, as well as a gymnasium, swimming pool, and changing rooms on the roof, with building services taking up two floors.

The car park consists of nine floors with an overall capacity of 412 parking bays. Building services are accommodated in the car park building.

1

1 *At 270 metres, the 21st Century Tower was the tallest residential building in the world, at the time of completion*

2 *Curved 'wing' element of front façade*

3 *Entrance detail*

4 *Entrance reception lobby*

5 *Typical floor plan*

Photography: *Nick Otty (1); courtesy Atkins (2,3,4)*

21st Century Tower | **Location** Dubai, United Arab Emirates | **Completion date** 2003 | **Architect** Atkins | **Client** Al Rostamani Group of Companies | **Structural engineer** Atkins | **Mechanical engineer** Atkins | **Contractor** Arabtec & Al Rostamani Pegel (JV) | **Height** 270 m/886 ft | **Above-ground storeys** 55 | **Basements** 1 | **Above-ground useable levels** 54 | **Mechanical levels** 4 | **Use** Residential | **Site area** 1319 sq m/14,200 sq ft | **Area of above-ground building** 86,000 sq m/925,360 sq ft | **Structural materials** Reinforced concrete | **Other materials** Reflective grey and blue glass and aluminium panel cladding

2

3

4

5

CAPITAL CITY MOSCOW RUSSIA

Capital City is part of the Moscow International Business Center (MIBC), an investment-construction project known as Moscow-City. This multifunctional complex is one of the largest investment and construction projects in Europe, with an area of almost 27 million square feet. Its implementation is a sign that Moscow is taking its place as one of the world's leading international business centres.

The complex is located on the Krasnopresnenskaya embankment, just 2½ miles from the Kremlin. This location provides residents with panoramic city views, including the Kremlin and Moscow skyscrapers, river views, and views of the entire Moscow International Business Center development.

Capital City is composed of two residential towers, of 73 and 62 floors, named after the two capitals – Moscow and Saint Petersburg – and an adjacent office complex. The architectural approach to the complex is rooted in 20th-century Russian Constructivism, with its clear and distinct geometric forms. The square towers are twisted on axis at the technical floor levels, adding motion to their silhouette. The unusual geometrical design of the two towers provides structural strength and allows the creation of spacious apartments with panoramic windows. Echoes of Russian Constructivism can be seen not only in the proportion of the sizes of the podiums and the towers, but also in the design of the façade. The vertical lines are highlighted by a 'mosaic' made of dark and light terra cotta tablets. The tablets also emphasise the residential part of the building, where there is again a combination of smooth and rough surfaces on the podium façade.

The building program includes 1,125,840 million square feet of apartments from the 19th to 73rd floors; 907,300 square feet of offices on floors 4–17; a 238,765-square-foot shopping mall on the ground and first floors; a fitness centre, swimming pool and spa on the third floor; and 1,013,110 square feet of parking on the 1st–6th floors. The apartments in Capital City are divided into six types, with floor areas ranging from 1130 square feet for the one-bedroom Deluxe apartments to 2375 square feet for the two-bedroom Royal apartments.

1 *General view*
2 *Typical office floor plan*
3 *Typical residential floor plan*

Rendering: *Courtesy Capital Group Holding/NBBJ*

1

Capital City | **Location** Moscow, Russia | **Completion date** 2008 | **Architect** NBBJ | **Client** Capital Group Holding | **Structural engineer** Arup | **Mechanical engineer** Arup | **Vertical transportation engineer** Arup | **Height** 286 m/938 ft (Moscow Tower); 245 m/804 ft (St Petersburg Tower); 71 m/233 ft (office complex) | **Above-ground storeys** 73 (Moscow Tower); 62 (St Petersburg Tower); 18 (office complex) | **Above-ground useable levels** 68 (Moscow Tower); 58 (St Petersburg Tower); 17 (office complex) | **Basements** 6 | **Use** Residential, offices, retail, leisure | **Site area** 1.27 ha/3.14 acres | **Area of above-ground building** 211,066 sq m/2,271,895 sq ft | **Principal structural materials** Reinforced concrete with mega columns | **Other materials** Glass, terracotta, stone, aluminium, granite

THE BISHOPSGATE TOWER LONDON UNITED KINGDOM

The Bishopsgate Tower will be a major new development on land in the City of London at Bishopsgate and Crosby Square owned by German international capital investment company, DIFA Deutsche Immobilien Fonds AG. The Bishopsgate Tower has been designed by architects Kohn Pedersen Fox Associates.

The proposed building is 288 metres high and comprises 84,000 square metres of offices, retail and public space, which, together with sustainable energy systems, form a symbiotic part of the refined architectural design. The Bishopsgate Tower has the potential to become one of the most significant new buildings in the City with a design that will strengthen the overall character and identity of the emerging cluster of tall buildings in this location. The proposal will also make a substantial contribution to the public realm, opening up the ground level area to pedestrians and providing an important new public amenity that will enhance the immediate area and the wider environment. Inside The Bishopsgate Tower, restaurant facilities planned for the sky lobby on the 42nd and 43rd floor will be higher than any existing public space in London.

This building is a specific response to the site's unique location within the City of London. In its form, it could not exist in any other place. KPF's design unites and balances the new and emerging tall buildings within the City by completing the apex to the cluster. Equally important to the building's contribution to London's skyline is its contribution to the public realm. The design provides magnificent new public spaces at the sky lobby and ground levels and also links a number of important urban spaces along Bishopsgate and St. Mary Axe.

1

2

3

The Bishopsgate Tower | **Location** London, United Kingdom | **Completion date** Planning consent granted | **Architect** Kohn Pedersen Fox Associates | **Client** DIFA Deutsche Immobilien Fonds AG | **Structural engineer** ARUP | **Mechanical and electrical engineers** Hilson Moran | **Height** 288 m/945 ft | **Above-ground storeys** 60 | **Basements** 3 | **Above-ground useable levels** 54 | **Mechanical levels** 6 | **Use** offices, retail and public space | **Area of above-ground building** 84,000 sq m/903,840 sq ft

4

5

1 *View from Tate Modern*
2 *View from Threadneedle Street*
3 *Entrance*
4 *Ground floor plan*
5 *Typical floor plan*

Photography: *Courtesy Kohn Pedersen Fox Associates and Cityscape*

COMMERZBANK FRANKFURT GERMANY

The Commerzbank was considered to be the world's first ecological office tower. The outcome of a limited international competition, the project explores the nature of the office environment, developing new ideas for its ecology and working patterns. Central to this concept is a reliance on natural systems of lighting and ventilation. Every office in the tower is daylit and has openable windows. External conditions permitting, this allows occupants to control their own environment for most of the year, resulting in energy consumption levels equivalent to half those of conventional office towers.

The plan form is triangular, comprising three 'petals' – the office floors – and a 'stem' formed by a full-height central atrium. Pairs of vertical masts enclose services and circulation cores in the corners of the plan and support eight-storey Vierendeel beams, which in turn support clear-span office floors.

Four-storey gardens are set at different levels on each of the three sides of the tower, forming a spiral of gardens around the building. As a result, on any level only two sides of the tower are filled with offices. The gardens become the visual and social focus for village-like clusters of offices. They play an ecological role, bringing daylight and fresh air into the central atrium, which acts as a natural ventilation chimney up the building for the inward-facing offices.

The gardens are also places to relax during refreshment breaks, bringing richness and humanity to the workplace. From the outside they give the building a sense of transparency and lightness.

The tower has a distinctive presence on the Frankfurt skyline but it is also anchored into the lower-scale city fabric. It rises from the centre of a city block alongside the original Commerzbank building. Through restoration and sensitive rebuilding of the perimeter structures, the traditional scale of this block has been reinforced. The development at street level provides shops, car parking, apartments and a banking hall, and forges links between the Commerzbank and the broader community. At the heart of the scheme a public galleria with restaurants, cafés and spaces for social and cultural events forms a popular new route cutting across the site.

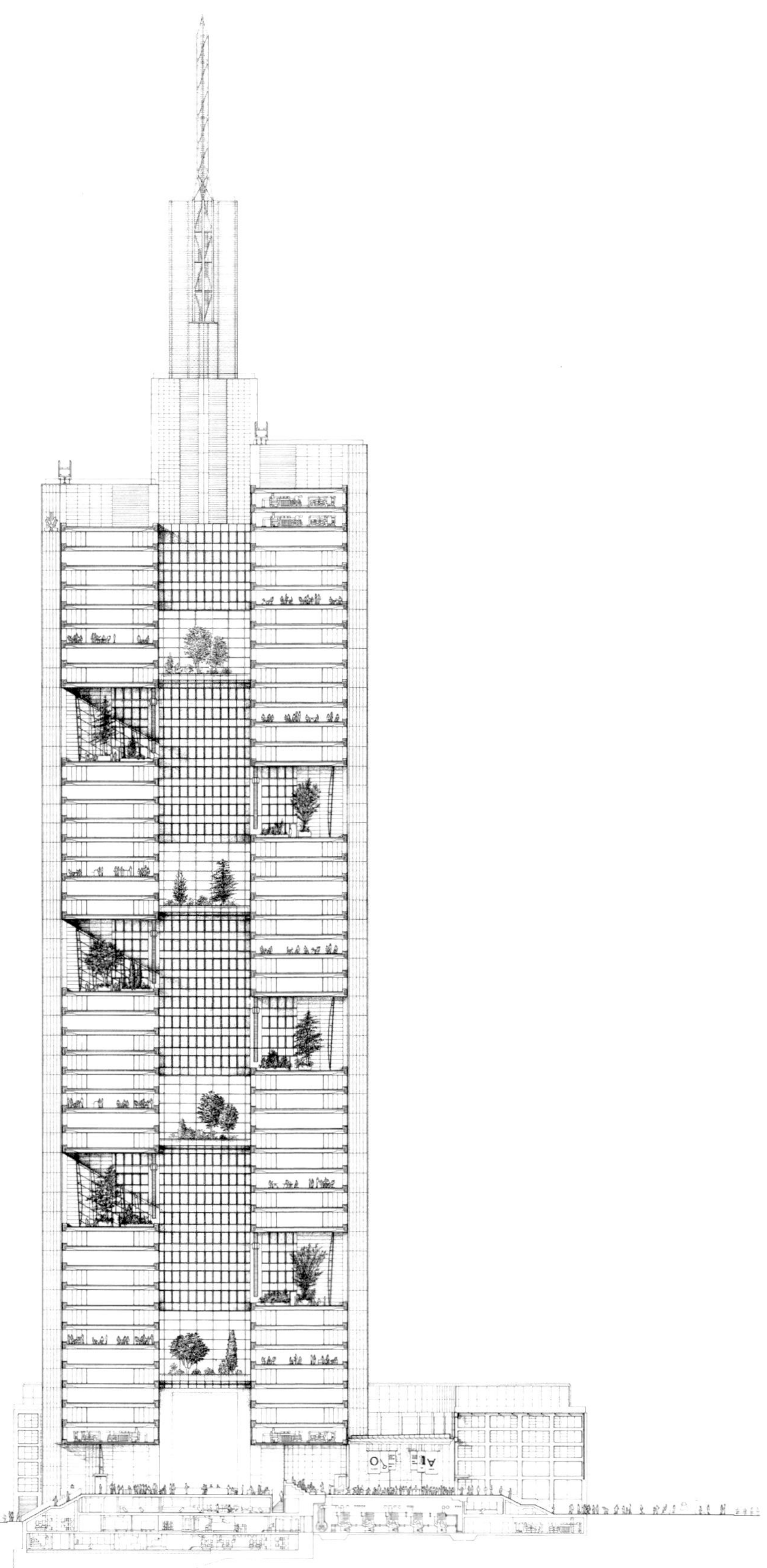

1

1 *Section*

2 *Interior view looking up from the lobby through 48 stories of the central atrium*

3 *Typical floor plan*

4 *Interior view of sky garden*

5 *Interior view of restaurant*

Photography: *Nigel Young/Foster and Partners*

Commerzbank | **Location** Frankfurt, Germany | **Completion date** 1997 | **Architect** Foster and Partners | **Client** Commerzbank AG | **Structural engineer** Ove Arup & Partners; Krebs & Kiefer | **Mechanical engineer** J Roger Preston & Partners; Petterson & Ahrens | **Landscape architect** Sommerlad and Partners | **Height** 258.7 m/849 ft (without aerial); 298.74 m/980 ft (with aerial) | **Above-ground storeys** 51 | **Basements** 2 | **Mechanical levels** 6 | **Above-ground useable levels** 57 | **Use** Office | **Area of building** 85,503 sq m/920,012 sq ft (tower) | **Structural materials** Reinforced concrete, steel

2

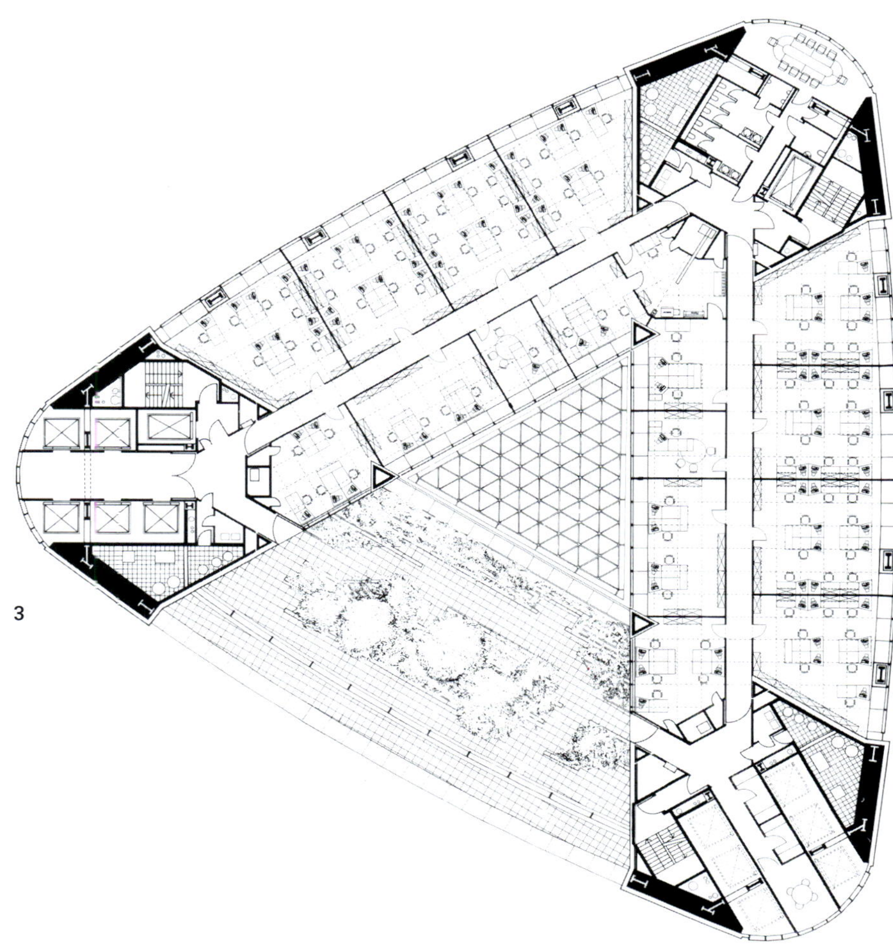

3

4

5

MOSCOW INTERNATIONAL BUSINESS CENTER

MOSCOW
RUSSIA

Swanke Hayden Connell Architects was commissioned by the Turkish Development Company, SUMMA, working with Russian investors, to design a 2-million-square-foot, mixed use, 67-storey tower on a 1.5-million-square-foot site. The building will have 31 floors of commercial office space based on a class 'A' US occupancy standard. Above the office space will be a sky lobby with amenities for the offices as well as the residents of the 19 floors of apartments above the sky lobby. At the base of the building, four floors of retail will relate to a huge retail complex in the centre of this site in central Moscow, not far from the Kremlin.

The overall mixed-use development, covering 148 acres, will house 30 million square feet of retail, residential, hospitality, commercial, government offices and a major transportation centre, and is divided into 16 parcel sites that ring the retail complex. These sites are being bought and developed individually by international consortiums under the unique requirement that all the parcels must be completed by the end of 2007.

1

2

3

4

Moscow International Business Center | **Location** Moscow, Russia | **Expected completion date** 2007 | **Architect** Swanke Hayden Connell Architects | **Client** ZAO Tekinvest | **Structural engineer** Thornton-Tomasetti Engineers Division | **Mechanical engineer** Consentini Associates | **Height** 300 m/984 ft | **Above-ground storeys** 67 | **Basements** 5 | **Above-ground useable levels** 64 | **Mechanical levels** 3 | **Use** Mixed, primarily office and residential | **Site area** 10,970 sq m/118,037 sq ft | **Area of above-ground building** 158,000 sq m/1,700,080 sq ft | **Structural materials** Structural steel, reinforced concrete | **Other materials** Stainless steel, granite | **Cost** F 275 M

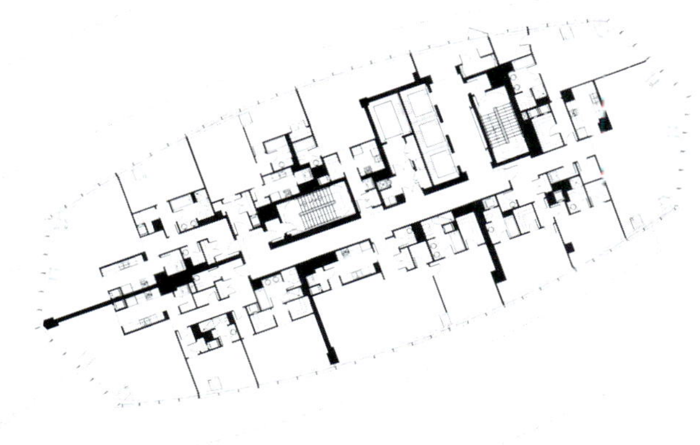

5

1 *General view*
2 *Tower base*
3 *Main lobby for office floors*
4 *Galleria overlooking lobby*
5 *Typical residential floor plan (48–66)*

***Renderings:** Courtesy Swanke Hayden Connell Architects*

KINGDOM CENTRE

RIYADH
KINGDOM OF SAUDI ARABIA

The Kingdom Centre is one of the Middle East's tallest buildings, occupying a 100,000-square-metre site in the heart of Riyadh's retail district. The three principal elements of the project, the Tower, the East Podium and the West Podium have a gross built-up area of 185,000 square metres plus 115,000 square metres of parking space for up to 3000 cars.

Unlike most podium and tower assemblages, where the tower rises from the podium roof, the Kingdom Tower actually rises from ground level, with the two podiums flanking it. This gives the tower an individual identity at the arrival apron, while still giving the impression from a distance of a tower resting on a single podium.

The East Podium accommodates a shopping mall, and the West Podium accommodates a wedding hall/banquet facility, conference hall and sports facilities. The upper third of the total tower height comprises a monumental inverted parabolic arch spanned by an enclosed observation bridge.

The deliberate use of butt-jointed glazing on the tower, coupled with the vast amount of space around it, gives the tower an enhanced scale, adding to its monumental character. The absence of scale-relating elements such as mullions and transoms or floor lines gives the tower, which is relatively small by global standards, the awe-inspiring scale and iconic quality inherent in very tall buildings.

In contrast to typical high-rise construction in western countries, the substructure and greater part of the superstructure of the tower are designed as a reinforced concrete frame. The top third of the tower is constructed in tubular steel frame, triangulated for stability against lateral wind forces. The connections between the reinforced concrete lower frame and the steel structure above incorporate specially designed high-strength steel anchor bars extending two storeys in height. The tower foundations comprise a reinforced concrete mat bearing on rock.

The building uses materials of silver reflective glass, concrete, granite and brushed aluminium. These materials, combined with variations in the reflection of the sky on the curved glass form, give the tower an unusually rich visual character.

1

2

3

4

1 *Night context view*
2 *Tower view*
3 *Detail of inverted parabolic arch*
4 *Podium detail*
5&6 *Tower's mix of materials adds to its monumental character*
7 *Floor plans (top to bottom): observation deck; level 24; level 22; level 14; levels 7–13; levels 1–6*

Photography: *Courtesy Ellerbe Beckett*

Kingdom Centre | **Location** Riyadh, Kingdom of Saudi Arabia | **Completion date** 2002 | **Architect** Consortium of: Ellerbe Becket, Inc., Minneapolis, USA and Omrania & Associates, Riyadh, KSA | **Client** HRH Prince Alwaleed bin Talal bin Abdulaziz Al Saud (Kingdom Holding Company) | **Structural engineer** Ove Arup & Partners | **Mechanical engineer** Ellerbe Becket | **Contractor** El-Seif Engineering Company | **Height** 302.3 m/992 ft | **Above-ground storeys** 38 | **Basements** 3 | **Above-ground useable levels** 34 | **Mechanical levels** 4 | **Use** Mixed-use: offices, hotel, residential, retail | **Site area** 9.3 ha/23 acres | **Area of above-ground building** 306,570 sq m/3,300,000 sq ft | **Structural materials** Reinforced concrete, steel, curtainwall | **Other materials** Glass, granite, brushed aluminium | **Cost** SAR 1.7 billion

5

6

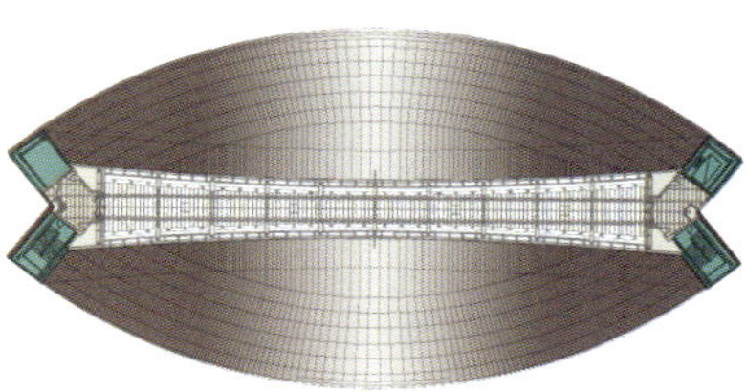

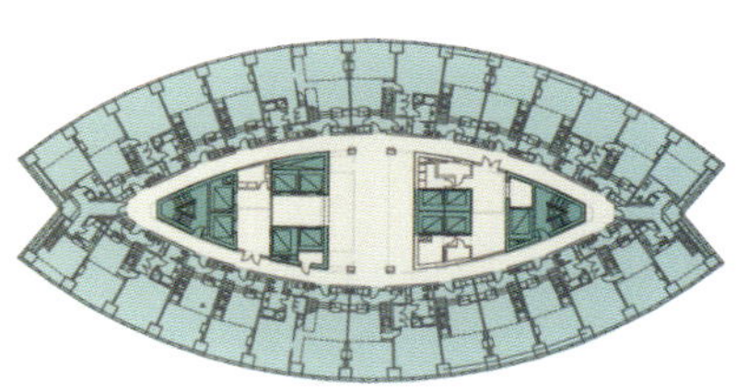

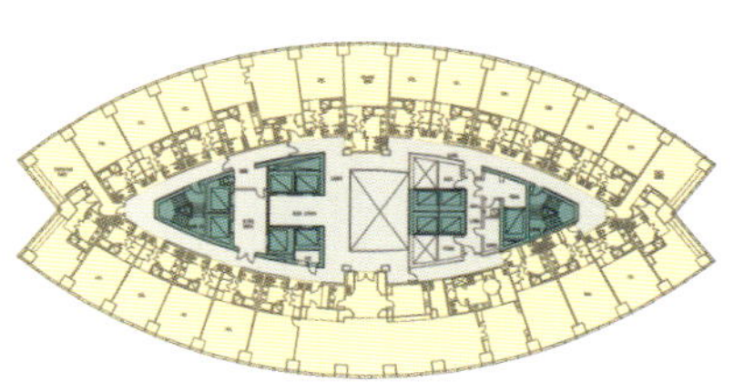

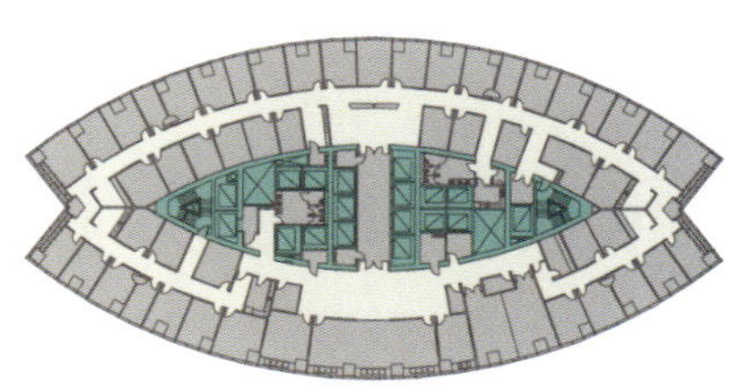

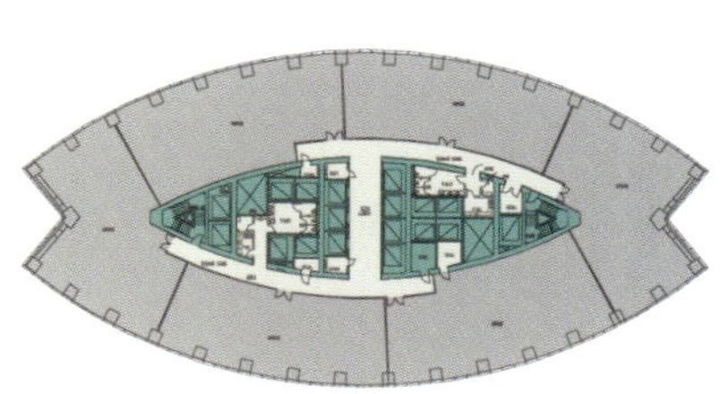

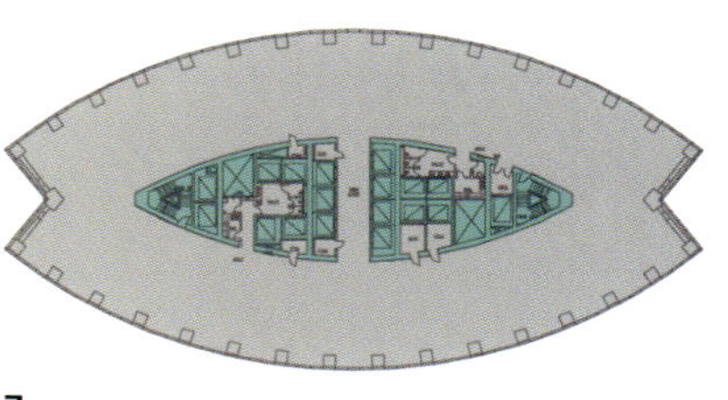

7

THE SHARD AT LONDON BRIDGE

LONDON
UNITED KINGDOM

Rising 310 metres above London's skyline, The Shard at London Bridge (also known as London Bridge Tower) will provide more than 125,000 square metres of commercial, residential and public space over 72 floors. At the station concourse level, a public piazza will incorporate a dramatic upgrading of the entrance to London Bridge Station. This level will also incorporate retail facilities; a café, restaurant and health club; and a learning centre.

A total of 54,352 square metres of offices will occupy the next 27 floors, followed by the three-storey mid-level public piazza. The piazza will provide visitors with not only spectacular views of London but also a range of leisure activities including an auditorium, exhibition space, bars and restaurants.

Directly above the mid-level piazza is the six-star Shangri-La hotel, occupying floors 34 to 52 and offering guests some of the finest views of any hotel in the United Kingdom, if not Europe. The hotel will provide 195 rooms and occupy 17,500 square metres of space in the tower.

The apartments will be constructed on floors 53 to 65, some occupying entire floors and affording unprecedented views of the capital and surrounding countryside. On a clear day residents will be able to see for more than 30 miles.

Finally, on floor 72, 224 metres above the street, the viewing gallery provides Londoners and visitors alike a view of the capital that has never been accessible to the public. The remaining height of the London Bridge Tower will comprise the building's cooling radiator.

The London Bridge Tower will also have a major positive impact on the streetscape of St. Thomas and Joiner Streets, replacing brick walls and service yards with retail street frontages and building entrances. The proposed canopy over the piazza will protect from wind and is intended to alleviate the problem that exists there today.

1

The Shard at London Bridge | **Location** London, United Kingdom | **Scheduled completion date** 2010 | **Architect** Renzo Piano Building Workshop | **Client** Sellar Property Group | **Consultant structural engineer** WSP Cantor Seinuk | **Consultant service engineer** Ove Arup & Partners | **Fire engineering** Arup Fire | **Vertical transportation engineer** Lerch Bates & Associates | **Height** 310 m/ 1016 ft | **Above-ground storeys** 72 | **Basements** 3 | **Use** Office, residential, hotel, observation deck | **Area of above-ground building** 125,000 sq m/1,340,000 sq ft | **Structural materials** Concrete, steel | **Other materials** Glass

2

3

1,3 *General views*

2 *London skyline by day, evening and night*

Renderings: *Hayes Davidson and John Maclean, courtesy Sellar Property Group*

OCEAN HEIGHTS DUBAI UNITED ARAB EMIRATES

Dubai Marina will soon have a new structure added to its skyline in the form of Ocean Heights, a 310-metre tower that will possibly be the tallest residential building in the United Arab Emirates.

The 82-storey tower will be easily distinguishable by its twisting form that allows each apartment unit – even those in the back – sweeping ocean views. The building immediately starts its twist from the base. As it rises, the tower's floor plates reduce in size, allowing the twist to become even more pronounced. At 50 storeys, the building rises over its neighbours, allowing two faces unobstructed views to the ocean. The tower breaks away from the orthogonal grid and reorients the project towards one of Dubai's Palm Islands to the north.

The most challenging aspect of the design was accommodating the client's strict requirement of unit layouts within a changing envelope. The result was a rational 4-metre module, which tracks its way down through the entire building and only changes at the façade. This also considerably simplified the structural system of the project.

Minimising wind affect on the tower was the main structural challenge. The building's overall height, with its sharp edges, could have high levels of motion when subject to either low-speed, steady synoptic winds, or short duration, high-velocity thunderstorm downbursts. The wind climate in Dubai is dominated by steady afternoon sea breezes and strong smooth seasonal 'Shamal' winds that can cause considerable motion in tall buildings in Dubai unless appropriate measures are incorporated into the design of the project. The proposal is to construct a system of continuous shear walls as 'outrigger stiffening walls' from the core to significantly reduce this motion. A central reinforced concrete core of maximum perimeter up the full height of the building will provide a significant contribution to the lateral and torsional stiffness of the tower. The outrigger walls will be coupled to the core with post-tensioned reinforcement. This technique allows the differential movement of the core and outrigger walls to occur during construction prior to locking them together. The floors will incorporate post-tensioned reinforcement to allow early stripping of the floor formwork and further reduce the construction time.

To ensure the stability of the tall structure on sand, the tower will be launched from a piled raft, 2.5 metres thick with 1.2-metre-diameter piles anchored into the sand and soft rock formations at approximately 15 metres below ground level.

1

Ocean Heights | **Location** Dubai, United Arab Emirates | **Completion date** 2008 | **Architect** Aedas Ltd. | **Developer** DAMAC Properties Co. LLC | **Structural engineer** Meinhardt, Singapore | **Mechanical engineer** M/S Engineering Associates, Dubai | **Height** 310 m/1017 ft | **Above-ground storeys** 82 | **Basements** 3 | **Above-ground useable levels** 82 | **Mechanical levels** Levels 35/36; levels 65/66 | **Use** Residential (601 units) | **Site area** 3476 sq m/37,402 sq ft | **Floor area** 79,771 sq m/858,336 sq ft; typical floor plate 1290 sq m/13,880 sq ft | **Structural materials** Reinforced concrete, curtain wall | **Other materials** Aluminium cladding, glass | **Cost** AED 500 M

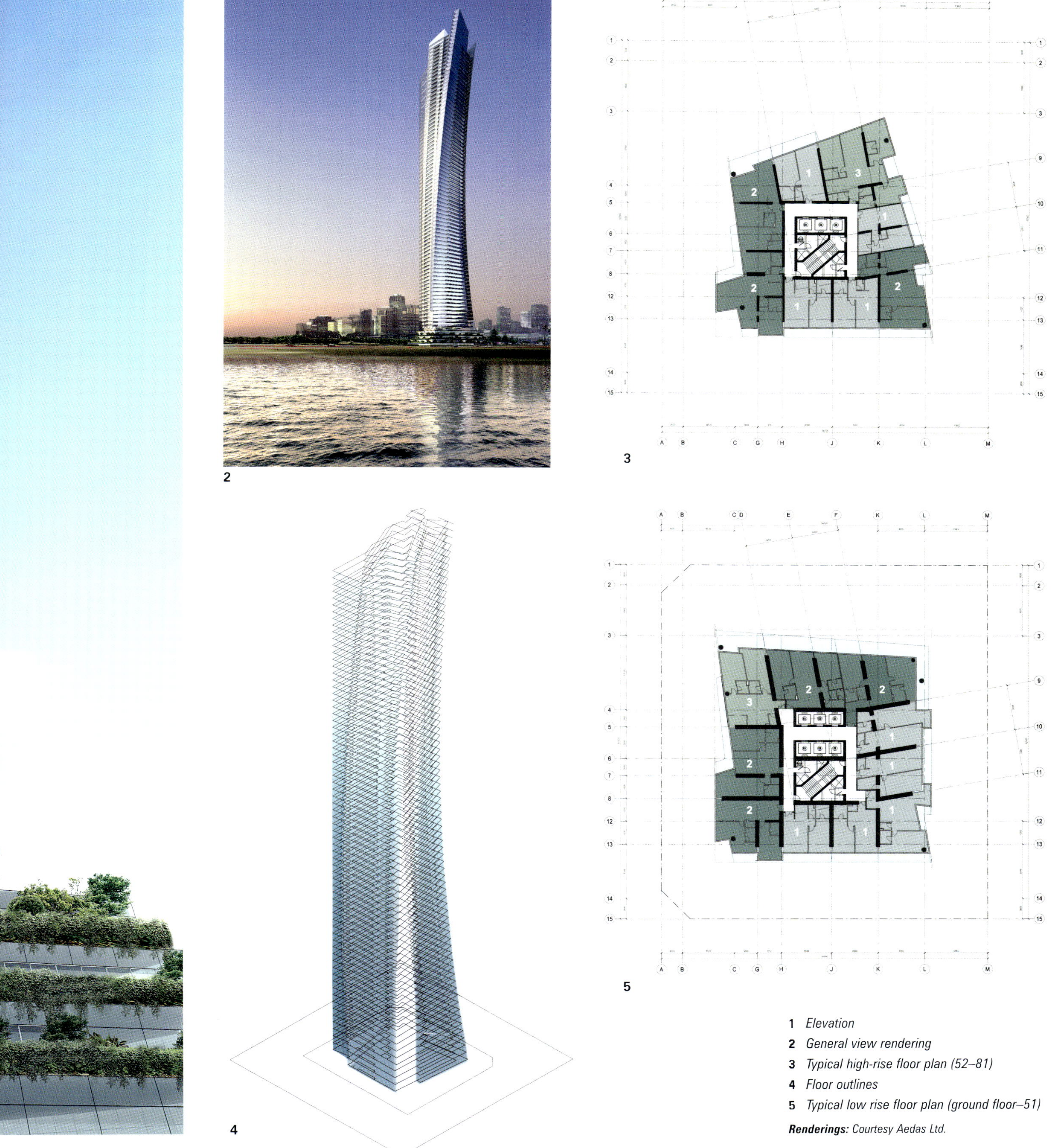

1 *Elevation*
2 *General view rendering*
3 *Typical high-rise floor plan (52–81)*
4 *Floor outlines*
5 *Typical low rise floor plan (ground floor–51)*

Renderings: *Courtesy Aedas Ltd.*

BURJ AL ARAB DUBAI UNITED ARAB EMIRATES

Dubai's Burj Al Arab is located offshore on a man-made island in the Arabian Gulf. The tallest all-suite hotel in the world at 321 metres, it forms the centrepiece of Atkins' design for the world-class Chicago Beach Resort Development that includes the Jumeirah Beach Resort, the Wild Wadi aqua park and the Beit Al Bahar Villas.

The design for the hotel resembles the spinnaker sail of a J-Class yacht and reflects the seafaring heritage of Dubai. By a combination of innovative and efficient structural design, complemented by and integrated with dramatic architecture, the resulting unique building is now globally recognised as an icon of Dubai.

Extending up to the underside of the 26th duplex floor level, the dramatic and glittering 182-metre-high atrium is the tallest of its kind in the world and addresses the space that is the core of the Burj Al Arab. It is flanked on two sides by the balconies of hotel suites and on the third side by a sail-shaped geometric membrane of PTFE-coated fibreglass. Internally, the 202 luxury duplex bedroom suites are the height of opulence.

As well as providing a natural light source and insulating the atrium space, the membrane also acts as a 'canvas' for the myriad lighting effects, generated by the luminaries concealed in the main access bridge that project onto the front face to highlight the hotel at night. The membrane also provides a screen for the long-range 'light cannon' projectors that operate from the mainland to cast pictorial images onto the Burj.

A further sense of interior luxury is provided by a circular atrium water feature, composed of 24 white fibre-optically lit water arches with a central 50-metre-high jet and a two-storey-high tropical aquarium extending to a 'submerged' restaurant which contrasts with the 190-metre-high elevated sky view restaurant offering panoramic views of the city and Arabian Gulf.

State-of-the-art technology is prevalent throughout the hotel from the electromechanical design to the guest and operational interfaces and the amazing water and flame feature at the main entrance.

1

2

1 *Innovative structure with a dramatic architecture*
2 *Night view from causeway*
3 *Level 16 floor plan*
4 *View of the exoskeleton*
5 *Atrium*

Photography: *Courtesy Jumeirah (1,2); courtesy Atkins (3–5)*

Burj Al Arab | **Location** Dubai, United Arab Emirates | **Completion date** 1999 | **Architect** Atkins | **Structural engineer** Atkins | **Mechanical engineer** Atkins | **Landscape architect** Al Khatib Cracknell | **Contractor** Al Habtoor Murray & Roberts | **Height** 321 m/1053 ft | **Above-ground storeys** 52 | **Basements** 3 | **Mechanical levels** 3 | **Use** Hotel | **Area of above-ground building** 120,000 sq m/1,291,200 sq ft | **Site area** 5060 sq m/54,445 sq ft | **Structural materials** Steel, curtain wall, reinforced concrete | **Other materials** Aluminium cladding, Teflon-covered glass, fibre fabric wall

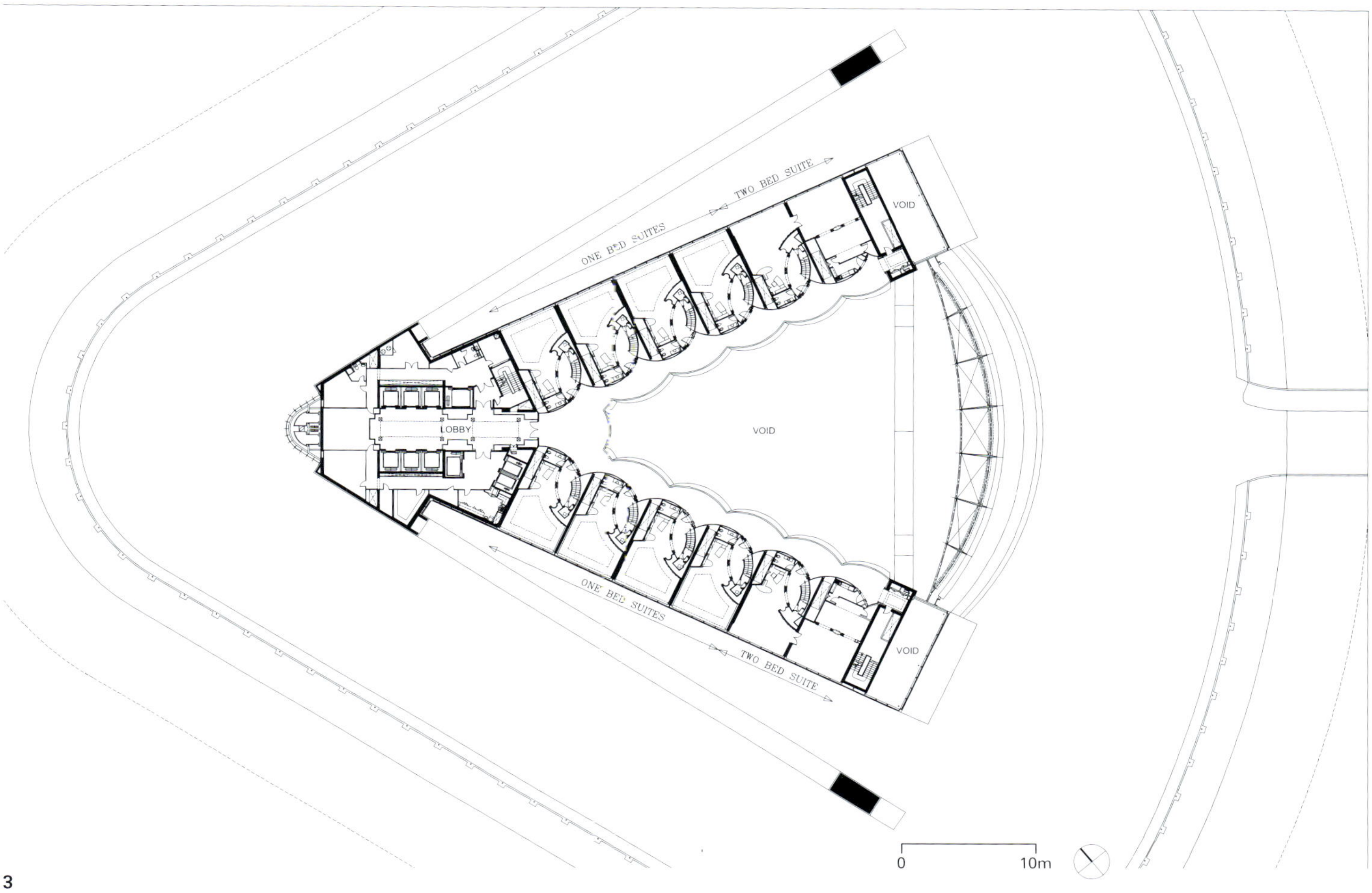

TWO BED SUITE
ONE BED SUITES
VOID
LOBBY
VOID
ONE BED SUITES
TWO BED SUITE
VOID
0 10m

3

4

5

ROSE ROTANA SUITES DUBAI UNITED ARAB EMIRATES

The project is a prestigious, hospitality sector development consisting of a 333-metre-high tower offering 482 quality hotel-style apartments with both studio and single-bedroom configurations. The ground floor provides main reception and front office areas and the mezzanine floor accommodates administration and services sections. The restaurant and main kitchen are located on the first floor and the second and third floors are devoted to meeting rooms and conference hall. The fourth through to seventh floors comprise housekeeping and staff facilities, furnished office units and studio-style residential accommodation.

A separate six-storey car-park structure with health club, roof-level swimming pool and MEP systems installation is included in the scope of the design.

1 *General view*
2 *Typical suites floor plan (9–28); (31–51)*
3 *Ground floor plan*
4 *Typical suites floor plan (54–65)*

Renderings: *Courtesy Khatib & Alami CEC*

1

Rose Rotana Suites | **Location** Dubai, United Arab Emirates | **Completion date** 2007 | **Architect** Khatib & Alami C.E.C. | **Client** Sh. Maktoum Bin Khalifa Bin Saeed Al Maktoum | **Structural engineer** Khatib & Alami C.E.C. | **Mechanical engineer** Khatib & Alami C.E.C. | **Contractor** ABBCO Company | **Height** 333 m/1093 ft | **Above-ground storeys** 67 | **Basements** 1 | **Above-ground useable levels** 60 | **Mechanical levels** 7 | **Use** Hotel | **Area of above-ground building** 50,817.95 sq m/547,004 sq ft | **Structural materials** Steel, concrete

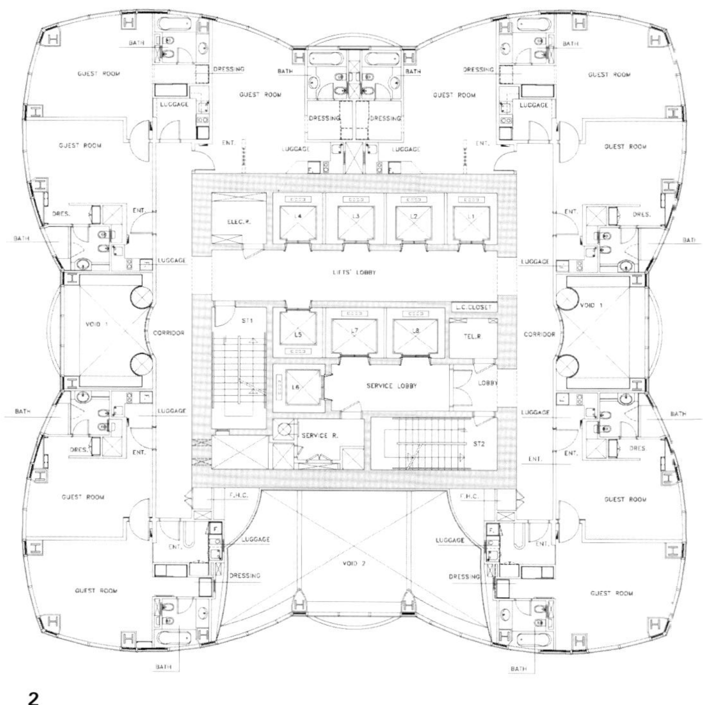

2

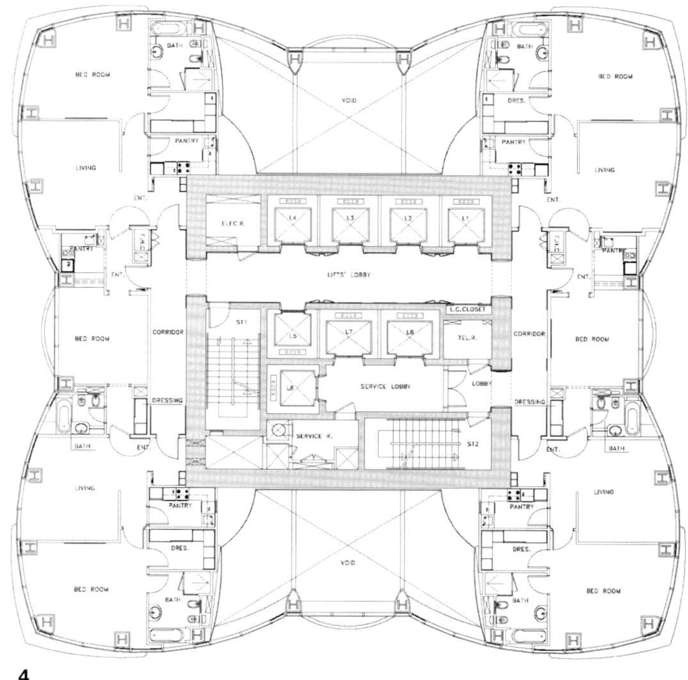

4

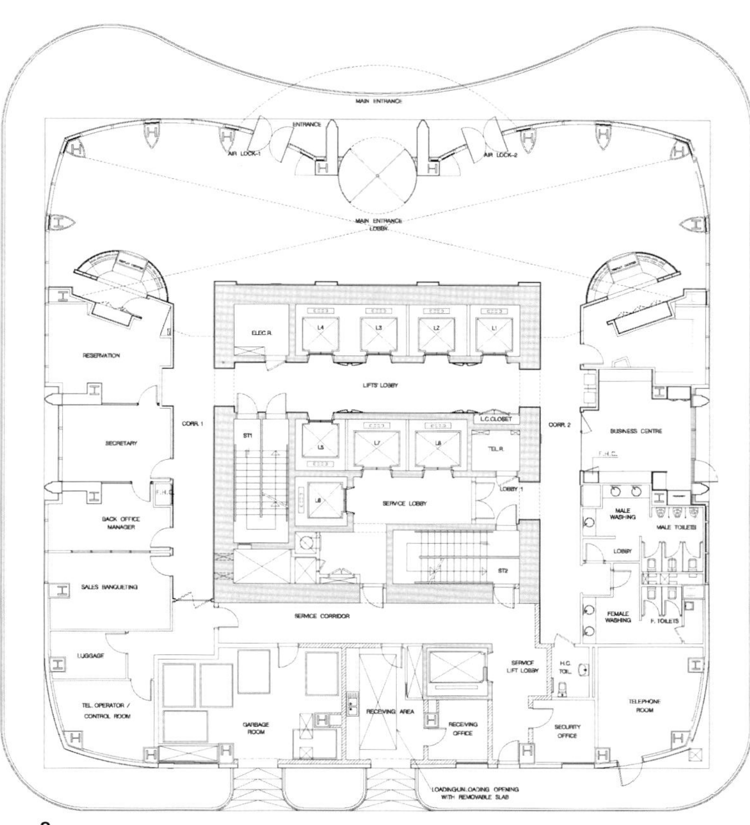

3

JUMEIRAH EMIRATES TOWERS

DUBAI
UNITED ARAB EMIRATES

A major landmark in Dubai's thriving central business district, Jumeirah Emirates Towers (originally Emirates Towers) is a symbol of the city's growing prominence. The twin silver-grey metal and glass towers rise from a stepped granite base. At night, lighting effects reinforce the drama of the unique soaring forms.

Flanking each tower at its base is a low curvilinear structure, designed in a form reminiscent of massive shifting sand dunes, which houses parking for 1800 cars and service elements. Connecting the two towers is Boulevard at Jumeirah Emirates Towers, a two-storey retail development with walkways lined by skylit courtyards, high-end retail shops, restaurants and cafés.

Equilateral triangles in plan, the towers are inspired by Islamic geometric themes, and the triangular pattern is visible at various levels of detail throughout the project, from the tower roofs, triangular skylights and canopy structures with their repeating positive-negative patterns in ceramic fritted glass, to various interior and exterior paving patterns. Balancing the rigid geometry are the soft curves of the base structure's north and south granite-clad walls, a large cascading waterfall in front of the hotel entrance and the gentle lines of the retail mall's precision-cut paving pattern.

The 355-metre 52-storey office tower has a spacious lobby formed by circular floor plates, creating an eight-storey-high drum of clear glass. The triangular geometry of the tower above is made apparent at the drum levels by the three structural legs that straddle these circular floors. The 16 elevators, travelling at speeds of up to 7 metres per second, are divided into four banks serving respective zones of the tower. A typical floor plate provides 1334 square metres of gross floor area and is designed to provide maximum efficiency with a minimum number of columns.

The 52-storey hotel tower rises to a height of 309.1 metres. Above the eight-storey atrium are 400 luxurious guestrooms and suites served by four glass-enclosed elevators and organised around a 31-storey glazed atrium facing the waters of the Gulf. An exclusive restaurant is located on the penthouse level, offering dramatic views of the coastline.

1

2

Emirates Towers | **Location** Dubai, United Arab Emirates | **Completion date** 2000 | **Lead consultant** Hyder Consulting Middle East Ltd | **Architect** NORR Group Consultants International (design architect Hazel WS Wong) | **Client** The Office of HH General Sheikh Mohammed Bin Rashid Al Maktoum, Crown Prince of Dubai | **Project manager** Turner International | **Structural engineer** Hyder Consulting Pty. Ltd. | **Mechanical engineer** Donald Smith Seymour Rooley | **Mechanical design** The Mitchell Partnership | **Contractor** BESIX and SsangYong Engineering & Construction Co., Ltd. (hotel); Nasa Multiplex LLC (offices) | **Height** Hotel: 309.1 m/1014.1 ft; offices: 354.8 m /1164 ft | **Above-ground storeys** Hotel: 52 above 2-level podium; offices: 52 above 1-level podium | **Basements** 1 (semi-grounded) | **Use** Office, hotel, retail | **Site area** 169,000 sq m/1,818,440 sq ft | **Area of above-ground building** 140,000 sq m/1,507,000 sq ft; hotel: 50,360 sq m/541,873 sq ft; offices: 68,500 sq m/737,060 sq ft | **Structural materials** Hotel: concrete; offices: mixed | **Other materials** Brazilian Kinawa granite, aluminium panels, glass

3

5

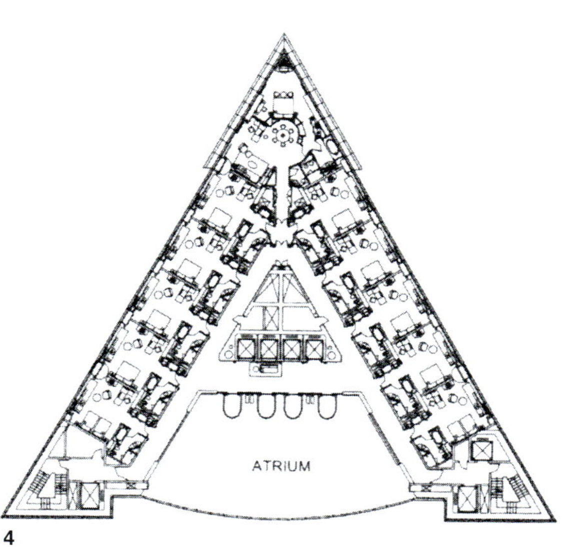

4

1–3 *General views*

4 *Typical hotel floor plan*

5 *Hotel lobby atrium*

Photography: *Courtesy Jumeirah*
Typical office plan: *from Council on Tall Buildings and Urban Habitat/CTBUH Sixth World Congress –* Cities in the Third Millennium, *Melbourne, Australia, Spon Press, London/New York, 2001*

AL MAS TOWER DUBAI UNITED ARAB EMIRATES

Located 20 kilometres south of Dubai and at the centrepiece of the Jumeirah Lakes development, the 68-storey Al Mas Tower has been designed by Atkins to reflect the character and uniqueness of the Diamond Exchange facility accommodated within. The 360-metre-tall building offers prominent views both of the Lake and the central spine of the development. The tower accommodates 63 commercial office floors above the three-storey podium. Car parking for 1800 cars is provided within the five-level basement.

The design of this tower has been inspired by the requirement for an optimal environment for viewing precious stones and responds in providing two oval-shaped towers of varying height that overlap along their east–west axis. The lower, north-facing tower has a semi-transparent elevation in order to benefit from the cool, ambient north light. The taller, south-facing tower is protected by a high-performance treatment to its exterior.

Various aspects of the building design combine to express the tower's tendency to become lighter as it ascends. This is emphasised by the continuing height of the taller tower, the further prominence of the mast and the tapering of the narrow side elevation of both towers.

The podium design is inspired by the cut of a diamond with projecting facets. Each facet cantilevers out over the lake, making them visible from all aspects of the tower and surrounding buildings when viewed from above. The glazed elements of the retail area reflect the water surrounding the tower, creating an animated façade.

The podium accommodates a mall, conference rooms and health spa on the first floor and the Diamond Exchange Centre on the second floor. The mall extends from ground to first floor and offers magnificent views of the lake from its double-volume atrium space. The north-facing Diamond Exchange is externally treated with a high colour spectrum glazing that will facilitate world-class diamond inspection and trading.

1 *Tower perspectives*
2 *Typical floor plan*
3&4 *Elevations*

Renderings: *Courtesy Atkins*

1

Al Mas Tower | **Location** Dubai, United Arab Emirates | **Expected completion date** 2008 | **Architect** Atkins | **Client** Nakheel | **Structural engineer** Atkins | **Mechanical engineer** Atkins | **Landscape architect** Al Khatib Cracknell | **Height** 360 m/1181 ft | **Above-ground storeys** 68 | **Basements** 5 | **Above-ground useable levels** 68 | **Mechanical levels** 3 | **Use** Office | **Site area** 15,393 sq m/165,700 sq ft | **Area of above-ground building** 183,400 sq m/1,973,384 sq ft | **Structural materials** Reinforced concrete | **Other materials** Reflective grey and tinted green glass, aluminium panel cladding

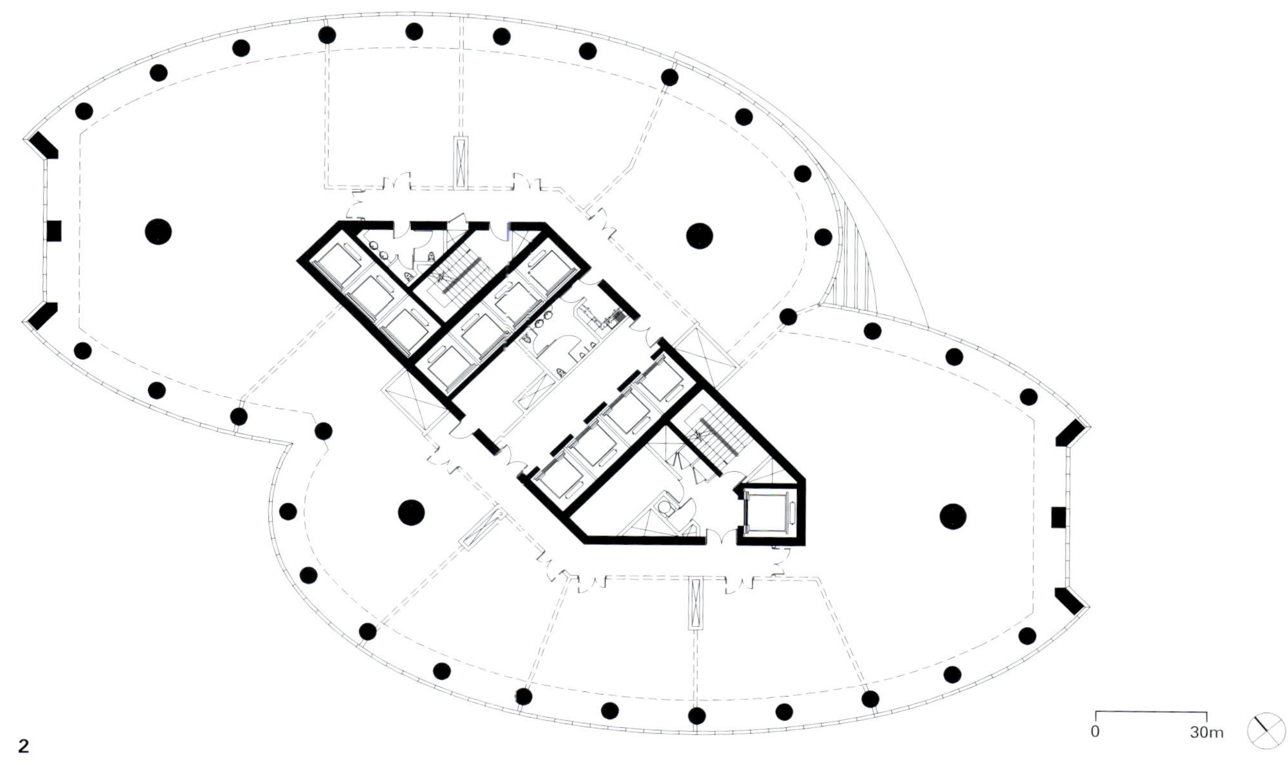

2

3

4

HAYDARPASA 'DA ISTANBUL

ISTANBUL
TURKEY

Located along Istanbul's Golden Horn on the former Haydarpasa railway site, the project comprises seven hills crowned by seven towers. The whole project is nestled in a landscaped urban environment re-created according to typical local seacoast districts.

The seven towers with their slender organic shape and their multiple detachments will become a metaphor recalling the silhouette of Istanbul's cypress tree. The use of oxidised green copper will reinforce the organic expression.

The programming will ensure coherence between the various functions such as residential accommodation (583,000 square metres); hospitality projects (149,000 square metres); hospitals and housing for seniors (35,000 square metres); offices (280,000 square metres); retail shops (197,000 square metres); (196,000 square metres) and other functions such as fairs (134,000 square metres), convention centres (99,000 square metres), sports events (14,500 square metres), yacht clubs (9,000 square metres), museums (6,000 square metres), theme parks and other socio-cultural activities including theatres and cinemas.

An important aspect of the project is the outcome for traffic, in terms of extending both the existing road network and public transport system. The larger facilities developed on the site are concealed and integrated into the landscape through the use of the seven man-made hills laid out as landscaped parks. Smaller buildings housing a rich array of diverse activities will be located on the peripheral roads.

Haydarpasa 'da Istanbul, together with the development of the surrounding districts aims at creating a new hub for Istanbul as well as a major landmark along the Bosphorus.

1

1 *Haydarpasa 'da Istanbul's main 74-storey building and its cantilevered wings add drama to the Istanbul skyline*

2 *General view, day*

3 *Site plan*

4 *General view, night*

Digital renderings: *Détrois sa (1,2); Atelier d'Art Urbain, Architects (4)*
Drawing: *Atelier d'Art Urbain, Architects (3)*

Haydarpasa 'da Istanbul | **Location** Istanbul, Turkey | **Completion date** Design phase | **Architect** Atelier d'Art Urbain, Architects | **Client** Calik Holding A.S. | **Height** (to tip of spire) Towers 1, 2, 3: 218 m/715 ft; Tower 4: 381 m/1250 ft; Tower 5: 319 m/1047 ft; Towers 6, 7: 298 m/978 ft | **Above-ground storeys** Towers 1, 2, 3: 39; Tower 4: 74; Tower 5: 59; Towers 6, 7: 51 | **Basements** 7 | **Use** 1, 2, 3: housing; Towers 4, 5: offices, housing; Towers 6, 7: hotels | **Total built area** 2,218,664 sq m/23,872,824 sq ft, including 394,773 sq m/4,247,757 sq ft of parking spaces | **Structural materials** Steel | **Other materials** Oxidised green copper, glass

2

3

4

FEDERATION TOWER MOSCOW RUSSIA

Federation Tower is part of the Moscow International Business Centre, 'Moscow-City', that includes 2.5 million square metres of office, hotel, retail and entertainment areas in several skyscrapers.

Federation Tower is a dynamic composition of two upward-reaching glass towers. The towers are formed as two spherical, equilateral triangles that narrow towards the top and grow out of a four-storey stone base. The rift between the base and the towers is enhanced through a rebounding, three-storey-tall lens. The central vertical axis of the complex is formed by a 'needle', comprised of glass elevators, that extends over the skyscraper and is connected to the two towers by several bridges.

Inside the base and lens is a spacious, 14-storey atrium with supermarkets, conference halls, banks, shopping malls, airline offices, cafés and restaurants.

The complex has many functions: it includes approximately 250,000 square metres of office space; apartments and a hotel; retail and restaurant areas; several entertainment and wellness areas, as well as a panoramic restaurant atop the taller tower that has a spectacular view over the entire Russian capital.

1

2

Federation Tower | **Location** Moscow, Russia | **Completion date** 2008 | **Architect** 'Federation Tower' Planning Association mbH: Prof. Peter Schweger, ASP Schweger Assoziierte Gesamtplanung GmbH and Sergei Tchoban, nps tchoban voss GbR Architekten BDA; AM Prasch; P Sigl; S Tchoban; E Voss | **Client** Mirax-City | **Structural engineer** Thornton-Tomasetti Engineers, New York | **Height** Tower A: 354.33 m/1162.5 ft; Tower B 242.4 m/795.3 ft (with antenna 448.25 m/1470.7 ft) | **Above-ground storeys** Tower A 93; Tower B 62 | **Basements** 4 | **Use** Mixed: office, hotel, apartments, retail, entertainment | **Site area** 10,840 sq m/116,638 sq ft | **Area of above-ground building** 423,000 sq m/4,551,480 sq ft | **Structural materials** Reinforced concrete

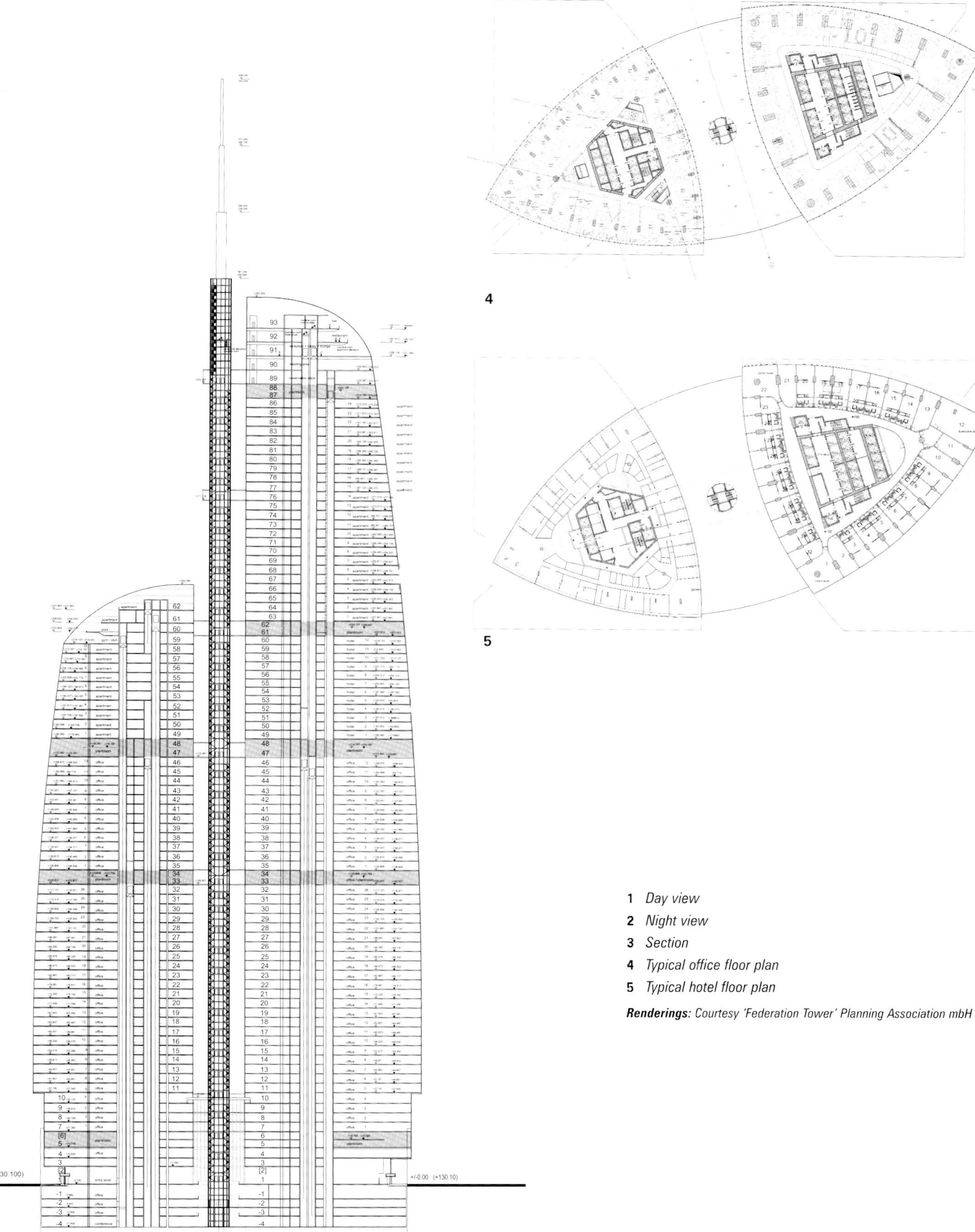

4

5

3

1 *Day view*
2 *Night view*
3 *Section*
4 *Typical office floor plan*
5 *Typical hotel floor plan*

Renderings: *Courtesy 'Federation Tower' Planning Association mbH*

MOSCOW CITY TOWERS

MOSCOW
RUSSIA

Foster and Partners' Moscow City Towers – taller than any other building in Europe – is a striking new addition to the dynamic high-rise skyline of Moscow City. The mixed-use project – incorporating apartments, hotel, office and leisure space – will have an 'energy cycle' that will pioneer sustainable architecture and reinforce the economic and social vitality of Moscow City.

Based on a highly efficient geometry derived from the triangular plan, the vertical city is a powerful triumvirate of three arms that meet at a central green spine running the full height of the tower. Wider at the base and tapering towards the top, the pyramidal form is elegant and slender in profile, and benefits from a highly efficient composition to achieve the maximum stability with the minimum structure. The tower is aided in resisting wind loads by a series of sloped fan columns extending diagonally upwards to the spine from the broad, triangular base. Overlaid by columns set at a reverse angle, this unusual oblique lattice carries the building's load while also giving it its distinctive geometric façade.

By harnessing the heat created by the offices in winter and the cooling properties of the ground in summer, the energy cycle is a hot water circuit that runs through the building, distributing the energy to regulate the temperature and heat water throughout the day and throughout the year. Rising up the centre of the building are a series of green skygardens that draw in natural ventilation and provide key circulation and social space.

The higher floors containing residential and hotel accommodation are designed as modular units that can be individually configured. Apartments benefit from fresh air, natural light, double- or triple-height volumes and access to skygardens, creating a unique lifestyle in the heart of Moscow. At the summit, a publicly accessible viewing deck with cafés and bars creates a magnetic new attraction for both visitors and residents of Moscow.

1 *Fan columns give the tower a distinctive façade*
2 *Section*
3 *Norman Foster concept sketch*
4 *Model*

Renderings and sketch: *Courtesy Foster and Partners*
Photography: *Nigel Young/Foster and Partners (4)*

1

Moscow City Towers | **Location** Moscow, Russia | **Design phase** | **Architect** Foster and Partners | **Client** STT Group | **Concept structure** Halvorson and Partners | **Structural and services engineer** Waterman International | **Vertical transportation consultant** Lerch Bates & Associates | **Height** 500 m/1640.5 ft (top occupied floor); 600 m/1968.6 ft (top of structure) | **Above-ground storeys** 118 | **Basements** 9 (3 retail, 6 basement) | **Use** Offices, hotel, retail, leisure, residences, observation deck, private gardens | **Site area** 21,935 sq m/236,021 sq ft | **Gross building area** 520,800 sq m/5,603,808 sq ft | **Structural materials** Steel, reinforced concrete

2

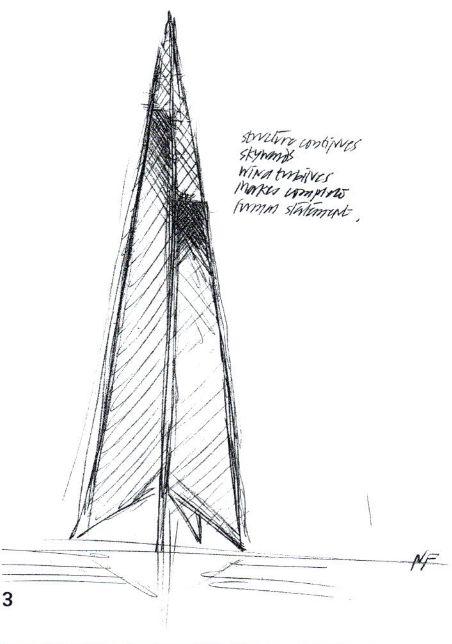

3

4

BURJ DUBAI
DUBAI
UNITED ARAB EMIRATES

The Burj Dubai, planned as the world's tallest building, will be the centrepiece of a large scale mixed-use development comprised of residential, commercial, hotel, entertainment, shopping and leisure outlets with open green spaces, water features, pedestrian boulevards, a shopping mall and a tourist-oriented old town in Dubai, United Arab Emirates.

The design of the tower is derived from the geometries of the desert flower, which is indigenous to the region, and the patterning systems embodied in Islamic architecture. It combines historical and cultural influences with cutting edge technology to achieve a high-performance building that will set the new standard for development in the Middle East and become the model for the future of the city.

The tower is composed of three elements arranged around a central core. As the tower rises from the flat desert base, setbacks occur at each element in an upward spiraling pattern, decreasing the mass of the tower as it reaches towards the sky. At the top, the central core emerges and is sculpted to form a finishing spire. A Y-shaped floor plan maximises views of the Persian Gulf.

Construction began in January 2004 and will be completed at the end of 2009.

1 *Front view rendering of Burj Dubai*
2 *Rendering of Burj Dubai in context of Dubai skyline*
3&4 *Y-shaped floor plans maximise views*

Renderings: *Courtesy Skidmore, Owings & Merrill LLP*

1

Burj Dubai | **Location** Dubai, United Arab Emirates | **Expected completion date** 2009 | **Architect** Skidmore, Owings & Merrill LLP, Adrian D Smith, FAIA, Consulting Design Partner | **Local consultant** Hyder Consulting Middle East Ltd | **Client** EMAAR Properties | **Structural engineer** Skidmore, Owings & Merrill LLP | **Mechanical engineer** Skidmore, Owings & Merrill LLP | **Contractor** Samsung-BESIX-Arabtec | **Construction manager** Turner Construction International | **Height** More than 700 m/2300 ft | **Above-ground stories** More than 150 | **Use** Mixed: hotel, residential, resort | **Area of above-ground building** 464,500 sq m/5,000,000 sq ft | **Number of parking spaces** 3000 | **Principal structural materials** Reinforced concrete | **Other materials** Exterior: aluminium, glass; interior: granite, stainless steel, wood

2

3

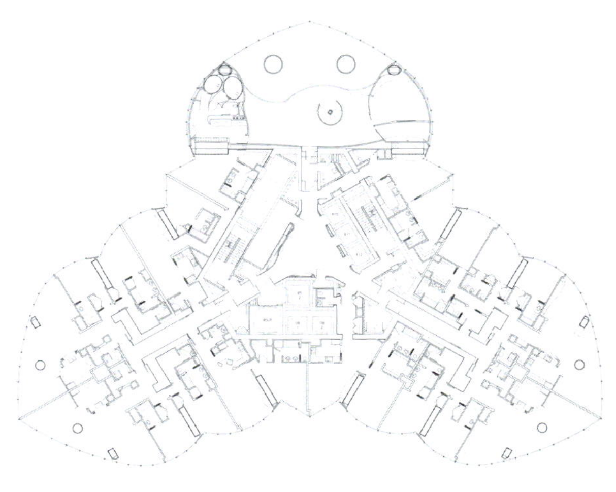

4

50 TALLEST BUILDINGS OF EUROPE, THE MIDDLE EAST AND AFRICA IN 1996

Completed as of 31 December 1996

	Name	City	Country	Year	Storeys	Metres	Feet	Use	Architect
1	Commerzbank	Frankfurt	Germany	1997	57	299*	980*	Office	Foster and Partners
2	MesseTurm	Frankfurt	Germany	1990	63	257	842	Office	Murphy/Jahn, Inc.
3	Moscow State University	Moscow	Russia	1953	36	240*	787*	Educational	Lev Rudnev, Sergei Tchernitchev, Pavel Abrosimov, Alexander Khriakov
4	One Canada Square	London	United Kingdom	1991	48	236	775	Office	Cesar Pelli & Associates; Adamson Associates
5	Palace of Culture and Science	Warsaw	Poland	1955	43	231*	758*	Mixed-use	Lev Rudnev
6	Carlton Centre	Johannesburg	South Africa	1973	50	222	730	Office	Skidmore, Owings & Merrill; W. Rhodes-Harrison, Hoffe and Partners
7	Tour Maine-Montparnasse	Paris	France	1973	58	209	686	Office	Eugène Beaudouin, Urbain Cassan, Louis de Hoym de Marien and Jean Saubot; A. Epstein and Sons
8	DG Bank (now DZ Bank)	Frankfurt	Germany	1993	52	208	682	Office	Kohn Pedersen Fox Associates; NHT Nägele Hofmann Tiedeman und Partner
9	Ukraina Hotel	Moscow	Russia	1957	34	198*	650*	Hotel	A. Mordvinov, V. Kalish and V. Oltarzhevskii
10	Trianon	Frankfurt	Germany	1993	47	186	610	Office	Novotny. Mähner & Assoziierte; HPP; Albert Speer & Partner
11	NatWest Tower (now Tower 42)	London	United Kingdom	1980	46	183	600	Office	R. Seifert & Partners
12	Tour Elf (now Tour Total)	Paris La Défense	France	1985	48	180	591	Office	The Webb Zerafa Menkès Housden Partnership; Saubot-Jullien
13	Tour FIAT (now Tour Areva)	Paris La Défense	France	1974	46	178	584	Office	Skidmore, Owings & Merrill; Saubot-Jullien
14	Mersin Metropol Tower	Mersin	Turkey	1987	52	177	580	Mixed-use	Cengiz Bektas
15	Kotelnicheskaya Naberezhnaya	Moscow	Russia	1952	32	176*	577*	Residential	D. Ceculian, S. Rostovovsky
16	Ponte City	Johannesburg	South Africa	1973	54	173	567	Residential	Manfred Hermer & Grosskopff
17	Ministry of Foreign Affairs	Moscow	Russia	1954	27	170*	558*	Office	Vladimir Gelfreikh, Mikhail Minkus
18	Tour Société Générale – Alicante	Paris La Défense	France	1995	38	167	548	Office	Michel Andrault, Pierre Parat, Nicolas Ayoub
19	Tour Société Générale – Chassagne	Paris La Défense	France	1995	37	167	548	Office	Michel Andrault, Pierre Parat, Nicolas Ayoub
20	Tour GAN	Paris La Défense	France	1973	44	166	545	Office	Harrison, Abramovitz et Bisseuil
21	Dresdner Bank (now Silver Tower)	Frankfurt	Germany	1980	32	166	545	Office	ABB Beckert + Becker und Partner
22	Baynunah Tower	Abu Dhabi	UAE	1995	42	165	541	Mixed-use	Arkan Architectural Consultants
23	La Tour Crédit Lyonnais	Lyon	France	1977	42	164	537	Mixed-use	Cossutta & Associates, Architects
24	Plaza Büro Center	Frankfurt	Germany	1976	44	162	531	Mixed-use	Siegfried Hoyer und Partner; Beratungsgesellschaft für Gewerbebau
25	RWE	Essen	Germany	1996	31	162*	531*	Office	Ingenhoven Overdiek und Partner
26	Kudrinskaya Square	Moscow	Russia	1954	22	160*	525*	Residential	Mikhail Posokhin
27	Sabanci Center	Istanbul	Turkey	1993	39	157	516	Office	Haluk Tümay; Ayhan Böke
28	Torre Picasso	Madrid	Spain	1988	44	157	515	Office	Minoru Yamasaki and Associates
29	Tour Assur (now Tour Axa)	Paris La Défense	France	1974	39	155	509	Office	Pierre Dufau; Dacbert and Stenzel, associated architects
30	Deutsche Bank Hauptverwaltung I	Frankfurt	Germany	1984	40	155	509	Office	ABB WalterHanig, Heinz Scheid, Johannes Schmidt, Gilbert Becker

	Name	City	Country	Year	Storeys	Metres	Feet	Use	Architect
31	Deutsche Bank Hauptverwaltung II	Frankfurt	Germany	1984	38	155	509	Office	ABB WalterHanig, Heinz Scheid, Johannes Schmidt, Gilbert Becker
32	Hotel Arts Barcelona	Barcelona	Spain	1992	45	154	504	Hotel	Skidmore, Owings & Merrill; Brufau, Obiol, Moya & Ass
33	Torre Mapfre	Barcelona	Spain	1992	40	154	504	Office	Ortiz Leon Arquitectos
34	Sanlamsentrum (now Marble Towers)	Johannesburg	South Africa	1973	32	152	499	Office	
35	Gebouw Delftse Poort	Rotterdam	The Netherlands	1991	41	151	496	Office	Ir. A. Bonnema, Bureau voor Architectuur en Ruimtelijke Ordening
36	Gazprom	Moscow	Russia	1994	35	151	495	Office	Tekeli & Sisa
37	Rembrandttoren	Amsterdam	The Netherlands	1995	36	150*	492*	Office	ZZ+P Architecten
38	Metropolitan Centre (now Metlife Centre)	Cape Town	South Africa	1993	28	150*	492*	Office	
39	Tour du Midi	Brussels	Belgium	1966	37	149	490	Office	Aerts & Ramon; Blomme & Petit; Bressers & Van Acker; Lambrichs & Van Doosselaere; A. Lipski, eng.
40	International Trade Centre (WTC)	Dubai	UAE	1979	39	149	489	Office	John R Harris Partnership
41	BfG (now Eurotower)	Frankfurt	Germany	1977	39	148	486	Office	Richard Heil
42	South African Reserve Bank	Pretoria	South Africa	1988	38	148	485	Office	Burg, Doherty, Bryant & Partners
43	Colonia-Haus (Axa-Hochhaus)	Cologne	Germany	1972	46	147	482	Residential	Henrik Busch
44	88 on Field	Durban	South Africa	1986	26	147	481	Office	Murphy/Jahn, Inc.; Stauch Vorster
45	Tour de Bretagne	Nantes	France	1976	32	144	472	Office	Claude Devorsine
46	City-Haus	Frankfurt	Germany	1976	43	143	469	Office	Johannes Krahn and Richard Heil
47	Ministry of Foreign Affairs	Cairo	Egypt	1994	40	143	469	Office	
48	Guy's Hospital	London	United Kingdom	1970	32	143	468	Hospital	
49	Frankfurter Büro-Center	Frankfurt	Germany	1980	40	142	467	Office	Richard Heil
50	El Gezira Tower (now Sofitel)	Cairo	Egypt	1996	43	142	466	Hotel	

Source: © Georges Binder/Buildings & Data SA with Marshall Gerometta

* Spires are included in the height count when they are part of the overall design

In 1996, the 50 tallest completed buildings in the Europe/Middle East/Africa regions comprised 39 buildings in Europe, 3 buildings in the Middle East and 8 buildings in Africa, while 72 percent of the projects were office buildings.

50 TALLEST BUILDINGS OF EUROPE, THE MIDDLE EAST AND AFRICA IN 2006

Completed and under construction as of 1 July 2006

	Name	City	Country	Year	Storeys	Metres	Feet	Use	Architect
1	Burj Dubai	Dubai	UAE	2009*	150+	700+**	2300+**	Mixed-use	Adrian Smith of Skidmore, Owings & Merrill
2	Abraj Al Bait Hotel	Makkah	Saudi Arabia	2008*	76	485**	1591**	Hotel	Dar Al-Handasah (Shair and Partners)
3	Burj Al Alam (The World Tower)	Dubai	UAE	2009***	108	484	1588	Mixed-use	Nikken Sekkei; Theo A. Khing design consultants
4	Federation Tower A****	Moscow	Russia	2008*	93	448**	1471**	Mixed-use	Federation Tower Planning Association
5	Dubai Towers – Doha	Doha	Qatar	2008*	86	445**	1460**	Mixed-use	RMJM Dubai (concept design: Hazel WS Wong)
6	Princess Tower	Dubai	UAE	2009*	102	414**	1358**	Residential	Eng. Adnan Saffarini Office
7	Al Hamra Tower	Kuwait City	Kuwait	2009*	77	412	1352	Office	Skidmore, Owings & Merrill; Al Jazeera
8	23 Marina	Dubai	UAE	2008*	90	389**	1276**	Residential	Architect Hafeez Contractor; KEO International Consultants
9	Najd Tower	Dubai	UAE	2008*	82	375**	1230**	Residential	Eng. Adnan Saffarini Office
10	Al Mas Tower	Dubai	UAE	2008*	68	360**	1181**	Office	Atkins
11	Jumeirah Emirates Towers	Dubai	UAE	2000	53	355**	1164**	Office	Hyder Consulting Middle East; NORR Group Consultants International (design architect Hazel WS Wong)
12	The Square Capital Tower	Kuwait City	Kuwait	2008*	63	351**	1150**	Office	NORR Group Consultants International
13	The Torch	Dubai	UAE	2008*	80	345**	1132**	Residential	Khatib & Alami
14	Rose Rotana Suites	Dubai	UAE	2007*	67	333**	1093**	Hotel	Khatib & Alami
15	The Index	Dubai	UAE	2008*	80	328	1076	Mixed-use	Foster and Partners; Khatib & Alami
16	Al Yaquob Tower	Dubai	UAE	2008*	69	328**	1076**	Mixed-use	Eng. Adnan Saffarini Office
17	Burj Al Arab	Dubai	UAE	1999	52	321**	1053**	Hotel	WS Atkins
18	Ocean Heights	Dubai	UAE	2008*	82	310	1017	Residential	Aedas Limited
19	Jumeirah Emirates Towers	Dubai	UAE	2000	54	309**	1014**	Hotel	Hyder Consulting Middle East; NORR Group Consultants International (design architect Hazel WS Wong)
20	Infinity Tower	Dubai	UAE	2008*	73	307	1007	Residential	Skidmore, Owings & Merrill; Khatib & Alami
21	Burj Dubai Lake Hotel & Serviced Apartments	Dubai	UAE	2008*	61	306**	1004**	Mixed-use	Atkins
22	Kingdom Centre	Riyadh	Saudi Arabia	2002	38	302	992	Mixed-use	Consortium of Ellerbe Becket and Omrania & Associates
23	Ahmed Abdul Rahim Al Attar Tower	Dubai	UAE	2007*	76	301**	988**	Residential	Gulf Engineering & Consultants
24	Moscow International Business Center – Plot 12	Moscow	Russia	2007*	67	300	984	Mixed-use	Swanke Hayden Connell Architects
25	Arraya 2	Kuwait City	Kuwait	2008*	56	300**	984**	Office	Fentress Bradburn Architects
26	Sports City Tower	Doha	Qatar	2007*	51	300	984	Mixed-use	Hadi Simaan; AREP
27	Commerzbank	Frankfurt	Germany	1997	51	299**	980**	Office	Foster and Partners
28	Emirates Crown	Dubai	UAE	2008*	63	296**	971**	Residential	DAR Consult
29	Khalid Al Attar Tower 2	Dubai	UAE	2008*	66	295	966	Mixed-use	Eng. Adnan Saffarini Office
30	I & M Tower	Dubai	UAE	2008*	54	290**	952**	Office	P & T Architects & Engineers; Alex Vacha Architects
31	Dubai Pearl Hotel Tower	Dubai	UAE	2008*	60	287	942	Hotel	NORR Group Consultants International Ltd.
32	Capital City – Moscow Tower	Moscow	Russia	2008*	73	286	938	Mixed-use	NBBJ
33	Bright Start Tower	Dubai	UAE	2006*	60	280**	919**	Residential	Atkins

	Name	City	Country	Year	Storeys	Metres	Feet	Use	Architect
34	Mag 218 Tower	Dubai	UAE	2008*	66	275	902	Residential	Dar Al-Handasah (Shair and Partners)
35	Hotel JAL Tower Dubai	Dubai	UAE	2007*	57	270	886	Hotel	BRT Architekten
36	21st Century Tower	Dubai	UAE	2003	55	270**	886**	Residential	Atkins
37	Al Faisaliah Complex	Riyadh	Saudi Arabia	2000	33	267**	876**	Office	Foster and Partners
38	Al Kazim Tower 1	Dubai	UAE	2008*	53	265**	869**	Residential	National Engineering Bureau
39	Al Kazim Tower 2	Dubai	UAE	2008*	53	265**	869**	Residential	National Engineering Bureau
40	Triumph-Palace	Moscow	Russia	2005	57	264**	867**	Residential	TROMOS
41	Marina Pinnacle	Dubai	UAE	2007*	67	260**	853**	Residential	National Engineering Bureau
42	Dual Towers – East Tower	Manama	Bahrain	2006*	57	260**	853**	Office	Ahmed Janahi Architects
43	Dual Towers – West Tower	Manama	Bahrain	2006*	57	260**	853**	Office	Ahmed Janahi Architects
44	Abraj Al Bait Hajar Tower	Makkah	Saudi Arabia	2007*	48	260	853	Residential	Dar Al-Handasah (Shair and Partners)
45	Abraj Al Bait ZamZam Tower	Makkah	Saudi Arabia	2006*	48	260	853	Residential	Dar Al-Handasah (Shair and Partners)
46	MesseTurm	Frankfurt	Germany	1990	63	257	842	Office	Murphy/Jahn, Inc.
47	Latefa Tower	Sharjah	UAE	2006*	52	255**	837**	Residential	Dimensions Engineering Consultants
48	Emirates Marina Serviced Apartments & Spa	Dubai	UAE	2006*	63	254**	832**	Residential	Khatib & Alami
49	Naberezhnaya Tower C	Moscow	Russia	2007*	57	252	825	Office	RTKL – ENKA Architectural Office; ENKA Architectural Office
50	Chelsea Tower	Dubai	UAE	2005	51	251**	824**	Residential	Atkins

Source: © Georges Binder/Buildings & Data SA with Marshall Gerometta

* Projects under construction

** Spires are included in the height count when they are part of the overall design

*** At the time of printing, construction of Burj Al Alam was scheduled to start in July 2006

**** Federation Tower A is ranked according to the adjoining 448-metre central mast while the building itself reaches 354 metres

In 2006, the 50 tallest completed buildings, including those under construction in the Europe/Middle East/Africa regions comprise 7 projects in Europe, 43 buildings in the Middle East and no buildings in Africa while only 24 percent of the projects are office buildings, down from 72 percent ten years ago.

Also of note is the domination of the Middle East – 60 percent of the projects are located in Dubai alone – which is slightly above the European domination observed in 1996. Dubai, with 17 projects above 300 metres already scheduled to be completed by the end of the current decade, will soon have more such projects than did the entire world at the end of 1996.

INDEX OF PROJECTS

INDEX OF ARCHITECTS